LEGAL EDUCATION IN THE GLOBAL CONTEXT

Emerging Legal Education

Series Editors:
Paul Maharg, *Australian National University, Canberra, Australia,*
Caroline Maughan, *University of the West of England, Bristol, UK* and
Elizabeth Mertz, *University of Wisconsin-Madison/American Bar Foundation, USA*

Emerging Legal Education is a forum for analysing the discourse of legal education and creating innovative ways of learning the law. The series focuses on research, theory and practice within legal education, drawing attention to historical, interdisciplinary and international characteristics, and is based upon imaginative and sophisticated educational thinking. The series takes a broad view of theory and practice. Series books are written for an international audience and are sensitive to the diversity of contexts in which law is taught, learned and practised.

Other titles in this series:

Legal Education
Simulation in Theory and Practice
Edited by Caroline Strevens, Richard Grimes and Edward Phillips

The Calling of Law
The Pivotal Role of Vocational Legal Education
Edited by Fiona Westwood and Karen Barton

Law and Leadership
Integrating Leadership Studies into the Law School Curriculum
Edited by Paula Monopoli and Susan McCarty

The Moral Imagination and the Legal Life
Beyond Text in Legal Education
Edited by Zenon Bankowski and Maksymilian Del Mar

The Arts and the Legal Academy
Beyond Text in Legal Education
Edited by Zenon Bańkowski, Maksymilian Del Mar and Paul Maharg

Affect and Legal Education
Emotion in Learning and Teaching the Law
Edited by Paul Maharg and Caroline Maughan

Legal Education in the Global Context

Opportunities and Challenges

Edited by

CHRISTOPHER GANE
Chinese University of Hong Kong

ROBIN HUI HUANG
Chinese University of Hong Kong

Routledge
Taylor & Francis Group
LONDON AND NEW YORK

First published 2016 by Routledge

2 Park Square, Milton Park, Abingdon, Oxfordshire OX14 4RN
711 Third Avenue, New York, NY 10017

Routledge is an imprint of the Taylor & Francis Group, an informa business

First issued in paperback 2017

British Library Cataloguing in Publication Data
A catalogue record for this book is available from the British Library

The Library of Congress has cataloged the printed edition as follows:
Legal education in the global context : opportunities and challenges / edited by Christopher Gane and Robin Hui Huang.
pages cm. -- (Emerging legal education)
Includes bibliographical references and index.
ISBN 978-1-4724-4496-7 (hardback) -- ISBN 978-1-4724-4497-4 (ebook) -- ISBN 978-1-4724-4498-1 (epub) 1. Law--Study and teaching. 2. Law and globalization. I. Gane, Christopher H. W., editor. II. Hui Huang, Robin, editor.
K100.L447 2015
340.071--dc23

2015024503

ISBN: 978-1-4724-4496-7 (hbk)
ISBN: 978-0-8153-9345-0 (pbk)

Contents

PART II: SHIFTS IN TEACHING PHILOSOPHIES AND METHODS

PART III: INTERNATIONAL EXPERIENCES

List of Figures

List of Tables

Notes on Contributors

David Camarotto

Adjunct Professor, William Mitchell College of Law

Professor David Camarotto is a shareholder at Bassford Remele, a professional association. He is also an Adjunct Professor at William Mitchell College of Law and at the University of St. Thomas Law School. He has taught trial advocacy and legal practicum at law schools for over a decade, teaches classes and seminars for bar associations and other professional organizations, and is a recognized author of many published works.

Professor Camarotto is an accomplished litigator and focuses his practice on general liability, construction litigation and product liability matters. He has been repeatedly named in the *Minnesota Rising Stars* list, is a Barrister in the Douglas K. Amdahl Inn of Court, and is a member of the Association of Defense Trial Attorneys. Professor Camarotto received his law degree from William Mitchell College of Law and received his undergraduate degree from Saint John's University.

Bassford Remele, a professional association, is a full-service litigation firm located in Minneapolis, Minnesota. Founded in 1882, the firm represents local, national and international clients in all areas of civil litigation and dispute resolution.

Johannes M.M. Chan

Former Dean, Faculty of Law, University of Hong Kong

Professor Johannes M.M. Chan, SC (Hon) (陳文敏), former Dean of the Faculty of Law, The University of Hong Kong, specializes in human rights, constitutional and administrative law, and has published widely in these fields, including *The Law of Hong Kong Constitution* (Sweet and Maxwell Hong Kong, 2011) and the rewrite of *Halsbury's Laws of Hong Kong on Constitutional Law and Human Rig*hts (vol. 16, LexisNexis Hong Kong, 2015). He has appeared as counsel in many leading human rights and constitutional law cases, and was appointed as the first (and so far the only) Honorary Senior Counsel in Hong Kong in 2003. He was the BOK Visiting Professor of University of Pennsylvania Law School (2014), Herbert Smith Freehills Visiting Professor at Cambridge University (2015), and Visiting Fellows of Gonville and Caius College, Cambridge University (2015).

Yen-Chia Chen

Adjunct Assistant Professor of Law, Aletheia University Department of Law
Manager, Legal and Compliance Division, Bank SinoPac Ltd

Professor Yen-Chia Chen holds a manager position at the legal and compliance division of Bank SinoPac, Ltd, where his daily work involves conducting extensive legal research and drafting legal memorandum on a broad range of corporate and banking legal matters. He also serves as an Adjunct Assistant Professor of Law at Aletheia University Department of Law and teaches upper-level law classes on the laws and regulations of banking, securities, asset securitization, generic top-level domain and third-party payment services. Professor Chen's research and teaching interests include financial and business law, criminal justice, human rights and constitutional law.

Simon Chesterman

Dean, Faculty of Law, National University of Singapore

Professor Simon Chesterman is Dean of the National University of Singapore Faculty of Law. He is also Editor of the *Asian Journal of International Law* and Secretary-General of the Asian Society of International Law. His teaching experience includes periods at the Universities of Melbourne, Oxford, Southampton, Columbia and Sciences Po. From 2006–2011, he was Global Professor and Director of the New York University School of Law Singapore Programme. Prior to joining NYU, he was a Senior Associate at the International Peace Academy and Director of UN Relations at the International Crisis Group in New York. He has previously worked for the UN Office for the Coordination of Humanitarian Affairs in Yugoslavia and interned at the International Criminal Tribunal for Rwanda. Professor Chesterman is a recognized authority on international law and author or editor of fourteen books including *One Nation Under Surveillance* (OUP, 2011) and *Law and Practice of the United Nations* (with Thomas M. Franck and David M. Malone, OUP, 2008).

Carolyn Evans

Dean, Faculty of Law, University of Melbourne

Professor Carolyn Evans is Dean of Melbourne Law School. Carolyn has degrees in Arts and Law from Melbourne University and a doctorate from Oxford University where she studied as a Rhodes Scholar and where she held a stipendiary lectureship for two years before returning to Melbourne in 2000. In 2010, Professor Evans was awarded a Fulbright Senior Scholarship to allow her to travel as a Visiting Fellow at American and Emory Universities to examine questions of comparative religious freedom.

Professor Evans is the author, co-author or editor of six books on religious freedom and human rights. She is an internationally recognized expert on religious freedom and the relationship between law and religion and has spoken on these topics in the United States, United Kingdom, Russia, China, Greece, Vietnam, India, Hong Kong, Switzerland, Malaysia, Nepal and Australia.

John Flood

Professor of Law and Director of Law Futures Centre,
Griffith University Law School

Professor John Flood studied law and sociolegal studies at the LSE, Warwick and Yale Law School. He took his PhD in sociology at Northwestern University in Chicago under the supervision of Howard Becker, Jack Heinz and Art Stinchcombe. He worked at the American Bar Foundation as a research associate and Indiana University-Bloomington, the University of Westminster and University College Dublin before joining Griffith University. He has been an Exxon Fellow in Ethics in the Poynter Center at Indiana University, an Academic Visitor in the Sociology Department at LSE, a Jean Monnet Fellow at the European University Institute in Florence, a Visiting Fellow at the Institute of Advanced Legal Studies, and TranState Adjunct Professor at the University of Bremen. He is currently Honorary Professor of Law at University College London and Visiting Professor of Law and Sociology at the University of Westminster. Since 2010 he has been a member of the Legal Services Board's Research Strategy Group. From 2012 to 2014 he held a Leverhulme Research Fellowship to study the new legal services market. www.johnflood.com.

Kate Galloway

Senior Lecturer, College of Law, Business & Governance, James Cook University

Professor Kate Galloway is Senior Lecturer in Law at James Cook University, Cairns, Australia. Her substantive law interest is property law, but she also researches and writes on legal education, particularly on the law curriculum. She has led a number of teaching and learning projects over a decade, including flexible learning, Indigenous perspectives and sustainability in the law curriculum, and won a national teaching award for her leadership in legal education. Professor Galloway is presently part of an Australian Government-funded project creating professional development modules for sessional law teachers. She was the inaugural co-convenor of the Australian Legal Education Associate Deans Network and serves on the editorial committee of the *Legal Education Review*. Professor Galloway blogs at http://katgallow.blogspot.com.au/.

Christopher Gane

Dean, Faculty of Law, Chinese University of Hong Kong

Professor Christopher Gane is Dean at the Faculty of Law, Chinese University of Hong Kong. His research and teaching interests include Domestic Criminal Law and Procedure, International Criminal Law and Human Rights. He is author of 12 books and more than 50 scholarly articles and papers.

Rick Glofcheski

Professor, Faculty of Law, University of Hong Kong

Professor Rick Glofcheski obtained his BA at Wilfrid Laurier University, his LLB at University of Windsor and his LLM at Cambridge University, England. After practising law in Canada, he joined the University of Hong Kong. His primary areas of teaching and research are in tort law, labour and employment law, and teaching and learning in higher education. He has also taught criminal law, contract law, legal system and medical law. Professor Glofcheski is the Editor-in-Chief of *Hong Kong Law Journal*. He was Head of the Department of Law from 1996–1999. He is the author of *Tort Law in Hong Kong* (Sweet and Maxwell Asia, 2012). He is author and co-editor of *Employment Law and Practice in Hong Kong* (Sweet & Maxwell Asia, 2010), for which he was awarded (jointly with Farzana Aslam) the University Research Output Prize 2011. Professor Glofcheski was selected for the award of University Teaching Fellow (2004), the inaugural University Outstanding Teaching Award (2009), the inaugural University Distinguished Teaching Award (2010) and the inaugural Hong Kong-wide University Grants Committee Teaching Excellence Award (2011), in recognition of outstanding teaching and his leadership and contributions to the advancement of teaching and learning.

Robin Hui Huang

Professor, Faculty of Law, Chinese University of Hong Kong

Professor Robin Hui Huang is a Professor and Assistant Dean at the Faculty of Law, Chinese University of Hong Kong. He specializes in corporate law, securities regulation, financial law, financial dispute resolution and foreign investment, with a particular focus on Chinese and comparative law issues. He has held visiting posts at prestigious institutions including Harvard Law School and Cambridge Law School, and has been engaged as an expert by international organizations such as the World Bank.

Weidong Ji

Dean, Shanghai Jiao Tong University KoGuan Law School

Professor Ji Weidong is Dean and KoGuan Chair Professor of the Law School, Shanghai Jiao Tong University (SJTU), China, since 2008; Vice Chairman of the Guiding Committee of Legal Education, the Ministry of Education, China since 2013; Co-Editors-in-Chief of Asian Journal of Law and Society, since 2014; Member of the Global Agenda Council on Justice, World Economic Forum, since 2014. Prior to joining SJTU, he was a professor of Graduate School of Law, Kobe University, Japan.

His major works include: *A Hypermodern Law* (Minerva Press, 1999), *Constructing Rule of Law* (China University of Law and Political Sciences Press, 1999), *Legal Change in Modern China* (Japan Review Press, 2001), *New Views on Constitutionalism* (Peking University Press, 2002, enlarged edition, 2005), *The Composition of Chinese Judicial System* (Yuhikaku Press, 2004), *Orbit of Thinking Justice* (Law Press, 2007), *At Critical Point of Order and Chaos* (Law Press, 2008), *Switching the Institutions* (Zhejiang University Press, 2009), Rule of Law in Perspective (Law Press, 2012), *Great Transformation and Rule of Law in China* (Peking University Press, 2013), *The Road to The Rule of Law: Social Diversity and Authority System* (Law Press, 2014), among others.

Leigha Lattner

Professor, William College of Law, spring 2014

Xiaohong Liu

Vice President, East China University of Political Science and Law

Professor Liu Xiaohong is a Professor of Law at the East China University of Political Science & Law (ECUPL). She is now the Vice President of ECUPL. She is the Vice Chairman of Chinese Private International Law Society and Vice Secretary-General of China Academy of Arbitration Law. She is an Arbitrator of many arbitration institutions, including China International Economic and Trade Arbitration Commission, Arbitration Foundation of South Africa and

Cairo Regional Center for International Commercial Arbitration. Professor Liu has written extensively in many fields, and has been the author and co-author of 10 books and the author of more than 70 articles in reputable law journals at home and abroad. She has lectured as a Visiting Professor in many law schools, including the Law School of University of Wisconsin, University of San Francisco and Temple University in the United States. She won the Award of Excellent University Young Teacher of Shanghai Municipality and the Annual Excellent University Young Teacher Scholarship of Huo Yingdong Education Fund by the Ministry of Education Of China. In 2009, she was elected as one of the "Top Ten Excellent Young Lawyers in Shanghai" by Shanghai Law Society.

Hans-Wolfgang Micklitz

Head of Department, Department of Law, Professor of Economic Law, European University Institute

Since 2007, Professor Hans-Wolfgang Micklitz has been Professor for Economic Law at the European University Institute, Jean Monnet Chair of Private Law and European Economic Law at the University of Bamberg, Germany (on leave). He is the Head of the Institute of European and Consumer Law (VIEW) in Bamberg. He studied law and sociology in Mainz, Lausanne/Geneva (Switzerland), Giessen and Hamburg. Professor Micklitz is a consultant for OECD in Paris, UNEP Geneva Switzerland/Nairobi Kenya and CI (Consumers International) Den Haag Netherlands/Penang Malaysia. He has made study visits to the University of of Michigan, Ann Arbor, is a Jean Monnet Fellow at the European University Institute Florence, Italy, is a Visiting Professor at Somerville College at the University of Oxford, and is co-founder of the Centre of Excellence at the University of Helsinki. He is a holder of an ERC Grant 2011–2016 on European Regulatory Private Law and from 2016–2020 Finisch Distiguished Professor.

Emily Parks

William Mitchell College of Law

William Mitchell College of Law, May 2015. Bachelor degree in German studies from Macalester College in 2008.

Paul Redmond

Emeritus Professor, Faculty of Law, University of New South Wales

Professor Paul Redmond AM is Sir Gerard Brennan Professor of Law at the University of Technology, Sydney. While he was Dean of the Faculty of Law at the University of New South Wales, he co-authored a significant report on the reform of legal education and training in Hong Kong. He is Chair of the Diplomacy Training Program, a regional human rights training body, was a founding member of Australian National Pro Bono Resource Centre and has participated in a number of other national and international initiatives in legal education. He has written widely on corporate law, corporate governance and standards of responsibility.

Joellen Riley

Dean and Professor of Labour Law, Faculty of Law, University of Sydney

Professor Joellen Riley, Dean at the Faculty of Law at the University of Sydney, holds degrees in law from the Universities of Sydney and Oxford, and has been teaching and researching in the field of employment and labour law since 1998. She studied law after a number of years as a financial journalist, and spent some time in commercial legal practice before joining the University of Sydney. Her academic career includes some years on the staff of the Law Faculty of the University of New South Wales, where she taught principally in corporate and commercial law. Professor Riley is a Fellow of the Commercial Law Association. She was a co-editor of the *Australian Journal of Labour Law* from 2008 till 2012.

Rita Shackel

Associate Professor, Faculty of Law, University of Sydney

Professor Rita Shackel is a permanent academic based at Sydney Law School. In addition to a broad interdisciplinary research programme in the field of criminal justice, She is an active researcher in legal education, legal professionalism and ethics. She is a former Associate Dean Learning and Teaching at Sydney Law School and is currently Chair of the Human Research Ethics Committee, The University of Sydney. She is also a long-standing teacher in legal professional responsibility and has delivered a range of CLE programmes to the profession including the judiciary in Australia and internationally. She has published widely across a number of fields relevant to legal education and lawyering. Currently she is engaged in collaborative research on the wellness of law students and legal professionals.

Avrom Sherr

Emeritus Professor, Institute of Advanced Legal Studies, University of London

Professor Avrom Sherr qualified as a solicitor in commercial litigation with Coward (now Clifford) Chance. From 1974 to 1990 at Warwick University he pioneered clinical legal education. His PhD from Warwick University was on "The Value of Experience in Legal Competence".

In 1990 he became the first Alsop Wilkinson Professor of Law at the University of Liverpool and subsequently Director of the Centre for Business and Professional Law. In 1995 he was appointed as the founding Woolf Professor of Legal Education at the Institute of Advanced Legal Studies. From 2004 to 2012 he was Director of the Institute of Advanced Legal Studies. His main areas of research have been in legal education, professional competence and human rights. He developed and runs the Independent Peer Review of all legal aid lawyers in England and Wales, and is current Chair of the Hamlyn Trust and the Quality Project Committee for Legal Advice centres.

Yan'an Shi

Vice Dean, School of Law, Renmin University of China

Professor Shi Yan'an is currently Professor in Law and Vice Dean of Renmin University of China (RUC) Law School, and Deputy Director and a Senior Fellow of the Research Center for Criminal Justice of RUC, one of the key national research institutes of humanistic and social sciences in universities of China.

His research field is criminal law, criminal justice and international cooperation in criminal matters. He has published one book on the Inter-regional Concurrent Criminal Jurisdiction in China, one book on jurisdiction and another book on offences of violating decency. Since 2000, he has published dozens of papers on criminal law and criminal justice, and translated *Gotham Unbound* (by Professor James Jacobs, NYU) and several English papers into Chinese. He and other two professors have just finished the translation of a book *Public Criminology?* written by Professor Ian Loader and Professor Sparks. He is currently writing a textbook on American–British criminal law.

Ming-Yan Shieh

Professor of Law and Former Dean of National Taiwan University College of Law, College of Law, National Taiwan University

Professor Ming-Yan Shieh is a leading expert who has devoted substantial scholarly effort in the field of intellectual property law in Taiwan. He received his Bachelor of Laws degree and Master of Laws degree from National Taiwan University College of Law before earning his Doctor of Laws (Dr. jur.) degree at the Ludwig Maximilian University of Munich (German: Ludwig-Maximilians-Universität München) in 1990. In the same year Professor Shieh joined the law faculty of his alma mater in Taiwan and has served as a Professor of Law since then. Moreover, he served as Dean of National Taiwan University College of Law between August 2012 and August 2015.

Professor Shieh's research interests include intellectual property law, fair trade law, internet law and civil law. So far Professor Shieh has published 10 books. More than 100 of his articles have appeared in numerous leading law journals. As a legal activist committed to the development of Taiwan's intellectual property law, Professor Shieh has actively engaged in the formulation of policy and legislation of intellectual property law in Taiwan. Over the past few years several intellectual property law amendments in Taiwan have taken place as a result of Professor Shieh's initiatives.

John Sonsteng

Professor of Law, William Mitchell College of Law

Professor John Sonsteng received his BA and JD degrees from the University of Minnesota. At William Mitchell College of Law he developed the college's lawyering, advocacy and practicum classes and has taught Advanced Advocacy, Criminal Law, Criminal Procedure and the Legal Practicum course during his 30 years at the college.

His commitment to educating law students and lawyers was recognized by the National Institute for Trial Advocacy with the Honorable Prentice H. Marshall Faculty Award. He was the first recipient of the "Advocate" Award from the Minnesota State Bar Association for Outstanding Achievement and Contribution to the bar. The National College of Trial Lawyers honoured Professor Sonsteng with the Emil Gumpert Award for excellence in Teaching Trial Advocacy.

Professor Sonsteng was a Fulbright Lecturer in Aberdeen, Scotland and a City Solicitors Education Trust Visiting Professor in Litigation Advocacy at England's Nottingham Law School. He has taught advocacy skills throughout the United States, Canada, Ireland, Northern Ireland, Scotland, Wales, Singapore, Columbia and Turkey.

He has authored or co-authored dozens of books, articles, videos and manuals on advocacy, juvenile law and practice and criminal procedure prepare students for practice.

Seow Hon Tan

Associate Professor of Law, Associate Dean (Research), School of Law, Singapore Management University

Professor Tan Seow Hon is an Associate Professor and Associate Dean (Research) at the School of Law, Singapore Management University (SMU), where she teaches Jurisprudence as an upper year elective as well as a mandatory upper year course. She is the winner of the SMU Innovative Teacher Award 2012–2013 and the SMU School of Law Most Outstanding Teacher Award 2012–2013, and has won several other teaching awards from the school and from the National University of Singapore where she was previously tenured. She completed her doctoral studies at Harvard Law School in 2004, specializing in Jurisprudence. She has undertaken several empirical projects, which examined the impact of legal education and of internships on the moral transformation and formation of the professional identity of lawyers and written numerous articles on pedagogy.

Zhenmin Wang

Dean, School of Law, Tsinghua University

Professor Wang Zhenmin received his LL.B. from Zhengzhou University (1989), LL.M. and PhD in Law from Renmin (People's) University of China (1992 and 1995). He also studied in the Law Faculty of Hong Kong University from 1993 to 1995. He was a Fulbright Visiting Scholar at Harvard Law School in 2000–2001. Professor Wang joined Tsinghua University law faculty in 1995. In 2008 he was appointed Dean of Tsinghua University School of Law.

In 2004, 2009 and 2014 he was appointed member of the Committee for the Macao Basic Law under the Standing Committee of the Chinese National People's Congress (and concurrently a member of the paralleling Committee for Hong Kong Basic Law in 2006). Professor Wang is Vice President of China Research Association of Constitutional Law, President of China Research Association for Hong Kong and Macao Basic Laws, and President of China Research Association for Judicial Cases. He is a Member of the Forum of Young Global Leaders of World Economic Forum, and member of American Law Institute since 2013. In 2010 he was awarded the Top 10 Outstanding Young Jurist Prize by China Law Society. His teaching and research mainly focus on constitutional law and the Basic Laws of HK and Macao. He is the author of Central-Special Administrative

Region Relationship in China – from a Legal Perspective (Tsinghua University Press, 2002, Joint Publishing 2014) and Constitutional Review in China (China University of Political Science and Law Press, 2004). He has published over 90 articles and presented papers at many regional and international conferences on Chinese constitutional law, legal reform and so on.

Rainer Wernsmann

Dean, University of Passau, Faculty of Law

Professor Dr Rainer Wernsmann took his First Legal State Examination in 1993 and his Second Legal State Examination in 1996 after law studies in Münster and Paris. From 1993 until 2004 he worked as an academic assistant and lecturer at the University of Münster. In 1999 Professor Dr Wernsmann was conferred the degree Dr. iur., whereupon he habilitated in 2003 and hence received the venia legendi for Public Law, Tax Law and European Law. After one and a half years at the Helmut Schmidt University in Hamburg, Professor Dr Wernsmann accepted an offer for the Chair of Constitutional, Administrative, Public Finance and Tax Law at the University of Passau in 2006. He has rejected two further offers for Chairs of Public Law since then. After having served as Vice-Dean (2010–2012) and Dean of the Faculty of Law (2012–2014), he was elected Vice President of the University of Passau in 2014.

Professor Dr Wernsmann is co-author of some important commentaries on legal codes. He has litigated in numerous constitutional and administrative cases, for example, on behalf of the German federal government and several states at the Federal Constitutional Court of Germany and other Constitutional Courts of German states ("Länder").

Introduction

Christopher Gane[1] and Robin Hui Huang[2]

This volume brings together academic leaders and scholars interested in legal education from China, the Asia–Pacific Region, Europe and North America[3] to discuss and reflect upon developments in legal education in the first years of the twenty-first century. Given the extensive experience of the contributors, in many different jurisdictions, one might have expected that a huge range of issues would have emerged during the discussions, and certainly there was considerable diversity in the subjects addressed and the opinions expressed. But what is perhaps most striking is the commonality of experience and concerns reflected in these chapters, concerns that are expressed by contributors often from very different legal, social and political backgrounds. All of which suggests that in legal education, as in so many other fields, our commonalities are more significant than our differences. This introductory chapter, then, will try to draw out some of those common experiences, as well as highlighting particular aspects of "local" experience where appropriate,[4] including the experience of the Faculty of Law at the Chinese University of Hong Kong where we both work.

Law Schools and Professional Education and Training

"What are law schools for?" is an abiding question. Of course this can be a very broad question, or one that is more narrowly focused, and in particular the question of the role of the law schools in relation to professional legal education, or education for the practice of law, is perennial, and reflected in several contributions.[5] Simon Chesterman[6] suggests that "Legal education has always been influenced by the

---

1 Simon F.S. Li Professor of Law and Dean of the Faculty of Law, The Chinese University of Hong Kong.

2 Professor of Law, Faculty of Law, The Chinese University of Hong Kong.

3 A full list of participants and their affiliations is set out in the Notes on Contributors.

4 References to contributions are by name of the author (e.g., "Chan", "Flood" and so on).

5 See in particular Chan, Chapter 19 (Hong Kong), Chesterman, Chapter 5 (Singapore), Flood, Chapter 2 (England), Sherr, Chapter 13 (England).

6 Professor Simon Chesterman is Dean of the Faculty of Law, National University of Singapore.

tension between being an academic pursuit and a professional qualification",[7] a view shared by John Flood[8] who observes that "Legal education has always occupied an uneasy position between the theoretical and the vocational".[9]

Whether the "tension" is as long standing as these comments suggest is perhaps open to question. It is worth recalling, in this regard, that in many jurisdictions a law degree was not, until relatively recently, a pre-requisite for legal practice, and indeed it remains the case that an aspiring solicitor or barrister in England and Wales does not have to have a law degree. Equally, it is probably the case that "academic" legal education – in the sense that it now manifests itself at the global level – is a relatively recent phenomenon. Certainly in the United Kingdom the emergence of programmes of study whose focus was not primarily the preparation of students for eventual admission to practice has been a fairly recent development. That said, it is clear that the competing demands of the academy and the legal professions have produced a problem of crowded curricula, competing claims for priority in objectives, and a consequent risk of the law schools collectively producing graduates who have had insufficient time to reflect on what they study from course to course and year to year.

The "tension" referred to above is likely to be greatest in those jurisdictions – such as Hong Kong – where the legal professions have traditionally had a significant "say" in the content of the university law degree. In some jurisdictions – most of the states of the United States, for example – the presence of a professionally-required "bar exam" as part of the process of admission to practice, and the fact that candidates will not necessarily seek admission in a state where they have studied law – the law schools are insulated from professional influence over the content of the law degree. By way of contrast, in a jurisdiction such as Hong Kong, the legal professions determine to a large extent the content of the law degree, at least to the extent of prescribing courses that must be taught if the degree is to be a "qualifying degree". In Hong Kong the law degree,[10] in order to be recognized for admission to practice as a solicitor or barrister, must contain the following subjects: contract, tort, constitutional law, criminal law, land law, equity, civil procedure, criminal procedure, evidence, business associations and commercial law. This is a relatively long list of required courses, and Hong Kong is at least unusual in common law jurisdictions in requiring the study of civil and criminal procedure as part of the undergraduate law degree.[11]

7 Chesterman, Chapter 5.

8 Professor John Flood is Leverhulme Research Fellow and Professor of Law and Sociology, University of Westminster.

9 Flood, Chapter 2.

10 In Hong Kong there are two "qualifying" law degrees – the four-year undergraduate bachelor of laws degree (LLB) degree, and the two or three-year graduate *Juris Doctor* (JD) degree. Both degrees are offered by The Chinese University of Hong Kong, the University of Hong Kong and the City University of Hong Kong.

11 Similar requirements are, however, to be found in Australia.

In some jurisdictions it appears that the legal profession is concerned not only with *what* is taught, but *how* it is taught. Joellen Riley's[12] discussion of the potential impact of Massive Open Online Courses (MOOCs) on traditional legal education[13] highlights an even greater level of engagement by the profession on the delivery of the law degree. In New South Wales the Legal Profession Admission Board has asked all law schools in New South Wales to provide them with information which indicated "the extent to which [their] degree programs provided adequate learning in statutory interpretation". The request from the Board asked for information not only on how this aspect of legal study was taught, but also how competency in statutory interpretation skills was assessed. "The LPAB is concerned not only with course content, but with graduate outcomes".[14] While it is entirely understandable, and commendable, that the professions understand the importance of outcomes in the education process, professional bodies do need to appreciate that this is precisely the kind of question that educators are concerned about all the time, and are required by their own institutions to demonstrate as part of the ordinary processes of course and programme preparation and evaluation.

What is perhaps most striking in considering the impact of professional recognition on the content of law degrees, at least in the context of the "globalization" of legal education, is the apparent absence of an appreciation of these issues on the part of the legal profession in many jurisdictions. Where, for example, is the study of international law in the "core curriculum" of most common law systems? To what extent do the professions recognize that future legal practice will require an understanding of how lawyers from other jurisdictions think, how they conceptualize legal problems and how they construct solutions to those problems? Where are comparative legal studies in the "core curriculum" of legal professions? To the extent that subjects such as these have been identified as a required part of a modern legal education, this is almost entirely due to movements from within the law schools, who clearly have a job to do in persuading their professional counterparts of the importance of such topics of study.

The Ethical Dimension of Legal Study

A related, but distinct, concern about the ethical dimension of legal education is raised by a number of contributors, with a concentration of interest in this issue coming from Mainland China legal scholars,[15] although the contributions from Redmond and Seow illustrate that this is not a "jurisdiction-specific" concern.

---

12 Professor Joellen Riley is Dean and Professor of Labour Law, Sydney Law School.

13 Riley, Chapter 14 (Australia).

14 Riley, Chapter 14.

15 Ji, Chapter 18 (China), Xiaohong, Chapter 6 (China), Redmond, Chapter 7 (Australia), Shi, Chapter 11 (China), Tan, Chapter 8 (Singapore), Wang, Chapter 17 (China).

Against a background of the rapid – and unregulated[16] – expansion of legal education in China, Ji calls for a two-level programme of legal education in which the cultivation of legal talent is not confined to the inculcation of legal professional skills. While the foundations of (undergraduate) legal education ought to provide students with a sound grasp of basic legal subjects, as well as certain important transferable skills (such as IT and language proficiency), a more advanced, graduate programme of legal education should be offered, on a more selective basis, the purpose of which would be to "cultivate excellent legal talents with a strong sense of justice and responsibility as well as superior knowledge, international vision and creative thinking ability".[17] Against a similar background of economic expansion and the growth of legal education in China, Lin likewise emphasizes the need for a more structured system of legal education, and one that places an emphasis on "belief in law, the sense of social responsibility … as well as good professional morality". In somewhat similar vein Shi laments the "waning" of the "spirit of humanism" in China's law schools, which have been "somewhat transformed into a factory-line" which will generate "law craftsmen" whose interest in legal training will be dominated by economic concerns, as opposed to the "humanistic" dimension of legal education. But Shi does not blame the students: "With the law schools transforming into such icy processing workshops isolated from humanistic concerns, what can we expect from them."

As noted above, such concerns are not confined to development in China. Redmond's chapter reflects concerns in the United States, Australia and the United Kingdom about a direction of legal education in which "a cynical, game-oriented consciousness replaces student idealism and social justice commitment".[18] This chapter also contains one of the most poignant and challenging observations on contemporary legal education from a student at Loyola University New Orleans: "[y]ou know, the first thing I lost in law school was the reason that I came."[19] Likewise, Seow notes that while student preparedness for, and understanding of, the globalized context of legal practice are important aims of legal education, "the role of legal education in shaping the lawyer's understanding of the foundational ideals of law has received, in comparison, short shrift".

The central message of these chapters is that the law schools can, and must, adopt educational strategies that at least present students with different visions or understandings of what studying and practising law is meant to be about. It is not inevitable that the requirements of a professionally accredited degree should be driven by what are perceived to be the demands of a particular form of legal

16 *Cf.* in this regard Wang, Chapter 17.

17 Ji, Chapter 18.

18 Redmond, Chapter 7.

19 Redmond, Chapter 7, quoting William P. Quigley, "Letter to a Law Student Interested in Social Justice" (2007) 1 *DePaul Journal of Social Justice* 7, at p. 8. The student did, however, go on to note that his involvement with victims of hurricane Katrina helped to "get back on track".

practice. At the very least, law schools need to offer their students choices, a vision of practice that is not driven entirely by the demands of the marketplace or the needs of major international law firms.

How Should We Deliver Our Programmes?

The two issues highlighted above concern *what we do*. A number of contributors focus on *how we do it*, and in particular the challenges and opportunities offered by information technology.[20]

Flood's observations that "[t]echnology has not yet permeated legal education in a substantive way", that "[l]aw is still largely taught with traditional techniques" and that "[l]aw faculty have not embraced the varieties of e-learning available to them nor have they been trained in their use", will probably ring true for most law academics – or at least those of a certain age. There are no doubt excellent exceptions to be found in many law schools, but they are just that – exceptions. The more interesting question, however, is why this should be so.[21] Joellen Riley tackles the challenge of MOOCs in the context of legal education and poses the straight question "[w]ill the phenomenon of the 'Massive Open Online Course' or 'MOOC' ... radically change the delivery of legal education, in the way that it promises to revolutionize the delivery of computer science and business degrees?" Her answer to this question is equally straightforward: "I doubt it." Her explanation for this position takes us back to the relationship between what is done in law schools and the demands of professional legal practice. For the time being at least, it is unlikely that MOOCs, as currently delivered, would satisfy the demands of the legal profession who are provided with certain guarantees in terms of knowledge skills and standards through the delivery by law schools of "accredited" law degrees. She concludes: "So until it is possible to obtain an accredited law degree through MOOCs, 'real-time', in-person enrolment in law schools is likely to remain the norm. It will take a considerable revolution in the thinking of admission authorities to change this situation."[22]

This is not to say, of course, that "remote" delivery of legal education acceptable to the legal profession is not realistic. The Law School of the Open University of the United Kingdom offers a law degree that is recognized as a qualifying law degree in England and Wales. It has over 6,000 students, and students graduating with the OU's degree are guaranteed a place on the Legal Practice Course offered by the University of Law. Of course the OU's degree is delivered against a background of several decades of experience in the remote delivery of higher education, and

20 Flood, Chapter 2, Glofcheski, Chapter 9, Riley, Chapter 14, Shackel, Chapter 12.

21 And, indeed, whether law schools are very much different in that regard from other disciplines in the humanities and the social sciences.

22 Riley, p. 223.

differs from the typical MOOC in that the University offers individualized and group teaching support which is "face-to-face" or at least "voice-to-voice".

Of course, once one moves away from the constraints of professional recognition and accreditation, the opportunities offered by online delivery become more interesting. One of the most important suggested by Riley is to relieve pressure in the delivery of an already very crowded curriculum.[23] Online delivery of courses, or parts of courses, also offers the possibility of better use of face-to-face classroom interaction between faculty and students. This is especially important in the context of the Chinese University of Hong Kong where teaching in the Master of Laws (LLM) and Juris Doctor (JD) programmes is exclusively by lectures (some more or less Socratic) with very little scope for small group delivery. The typical LLM or JD class is delivered by means of a three-hour lecture once a week over 13 weeks. Online delivery offers the possibility of replacing at least some of the classroom time devoted to lecturing and breaking the classroom time into smaller group classes. However, all such notions are subject to institutional constraints. Thus in Hong Kong, while the universities are encouraged to explore the opportunities afforded by e-learning, they are under fairly clear instruction that these opportunities should not be used to reduce the total face-to-face contact time between faculty and students.

Rita Shackel,[24] reviewing the landscape of e-learning more broadly, offers a relatively positive conspectus:

> E-based learning thus can be seen to encourage flexible and independent student learning and facilitates individualized, student-driven learning by permitting students to work at their own pace outside of the classroom, when and how they find most productive. The e-learning space creates a cradle for students to explore and engage with new information and knowledge. This effectively flips the traditional teacher–student dynamic from teacher-centred to student-centred.[25]

These are valuable possibilities. They are not, of course, necessarily related to e-learning as such. The "flipped" classroom as it is commonly described today – in which students are expected to come to class prepared to engage with each other in the discussion of material that they have previously read, looked at or listened to, is essentially the model of delivery used in the honours stage (typically third and fourth year) of the four-year Honours Bachelor of Laws (LLB) programme in the Scottish universities, and has been for many years now. (It is certainly the way the present writer was taught at Edinburgh in the early 1970s and the way he delivered his honours electives at Edinburgh and later Aberdeen from the late 1970s to the first decade of the present century.)

---

23 Riley, p. 223.

24 Rita Shackel is Associate Professor, Sydney Law School.

25 Shackel, p. 210.

Moreover, the shift to increased independent learning needs to take account of the wider cultural context in which the learning takes place. This can be especially problematic where students' previous educational experience has not promoted independent learning, and also where students may not be wholly confident in their own use of language. Contrary to popular assumptions, Hong Kong students are not typically "rote learners". Research conducted nearly 20 years ago suggested that Hong Kong students were in fact "deep" learners, but that language skills and language confidence may affect the willingness as well as the ability of students to engage in the kind of deep learning that is pursued through the "flipped classroom" paradigm. This can be especially challenging given the range of practical linguistic skills amongst Hong Kong law students, many of whom have pursued the entirety of their schooling or secondary schooling in an English-speaking environment, while others have come to law school from a predominantly Chinese-speaking environment. (It should be noted that the medium of instruction in all of the Hong Kong Law Schools is English.)

The Globalized Law School

It is something of a commonplace today that law schools – whether at their initiative or under the "guidance" of their parent institutions – are increasingly "international" or "globalized" (depending on the local preference). While several of the chapters in this collection locate their discussions against this background, what this means in a practical sense for students within the law schools is not much touched upon.

An excellent, and challenging, exception to this is Carolyn Evans' chapter on "Learning Opportunities in Multi-National Law School Classes: Potential and Pitfalls".[26] As well as exploring a number of valuable practical considerations when addressing the issues that arise now that, increasingly, our classrooms are no longer nationally, culturally or linguistically homogenous, Evans flags up some of the important ethical considerations that arise from the increased recruitment of international students. Although it is not discussed at length, the "economic" incentive for international recruitment is a significant one in many jurisdictions. Evans points out that in Australia "higher education is a multi-billion dollar industry"[27] and the financial incentives to recruit international students are powerful, not least where universities and governments consider it acceptable to charge international students higher tuition fees. Whether from a commitment to internationalization, or for less worthy motivations, law schools are expanding their international intake without necessarily having the appropriate experience

26 Professor Carolyn Evans is Dean and Harrison Moore Professor of Law, Melbourne Law School.

27 Evans, Chapter 4, p. 62.

in handling the important pedagogical and pastoral considerations to which the diversification of their student body gives rise.

As Evans points out, one of the "most complex" issues facing students who chose to study abroad is the cultural differences between the students' experiences in their system of origin, and that of the host. So, for example, international students may find the "relatively informal culture that prevails in most Australian law schools" "unsettling and unclear" if they come from a "more formal learning culture" (which she suggests, is "almost everywhere").[28]

A similar, but rather different, question[29] arises where the faculty member is a newcomer to the "local" culture – which is very frequently the case in a law faculty such as that of the Chinese University of Hong Kong. At the time of writing, the Faculty has 49 academic staff, of whom 44 are non-Hong Kong passport holders, and 12 are ethnically Chinese, and while several faculty members are Hong Kong permanent residents,[30] the vast majority of recent appointees are newcomers to Hong Kong, and, indeed, to Asia. What this means is that for teachers as well as students, there may need to be a period and process of "cultural acclimatization" during which different norms of behaviour and understanding need to be addressed. And so, for example, it has been necessary for the Faculty to discuss, in a formal sense, the expectations that lie behind the offering of gifts to staff by students,[31] and to adopt a practice of declining such gifts (even where they would probably not be caught by the University's general guidelines on the receiving of gifts.) Equally, the process of induction into the Faculty may involve countering some of the widely held beliefs about the "reticence" of Asian students in the classroom lest these become expectations on the part of both teacher and student.[32]

The question of "cultural diversity" has its own local complications in Hong Kong. While the undergraduate population of the Law Faculty at The Chinese University of Hong Kong is predominantly (but not exclusively[33]) drawn from Hong Kong, it admits a substantial number of students into its graduate programmes from the rest of China. Regrettably, there is a vocal element in Hong Kong society (including the Legislative Council) that is willing to accuse the Hong Kong universities of admitting Mainland students to the detriment of local students.[34] There are of course good reasons for not over-admitting from any one

28 Evans, Chapter 4, p. 67.

29 Not discussed by Evans.

30 Subject to certain exceptions, the status of "permanent resident" may be granted to persons who have been lawfully resident in Hong Kong for seven years.

31 And this being Hong Kong, the ever-present legal rules relating to corruption.

32 The experience of "foreign" faculty in law schools appears largely to have escaped the attention of pedagogical researchers.

33 The Faculty admits a small number of students from Mainland China each year, and an even smaller number of "international" students.

34 See, e.g.: "CityU protest demands curb on mainlanders", *South China Morning Post*, 22 April 2014; Chinese students flood Hong Kong universities' graduate programmes", *South China Morning Post*, 11 November 2013.

"foreign" jurisdiction,[35] but the universities (and hence law schools) in Hong Kong are facing the odd situation of being the only universities, perhaps in the world, that are effectively being discouraged from admitting students from China!

Law schools established at the national level have been founded, at least in origin, to serve the needs of the local community by providing appropriately qualified graduates for the local legal profession(s). Many law schools now offer non-qualifying degrees, and graduate programmes which are not linked to professional qualification. But it is still very unusual to see law programmes that are fully transnational in their philosophy and execution at the undergraduate level.[36] Hans Micklitz's[37] contribution to these chapters explores the issues that arise from a transnational legal programme of study, and in particular the potential for a "disconnection" between national and transnational legal education: "The longer the researcher remains in a transnational legal environment, the deeper he indulges into transnational perspectivism and transnational law, the more difficult it becomes to bring the two dimensions, the national and the transnational together."[38] Micklitz goes on to raise the question of whether there will in the future evolve two distinct types of legal education – the "national" and the "transnational" – the former "embedded into the national legal culture, tradition, history, language" and the latter "for transnational needs, for supranational and international organizations, law firms and NGOs, which remains disconnected from national legal education and which develops its own rationales".[39] Micklitz offers two possible conclusions.

One is that that a "free-standing" transnational legal education may well emerge if certain conditions and considerations are met, but points out that there is "a price to pay for transnational law and transnational legal education which is more and more disconnected from national legal education and from national legal systems". The "price" is potentially to be paid by the national legal order: "The fine and nice national legal doctrine, the sophisticated inner structure of a national legal system might suffer from such an open educational training which oscillates between abstract theories and concrete problems".

The alternative conclusion is that the two domains of legal education will remain separate, but co-existent, in which the national legal education becomes "less a goal in itself" and more of a laboratory for the development of transnational law. But even if this were to emerge, Micklitz asks, would all legal systems be able to respond – and in particular, would the differences of philosophy and method tend to result in an increasing influence of the common law world: "In other words, is the common law legal education more apt and more open to transnationalism of

35 As noted by Evans, Chapter 4, p. 61.

36 Programmes at the Univerities of Maastricht and Tilburg offer exceptions.

37 Hans-Wolfgang Micklitz is Professor for Economic Law and Head of the Law Department at the European University Institute in Florence.

38 Micklitz, Chapter 3, p. 57.

39 Micklitz, Chapter 3, p. 58.

legal education? Are the continental legal systems stuck in their post-Westphalian boundaries?"[40] Micklitz offers some further questions which might help formulate a response. Tantalizingly, he concludes: "I will leave for a later occasion to develop these thoughts … ".[41]

Legal Education in Asia's World City – Where Next for the Chinese University of Hong Kong?

The Faculty of Law at the Chinese University of Hong Kong is the newest law school in Hong Kong, and, indeed, the youngest law school represented at the conference from which this collection of chapters derive. It was established as a School of Law in 2004, admitted its first students in 2006, and was granted Faculty status in 2008. It is now, in terms of total student numbers, the largest provider of degree-level legal education in Hong Kong, with over 1,300 students studying for LLB, JD, LLM, Postgraduate Certificate in Laws (PCLL) and Doctor of Philosophy (PhD) degrees. In its relatively short period of development, the Faculty has had to address a number of significant challenges, which largely derive from the circumstances of its establishment.

Undergraduate education, including the LLB degrees offered at The Chinese University, Hong Kong University and City University, and research postgraduate education, are heavily subsidized by the Hong Kong taxpayer,[42] and therefore there is at least an indirect control over the numbers of students admitted to undergraduate programmes. When the Chinese University LLB was established it was pegged at an admission of 60 local students per year (now 70 students). It was quickly appreciated that a programme of that size would not be sustainable, or at least would not allow legal studies to develop significantly in the University, and the decision was taken to pursue growth through the establishment of a number of taught postgraduate programmes – the *Juris Doctor* programme (which was already established at the City University of Hong Kong and which was designed to be a qualifying law degree), and three LLM programmes (Common Law, International Economic Law and Chinese Business Law).

The significance of going down this route was two-fold, and derives from a key part of Hong Kong Government policy on the funding of tertiary education. In Hong Kong, with only a few exceptions, taught postgraduate education does not receive support from public funds. All such programmes are, therefore, self-financed, that

40 Micklitz, Chapter 3, p. 59.

41 Micklitz, Chapter 3, p. 60.

42 At the time of writing, Hong Kong LLB students pay a tuition fee to their university of HK$46,000 per annum which must make them the envy of their counterparts in most other common law jurisdictions. Many European countries do not charge tuition fees. Scotland (somewhere between the Continent and the Common Law as always) does not charge local students any tuition fee.

is, paid for by the student in the form of tuition fees. Furthermore, since these self-financed programmes are not publicly funded, they are not subject to the kind of control on numbers that applies in the case of undergraduate programmes. The University also decided to offer the Postgraduate Certificate in Laws – which in Hong Kong provides a skills-based "bridge" between the qualifying law degree and practical professional training as a trainee solicitor or pupil barrister. Although this is a programme for which government support is available, the Faculty was only afforded support for 36 student places (out of a planned intake of 130, now at 150), with the result that the Postgraduate Certificate in Laws Programme is predominantly self-financed, like the JD and LLM programmes.

The development of successful taught postgraduate programmes has therefore allowed the Faculty to expand significantly beyond the size that would have been sustainable if restricted to publicly funded student numbers. The development and funding strategy pursued by the Faculty, while highly successful, does present some risks. In the first place, it is dependent upon the market for well-qualified law graduates, and its continuing attractiveness as a destination for such students. That market will have to be increasingly global, since it cannot be supplied by the numbers of local students pursuing graduate legal studies. Secondly, local political concerns (driven largely by misconceptions about the admission of students from Mainland China)[43] have led to calls for the reduction in the number of international students admitted to Hong Kong universities. The Faculty of Law at the Chinese University would certainly be at risk if the number of international students were to be restricted.[44]

The other major challenge faced by the Faculty of Law in its development has been to differentiate itself from the already established Faculty of Law at Hong Kong University and the School of Law at the City University of Hong Kong. Both have established leading positions as providers of legal education and research in Hong Kong. The Faculty of Law at Hong Kong University has established a pre-eminent position in the study of public law issues in the region, and in particular Hong Kong constitutional law and Basic Law studies. The School of Law at City University has very effectively engaged with Mainland China and developed close working relations with law schools and public agencies in the People's Republic of China (PRC).

Given its diverse faculty profile, and its capacity to draw on experience of a wide range of national jurisdictions[45] and transnational law, the Faculty's strategy

---

43 See above, p. 9.

44 It is important to note here that the Faculty does not differentiate between local and non-local students in determining tuition fee levels for its taught postgraduate programmes, although such differentiation is to be found in other programmes across the sector in Hong Kong.

45 At the time of writing (and in no particular order): England and Wales, France, Hong Kong, India, Italy, New Zealand, the United States of America, Northern Ireland, Canada, China, Australia, Taiwan, Spain, Finland, Scotland, Germany.

has been to promote an internationalized profile, especially in its research activities. The Faculty is thus rooted in Hong Kong – and that is necessarily the case when it comes to the delivery of the LLB and JD degrees – but pursues research (and teaching) in areas that are of significance beyond Hong Kong.

In order to carry forward its strategy the Faculty has recently adopted a wide-ranging "Globalization Strategy" which is ambitious in its breadth and its depth. Elements of the strategy range from the funding of global scholarships for students, the establishment of new visiting professorships and fellowships to the re-design of the curricula of all of its programmes (with the exception of the Postgraduate Certificate in Laws). The LLB has been re-designed to allow all students to complete the "required" courses for the LLB in years 1 and 2 of the degree, thus leaving years 3 and 4 as wholly elective years with freedom for students to choose different directions in their study, and in particular enhancing the opportunities for students to take advantage of more than 200 study abroad possibilities offered by the University. By a combination of courses in their third and fourth years, students may elect to graduate with a specialism (or specialisms) in such areas as "Global Law", Chinese Law or International Commercial Law. The Faculty recognizes that many students will, of course, spend their third or final year completing the requirements for admission to the Postgraduate Certificate in Laws, but even for students who choose the "professional" route there remains the opportunity to pursue a specialism in another area. A review of the JD programme was instituted in 2014 and will be completed in 2015, and elements of the philosophy pursued in the LLB revisions will be incorporated, *mutatis mutandis*, into the JD programme.

One of the issues that had to be addressed in the development of this globalization agenda is how to deal with the comparative study of the law. Should we make all students follow a course on "comparative law", or should we adopt a policy of "embedding" comparative elements in other courses?[46] We have opted for the latter, and it is proposed that, over time, as many courses as possible in the LLB and JD programmes will have a comparative element. At the same time, the Faculty will offer an elective course on comparative law for students who wish to more fully develop their understanding of the theoretical problems to which the comparative study of law gives rise.

At the same time, we have not lost sight of the "ethical" dimension of the study of law. At present, the Faculty of Law at The Chinese University of Hong Kong is the only one of the three law schools in Hong Kong to make the study of ethics a compulsory part of both its LLB and JD programmes, recognizing that ethical issues arising from the study of law are by no means confined to "professional" ethics. Similarly, the Faculty encourages students not to lose sight of the issues of human rights and justice that figure in the range of considerations that brought them to law school in the first place and offers courses of study, including experiential

46 The debate is similar to that which surrounded the introduction of Common Market/EU law into the curriculum in the United Kingdom.

learning, that encourage students to engage directly with some challenging social issues in Hong Kong.[47]

Recently the Standing Committee on Legal Education and Training (a statutory body which has oversight of these broad areas in Hong Kong) announced its intention to undertake a comprehensive review of legal education and training in Hong Kong. While reviews of legal education are not the stuff that dreams are made of, the Faculty sees this as an opportunity to be fully involved in shaping the future direction of legal education in Hong Kong, having, in a sense, "inherited" a system which it was not party to shaping. Key issues that we will have to address include: (1) the relationship between the law degree and legal practice, and in particular the future of the Postgraduate Certificate in Laws as a "bridge" between the qualifying law degree and professional legal training; (2) the question of whether there should continue to be both an undergraduate and a graduate qualifying degree; (3) balancing the "open" nature of the legal professional market in Hong Kong with the understandable concerns of the profession about increasing international competition in the provision of legal services; (4) the implications of the already significant and growing importance of China as a consumer of legal services in Hong Kong – including the growth of Chinese law firms practising in Hong Kong; (5) the maintenance of the distinctive identity of Hong Kong's legal system.

It will be a busy time for all concerned in the future of legal education in Hong Kong!

---

47 These include: The Clinic for Public Interest Advocacy; Refugee Clinical Legal Assistance Programme; The Individual, the Community and the Law (a compulsory course which requires students to identify a significant social/policy issue in Hong Kong and to explore it through empirical study).

PART I
Theoretical Framework

Chapter 1

Getting Back to Our Roots: Global Law Schools in Local Context

Kate Galloway[1]

The contemporary law school sits at the intersection of global legal practice and global higher education. What was once a jurisdiction-specific endeavour is now ostensibly outward looking, driven by a call for international students, standards requiring equivalence of qualification, global rankings and the apparently borderless marketplace for graduates. At the same time though, there are calls for 'distinctive' graduates. While in one sense this relates to managerialist marketing of higher education, it is also relevant to grassroots community service and how a law school meets local community needs. This chapter frames a discussion of the direction of legal education around the dialectic of globalization and place, imputing not just geography and jurisdiction, but culture and community.

Introduction

There is no shortage of discussion around the meaning of globalization and internationalization of the law curriculum.[2] The topic is of interest to legal scholars and legal educators in both a discipline and pedagogical sense,[3] but also to universities in their quest for increased enrolments and to students who seek, so we are told, maximum portability of their qualification in the 'global employment marketplace'.

The position of the profession in this picture is somewhat more diverse. Organizations such as the Commonwealth Lawyers Association, ASEAN Law Association or Law Association for Asia and the Pacific (LAWASIA) have an

---

1 Senior Lecturer and Director of Teaching and Learning, School of Law, James Cook University, Cairns.

2 See e.g. Ronald Barnett, Gareth Parry, Kelly Coate, 'Conceptualising Curriculum Change' (2001) 6(4) *Teaching in Higher Education*, 435; Special edition; Simon Chesterman, 'The Globalisation of Legal Education' (2008) 58 *Singapore Journal of Legal Studies*; Stacey Steele and Kathryn Taylor (eds), *Legal Education in Asia* (Taylor and Francis, 2009).

3 See discussion in Stacey Steele and Kathryn Taylor 'Globalisation, Change and Contexts' in Steele and Taylor (eds), *Legal Education in Asia* (Taylor and Francis, 2009), 3; David Sugarman and Avrom Sherr, 'Editorial: Globalisation and Legal Education' (2001) 8(1) *International Journal of the Legal Profession*, 6; Jeff Waincymer, 'Internationalization of Legal Education: Putting the "Why" Before the "How"' in Steele and Taylor (eds) *Legal Education in Asia* (Routledge, 2009), 69; Qiang, Zha, 'Internationalization of Higher Education: Towards a Conceptual Framework' (2003) 1(2) *Policy Futures in Education*, 24.

interest in law in a transnational and international context, and increasingly the profession is calling for greater international engagement, including law graduates with knowledge of international contexts of law and prepared for global practice. However within particular jurisdictions it is the local profession that regulates entry to membership, and therefore the educational requirements of lawyers. This focus tends to be on the law of the jurisdiction in question, but also on the skills required to serve the community within that jurisdiction. This latter aspect of legal education presupposes an understanding of the community we serve. It plays out within Australia, where there are calls for development of skills and knowledge required for rural and regional practice: a particularly local context.

There is an additional local context that falls between the international and local 'at home': that of the 'locals' of an overseas jurisdiction. These people are not the clients of the international or transnational lawyer, but people who are affected by the consequences of international and transnational transactions. Consider the example of the Panguna Mine in Papua New Guinea (PNG).[4]

Australia's close northern neighbour, PNG, is rich in natural resources. Governed by Australia for many years until its independence in 1975, Australia has had an ongoing interest in PNG through both aid programs and investment – and the two are often inextricably linked – notably in mining. Bougainville Copper owns the Panguna open cut mine on Bougainville. The mine has been sitting idle since 1989 as a consequence of sabotage by the Bougainville Revolutionary Army, which sought secession from PNG and closure of the mine on environmental grounds.

To structure the acquisition and operation of the mine would have required an army of lawyers schooled in transnational dealings. Rio Tinto and the PNG Government are majority shareholders in Bougainville Copper. This structuring alone would have required sophisticated legal advice. Likewise, resources law itself in PNG required a lawyerly hand. It is significant that the framework for resource ownership echoes that of Australia, where resources are owned by the state, which differs from traditional Melanesian concept of land ownership, vested in traditional owners.

The structure of the mining rights and the mine's operation have resulted in severe environmental problems and impoverishment of the local people through lack of economic benefit flowing to them. This has contributed to armed resistance and ultimately a challenge to PNG's sovereignty through a bloody civil war. These issues could be thought of as representing the confluence of very local problems wrought by an abstracted transnational view of a legal transaction. Now that the mine has closed, this is also an economic issue for the company itself – an asset lying idle. Surely this was an unsustainable model that reflects a lack of understanding of local context.

4 The story of the Panguna mine is recounted in Antony Loewenstein, *Profits of Doom: How Vulture Capitalism is Swallowing the World* (Melbourne University Press, 2013).

What this illustrates is that what might be my 'international' experience is the local experience of someone else. The local and the international in this case, are inherently connected. For those lawyers who will advise in such matters, it is not enough to be educated in international laws, or simply in local laws. To have made a success of this project, for example, required different types of knowledge, skills and attitudes.

How are we to design curricula that meet these ostensibly divergent objectives? How can we address both the local – the local *here* and the local *there* – and the international?

This chapter recounts the ongoing path of the James Cook University ('JCU') Law School in Far North Queensland. The Law School has two regional campuses, separated by 350km. It serves the local community, including the local profession but is also cognizant of its relationship with the wider region, the state and the nation, as well as within the Asia–Pacific region.

In doing so, this chapter suggests ways in which we might think differently not just about what we do in the law curriculum, but why and how we do it – so that we can hope to reconcile the global and the local, as well as address the other imperatives of the contemporary law degree.

Internationalization and Other Imperatives in Australian Legal Education

Australian law schools are facing increasing calls to offer an internationalized curriculum. These calls come from two directions.

The first is the now international market for students. Universities are competing on a global scale and seek to attract a global cohort. The law degree, traditionally jurisdictionally based, now needs to find ways to respond to this market imperative. Additionally, our graduates seek qualifications that will serve them internationally – whether they are local or from overseas. To be competitive, our law degrees must offer a set of portable skills and knowledge.

But calls are coming also from the profession, which is itself becoming increasingly transnational and international. The Bentley Report, delivered in 2012, concluded that 'internationalization is having a significant impact on legal practice in Australia, and that legal education must change to reflect this reality'.[5] This reflects a consistent theme in conferences, judicial speeches and media reports over many years.[6]

---

5 *Education for Sustainable Development* (UNESCO) <http://www.unesco.org/new/en/education/themes/leading-the-international-agenda/education-for-sustainable-development/> accessed 15 August 2015.

6 *UN Decade of Education for Sustainable Development* (Department of Sustainability, Environment, Water, Population and Communities <http://www.environment.gov.au/education/decade/index.html> accessed 15 August 2015; Michael Rose, 'Rising to the Global Challenge in the Legal Profession' *The Australian* 21 February 2011; Robert French C.J., 'Horses for Courses' presented at *Internationalising the Australian Law Curriculum for Enhanced Global Legal Education and Practice: National Symposium*, Canberra, 16

Australian legal educators have not been complacent. The recent Threshold Learning Outcomes for Law[7] (TLOs) for example require graduates of the Bachelor of Laws to have a 'coherent body of knowledge that includes … fundamental areas of legal knowledge … including international and comparative contexts'.[8] The Bentley Report offers a framework for developing an internationalized curriculum,[9] and there is of course a healthy literature on this topic within legal education.

We have other imperatives also in the law curriculum. The TLOs incorporate the so-called 'Priestley 11' core Australian law subjects[10] within the knowledge to be acquired by graduates. These are required for accreditation with the admitting bodies in Australia. Also in the Australian context is the oversight of the new regulatory body of the Tertiary Education Quality Standards Agency, and the Australian Qualifications Framework. While these do not cover the content of the law degree per se, they do affect the level of student learning and require assurance of student learning reflecting discipline standards.

In terms of law specifically, there are choices to be made not just about internationalization of curriculum, but how much theory and jurisprudence is included and what will be the approach to law in context and critical perspectives.[11] The TLOs and the regulatory framework will require evidence of a variety of skills in addition to legal knowledge including collaboration and self-management.[12] Increasingly also our curricula incorporate not just the traditional problem-solving, research and mooting skills, but professional skills such as Alternative Dispute Resolution (ADR), client interviewing, professional writing and advocacy. These support an increasing move to 'work integrated learning' within the law school, scaffolded throughout the law degree.[13] There is a strong evidence-based argument

---

March 2012; Symposium Internationalisation, Curriculum and the Future Practice of Law at Bond University, Gold Coast, 23–24 November, 2012.

7 Sally Kift, Israel Mark and Rachael Field, 'Bachelor of Laws Learning and Teaching Academic Standards Statement' (Australian Learning and Teaching Council, 2010).

8 Ibid., 10, TLO 1.

9 UNESCO, above n. 5.

10 The 'Priestley 11' is the list of prescribed areas of legal knowledge identified by the Law Council of Australia that a student must cover within his or her law degree in order to be admitted to legal practice. See <www1.lawcouncil.asn.au/LACC/images/pdfs/LACC PrescribedAcademicAreasofKnowledge-June2008.pdf> accessed 13 August 2015.

11 Alex Steel, 'Good Practice Guide (Bachelor of Laws) Law in Broader Contexts' (ALTC, 2013).

12 TLOs 5 and 6. For examples on how these relate to curriculum design, see Elizabeth Handsley, 'Good Practice Guide (Bachelor of Laws) Collaboration Skills' (ALTC, 2011); and Judith Marychurch, 'Good Practice Guide (Bachelor of Laws) Self-Management' (ALTC, 2011).

13 Mandy Shircore et al., *'From the First Year to the Final Year Experience: Embedding Reflection for Work Integrated Learning in a Holistic Curriculum Framework'* (2013) 4(1) *International Journal of the First Year in Higher Education*, 125.

also for dealing with student psychological wellness through a variety of curricular innovations that challenge our view of the traditional law degree.[14]

There are further pressures also on what we teach and how we teach it. In higher education generally there has been a movement over recent years towards sustainability education and although this has not been highly visible in the Australian legal education context,[15] there is a growing literature both within substantive law and legal education.[16] Of greater visibility, but perhaps not yet with the desired impact, is the embedding of Indigenous perspectives into education. Again, there are a great many examples of scholarship and curriculum innovation in this area.[17]

For colleagues who are discipline experts in the traditional mould, the sheer scope of these developments in the focus of and approach to teaching in our discipline may seem overwhelming.[18] This is particularly the case if each curriculum innovation is seen as adding more content to an already crowded curriculum. Without careful planning, internationalization could seem to be yet another competing novelty in a long list.

In addition, the context of legal practice within Australia provides another priority for law schools. For all the calls from the profession for graduates conversant in international laws and contexts, local communities in Australia are crying out for competent lawyers to serve local needs. The Law Council of Australia in a 2009 survey ascertained that there was a serious shortage of lawyers in rural, regional and remote communities.[19] Firms in these areas have difficulty attracting and retaining staff and this is negatively affecting the ability of people in these areas to access justice.

This certainly reflects the experience in the catchment of the JCU Law School's campuses in Cairns and Townsville. These two small cities serve a wide region, including small towns and hamlets, as well as some of the remotest areas

14 See e.g., special edition on student wellness in (2011) 21(2) *Legal Education Review.*

15 Kate Galloway et al., *Using Sustainability to Inform Renewal of the LLB Foundation Curriculum: Knowledge Skills and Attitudes for the Future* (2012) 12(1) *QUT Law and Justice Journal*, 1.

16 See eg bibliography in Steel, above n11.

17 See eg Special Topic Issue: Incorporating Indigenous Perspectives in the Law Curriculum (2009) 19 (2) *Legal Education Review*; Special edition on Indigenous curricula (2012) 4 *Ngiya: Talk the Law*.

18 In the context of sustainability education, see e.g. Arjen E.J. Wals and Bob Jickling, '"Sustainability" in Higher Education: From Doublethink and Newspeak to Critical Thinking and Meaningful Learning' (2002) 3(3) *International Journal of Sustainability in Higher Education*, 221; Kerry Shephard, and Mary Furnari, 'Exploring What University Teachers Think About Education for Sustainability' (2012) *Studies in Higher Education*, 1.

19 *ALTC Learning and Teaching Sustainability, Sustainability Resources for Learning & Teaching in Higher Education* (ALTC <http://sustainability.edu.au/> accessed 13 August 2015).

of the state. The Law School inevitably supports the local profession and the local community by providing graduates ready to qualify as lawyers. The Law School works closely with the profession to take into account contemporary needs of legal practice and to provide both the profession and our students with networking opportunities.

The question in the JCU context has therefore become: how might we properly integrate these apparently competing ideas – localization and internationalization?[20] Are they reconcilable? I believe that they are and that in fact, they are two sides of the same coin. As the Panguna Mine story illustrates, one person's international is, after all, another person's local. Global economic dealings occur in a context, and they involve people and places. And this is the key to an integrated curriculum.

Resolving Tension in Curriculum Priorities

Despite the well-known focus in legal education on doctrine and problem-solving ostensibly driven by jurisdictional accreditation requirements ('black letter' law) there is scope for designing curriculum beyond black letter and doctrinal approaches.[21] Waincymer for example points out that there are choices and trade-offs as to the composition of legal education[22] and even in a traditional approach to curriculum there are decisions to be made about what content and how it is presented.

The Bentley Report, in the context of focusing on an internationalized curriculum,[23] identifies four key approaches to curriculum design: the aggregation approach involving separate internationalized or global subjects; segregation through establishment of a separate institute or centre of international or global aspects of law; integration by incorporating international and intercultural aspects within the whole curriculum and beyond; and immersion through student placement overseas.[24]

The Report provides a useful framework and process for development of such a curriculum – but this presupposes a decision already taken to internationalize as a priority within the curriculum. This part will focus on conceptualizing the curriculum to facilitate decisions that take place before that point. Investment in conceptualizing educational goals and curriculum at this early stage can assist in navigating the tension between what might seem to be competing priorities. This process involves articulating the degree's learning outcomes and teaching

20 Waincymer for example discusses the competing priorities in legal education. See above n. 3, 78.

21 See eg discussion in Kate Galloway and Peter Jones, 'Guarding Our Identities: The Dilemma of Transformation in the Legal Academy' (2014) 14(1) *QUT Law Review*, 15.

22 Waincymer, above n. 3, 71.

23 Bentley and Squelch, above n. 5.

24 Bentley and Squelch, above n. 5.

and learning approaches in terms of what we want our students to know, do and be like. They are therefore educational, rather than instrumental or managerial. While these other aspects do need to be taken into account, they are likely to be addressed through an effectively designed curriculum.

Curriculum through the Thematic Lens

Erickson provides a cogent argument for curriculum design through what she calls a thematic lens.[25] Vinson et al describe this as:

> an interdisciplinary approach to instruction. This approach focuses on one concept, and seeks to define and describe that concept through a variety of perspectives and fields of study ... The benefits of the thematic lens approach to learning are both the ability to look deeper into a single topic, and to gain a broad, cross-disciplinary understanding of said topic.[26]

In the law curriculum, this can be interpreted as providing a broad, overarching conceptual approach to the study of the various units (or subjects, sub-disciplines) within the degree. Aligned with contemporary imperatives within the discipline of higher education in Australia for example, a degree focusing on Indigenous perspectives,[27] sustainability[28] or of course internationalization, could provide a move away from thinking in terms of 'traditional' doctrinal approaches to substantive law taught within each of these concepts, and a curriculum that engages students in thinking broadly about the law through a particular perspective.

Once the curriculum is conceptualized in terms of learning through a concept, the possibilities afforded by the relationships between the different concepts ascendant in Australian higher education are evident. A key feature of sustainability for example, is interconnectedness. This is the case not just in environmental terms, but also in terms of the economy, and culturally. It is difficult to consider law in any of these domains in isolation without appreciating the flow-on effects. This is a useful lens for understanding the operation and the implications of the law. Such ideas may also require an appreciation of the effects of globalization on domestic law, but also the interrelationship between domestic contexts and international ones. Waincymer for example conceptualizes the law as 'an ever more intricate web of legal norms that apply to modern transactions'.[29] Likewise, globalization has affected Indigenous peoples since ancient times and the effects of colonization

25 H. Lynn Erickson, *Concept-based Curriculum and Instruction: Teaching Beyond the Facts* (Sage, 2002).

26 Emily Vinson et al., *Through the Looking Glass: Thematic Lenses, Rich Media, and the Texas Legacy Project* (University of Texas, 2009), 1.

27 See above, n. 17.

28 Galloway et al, above n. 15.

29 Waincymer, above n. 3, 77.

continue to resonate. This in turn affects sustainability of economies and cultures and the operation of the law.

This (very) brief example illustrates how it might be possible to construct a narrative around the law curriculum, providing contextual learning for students rather than solely relying on abstracted legal concepts. These ideas provide stimuli for questioning the 'ought' of the law[30] and a benchmark for comparing, measuring and testing the role of the law in society. In doing so, they do not detract from learning the text of the law. They simply frame why that text is learned, how it is learned and how it is assessed. This reflects a move away from purely vocational and market-driven educational outcomes, to one that focuses on student learning and a broad range of contextual and critical skills. Graduates will still be employable, but their skills will be enhanced by a curriculum that has reintroduced the 'unruliness of the social'.[31]

While the thematic lens is a useful tool through which to embrace a diverse range of conceptual approaches to learning the law, there is a further complementary strategy that offers a theoretical means by which to design a curriculum to support student engagement in both local and international dimensions of the law.

Place-Based Pedagogy

Pue observes that the most striking pattern apparent in writing in the area of internationalization is geographical.[32] He sees the experience of empire and colonization as informing more pessimistic responses to the idea of internationalization of the law curriculum. He postulates that where a law school is located informs that faculty's attitude towards internationalization either as a gateway to broader understanding, or as a means of homogenization. The Panguna Mine is an example of a worst-case scenario of globalization where local experiences do not seem to have been considered in drawing up the legal context. These issues could perhaps have been at least mitigated with a different approach to the structuring of the operations.

Esposito points out that '[p]lace plays an indelible role in the way we perceive and come to understand the world around us'.[33] Place is also regarded as a key learning tool for students and place-based pedagogies recognize this. Failure to take place into account (for example, in assuming a homogenous 'global' approach) runs the risk of alienating the local. A place-based pedagogy

---

30 Margaret Thornton, 'The Demise of Diversity in Legal Education: Globalisation and the New Knowledge Economy' (2001) 8(1) *International Journal of the Legal Profession* 37, 46.

31 Ibid., 45.

32 W. Wesley Pue, 'Globalisation and Legal Education: From the Outside-In' (2001) 8(1) *International Journal of the Legal Profession*, 87, 95.

33 Lauren Esposito, 'Where to Begin? Using Place-Based Writing to Connect Students with Their Local Communities' (2012) 101(4) *English Journal*, 70.

facilitates students' awareness and understanding of where they are and their role in society,[34] presupposing a connection with students' own experiences, implicitly related to place.

> [Place-based education] is ... an approach to curriculum development and instruction that acknowledges and makes use of the places where students live to induct them into the discourses and practices of any and all ... subjects ... Community and place become additional 'texts' for student learning. ... It can also act as an antidote to the experience of disconnection or alienation that sociologists from Emile Durkheim to Robert Bellah and Robert Putnam have associated with life in industrial and postindustrial civilizations ... Place-based education can address these gaps by providing ... people with opportunities to experience in visceral ways both the human and natural communities that surround them.[35]

Gruenewald goes so far as to suggest that a place-based pedagogy and critical pedagogy[36] are mutually supportive, and that a 'critical pedagogy of place offers a much needed framework for educational theory, research, policy, and practice'.[37] It is known also as a crucial component of a wider pedagogy of ecology or sustainability.[38]

Such a pedagogical approach may assist in addressing some of the more negative views of internationalization in the legal context, as well as opening up the curriculum to localized or regional perspectives also. Because place is more than simply jurisdictional boundaries, this approach also draws on cultural context and therefore cultural competencies. It invites a comparative approach through understanding not only the student's immediate vicinity, but also the relationship between *here* and *there*. Drawing on student understanding of place and how that plays out in both a local, regional, national and international legal context has potential to integrate what might otherwise form discrete ideas or components of curriculum. Like Erickson's thematic lens, place offers a vantage point from which to engage in the law, providing learning with context and otherwise divergent subject areas with a unifying theme.

---

34 David A. Gruenewald, 'Foundations of Place: A Multidisciplinary Framework for Place-Conscious Education' (2003) 40(3) *American Educational Research Journal*, 619.

35 Gregory A. Smith, 'Place-Based Education' in Robert B. Stevenson et al. (eds), *International Handbook of Research on Environmental Education* (Routledge, 2013), 213.

36 See eg the work of Paolo Freire, *Pedagogy of the Oppressed* (Myra Bergman Ramos Trans) (Penguin [Trans of: Pedagogia do Oprimido], 1972); Stephen D. Brookfield, *Becoming a Critically Reflective Teacher* (Jossey-Bass, 1995).

37 David A. Gruenewald, 'The Best of Both Worlds: A Critical Pedagogy of Place' (2008) 14(3) *Environmental Education Research*, 308.

38 Jennie Winter and Debby Cotton, 'Making the Hidden Curriculum Visible: Sustainability Literacy in Higher Education' (2012) 18(6) *Environmental Education Research*, 783.

Legal education is known for its abstraction – not necessarily from the 'real world' of practice, but from the real world altogether.[39] Characters in the appellate case law on which the study of law is based, are disembodied people stripped of their personality, their culture and, depending on the context, on their personal attributes as well.[40] Emotions are distanced and this is now recognized as an issue for the wellbeing of law students and practitioners alike.[41]

In contrast, place-based pedagogy recognizes that:

> Although culture and place are deeply intertwined, our relationship with places has been obscured by an educational system that currently neglects them. That is, schooling often distracts our attention from, and distorts our response to, the actual contexts of our own lives (places). (Citations omitted)[42]

While this statement is made in the context of schooling, the same could be said of higher education in general, and legal education in particular. A sense of place engages students not just with the physical environment around them, but community and culture. In the Australian context, there is a link between Indigenous culture and conceptions of place that is an important component of legal education. It represents the opportunity to develop cross-cultural competencies and to recognize the historical and contemporary impact of the law on Indigenous Australians. Through understanding the local, the gates of the university can be opened to Aboriginal and Torres Strait Islander communities thus generating community relationships that will serve both Indigenous and non-Indigenous students and staff. The same applies to residents of rural and regional Australia.

In the international or transnational context, 'place' recognizes that the effects of the law 'touch down' somewhere, and impact upon real (local) people in a particular cultural and ecological environment. The 'place' adapted in the JCU law curriculum is the tropics.

---

39 See e.g., Lucy Maxwell, 'How to Develop Law Students' Critical Awareness? Change the Language of Legal Education' (2012) 22(1) *Legal Education Review*, 99.

40 This has been a persistent feminist critique of the law. See e.g. Ngaire Naffine, *Law and the Sexes: Explorations in Feminist Jurisprudence* (Allen & Unwin, 1990).

41 See e.g., Colin James, 'Law Student Wellbeing: Benefits of Promoting Psychological Literacy and Self-Awareness Using Mindfulness, Strengths Theory and Emotional Intelligence' (2011) 21(1&2) *Legal Education Review*, 217; Norm Kelk et al., 'Courting the Blues: Attitudes Towards Depression in Australian Law Students and Lawyers' (2009); Molly Townes O'Brien, Stephen Tang and Kath Hall, 'Changing Our Thinking: Empirical Research on Law Student Wellbeing, Thinking Styles and the Law Curriculum' (2011) 21(1&2) *Legal Education Review*, 149; Kennon M. Sheldon and Lawrence S. Krieger, 'Understanding the Negative Effects of Legal Education on Law Students: A Longitudinal Test and Extension of Self-Determination Theory' (2007) 33 *Personality & Social Psychology Bulletin*, 883.

42 Gruenewald, above n. 34, 621.

The Tropics

JCU's mission is to engage in research and teaching 'in subjects of special importance to the people of the tropics'.[43] The educational concept of place-based pedagogies together with broader curriculum theory outlined above has supported the translation of this mission into a foundation for the law curriculum. Importantly it has allowed a multi-layered approach that draws in the strands of conceptual priorities in the contemporary law degree, including internationalization, localization, Indigenous perspectives and sustainability. Rather than being in tension, by looking at these areas as ideas through the thematic lens of the tropics, they resonate and reinforce student learning about the law, its role in society and their own place within both the law and society.

Each discipline at JCU has had to find its own level, its own means by which to represent place – the tropics – within the curriculum. For some, this has been easier than for others.[44] In the case of law, a place-based curriculum offers potential to identify *our* place as the tropics and our students the means by which to better understand the links between place and their discipline. This holds potential to elevate learning the abstracted ideas of the discipline to more closely represent experiential learning that could otherwise be subordinated to those abstracted ideas.

The framework for organizing curriculum through the thematic lens of the tropics provides the opportunity for an integrated approach to place – that encompasses both internationalization and localization.

In terms of developing curriculum, Erickson's framework identifies 'theory' as the highest conceptual level.[45] In the JCU context, this concept is the tropics. Through a review of the literature principally in tropical geography, it becomes clear that the notion of the tropics is deeply embedded with European notions of self. The persistent theme, since the times of the ancient Greeks, was to control the fertile but dangerous[46] tropics to provide materially for the European market – an imperative that fueled the exploration of the Age of Discovery. Associated with the perceived peril of tropical climates was also a perception of immorality of its people. The indolence associated with the foetid humid darkness of the region drove the science and the medicine of Victorian times. These ideas persisted

---

43 *James Cook University Act 1997* (Qld), s5(c).

44 See e.g., Kate Galloway, 'Refreshed in the Tropics: Developing Curricula Using a Thematic Lens' (2011) 4(1&2), 119.

45 H. Lynn Erickson, *Concept-based Curriculum and Instruction: Teaching Beyond the Facts* (Sage, 2002).

46 See e.g., David Arnold, '"Illusory Riches": Representations of the Tropical World, 1840–1950' 21(1) (2000) *Singapore Journal of Tropical Geography*, 6, 7; Stephen Frenkel, 'Geography, Empire, and Environmental Determinism' 82(2) (1992) *Geographical Review*, 143; Mike Hulme, 'The Conquering of Climate: Discourses of Fear and their Dissolution' 174(1) (2008) *The Geographical Journal*, 5; David Livingstone, 'Tropical Climate and Moral Hygiene: The Anatomy of a Victorian Debate' 32(1) (1999), 93.

almost unnoticed into the twentieth century in the work of the noted geographer Pierre Gourou.[47]

As this illustrates, place – represented here by the tropics – is more than simply location. It is people and culture, it is history and environment, and it is perception. The 'geographical imaginary of the tropics [is] an interpretive frame, constructed, enacted and disciplined in the process of European expansion into the tropical world'.[48] As a lens for development of the curriculum, we have sought to reconstruct this frame in a positive sense, resulting in a critical approach to the idea of place and the law that operates within that context.

To the extent that the tropics is *here* it also determines *there.* In Said's terms, the Orient is defined by its very otherness.[49] Its non-Europeanness from the perspective of a European hegemony reflects the sense of self of the observer. Through understanding one's immediate place and drawing links within the overarching concept of that locale, we aim to emphasize the importance of context in the operation and evolution of the law and its practice, providing opportunities for critique, comparison, inclusion, cultural competency and a grounded global – yet local – outlook.

For the JCU LLB, we have taken this lens as a cue for teaching and researching critically – challenging traditional parameters of colonialism and empire and focusing on models of sustainability in governance; economy and finance; community development; and the environment.[50] The tropics provides a common narrative around these key organizing principles, of the experience and vision of those from within the tropics rather than from those outside. And importantly, this idea of place allows for a linking of the local and the global.

While the latest iteration of our curriculum development is presently under construction, our next goal is to embed an understanding of our place within the Asia–Pacific region through exploration of the law. Place, and the domains of sustainability, remain central.

The local and the international context of the law, legal practice and legal institutions are introduced in the first year program through first a comparative approach drawing on the underlying principles of legal institutions and the very nature of the law, and then through a critical approach to the role of the lawyer in society, the nature of culture in the context of the law, and the impact of globalization on the law notably, as it is experienced in a local context.[51]

Using my own field of land law as an example in the second year, we use the idea of the cultures and environment of our region, both locally and

47 Pierre Gourou, *The Tropical World* (ED Laborde trans) (Longmans Green & Co, 1953), 1 [trans of: *Les Pays Tropicaux* (first published 1947)].

48 Felix Driver and Brenda Yeoh, 'Constructing the Tropics: Introduction' *Singapore Journal of Tropical Geography* 21(1) (2000), 1, 4, making reference to Livingstone.

49 Edward Said, *Orientalism* (Routledge, 1978).

50 See Galloway, above n. 44; Galloway et al., above n. 15.

51 Galloway et al., above n. 15.

internationally, to problematize the very concept of property. This affords the opportunity to explore Anglo–Australian, Indigenous and regional variations on concepts of property and how they support systems of land ownership. Students in this subject also engage in comparative systems of native title and Torrens land registration as well as the intersection between ecological concerns and property, all of which provide the opportunity for a deeper and more critical engagement with the black letter text of land law and its underlying principles. This broader approach generates thinking about both local and international contexts as well as an appreciation of cultural norms of the society being served – norms unacknowledged, but reflected within property and land law themselves.

In later years, a suite of elective subjects: environmental law, public international law, human rights, law of the sea and Indigenous people and the law provides an opportunity for a more specific engagement in the international arena, though based on an understanding of place – physical and cultural – that facilitates an engagement with the text of the law. The curriculum is thus designed to encourage students to learn about the law as well as learning the law, engaging with ideas and concepts bigger than the law itself.

Conclusion

This conceptual approach to the curriculum – through a thematic lens – offers a shift away from instrumental approaches to curriculum and traditional black letter law. Instead of looking at the 'business case' demands of local stakeholders as a driver for material educational outcomes, and instead of seeing internationalization solely as an instrumental push to support the export of Australian legal services or to meet a global higher education market, I propose a return to the true nature of the profession itself.

As Michael Coper has said, the purpose of the internationalized law curriculum is:

> … to enrich our thinking by consideration of diverse approaches to common problems, to learn from difference but to be alert for universals; … to cultivate the spirit and habit of open-mindedness and tolerance; and ultimately – consistently with our law reform and social justice ethos – to make a contribution to advancing the common good.[52]

The idea of service, of skills that meet client needs to the highest ethical standards, a wisdom borne of experience and a reflective approach to the self and one's own practice, are all hallmarks of good lawyering. Learning texts for the sake of the market may expose our students to these ways of practice, but this is left to chance.

---

52 Bentley and Squelch, above n. 5, 71, citing Michael Coper, 'Internationalisation and the ANU College of Law' Discussion Paper, March 2010, 2.

Understanding oneself and one's context in a personal and professional sense through a structured curriculum in which our place is embedded, seems a far more strategic way to engage our students in both a local and a global outlook.

My proposal here seeks to reflect these ideals, using the international to shine the light also on the local to bring out the best of the professionalism of the law. Legal education then generates the foundation for a profession of service to justice and community. Meeting the challenge of the so-called globalized profession can be achieved through a return to the roots of the profession.

Chapter 2
Global Challenges to Legal Education

John Flood[1]

In all parts of the world, legal education is under critical scrutiny as never before. In the US it is facing meltdown, in the UK it is under extensive review by the regulators, and elsewhere there are sustained moves to overthrow conventional wisdom and adopt more practice modes of legal education in the face of declining job markets in law. Yet new law schools are opening in many countries such as France, India, China, Australia and more. What is causing legal education to be so enmeshed in paradox?

In this chapter I suggest that legal education has always occupied an uneasy position between the theoretical and the vocational. It is redolent in some ways of Twining's personification of legal education as Pericles versus the plumber.[2] While this posits the extremes, the situation is more complex and subtle than that. The pressures on legal education are both endogenous and exogenous. On the one hand the academy is trying to justify a model that it has used for a number of years and is comfortable with, while on the other the economy is exerting huge pressures on legal services such that law jobs are no longer as plentiful as they were.

Various reports and analyses have suggested change. Among them the Carnegie Report,[3] the Legal Education and Training Review (LETR) report,[4] and the American Bar Association Section on Legal Education Task Force report.[5] None has yet provided a solution that commands wide enthusiasm from either the academy or the profession. The question "what is legal education for?" remains unanswered. For many in UK-style regimes legal education is presupposed to have elements

---

1 Leverhulme Research Fellow and Professor of Law and Sociology, University of Westminster.

2 William Twining, 'Pericles and the Plumber' (1967) 83 *Law Quarterly Review*, 396.

3 Anne Colby, William Sullivan and Judith Welch Wegner, *Educating Lawyers: Preparation for the Profession of Law* (Jossey-Bass, 2007).

4 See Legal Education and Training Review Independent Research Team, *Setting Standards: The Future of Legal Services Education and Training Regulation in England and Wales* (2013), <http://letr.org.uk/the-report/index.html>, accessed 27 February 2013.

5 See ABA Task Force *Report and Recommendations American Bar Association Task Force on the Future of Legal Education* (2014) <http://www.americanbar.org/content/dam/aba/administrative/professional_responsibility/report_and_recommendations_of_aba_task_force.authcheckdam.pdf>, accessed 27 February 2014.

of liberal education within it.[6] Proponents of US-style legal education view legal education as more practice-oriented. There are hybrids in between and all agree that one significant outcome of legal education is the production of lawyers.

There are three main challenges for legal education: globalization, technology and regulation. The academy is only beginning to get to grips with these and the profession is perhaps more advanced but finds itself resisting some changes, especially on the regulatory front. The one apparent effect of these changes and challenges is that they promote the deprofessionalization of law and its attendant careers. The result is that the twenty-first century lawyer is confused and in a state of some anxiety and seems ill prepared for the future.

Globalization

Globalization impinges on legal education in three ways. One is the content of legal education is becoming increasingly international, transnational and global. The second is students are more mobile and seek to study outside their home jurisdictions. While we have no specific statistics for law students, we have figures for all students and within them law is one of the key subjects.

According to the Organisation for Economic Cooperation and Development (OECD) the numbers of students studying outside their home countries has more than tripled in the last two decades, from 1.3 million in 1990 to 4.3 million in 2011.[7] The largest numbers of foreign students came from China, India and Korea with Asian students representing 53 per cent of foreign students engaged in tertiary education. The OECD says that its member states accommodated 77 per cent of all students registered outside their home states. If we examine their destinations, we see they reflect geopolitical realities combined with a desire to learn English. The US has 17 per cent, UK has 13 per cent, and Australia, Germany and France have 6 per cent each. Over 30 per cent come to study in social sciences, business and law. The traditional recipients of international education cannot be complacent, however, as newcomers are pushing forward. They include Canada, Japan, Russia and Spain. In addition, some countries are actively seeking students by balancing their higher tuition fees with more relaxed labour market opportunities.

The third impact is the change in legal practice and its globalization. This is especially marked in the growth of the large law firm during the late twentieth century into the present. We know that in the first half of the twentieth century law firms were small organizations with staff in the low hundreds at their biggest. In the

---

6 Tony Bradney *Conversations, Choices and Chances: The Liberal Law School in the Twenty-First Century* (Hart Publishing, 2003).

7 See <http://www.oecd-ilibrary.org/sites/eag_highlights-2013-en/02/05/index.html?contentType=/ns/Chapter,/ns/StatisticalPublication&itemId=/content/chapter/eag_highlights-2013–12-en&containerItemId=/content/serial/2076264x&accessItemIds=&mimeType=text/html>, accessed 17 January 2014.

1970s, with restrictions lifted on partner numbers, law firms grew exponentially.[8] Besides growing domestically law firms sought to expand overseas. Asia became the crucial market with Japan and China as the main markets. When the Iron Curtain collapsed Russia and Eastern Europe drew in many of the law firms from the UK and US. All of this was driven by the rise in international trade and the developments of capital markets. The Washington Consensus became the standard development model and law firms and lawyers did their best to help deliver the message.

Growth in law firms meant that the size of the biggest firms came to be measured in thousands rather than hundreds. Law firms were complex institutions that, despite their size, lacked sophisticated management and leadership.[9] They relied on traditional methods of governance, mainly partnership or patriarchal authority, which limited their development compared to the accounting and consulting firms. Even with moves towards more managerial forms of authority law firms remain small compared to other professional service firms. This necessarily placed a restriction on their ability to recruit large numbers of law graduates. And compared to other professional service firms law firms are monocultural in that there is little diversification from their core service.

The large law firm is an agent of globalization. Since much of global work revolves around the banks and capital markets the large law firms have conveyed these institutions into the world through the agreements they draft. In this respect it is not difficult to overestimate the importance of New York State law and English law as these are the basic normative systems that drive the work of the two main global capital markets: London and New York. Globalization in the legal sphere is represented by the export of these two systems by those trained in them. Much of this path dependency reflects mistrust in other systems as well as knowledge of English and New York law. This is made visible in the rise of the international arbitration system as one of the crucial – if not the crucial – forms of dispute resolution. Keen competition among countries to host arbitration centres and establish arbitration-friendly legislative frameworks enhances this. Even the alternative state-based systems appear to adopt the user-friendly style of arbitration. The Commercial Court in London has always been attractive to foreign parties, as evidenced by the number of Russian "oligarch" cases within its docket.

The big law firm has an over-reaching impact on legal education. Big law firms recruit large numbers of graduates and engage in a wide range of recruiting activities, including "milk rounds" at universities, social events for students and

---

8 Marc Galanter and Thomas Palay, *Tournament of Lawyers: The Transformation of the Big Law Firm* (University of Chicago Press, 1991).

9 Laura Empson, *Who's in Charge? Exploring Leadership Dynamics in Professional Service Firms* (Cass Business School, 2013) <http://www.cass.city.ac.uk/__data/assets/pdf_file/0004/181228/Empson-Exploring-Leadership-Dynamics-in-Professional-Service-Firms.pdf>, accessed 7 May 2014.

internships. This stereotype of the large law firm would be recognized in most countries, but especially in the UK, the US and Australia. Apart from maverick sole practitioners, for example, Perry Mason, Rake or Rumpole, successful lawyers are usually represented on television in large, corporate law firms, for example, *The Good Wife*, *Boston Legal* or *Ally McBeal*. The added allure of large law firms is their sponsorship for taking vocational courses and bar exams, but most of all is their remuneration system, which is generous to incoming lawyers.

The big law firm can be interpreted two ways by new lawyers. In the traditional mode it is a tournament for partnership[10] with the struggle for success as partner being the ultimate outcome.[11] In the mode more typical for Generation Y and the Millenials, the big law firm is a necessary item in a portfolio career that enables easy switching between firms and industries, for example, from law to banking or private practice to in house. The cachet of a stint at a big law firm carries much weight. The other side of this interpretation is that big law firms rely on a stable, relatively unchanging set of indicators for selecting candidates. These typically include university attended, grades, fathers' occupations and more. The result is that big law firms reproduce themselves with little variation. Even attempts at changing hiring processes as illustrated by Clifford Chance's "blind CV" approach do not bear scrutiny.[12]

The approach of the big law firms to education differs in the US and the UK/Europe. For US law firms the only entry qualification is an American Bar Association (ABA) accredited law degree followed by success in the appropriate state bar examination. The ABA tightly regulates legal education demanding 58,000 minutes of instruction for the award of the JD degree.[13] The JD is a professional degree, which generally follows some years of college education in another discipline. The typical route is four years college and three years law school. Disregarding outliers such as Wisconsin which has diploma privilege and

---

10 Galanter and Palay (n. 8); Marc Galanter and William Henderson, 'The Elastic Tournament: A Second Transformation of the Big Law Firm' (2008) 60 *Stanford Law Review*, 1867.

11 Henderson's recent work would indicate the tournament is a lost cause as law firms have changed from being pyramidal structures to being diamond shaped with the "fat" part composed of salaried partners and permanent associates, the top consisting of a shrunk equity partnership, and the bottom as a narrowing pipe for entry level associates seeking training (See William Henderson and Evan Parker-Stephen, 'The Diamond Law Firm: A New Model or the Pyramid Unravelling?' (2013) ,<http://lawyermetrics.com/2013/12/03/the-diamond-law-firm-a-new-model-or-the-pyramid-unraveling>, accessed 7 May 2014.

12 Richard Moorhead, 'Clifford Chance Change Ninjas' (2014), <http://lawyerwatch.wordpress.com/2014/02/03/clifford-chance-change-ninjas>, accessed 27 February 2014.

13 See *ABA Standards and Rules of Procedure for Approval of Law Schools 2013–2014*, <http://www.americanbar.org/groups/legal_education/resources/standards.html>, accessed 17 January 2014.

therefore does not require a bar exam pass from its graduates, this monocentric path into law practice is rigid.[14]

Within the UK and parts of continental Europe the route into practice is more fluid or polycentric. For UK students big law firms prefer a student to have either succeeded well in a law degree from a top-ranking university or to have gained a degree in another discipline and then taken a Graduate Diploma in Law, which typically takes one year to gain. Both of these paths are followed by a Legal Practice Course (LPC), a vocational course that imparts practical skills which takes anywhere between 7 and 12 months. UK students recruited into firms then undertake a two-year training contract that gives them opportunities to experience different departments and law within the firm. At this point they become qualified lawyers (solicitors).

A major distinction between big law firms and smaller ones is that big law firms invest heavily in education. Through their recruiting programmes they select their entrants early, usually during the first degree whether law or otherwise. Law students are then funded through their LPC and non-law students are funded through the Graduate Diploma in Law (GDL) and LPC. This is enhanced by the prevalence of bespoke LPC courses now run for the benefit of big law firms by some law colleges – University of Law and BPP. These are run on the basis that students become familiarized with the firm's documentation. During one interview with a senior telecommunications lawyer from Amsterdam at a major City law firm, he maintained that it mattered little where a lawyer was educated as the prime function of a firm lawyer was to be able to use the firm's documents: these were the knowledge base of the firm.

Faulconbridge, Cook and Muzio[15] have shown how big international law firms are increasingly involved in education, continuing professional development and knowledge transfer (with clients). The main point here is that global law firms are using education as a resource to intensify and deepen conceptions of professionalism within the firm. It guarantees quality and competency and also ensures everyone hues to common ethical standards. The firm's internal regulatory systems mirror and complement the external regulatory structures. In part, this to avoid the kinds of problems that ensued with the collapse of Arthur Andersen following the Enron debacle.[16] Large global law firms with over 4,000 lawyers and many more other kinds of staff are unwieldy and complex organizations to manage, so the role of education in inculcating firm-wide mores is vital. These

---

14 Russell Pearce and Samuel Levine, 'Rethinking the Legal Reform Agenda: Will Raising the Standards for Bar Admission Promote or Undermine Democracy, Human Rights, and Rule of Law?' (2009) 77 *Fordham Law Review*, 1635.

15 James Faulconbridge, Andrew Cook and Daniel Muzio, 'Institutional Legacies in TNCs and Their Management through Training Academies: The Case of Transnational Law Firms in Italy' (2012) 12 *Global Networks*, 48.

16 William Simon, 'Introduction: The Post-Enron Identity Crisis of the Business Lawyer' (2005) 74 *Fordham Law Review*, 947.

kinds of law firms cross cultures, values and other social systems that have to be brought into harmony with each other. For example, the use of *guanxi* may be acceptable in some cultures but in others it could be viewed as antithetical to arms-length dealing. In the next section I discuss the role of technology as it impacts on legal education.

Technology

We recognize how the internet has altered our systems of thinking and working. It is also affecting our delivery of education, with Massive Open Online Courses (MOOCs) and other online ideas like memrise.com or italki.com. Technology is altering the practice of law although lawyers are probably slower than other professionals to embrace its benefits. The key areas where technology has created an impact on legal practice is where practice can be standardized and routinized. Much of legal work can be unbundled and be fitted to algorithms so that it is automated. For example, document review for complex and large litigation is now frequently performed, not by first-year associates in New York at $160,000 a year, but by legally trained personnel in legal process outsourcers in Mumbai at $30,000 a year. Increasing amounts of legal work such as risk analysis of contracts and patent renewals are being outsourced to legal process outsourcers (LPOs) because of the availability of technology.

Within law firms, however, technology is mainly used in facilitating document production.[17] There are law firm companies that are exploiting this opportunity to create automated and simplified platforms for document and contract formation. Radiant Law, for example, has built systems to shorten the time it takes to produce contracts and to modify them during their lives.[18] Epoq Legal provides systems for users under "white label" conditions so that banks, insurance companies and even law firms can offer simplified access to their services.[19] Finally, we are seeing the development of some "intelligent" websites such as roadtrafficrepresentation.com that offer free diagnosis services to customers with the option to take premium services if wanted.[20]

Law firms have not yet understood how to make technology pay for them. Since they bill on hourly rates, procedures that reduce time can be seen as undermining their profit targets. Yet we see how Legal Hackathons are becoming more common as ways of providing solutions to legal problems for policy makers and how events

17 Mitu Gulati and Richard Scott, *The Three and a Half Minute Transaction: Boilerplate and the Limits of Contract Design* (University of Chicago Press, 2012).

18 See <http://www.radiantlaw.com>, accessed 3 January 2014.

19 See <http://www.epoq.co.uk >, accessed 3 January 2014.

20 See <http://roadtrafficrepresentation.com/RTR/PublicForms/Home.aspx>, accessed 3 January 2014.

like ReInvent Law are introducing new ways of thinking about legal activities. All of these are sustained by technology.

Technology has not yet permeated legal education in a substantive way. Although virtual learning environments are in use, their role is simple and ephemeral. Some scholars such as Paul Maharg at Northumberland have created online experiential programmes but these are in the minority.[21] A brief survey of legal MOOCs among the many thousands of courses available from providers such as Coursera and Udacity showed three extant courses: one in torts in the US, a Dutch course on intellectual property and one on introducing English law.[22] Law is still largely taught with traditional techniques. Law faculties have not embraced the varieties of e-learning available to them nor have they been trained in their use.

With the furore that surrounded Susskind's question, is it the end of lawyers? Little has been accomplished in the tech sphere.[23] Indeed Susskind has argued for a new kind of legal professional, a hybrid who would be able to use technology productively and profitably in the legal services market.[24] He draws on views of technology as replacing much of legal services along the lines sketched above. That which can standardized can be done by computer with little human interaction. As computing power increases, following Moore's Law it will exceed the capacity of human brains' processing power – the point of singularity predicted by Kurzweil.[25] Examples such as IBM's Watson winning the TV quiz programme, "Jeopardy", exemplify this approach. The preoccupation with technology highlights the tension again of law and practice and the proper role of legal education in them. This is not to deny that technology will not have a profound effect on legal education: it has not occurred yet.[26]

---

21 Paul Maharg, *Transforming Legal Education: Learning and Teaching the Law in the Early Twenty-first Century* (Ashgate, 2007).

22 See e.g., Justin Reich, Sergiy O Nesterko, Daniel Thomas Seaton, Tommy Mullaney, Jim Waldo, Isaac Chuang and Andrew Dean Ho, *ER22x: JusticeX – Spring 2013 Course Report* (21 January 2014) HarvardX Working Paper No. 4, <http://ssrn.com/abstract=2382248> or <http://dx.doi.org/10.2139/ssrn.2382248>, accessed 6 February 2014. This appears to have risen to around 20 courses now from the US, France, Russia, the UK, Holland and China, <https://www.coursera.org/courses?query=law>, accessed 14 September 2015.

23 Richard Susskind, *The End of Lawyers? Rethinking the Nature of Legal Services* (Oxford University Press, 2010).

24 Richard Susskind, 'Provocations and Perspectives', Briefing paper 3/2012, <http://letr.org.uk/wp-content/uploads/Susskind-LETR-final-Oct-2012.pdf>, accessed 24 August 2015.

25 Ray Kurzweil, *The Singularity is Near* (Gerald Duckworth & Co Ltd, 2006).

26 The number of technology-based educational programmes is rising, thus we have Law Without Walls (Miami), <http://www.lawwithoutwalls.org/>, ReInvent Law (MSU) <http://reinventlaw.com/>, LawMeets (Drexel), <http://www.lawmeets.com> and IronTech Law (Georgetown) <http://www.law.georgetown.edu/academics/centers-institutes/legal-profession/legal-technologies/iron-tech/index.cfm>, all accessed 7 May 2014.

Shifts in Regulation

The regulatory shifts in legal markets in the twenty-first century are proving tendentious times for legal education. Gone are the certainties of traditional professional boundaries and groups and in come new occupations such as legal apprentice or legal project manager. Australia, England and Wales are the laboratories for this experimentation and we learn most from them.

Australia introduced incorporated legal practices in the early 2000s and in 2007 Slater & Gordon of Melbourne became the first law firm to float on the stock exchange. The year 2007 was an explosive year for legal markets because it was when the Legal Services Act (LSA) was passed by the British Parliament after much debate and controversy. Both countries pushed similar agendas. Self-regulation was to give way to external regulation and the organizational categories that could provide legal services would expand to include "Alternative Business Structures" (ABS). There are now around 250 ABS providing different services but mostly still requiring lawyers to work for them. Having said that, the market for paralegals is growing and is prompted in part by the emergence of ABS and the constraints of the market. Three kinds have emerged as the dominant forms: Chartered Institute legal executives, legal apprenticeships and ordinary paralegals.

For the extant legal professions the LSA 2007 forced them to sever their professional bodies into two, one as representative and the other as regulator. The regulator was to be at arms length from the representative. Two shifts occurred in regulation – to entity regulation and outcomes-focused regulation. Along with external regulation of services the regulators investigated the state of legal education in England and Wales, setting up the LETR for this purpose. Its sponsors are still discussing the resulting report although the Solicitors Regulation Authority has begun to indicate that it might want to reimagine how legal education is regulated.

Despite 250 ABS, not much has changed in the delivery of legal services, except for online practice. Document assembly, for example online wills, is growing in scope and the use of online divorce services has increased because they are perceived as quicker and cheaper than lawyers' services.[27] And to date, the introduction of ABS has not had much impact on legal education. Cooperative Legal Services runs an academy to train future employees with Manchester Metropolitan University but this remains an outlier in the provision of legal education.

The regulatory push from Australia and the UK seems to have spilled over into other jurisdictions. Countries such as Canada, Singapore and Hong Kong are considering the introduction of new legal enterprises. The efforts of the Troika – the International Monetary Fund (IMF), the European Central Bank and the European Union – have demanded changes in legal services provision as part of debtor relief

27 Some online divorce services have Trustpilot reviews. See <http://www.trustpilot.co.uk/review/www.divorce-online.co.uk>, accessed 24 August 2015.

to such countries as Ireland, Greece and Portugal. Despite these initiatives there is considerable opposition to regulatory change in Europe.[28]

The Effect on Legal Education

It might be thought from what I have said that legal education is stuck in the doldrums and is not changing. This is not so. We are currently witnessing a global struggle over legal education. It is similar to the one taking place in the teaching of English as a second language where British English and American English are the two main contestants. Through the export of British culture and economy via the British Empire, English law and its education were firmly based in many countries. The Commonwealth countries adhered to British legal education until the late twentieth and early twenty-first centuries when they changed to American forms. The fact that the two forms of legal education are still paramount reflects the situation with respect to American and English law in international trade. These two are the principal forms of law used in transnational transactions.

The prototypical LLB degree (the British undergraduate law degree) as a precursor to further vocational training has transformed into a second US JD-type degree that incorporates forms of practical training within it. It is difficult to determine why this change has occurred but we can see what the results are in some countries. Take for example Japan, which has persistently kept the numbers of law students passing the bar examination low and so keeping the legal profession small. Since introducing a JD-style programme, the numbers have increased and there are more lawyers, which should be increasing access to justice.[29]

It is worth mentioning three other significant countries that have made this shift: Australia, China and India. We can argue that economic ties for these countries have veered towards the US and away from the UK with the result that American culture begins to dominate. The US–Australia bilateral free trade agreement includes provisions on the mutual acceptability of each other's legal qualifications.[30] China has received more legal input by way of US law firms and export of Chinese students to the US than from any other country. One exemplar of this is the establishment of the Peking University School of Transnational School

---

28 Jakob Weberstaedt, 'English Alternative Business Structures and the European Single Market' (2013) <http://papers.ssrn.com/sol3/papers.cfm?abstract_id=2333174>, accessed 24 February 2014.

29 Luke Nottage, 'Legal Education in Asia: Globalization, Change and Contexts – in Review' (2011) Sydney Law School Legal Studies Research Paper No. 11/05, <http://ssrn.com/abstract=1752646>, accessed 24 February 2014; Takahiro Saito, 'The Tragedy of Japanese Legal Education: Japanese "American" Law Schools' (2006) 24 *Wisconsin International Law Journal*, 197.

30 Laurel Terry, 'The Future Regulation of the Legal Profession: The Impact of Treating the Legal Profession as "Service Providers"' (2008) *Journal of the Professional Lawyer*, 189.

of Law, which teaches both the US JD programme and the Chinese Juris Master (JM) degree, yet the school has to be accredited by the American Bar Association.[31] India, like China, has many law colleges, of which few are considered of appropriate standard. To overcome this India has introduced national law schools to educate a cadre of elite lawyers. This has incorporated a move to US legal education principles as well in order to produce graduates ready to practice on taking the bar examination. Again we can see this exemplified in new institutions such as the Jindal Global Law School, which has adopted the American style.

These changes are reinforced by the numbers within the OECD statistics I introduced at the start of this chapter. The US is still the dominant power in the global educational sphere. It receives more foreign students than any other country.

It is possible to put forward an explanation for this move in educational outlook and pedagogy. The fundamental philosophical outlooks of American and British legal education are quite distinct. It is underpinned by the distinction between science and humanities. During the late nineteenth century the US started to change legal education. The Dean of Harvard Law School, Christopher Columbus Langdell, introduced ideas from Chemistry – the laboratory – which was transformed into the Socratic case method dialogue of the US law school classroom as epitomized by Professor Kingsfield in *The Paperchase.* This in conjunction with a system of grades assessed in class and in examinations meant prospective employers could select the best candidates by merit instead of relying on ascriptive methods like family connections. Editorial positions on law review and judicial clerkships bolstered the credentialing power of the law school.[32] With changes in pedagogical styles over the years the case method has been remarkably resilient. Even though it has been criticized by many law professors it endures.[33] There has been change, however, as movements such as the Legal Realists introduced forms of social science analysis into law. The apotheosis of this movement is the rise of law and economics as one of the dominant forms of analysis in the law school, especially through the agency of Judge Richard Posner.[34] Many areas of law have accepted economic analysis as the norm including antitrust, contracts, torts and securities law. The scientific approach to law is deeply embedded in the American academy.

---

31 See <http://blogs.wsj.com/law/2012/08/07/aba-council-votes-against-accrediting-foreign-law-schools>, accessed 7 May 2014.

32 Robert Stevens, *Law School: Legal Education in America from the 1850s to the 1980s* (University of North Carolina Press, 1987).

33 Russell Weaver, 'Langdell's Legacy: Living with the Case Method' (1991) 36 *Villanova Law Review*, 517; Lani Guinier, Michelle Fine and Jane Balin, *Becoming Gentlemen: Women, Law School and Institutional Change* (Beacon Press, 1997).

34 Robert Gordon, 'The American Legal Profession 1870–2000', in M. Grossberg and C. Tomlins (eds), *The Cambridge History of Law in America Volume III: The Twentieth Century and After (1920 –)* (Cambridge University Press, 2008), 73–126.

English legal education, although around in some academic institutions, depended more on a craft approach through apprenticeships and pupillages. The big law firm was not permitted until the late 1960s so the production of law graduates was low in number. English legal education relied on traditional methods of teaching, the exegetical lecture and the inquisitorial tutorial. There were no cases and materials books, rather textbooks were the norm. From an English perspective law fell into the humanities camp of the two cultures as articulated by C.P. Snow. Its research base was thin and it was closely aligned with philosophy. And today, as English law has firmly embedded itself in the academy, it hews more towards critique than scientific analysis. Law and economics is a minority interest.

The effect of these two approaches is to raise the impression that American legal education prepares students for practice. Whether it does or not is another question. On the other hand English legal education appears more theoretical and detached from practice. This is not to say one is better than the other, but that there are significant differences which policy makers around the world have utilized in their choice of educational form.

In the last few years both systems have been under intense scrutiny. For the US this has resulted from the crisis in legal education where law school applications have dropped substantially to the cost of the law school. Henderson and other analysts have shown the bimodal job market means graduates from law schools below the elite group are obtaining jobs at much lower salaries than the big law firms pay. Not only are they greatly dissatisfied, they are hugely in debt, as much as $200,000. Law schools, in order to fund increasingly expensive faculty, rely on the scheme of federally funded loans for law students. The *US News and World Report* law school rankings, however, prevent schools from raising their applicant numbers – indeed they force them to lower numbers – because the rankings are heavily influenced by Law School Admission Test (LSAT) scores. The American Bar Association Task Force on Legal Education has produced some mild reforms but nothing that will compel change. It failed to deal with the core problem of the three-year curriculum and its contested necessity. American legal education remains in crisis yet its dominion is still an extensive one when we examine global legal education.

English legal education is being examined because of the re-regulation of the legal services market and legal education falls under the remit of the LSA 2007. The examination has been conducted in a more rigorous way than in the US. The LETR covered the market, technology, pathways into law and more. The LETR report, while significant in its analysis of the situation, offered less in the way of solutions. The onus has now shifted from the academy to the legal regulators to shape the future of legal education. If anything this shows the tension inherent in English legal education. The legal profession and the academy have had a tense co-existence. This could be the period in which some harmony is achieved as the new arrangements are configured over the next few years.

Conclusion

Legal education is at the metaphorical cross roads. In global terms it is successful and in some parts of the world lawyer numbers are set to grow substantially. In others they are likely to shrink. There is great demand for post-graduate legal education and large numbers of students migrate across the globe to attend law schools, especially in the OECD countries. The problems exist in these key host countries. The US legal profession and education is in a highly uncertain position with little prospect of reforming itself. It appears economic forces will compel change. In the UK the legal profession is being restructured through government cutbacks on legal aid and new forms of law practice entering the market. Both solicitors and barristers feel under siege. In some ways the academy has been insulated from this and that insulation is now wearing thin as the reality of the market enters the consciousness of potential students and faculty. We have not yet worked out the answers, nor have we fully evaluated the scale of the problem. But the problems are no longer merely local ones; they have to be viewed in a global context, one of intense competition. I leave the last words to the Demos think tank:

> Professionals have never been more important nor under more pressure. Professionals 'profess' – promise – to deliver work of high standards and their promises keep us healthy and safe every day. But the promise of professionalism is struggling for credibility. As an institution, it faces a problem of legitimacy affecting not only doctors and lawyers but the success of governments and the freedom of their citizens … we depend on professionalism more than ever. The professional mediation of competing demands increasingly trumps the political process. As fields from medicine to the arts become more specialised and separate, so politicians can seem to lack the deep knowledge and the legitimacy that judgement calls require. As a result, the burden of conflict resolution is shifting from political decisions to professional norms. Professionals play a greater role than ever in shaping our public realm and our daily lives.[35]

---

35 John Craig, 'Production Values: Building Shared Autonomy' in John Craig (ed.), *Production Values: Futures for Professionalism* (Demos, 2006), 13, 13–14.

Chapter 3
The Bifurcation of Legal Education – National vs Transnational

Hans-Wolfgang Micklitz[1]

I will present thoughts, which will hopefully initiate a debate and even research to verify or falsify my observations on the future of legal education.[2] What I am presenting is in no way co-ordinated with my colleagues from the Law Department, let alone the other departments or the overall (EUI) community. I am expressing my personal opinion.[3]

This report is based on nearly eight years of teaching at the European University Institute in Florence, after more than 25 years of an academic life in Germany with scholarships beyond six months in Lausanne and Geneva (Switzerland), Montpellier and Paris (France), Michigan Ann Arbor (USA) and Somerville College in Oxford (UK). By training I am a private lawyer, educated in Germany, with experience in comparative legal studies, international private law, European Union law, transnational law and legal theory. In all these fields I have teaching experience. In 2007 I was appointed Professor of Economic Law at the European University Institute in Florence, Italy.

My argument is that the EUI provides a unique forum for the development of genuine transnational[4] education. Therefore, I will first introduce some basic information about the European University Institute, its institutional setting and its research identity. Secondly, I will look deeper into what I call the transnationalisation of legal education, taking the design of a seminar on the 'Fundamentals of European Private Law' as an example to explain that

---

1 Professor for Economic Law at the European University Institute since 2007, Head of the Law Department since 2012, holder of an ERC Grant on European Regulatory Private Law (2011–2016), see http://blogs.eui.eu/erc-erpl/project-description/, accessed 13 August 2015.

2 J. Smits, Law and Interdisciplinarity: On the Inevitable Normativity of Legal Studies, *Critical Analysis of Law*, 1:2014, 75 who gives an account of the state of the debate in the US and in Europe.

3 However, I could not have written without the many comments and discussions I had at the Law Department and outside the Law Department, with colleagues and researchers to whom I owe gratitude and whom I would like to thank.

4 I will not engage what transnational law is all about, but see the special issue in the *Revue Internationale du Droit Economique* which provides an overview of the different strands of theoretical approaches from constitutional over administrative to private law.

transnational education requires both a more abstract approach to law through a more theoretical orientation and a more concrete approach which requires a careful reconstruction of the factual and legal basis of a transnational conflict. Transnational education leads to an (un)-wanted and problematic (?) disconnection from national legal education. In the third part I will discuss (im)-possibilities of re-connecting national and transnational education.

The European University Institute

The EUI was established in 1973. It is a young institution. It was established by the Member States of the European Union (EU) – until today 22 out of the 28 decided to join the EUI. It is an institution established under international law.[5] The EUI is independent from and separate of the EU. Today the EUI hosts roughly 1,200 people: 600 researchers in four departments, economics, history, law and social and political sciences, 60 professors, 150 research assistants, post-docs and administrative staff. Today, the EUI rests on three pillars: the PhD programme, the Robert Schuman Centre for Advanced Studies which 'was set up in 1992 as a complementary initiative to develop interdisciplinary and comparative research and to promote work on the major issues facing the process of integration and European society'[6] and the Max-Weber Programme (a post-doctoral programme).[7]

The name European University Institute goes back to the political sensitivities, which its founding members encountered when they wanted to create a full European university with undergraduate students. There were technical problems: what should the curricula for undergraduates look like (in the early 1970s)? But there was also competition hanging in the air: the EUI as a potential competitor for

5 See Convention setting up a European University Institute, http://www.eui.eu/Documents/AboutEUI/Convention/ConsolidatedConventionRevising.pdf, accessed 13 August 2015.

6 See http://www.eui.eu/DepartmentsAndCentres/RobertSchumanCentre/Index.aspx, accessed 13 August 2015.

7 See http://www.eui.eu/ProgrammesAndFellowships/MaxWeberProgramme/AboutTheMWP.aspx, accessed 13 August 2015. The Max Weber Programme started in September 2006 and is now the largest international post-doctoral programme in the Social Sciences and Humanities in Europe. The Programme is located at the European University Institute in Florence. It is funded by the European Commission (DG Education and Culture), which provides bursaries of one or two years for over 40 Fellowships. These bursaries are open to scholars from anywhere in the world (not just nationals of an EU Member State) who have received a doctorate in economics, law, history, social and political sciences, or a related field, within the past five years. The Programme also includes a number of Fellows supported by other funders, such as national and other non-EU research bodies. Fellows are selected on the basis of their research accomplishments and potential, their academic career interests, and the availability of the EUI faculty to provide mentorship.

national universities. That is why the EUI is not just called 'European University'. Since its beginning it is only educating and training doctoral researchers, later post-docs, first as Jean Monnet Fellows,[8] and since 2006 also as Max-Weber Fellows,[9] together roughly 50 per year.

The Law Department is composed of 12 professors, holding chairs on EU law – constitutional, administrative and external relations – comparative constitutional law, international law, transnational law, human rights, labour and social law, private and economic law, competition law, information technology and legal theory. However, due to the limited capacity there are no chairs on criminal law, legal history, tax law and environmental law. The EUI resembles much more a research institute than a university in the traditional sense. The overall size of the EUI in general and the departments in particular allows for direct exchange between the professors and the researchers. In classes there are seldom more than 20–25 researchers.

The research identity of the Law Department is built around the Europeanization of law, which intrudes in more and more areas of law, not only in trade and competition law, but also in administrative law, constitutional law, human rights, private law, economic law and property rights. As the EU is a unique supranational entity, in that it has powers of secondary law-making, the investigation into the constitutionalization of the EU and into new modes of law-making and enforcement lies at the heart of the EUI research. The breakdown of the wall and the EU enlargement has shifted the focus even more strongly on the role and function of the EU in the world. This steadily growing strand of research is linked to the impact of globalization on international law, human rights and global governance. Both strands are embedded into social, linguistic and cognitive theories of law, law and science/technology, theories, processes and structures of interaction between legal systems between courts and judicial systems, between legislative and regulatory law-makers.

The international reputation of the EUI is built on three major achievements: the *Access to Justice* project run by Mauro Cappelletti,[10] the *Integration through Law* project by Mauro Cappelletti, Monica Seccombe and Joseph H.H. Weiler,[11] the *Constitutionalisation of Europe* after 1989, and its technical and theoretical implications.[12] Steadily but ever more intensively the research at the EUI

8 See http://www.eui.eu/ServicesAndAdmin/AcademicService/Fellowships/JeanMonnetFellowships/Index.aspx, accessed 13 August 2015.

9 See http://www.eui.eu/ServicesAndAdmin/AcademicService/Fellowships/MaxWeberFellowships/Index.aspx, accessed 13 August 2015.

10 Access to Justice and the Welfare State by Mauro Cappelletti, 1991.

11 Integration Through Law Europe and the American Federal Experience, M. Cappelletti/M. Seccombe/J.H. Weiler (eds), http://www.degruyter.com/view/serial/16479?rskey=QnKJT0&result=4, accessed 13 August 2015.

12 It is difficult to associate this strand with particular names as many members of the institute were involved in the constitutionalization of the last 20 years, developing and

has developed from an inward-looking perspective into an outward-looking perspective. This needs explanation. By inward-looking I mean focussing on the EU, the building of the Internal Market, the relationship between the EU and the Member States in the construction of the European legal order. However, an inward-looking perspective in EU law is still fundamentally different from an inward-looking perspective in national law. An inward-looking EU lawyer is still forced to look at how Member States interact with each other and with EU institutions. Outward-looking means leaving the inner process of EU law-making and focussing on the interaction of the EU with its outside world – the EU as a global actor in the concert of national, supranational and international global actors. This should not be misunderstood. The outward-looking perspective is already enshrined in the Integration through Law project through the comparison of US and EU external relations. It should be stressed that increasing weight and space is given to it in EUI research.

The Uniqueness of the European University Institute: Towards Transnational Legal Education

In Europe, legal (undergraduate) education is deeply tied into national legal culture, national legal traditions and national language. There are only a few exceptions to the dominant paradigm. The Universities of Maastricht,[13] Tilburg[14] and the European Law School[15] (Berlin/London/Paris/Rome/Amsterdam) are offering non-national European educational training for undergraduates. The EUI is running a Doctoral, an LLM programme and a post-doc programme. Each year there are approximately 30 PhD students with national grants and 10–15 self-financed LLM students, primarily from the Member States of the EU. However, there is an increasing number of PhD and LLM researchers from all over the world. Together they form the core of the EUI's educational training. The first two years of the doctoral programme are structured around seminars in which the researchers are obliged to participate. In the second two years – the doctoral programme takes four years – the researchers are free to engage in an exchange with other non-EU or EU universities, or to do an internship in European or international organizations.

---

promoting different approaches constitutional pluralism, deliberative supranationalism, comitology and so on.

13 See http://papers.ssrn.com/sol3/papers.cfm?abstract_id=1719118, accessed 13 August 2015.

14 See for example the Global law LLB at Tilburg University: https://www.tilburguniversity.edu/education/bachelors-programs/globallaw/, accessed 13 August 2015.

15 See http://www.european-law-school.eu/, accessed 13 August 2015.

This particular approach to law is *intra*disciplinary – in that it unites public law and private law, and *inter*disciplinary – in bringing together economics, social science (political science, sociology, international relations), philosophy and history. All this is not special in the sense that the EUI could claim to be the only place in the world where intra- and interdisciplinarity dominate the approach to law, both in research and in teaching. However, there are differences. First and foremost, the famous public/private divide is of much less importance. EU law does not know these boundaries.[16] Therefore, any lawyer who starts working on EU law necessarily crosses and escapes the boundaries of national boxes (private law, commercial law, competition law, administrative law, constitutional law, substantive and procedural law). What might be more striking is the attention to theoretical research both among professors and students in the interaction with legal practice.

The Classroom

In order to understand the requirements of a transnational education it suffices to imagine a typical situation in a classroom at the EUI: Stefan Grundmann, my colleague at the EUI, and I have been teaching a seminar on the 'Fundamentals of European Private Law' in Fall 2013. There are 15 researchers sitting around the table, coming from 15 different countries. Here is the challenge in designing and later in teaching such a seminar: the 15 participants have been educated in their home countries. They have a national background. They have learnt contract and tort law – to remain concrete – but they have learnt it in the framework of their national civil codes, in their national languages, through case books or any other material written in their own language, combined or not with cases decided by national courts. The challenge continues: the participants do not share a common understanding of 'legal methodology':[17] they have learnt their national variant of methodology, which might range from a politicized version of doctrinal research to very abstract and theoretical/epistemological perspectives on positive law;[18] they have or have not learnt to apply written or unwritten law (common law) to a concrete case; they only have knowledge about the law in the books

16 H.-W. Micklitz, Rethinking the public/private divide, in *Transnational Law: Rethinking European Law and Legal Thinking*, M. Maduro/K. Tuori/S. Sankari (eds), Cambridge University Press, 2014, 271–306.

17 What makes it even more complicated is that both students and professors understand different things by methodology. Many law professors, for example, still (implicitly) equate scholarly legal methodology with judicial legal interpretation.

18 Methodology is a booming topic. After years of silence, book after book is published dealing with variations of legal methodology; see our own contributions, R. v. Gestel/H.-W. Micklitz, Revitalising doctrinal legal research in Europe: what about methodology? in U. Neergard/R. Nielsen (eds), *European Legal Method – Paradoxes and Revitalisation*, 2011, 25–74v; R. v. Gestel/M.P. Maduro/ H.-W. Micklitz, *Methodology in the New Legal World, Liber Amicarum et Amicorum in Honour of Ruth Nielsen* (eds)

or they may have practical experience about the law in action. Their knowledge differs considerably in depth and breadth. Some might have heard of European private law, others have not. Some have basic knowledge, others have not: on the European institutions, on the European law-making process, on the European Court of Justice (now the Court of Justice of the European Union – CJEU), on the preliminary reference procedure before the CJEU or on the infringement procedure, on Secondary Community Law (mainly consumer law directives and international private law rules – the Brussels I and the Rome I and Rome II regulation)[19] and the much debated Draft Common Frame of Reference,[20] which is under discussion in the political fora as the Common European Sales Law (CESL).[21]

To be more concrete: discussing a private law case decided by the CJEU implies knowledge of the multi-level structure of the EU, of the role and function of the national courts in comparison to the European courts, of the substantive legal conflict enshrined in national laws which are meant to implement European private law directives or which are believed to be in breach of primary EU law. For many PhD students, capturing the complexities of a multi-level legal order, of the typical interpretation methods of the CJEU (for example, autonomous interpretation), poses a true challenge.

The argument might easily come up: is this really unique? Is this not the daily experience in classrooms today, which are meant to open up education to students coming from different legal backgrounds? My response is that in most seemingly comparable places, national law serves as a background to transnational legal education. The French are studying European law through French glasses, the Dutch through Dutch glasses and the Nordic countries have their own view on the EU, not to speak of the common law countries. This assessment can easily be underpinned by an endless list of publications on EU law which rarely contain transnational references.

The conclusion so far: there is no transnational coherent scholarly legal community that looks through the same lens at EU law. That is why the EUI is the perfect breeding ground for developing a new common understanding about what is European about European law. It is essential for understanding how and why EU law is different from national law to develop a common methodological framework that enables scholars from different countries, legal systems and cultures to communicate more effectively about why EU law develops as it does.

J. Fejø/U. Nedergaard/C.D. Tvarnø/G. Skovgaard Ølykke. København: Djøf/Jurist- og Økonomforbundet 2013, 373.

19 EC Regulation 44/2001 on jurisdiction and enforcement, EC Regulation 593/2008 Rome I, EC Regulation 864/2007 Rome II.

20 See http://ec.europa.eu/justice/policies/civil/docs/dcfr_outline_edition_en.pdf, accessed 13 August 2015.

21 Proposal for a REGULATION OF THE EUROPEAN PARLIAMENT AND OF THE COUNCIL on a Common European Sales Law COM/2011/0635 final.

The Seminar Design – More Abstract and More Concrete

What are the preconditions for designing a successful seminar with students from different backgrounds in such a heterogeneous multi-cultural environment as the EUI? Each design for such a seminar must necessarily be more *abstract* and at the same time more *concrete* than any national teaching seminar. The design for a seminar at the EUI has to be *more abstract* because of the differences in the background knowledge and culture. It is simply not possible, not feasible and probably not useful to transmit all the detailed knowledge of EU law, EU institutions, EU procedures and EU substantive law in the average time one has for doing a seminar without losing attention. Moreover, if one were to start every seminar with first looking for common ground, most of the lecture time would be spend on definitions, concepts and history.

Transferring knowledge, legal education in a transnational environment, is much more about learning techniques which can be applied largely independent from the concrete subject matter. The required abstraction strengthens the need for theorizing about the role and the function of European private law. The degree of abstraction may range from middle range legal theories on private law (for example, the concept of property or the rise of self-regulation in European private law) to political and moral philosophy (for example, social justice or constitutionalization of private law). I have observed in the last couple of years a steadily increasing interest of EUI PhD researchers in legal theory and legal philosophy, which helps to master the sheer masses of laws, legal levels and sources of laws.

At the same time, seminars must be more concrete, inductive, in order to be able to link abstract theories to the real world. That is why concrete examples based on current practice, not necessarily litigation but also contract-making or administrative practice, can serve as a perfect starting point for getting into the real world of law. How is the law being made and shaped, not only in courts but also in commercial arbitration, in negations between law firms and clients, in European regulatory agencies but also in monitoring and enforcement of law? In essence, designing seminars at the EUI requires a rather unique approach, one which requires more theory and abstraction as well as the need to start with a bottom-up perspective by looking at what's actually going on, by bringing the multi-facetted reality to the fore. Such an approach, however, leaves a certain gap in the transfer of knowledge, especially on the *substance* of European private law (for example, the respective directives and regulations). This is a gap which has to be filled by the participants themselves, which requires not only genuine curiosity but also self-discipline and perseverance. The same is true for any other subject, be it European law, administrative law or human rights. The outcome of such legal education might be a generation of lawyers who are better trained in legal theory and in a real life perspective on the law, but who might sometimes lack deep substantive knowledge of the various and increasingly sophisticated sub-fields of EU law.

Drafting and teaching goes hand in hand. Teaching in the EUI does not mean that professors are talking for an hour or even longer – teaching very much follows the Socratic method. Participants are supposed to have read the texts and the cases, which have been made available to them prior to the seminar session. Teaching then means summing up the text/cases and introducing them to the discussion via a set of prepared questions. Other possible variants are to ask the seminar participants to prepare and introduce the subject. Whatever way is chosen, the key problem of any such 'introduction' remains the same: how to catch the divergent horizons of the 15 suggested participants, who often do not have a common understanding of keys concepts of private law or common knowledge of what European private law is all about?

Two Examples to Illustrate Abstraction and Concretization

The solution is to formulate questions in a ***genuinely*** *transnational*, or *European* or *international* perspective.[22] A mere national approach to the questions must necessarily fail. Let me try to give two examples: one of the necessity of abstraction, the other of the necessity of concretization in order to illustrate what is meant.

Abstraction There is no common understanding in the room of what a 'contract' might mean. In the German understanding it is based on private autonomy, in France on liberté de la volonté, in the UK on freedom of contract.[23] For a comparative lawyer this is not really new. But Europe brings an additional layer. The ideology of private autonomy (Germany), liberté de la volonté (France) and freedom of contract (UK and Ireland) is enshrined in the four market freedoms, as can be seen by the case law of the CJEU.[24] Such an assumption, however, is ridden with preconceptions about ordo-liberal thinking and the idea of the European legal order as an economic constitution, a 'Privatrechtsgesellschaft' (a private law society) guaranteed by strong competition law and enforcement.[25] Secondary community law – consumer contract directives[26] or private international law regulations – belong to the category of *regulatory* law, implicitly suggesting that there is something like an idea of 'contract' behind it which could be shared

22 There is a certain resemblance to the so-called functional method in comparative law, see K. Zweigert/H. Kötz, The functions and aims of comparative law, in *Introduction to Comparative Law*, 3rd Edition Oxford University Press 1998, 16–31, I leave it for a later stage to develop this.

23 H.-W. Micklitz (ed.), *The Many Faces of Social Justice in Private Law*, Elgar 2011.

24 E. Steindorff, *E.G.-Vertrag und Privatrecht*, Nomos 1996, A. Hartkamp, *European Law and National Private Law*, Kluwer 2012.

25 F. Boehm, Private law society and market order, in A. Peacock/H. Willgerodt (eds) *Germany's Social Market Economy: Origins and Evolution*, Macmillan 1989, pp. 46–67.

26 H.-W. Micklitz/N. Reich/P. Rott/K, Tonner, *European Consumer Law*, 2nd Edition Intersentia 2014.

by everybody. That is why studying European private law implies the need to understand and to be familiar with 'regulation', with theories on the regulatory and the welfare state, with the implications of, opportunities for and failures of regulation.

Maybe an example is necessary to explain the interplay between contract and regulation. Over time the EU has turned into the most important promoter of consumer law regulation. A whole set of mandatory rules aim to protect consumers, who are considered as the weaker parties in contractual relations. The traditional reading goes like this: parties are free to conclude a contract and to design the content of a contract, with the only limit being – in a continental understanding – bones mores. Consumer regulation restricts party autonomy and freedom of contract. Consumer regulation introduces information obligations and mandatory remedies which are intended to secure the position of the consumer in the Internal Market. Consumer law has its origin in the idea of the welfare state. Europe, however, is not a state, so Europe cannot regulate consumer protection on the basis of the same philosophy. This means consumer regulation in the EU is different from national consumer legislation, both in its ideology and in the philosophy behind it. National consumer law aims at social protection, EU consumer law at market efficiency. There is no need to go deeper, what remains to be recalled is that European private law cannot be seriously discussed and analysed without looking into 'regulation' and regulatory theories.

The initiative launched by the European Commission in 2001[27] on a European contract law, which eventually led to the Draft Common Frame of Reference – which has now been turned into the pending project of a CESL – marks the first – mainly academic attempt so far – to seek and define a positive, if not positivistic, understanding of what a 'European contract' is all about. What is at stake is the development of a genuine European understanding of contract, not in a vertical but in a horizontal perspective. Horizontal is referring to the understanding of a European legal order, which lies in a way on top of the 28 vertical national legal systems.

The different drafts rely on a comparative perspective; they do not embark on an unknown journey into what is called the acquis communautaire of European private law.[28] Two recent publications[29] link the existing national private law rules to the rules enshrined in the Draft Common Frame of Reference. Whilst these impressive exercises are valuable from a national vertical perspective – from the

---

27 COM (2001) 398 final, http://eur-lex.europa.eu/legal-content/EN/ALL/;jsessionid=D78LTBqZfqQ7GcvG1R0n6JyDNGjw1Ny4GmGdPBy8SHNT384LWwdL!404326324?uri=CELEX:52001DC0398, accessed 13 August 2015.

28 H.-W. Micklitz/F. Cafaggi (eds), *The European Private Law after the Common Frame of Reference*, Elgar 2010.

29 G. Dannemann/S. Vogenauer (eds) *The Common European Sales in Context, Interactions with English and German Law*, Oxford University Press 2013; S. Leible/M. Lehmann (eds), *European Contract Law and German Law*, Kluwer International 2014.

perspective of the nation state legal system to the supreme European legal order, they downsize the overall project of a genuine transnational character of 'contract'. In a way they fall back into 'silo-thinking'.

Highlighting the differences between national concepts of contract, concepts in Primary and Secondary Community law and even in academic or political projects demonstrates that the rather innocent reference to a contract in a seminar on 'the Fundamentals of European Private Law' requires clarifications of the very basic historical, economic, social and theoretical function of contract and of regulating contracts.[30] Ignoring this dimension would imply the existence of a common world-wide understanding of contract which cuts across the boundaries of national private legal systems, of different levels of law-making – national, supranational and international – of different legal cultures and traditions.[31] Such a concept does not (yet) exist and the attempt to codify European private law is the best possible evidence that this is the case, even with the deficient approach chosen by the drafters.

Only at a reasonable level of abstraction can the different preconceptions, implicit assumptions, the knowledge and half-knowledge of other legal systems or of European private law be brought together. There is no way out, unless a deeper knowledge of history and theory is replaced by a diffuse common sense of legal concepts.

Concretization The same is true with regard to the counterpart of abstraction – the need for concretization. Let us again take an example from contract law. *CMC Motorradcenter*[32] and *Alsthom Atlantique*[33] are landmark cases, decided by the CJEU in the early 1990s. They both concern the question whether and to what extent national mandatory private law, more specifically private law remedies – in *CMC Motorradcenter* culpa in contrahendo – liability for pre-contractual damages – and in *Alsthom Atlantique* the action directe under the French Civil Code – come within the scope of the freedom to trade in Article 30 TFEU. If the answer is in the affirmative, national private law and national private law remedies are to be regarded as potential barriers to trade whose compatibility with EU law requirements has to be tested. They can survive the grip of EU law only if they can be regarded as mandatory requirements in the meaning of Article 34 TFEU (former Art. 36 CEE). Mandatory requirements can roughly be equated with non-economic reasons, such as health, safety, environmental and (social) consumer protection, and are subject to the proportionality test.

Again deepening the example might help to increase the understanding. In *Alsthom Atlantique* the claimant argued that the strict French liability regime (the action directe) infringes Article 30 in that it sets a barrier to trade because other

30 On the last point H. Collins, *Regulating Contracts*, Oxford University Press 1999.

31 G. Helleringer/K. Purnhagen, *Towards a European Legal Culture*, Hart 2014.

32 ECJ Case 93/92 CMC Motorradcenter [1993] ECR I-5009.

33 ECJ C-339/89 Alsthom Atlantique [1991] ECR I-107.

national liability regimes are less strict and, therefore, impose a lesser burden on business. The CJEU had to face the challenge that confirming the applicability of Article 30 would open up the floodgates for all sorts of claims where traders could refer to national private law rules as barriers to trade. The CJEU would then have to test whether the Member States could bring non-economic arguments forward which could justify a limitation to trade under Article 34 TFEU. In the case at stake the question would be whether the stricter French liability regime could be justified – for example, by reference to consumer protection in contracts between consumers and business, but not in contracts between businesses. The CJEU wisely avoided getting into such a sort of balancing and rejected the applicability of Article 30.

What is at stake in such a conflict and how can it be used to bring down abstract theories of contract law to the reality of preliminary rulings submitted by national courts to the CJEU? In the seminar room what has to be made clear is how the national private legal systems are linked or not linked to the European legal order. The national private legal systems should be understood as 28 *vertical* closed silos, which follow their own rationale, their own particular national legal doctrine. The EU instead establishes a horizontal legal order. The CJEU does not decide cases, it provides for an authoritative interpretation of EU law, which is addressed not only to the referring court but also to the national courts of all 28 Member States. Whenever the national and the European legal order clash – like in *CMC Motorradcenter* and *Alsthom Atlantique* – there is a need to dig deeper and to ask why they clash and what the clash looks like (what is behind it).

The first aspect is strongly related to the level of abstraction and can be ignored here. The second sounds easy, but is not in fact easy. How could it be that a national private legal system, enshrined in a value system of the nation state and bearing its own history, is confronted with the rationale of European integration, of a supranational court which has been given jurisdiction on the interpretation of EU law, which supersedes national law? National private law and national contract is dealing with a conflict between parties on non-payment, late payment or compensation claims. The European Treaty has been concluded between nation states. It is an international treaty with no direct impact on private parties. In order to bring a classical private party conflict before the CJEU, the lawyers involved in formulating the references must twist the case so as to give it an outlook which makes it possible to test its compliance with EU law. What is then at stake is the public law character of private law. By this I mean that a national remedy granted under private law can only reach the CJEU if the Treaty applies directly to private parties – a much discussed issue under the notion of horizontal direct effect[34] – or (what happens more often) if the national rules are challenged before the CJEU as public rules, similar to any other national regulation which impedes the access

34 There is an abundant literature on this, T. Tridmas, *The General Principles of EU Law*, 2nd Edition Oxford University Press 2006, 3rd Edition under preparation.

to the European market (food and cosmetic regulation such as the conflict in the famous *Cassis de Dijon* case[35]).

This twist, this change in perspective can only be understood if the cases are carefully reconstructed.[36] What does this mean? First and foremost what is needed is a solid understanding of the facts behind the case. This is admittedly difficult, as the CJEU judgments are often quite incomplete and the full text of the referring judgment is often not publicly accessible. Be that as it may, it is possible though painful. Nearly each and every case reaching the CJEU under Article 30 TFEU is going back to a contract. A party seeks access to the European market and realizes that there are barriers.[37] Researchers tend to ignore both the concrete facts and the contractual dimension, which is often not so obvious from the facts and from the way the case is presented for a preliminary reference. Seminar participants tend to jump to EU law, discussing in our examples of *CMC Motorradcenter* and *Alsthom Atlantique* the scope of Article 30 and the possible justifications under Article 34 TFEU for exemptions to freedom of trade. Concretization under the particular circumstances of a seminar on EU private law then means putting emphasis on the facts behind the reference, understanding the private law dimension behind the reference, getting to grips with the European legal dimension of the case and last but not least looking into the follow-up judgment of the national court after the decision of the CJEU.[38]

An intermediary conclusion: I hope that the confrontation between the parallel need for abstraction and the need for concretization has highlighted the specificities of a genuine European approach to teach a topic such as contract law. Abstraction and concretization could be understood as a particular method – one which combines legal theory and legal techniques to solve conflicts with a transnational European dimension. What becomes equally clear is that the concrete knowledge of the different 'legal quantities' (contract law, pre-contractual remedies (*CMC Motorradcenter*) or concepts of liability (*Alsthom Atlantique*) have to be reconstructed and studied ad hoc). This is more or less what the Advocate Generals are doing in their Opinions.[39]

---

35 ECJ C-120/78 ECR 1979, 649.

36 H.-W. Micklitz, *The Politics of Judicial Co-operation in the EU – the Case of Sunday Trading, Equal Treatment and Good Faith*, Cambridge University Press 2005.

37 G. Davies, Freedom of contract and the horizontal effect of free movement law, in D. Lezykiewicz/Stephan Weatherill, *The Involvement of EU Law in Private Law Relationships*, Hart Publishing 2013, 53.

38 Strangely enough the follow-up decisions of national courts are not available on the website of the CJEU although the Member States' courts are reporting their decisions to the CJEU.

39 AG V. Trstenjak laid the ground for the basics of European private law, see for a short summary of her contribution through her own eyes, V. Trstenjak/E. Beysen, 'European Consumer Protection Law: Curia Semper Dabit Remedium?, (48) 2011 *Common Market Law Review*, 119.

Perspectives and Perspectivism

What has to be taught and trained is thinking in different perspectives, linked to two different legal system/orders: the vertical intellectual edifice of the private legal system versus the horizontal European legal order. The jiggling around with perspectives, the jumping from national to European, back and forth, might sound manageable and feasible, but in current teaching practice it turns out to be rather difficult. With my colleague Carla Sieburgh I am currently running a project where the research question is how EU primary community law affects national private legal systems.[40] The participants of the project, all post-docs from different European Member States, have found it extremely difficult to combine the two different perspectives. They either fall back on national private law – if they are private lawyers by training – or they focus exclusively on EU law and ignore the private law dimension, in particular the facts of the cases.

Therefore, concretization means the miniscule reconstruction and rebuilding of the transnational factual and multi-facetted legal dimension of a preliminary reference. Such an exercise is not one of legal knowledge, but one of having been trained and educated in handling different perspectives (for example, studying national law remains important not so much from a substantive perspective but because it show that similar legal problems are dealt with via different legal concepts, constructs and theories), in short studying the role and function of perspectivism.[41] I focussed on European private law, but the same is true for any other subject matter in EU law or international law. It does not matter whether the decision to be analysed is one from the CJEU, from the European Court of Human Rights of from the International Court of Justice.

The Effects and Practical Consequences of Transnational Education

What makes the EUI special if not unique is the institutional pressure, which is the result of its mandate, to educate researchers in such a transnational spirit. The EUI's treasure trove is 40 years of experience and hundreds of PhDs in which this transnational thinking is (sometimes more, sometimes less) enshrined. It would

40 We held a conference in Florence in 2013 and we will have a second one in Nijmegen in November 2014.

41 'In so far as the word "knowledge" has any meaning, the world is knowable; but it is interpretable otherwise, it has no meaning behind it, but countless meanings – "Perspectivism". It is our needs that interpret the world; our drives and their For and Against' [emphasis added]. Every drive is a kind of lust to rule; each one has its perspective that it would like to compel all the other drives to accept as a norm – F. Nietzsche; trans. Walter Kaufmann, *The Will to Power*, §481 (1883–88).

be a research project in itself to investigate the PhD writings over four decades at the EUI in order to give the transnational dimension of legal education more bite.[42]

The EUI has built its own legal community and network of alumni over the last 40 years. Seventy per cent of EUI researchers end up in academic positions, most of them outside their home countries. The result is the gradual development of some sort of a European legal – educational – culture and maybe even more a European conscience. It is the training for four years during the PhD which offers the opportunity to change perspective, from a vertical one – the national legal system up to Brussels and Luxemburg, to a horizontal one – the European legal order – and what might be even more important to learn is how to handle different perspectives. The deeper level of transnational legal education lies in the combination of the need for abstraction, the pressure for concretization and the methodology to combine both perspectives (for example, by thinking in terms of different possible problem definitions, of alternative explanations and of multiple strategies to deal with the problems). No lawyer having enjoyed transnational education may know all the subjects he has to deal with equally well. The 'hole in the donut' – the lack of knowledge resulting from the sheer mass of rules over different law-making levels – might be filled occasionally but it cannot be filled systematically by way of reference to abundant national laws and national legal systems or the equally abundant international rules and regulations.

What is often overlooked is that transnational legal education goes hand in hand with the rise of transnational law. This means that the gap, which remains between the two poles, is gradually filled by rules having their own legal origin. In the EU, and more specifically in European private law, this is the mixture of European primary and secondary community law, but also the new forms of soft law and co-regulation, of contract governance, networks and new modes such as Lamfalussy and the open method of co-ordination. Overall, researchers are not paying enough attention to what is 'really new'. A contract in a transnational dimension is more than a German, French or UK contract – it combines elements of the three but equally yields a new understanding of contract as it must be reconstructed in light of the particular European legal environment, the Treaties, the case law of the CJEU, and legal and administrative practices.[43] If they do so, they gain a transnational dimension – they achieve what I called transnational education and put it into action.

---

42 R. van Gestel, Professor in Tilburg, with whom I am co-operating in legal methodology brought up the idea. Hopefully he will find the resources.

43 See our certainly still incomplete approach G. Comparato/H.-W. Micklitz, *Regulated Autonomy between Market Freedoms and Fundamental Rights in the Case Law of the CJEU, in General Principles of EU Law and European Private Law*, edited by U. Bernitz/X. Groussot/F. Schulyok, Ashgate 2013, 121–54; H.-W. Micklitz, The European Union Project, in *The Philosophical Foundations of European Union Law, Yearbook of European Law*, J. Dickson/P. Elfetheriadis (eds), Oxford University Press 2013, pp. 1–17.

However, there is a downside of transnational legal education – one which can be observed in legal education at the EUI. Transnational legal education results in a gradual disconnection from the national legal environment, from national law, from national legal doctrine, from the national social environment, but also in a deeper sense from national legal culture. The longer the researcher remains in a transnational educational environment, the deeper he indulges into transnational perspectivism and transnational law, the more difficult it becomes to bring the two dimensions, the national and the transnational together. Disconnection leads to a gulf between transnational and national legal education. Transnational and national legal education, and that is why I am using the bifurcation as a paradigm, are drifting further apart. The gulf between the two becomes deeper and broader.

Again I have no hard evidence or empirical data, but I may provide for a short narrative, which underpins my assumption. At the EUI I can observe a development which occurs in two phases. During the first phase researchers from all over Europe (to a lesser extent the world) graduated from the EUI. They had enjoyed solid educational training at their home country but ran into difficulties once they wanted to return with their PhD to their home country. Transnational education works as a barrier to the reintegration into the national academic environment. A PhD is to be located somewhere in between the German Doktorarbeit und Habilitation. As a result, having written a PhD at the EUI means that Germans have to return to Germany and then have to write a habilitation in the traditional German sense – if this opportunity is created. This is an exercise similar to shifting the perspective back from horizontal to vertical, back to the national silo-thinking.

However, there is no right to return, not even an entitlement. So even if the researcher is ready to return, ready to readjust his thinking to the national vertical requirements, he may in practice often be barred from access to the national academic market. In theory, the alternative would be to look for a job in another Member State. However, it is an open secret that in Europe only the UK and the Netherlands offer job opportunities to non-nationals who are not familiar with the common law or Dutch law. If the PhD researchers are lucky enough to be offered a job in that country they are no longer compatible with the national legal system. To put it bluntly: having a German undergraduate state exam, a PhD from the EUI and work experience in the UK does not necessarily qualify one for the German academic labour market. The result is disconnection and in fact more than 60 young German academics have held academic positions outside Germany.[44]

The second phase creates even more conflicts. I observe that more and more young scholars who apply for a PhD at the EUI come from the few universities which offer transnational undergraduate education, for example University of

44 See http://siemslegal.blogspot.de/2008/08/germans-in-us.html; http://siemslegal.blogspot.de/2008/06/german-legal-academics-in-uk.html, accessed 13 August 2015.

Maastricht.[45] We then find a situation in which a student with German nationality who studied in the Netherlands and wrote his PhD at the EUI is practically barred from the German academic labour market. Here the so-called state exam is a mandatory requirement for being admitted to teaching. This means that a German, with a non-German undergraduate exam, is regarded as being incompetent to teach German law, even if the undergraduate degree comes from the best universities, such as Oxford or Cambridge.

It is true that there are differences between the Member States and that each country in Europe has its own tradition, history, access barriers and integration strategies. However, there is enough anecdotal evidence available to point to the existence of undesired consequences of transnational legal education. Once they have left the safe harbour of their national legal educational systems, researchers are exposed to transnationalization of legal education and are catapulted into a different space.

Reconnection of Transnational to National Education

If my observation is correct, legal education is undergoing a transformation which raises follow-up questions that I will sketch without going into detail.[46]

Are we approaching a world in which we need two types of legal education, one for the national needs, embedded into the national legal culture, tradition, history, language, and another one for transnational needs, for supranational and international organizations, law firms and Non-Governmental Organizations (NGOs), which remains disconnected from national legal education and which develops its own rationales? If my observation of the ever deeper bifurcation is correct – if the two types of legal education are turning into ever stronger self-sufficient systems/orders shielding themselves mutually from outside influence – are there ways and means to bridge the gulf? Is it possible and feasible – do we have means and tools to overcome the differences?

- The first set of question implies that transnational legal education is self-standing and can exist without borrowing from national legal education.
- Transnational legal education implies solid training in legal theory and legal philosophy, more particularly in moral philosophy, which suggests

45 Hans Peter Blossfeld, Student admission, PhD programme structuration and completion rates, a longitudinal study of changes at the European University, 1977–2012, on file with the author.

46 I will use national legal systems and transnational legal order, without explaining here the difference between system and order, see for a deeper analysis on the differences between systems and orders the contributions of J. Dickson and K. Cutler/M. Guidice in J. Dickson/P. Elfetheriadis (eds), *The Philosophical Foundations of European Union Law, Yearbook of European Law*, Oxford University Press 2013.

that law is linked to 'justice'. Only familiarity with the grand ideas of law allows us to fight the jungle of rules and levels, not to mention the struggle over models of justice, rationalities and efficiency.

- Transnational legal education guarantees solid methodology in finding and applying the law, law finding refers to perspectivism, law application to the necessary sensitivity in handling various levels of rules, contradicting values.
- Transnational legal education rebuilds the substance of law around areas which are broad enough not to get lost in over-complexity, which is only possible if law opens up to interdisciplinarity. For example, the law on telecommunications, energy law, transport and financial services can only be understood in a transnational dimension by integrating the necessary knowledge from economics, political science and so on.
- It seems there are arguments in favour of such a possibility, of the feasibility of a self-standing transnational legal education.

However, there is a price to pay for transnational law and transnational legal education, which is more and more disconnected from national legal education and from national legal systems. The fine and nice national legal doctrine, the sophisticated inner structure of a national legal system might suffer from such an open educational training, which oscillates between abstract theories and concrete problems. In such training, law-making in law firms and companies and dispute resolution and mediation prevails over litigation in courts. It is not more or less focussed on the 'national judge', who decides a 'national problem', but on law-makers in international fora (not only international organizations but also public and semi-public fora) and on mediators and arbiters in mediation and arbitration bodies.

The second set of questions starts from the premise that the two worlds of transnational and national legal education are staying apart, but co-exist and can be held together. This might certainly be the prevailing view. National law and national legal education may then become less a goal in itself. National legal systems turn into 'laboratories' for the development of transnational law (see *Justice Brandeis*[47] 'states as laboratories metaphor'). They deliver fuel through the fact that they are an experimental breeding ground for what sort of interventions work and do not work – and why – and national law will stay important from a comparative law perspective.

This sounds promising and reassuring, but how can this be achieved and are all national legal systems in an equal position, or is the old difference between the continental law and common law reappearing? In other words, is the common law legal education more apt and more open to transnationalization of legal education? Are the continental legal systems stuck in their post-Westphalian boundaries?

47 See J.A. Gardner, The 'States-as-Laboratories' Metaphor in State Constitutional Law, 30 *Valparasiso University Law Review* 475:1996. Available at: http://scholar.valpo.edu/vulr/vol30/iss2/3, accessed 13 August 2015.

- One might think of particular educational training to improve reconnection, to strengthen the links between supranational educational institution like the EUI and national legal educational systems. But how can it be avoided that transnational legal education, which is intended to escape the boundaries of the vertical silos, is not simply readjusted to the inner rationale of a particular national legal system, whatever it might be?
- The EUI has trained and educated researchers for more than 40 years. Seventy per cent ended up in universities and international organizations. In order to answer the question of compatibility, it would be important to know whether these transnationally trained researchers remained strangers in the 'foreign' national legal system, whether they 'fuelled' it or whether they were re-educated in the national boundaries.
- Most of them went to common law countries and to the Netherlands, although we do not have exact figures. The willingness of the common law system to integrate non-national elements is well documented. But does this mean that the common law is the better breeding ground for new legal education that unites national and transnational? What about the Netherlands? They belong to the continental legal systems and they are the ones who are at the forefront of providing genuinely transnational education (Maastricht and Tilburg).

In the meanwhile M. Reimann argued on the American advantage in global lawyering.[48] The question remains whether there is a European Advantage in legal scholarship and maybe in legal education. I will leave it for a later occasion to develop these thoughts.[49]

48 M. Reimann, The American Advantage of Global Lawyering, *RabelsZ* (78) 2014, 1–36.

49 See H.-W. Micklitz, Is There a European Advantage in Legal Scholarship? in Rob van Gestel/H.-W. Micklitz/Ed Rubin (eds), *Rethinking Legal Scholarship: A Transatlantic Dialogue*, Cambridge Massachusetts, 2016.

Chapter 4
Learning Opportunities in Multi-National Law School Classes: Potential and Pitfalls

Carolyn Evans[1]

Introduction

Globalization is a buzzword of the university sector. In mission statements, advertising, webpages and business plans, most universities now describe themselves as being 'global'. What this means in practice can be anything from having a modest exchange program to a wide range of learning, research and engagements activities with a web of international partners. It is very easy to state that a law school is global or international in its outlook. It is generally also quite easy to sign a large number of Memoranda of Understanding with a wide range of partners under which little is promised and nothing is delivered. The hard work of creating more cosmopolitan law schools where the real benefits of internationalization are felt by a wide range of students, staff and stakeholders is much more difficult.

This chapter addresses one aspect of globalization that is often overlooked – the importance of the experience of international students in host institutions. Too often it is easiest to focus on glamorous mobility experiences or opportunities that take our students to other parts of the globe – exchange, internationally taught courses, dual or joint degrees and so forth. However, the number of students who seek to travel overseas for the whole of their university education or some part of it has been increasing rapidly in recent years. Universities and law schools have tended to embrace this trend for a whole range of reasons. Some of these reasons are educationally focused – creating more intellectually and culturally diverse classrooms; creating closer ties between students from various countries; and selecting the best students wherever they may be found in the world. There is little doubt that when international students are seen as a valuable part of the law school community with thought and effort put in to integrating them into the life of the school that the results can be beneficial to all. The ideal is nicely encapsulated by Professor Spanbauer who writes that:

---

1 Professor Carolyn Evans, Dean and Harrison Moore Professor of Law, Melbourne Law School.

> If common ground is recognized in teaching both groups of students [international and domestic], and if differences are simultaneously respected and cultivated, legal educators will enrich their classrooms and be enriched as teachers.[2]

Other motives for encouraging international students may be less pure, but are quite common – in particular, the desire for the fees paid by international students which can assist law schools struggling in the difficult economic environment to make ends meet. Many countries are now beginning to see the economic benefits that international students can provide; higher education is a multi-billion dollar industry in Australia, for example.[3] Some countries are also aware of the considerable soft power that can be exercised by providing educational experiences for bright students who may go on to hold leadership positions in their home countries.

Whatever the motives, the outcome is that some law schools which have little or no experience of hosting international students are now rapidly increasing or seeking to increase their international intake. Australia has been engaged in taking in relatively high percentages of international students by global standards for many years – in part, because the way in which higher education funding has worked in Australia meant that universities need to attract reasonably high numbers of international students to have sufficient funding to run high quality programs.

There are some lessons that can be learnt from that experience and from experiences elsewhere about both the potential and the pitfalls such multi-national classrooms can bring. In the worst case, international students are treated as cash cows – brought in large numbers, charged high sums, abandoned to make their way as best they can without much support or guidance, sometimes the objects of overt racism[4] and more often simply marginalized or

---

2 Julie M. Spanbauer, Lost in Translation in the Law School Classroom: Assessing Required Coursework in LLM Programs for International Students, 35 *Int'l J. Legal Info.* 396, 403 (2007).

3 'The [international education sector] is Australia's fourth largest export industry, earning $15.7 billion during 2011. This is largely driven by the higher education sector, representing 65.6 per cent of total revenue during this period.

International education and training is Victoria's top export ahead of personal travel and wool, earning $4.82 billion in the 2010/11 financial year. In 2012 there were nearly 150,000 international student enrolments in Victoria from over 160 nations. In New South Wales, international education and training is the second top export earner after coal, earning $5.82 billion in 2010/11'.

International Education Advisory Council, *Australia – Educating Globally* (2013), *available at* https://aei.gov.au/IEAC2/theCouncilsReport/Documents/Australia%20%E2%80%93%20Educating%20Globally%20FINAL%20REPORT.pdf, accessed 9 December 2013. It should be noted, of course, that some countries fully or largely subsidize international students and for them the benefits of such students are purely educational or soft power related.

4 This aspect, while not explored in detail here, can loom large for some students. See Jenny J. Lee, International Students' Experiences and Attitudes at a US Host Institution: Self-Reports and Future Recommendations, 9 *J. Res. Int'l Educ.* 66 (2010).

ghettoized in their learning environment.[5] Some manage to thrive despite this, but for some it is a gruelling and unpleasant struggle through the degree (and sometimes not through, as failure looms as a real possibility, particularly at elite institutions) with none of the benefits for either the international student or the host institution that can come from a well thought through international student experience. In the best case, international students are well integrated with their fellow international and domestic students. They are provided with the personal, cultural and learning support that they need to perform well and they bring diverse voices to the classroom and extra-curricular activities that enhance the Law School experience for everyone.[6]

While not every aspect of the international student experience is in the hands of the Law School, there is a clear ethical obligation on universities which bring in international students to consider carefully how to assist those students to make their experience an intellectually and personally rich one. Even institutions that are purely pragmatic and profit driven should consider that the competition for international students is now intense, and that over time universities that treat their international students as cash cows may find that the milk dries up.

This chapter gives an overview of a number of considerations that law schools should take into account when thinking about how to ensure that having a multi-national student body enhances the experience of all students and integrates into the wider strategic internationalization aims of the school rather than sitting awkwardly aside them.

Diversity and Selection

The first issue for law schools to take into account when trying to create a high quality multi-national classroom is the make-up of the student body. When it is possible, it is good to aim for an international student cohort that is diverse rather than over-relying on one or two nationalities exclusively or overwhelmingly. At present, there are a small number of countries from which there are likely to be a steady stream of high quality students for many years. China is currently dominant in this space but it is likely that countries including India will play a

5 The dangers here, including of irresponsible recruiting of people who are not ready for law studies, have been recognized for a long time. *See* Wendy Addison and Fiona Cownie, Overseas Law Students: Language Support and Responsible Recruitment, 19 *J.L. & Soc'y* 467 (1992).

6 While some of these issues are particularly salient in law, a number apply equally across various disciplines. For a good early identification of the issues, see D.J. Phillips, Solution to the Dilemmas and Concerns of Teaching International Students in Universities, 5 *Legal Educ. Rev.* 47 (1994).

more significant role in years to come.[7] While the interest level and commitment of students from these countries opens up significant opportunities, there is the prospect of some classrooms being bi-cultural – dominated by the domestic students and students of one other nationality. While this can be a rich student experience if handled well, it does not bring with it the full benefits of a multi-nationality classroom with a variety of cultural, linguistic and educational perspectives represented.

This is a point at which the pragmatic, financially driven aspects of international student recruitment may be in tension with the educational focused approach to multi-national classrooms. From the point of view of those charged with bringing in international students, it is simpler and cheaper to focus in on a small number of countries from which there will be significant return on the investment of recruitment dollars. In a time when most universities are feeling the pressure of decreasing or limited resources, it is understandable that such an approach might be taken even if it comes at the expense of more diverse classrooms. However, there are pragmatic concerns that might also argue in favour of a more diverse approach to recruiting international students. Too significant a reliance on a single country or small number of countries creates a risk if something occurs to place that market in danger. Such risks may be wholly outside the control of law schools and can only be mitigated by developing diverse markets. Australian higher education generally, for example, saw a sharp decline in applications from Indian students after a series of attacks on Indian students was given a high degree of publicity in the Indian media. It has taken several years to recover from the damage that these incidents and the media storm that accompanied them caused.[8]

This is an area in which a compromise may be needed between idealism and pragmatism in terms of marketing and strategic recruitment. Some high profile law schools may effortlessly attract the highest quality students from around the globe and they can then simply select a well-rounded cohort from this group. Others will have to make decisions, constrained by resources, about where best to focus recruitment efforts. If those efforts end up with a single group pre-dominating the international cohort, this is not inherently problematic but it may give rise to complications that need to be managed. In particular, it is fairly easy in these circumstances for students to divide into two groups that have little to do with

---

7 In Australia, for example, over a third of all international students come from China and more than half of the international student body is made up of students from China and India. See International Education Advisory Council, *supra* note 3, at 12.

8 After the attacks were publicized in 2009, the number of applicants from India to Australia halved and, while they have been regaining ground, they are not yet back to the numbers before the attacks. *See* Australian Bureau of Statistics, International Students (2011), available at http://www.abs.gov.au/AUSSTATS/abs@.nsf/Lookup/4102.0Main+Features20Dec+2011, accessed 9 December 2013.

one another, so more focus might need to be given to ensuring that this does not happen (see further below).

Induction and Welcome

All students benefit from an induction or orientation to their course of study that is welcoming, informative and helps them to create bonds with one another. International students, however, generally require some additional information and assistance in understanding their new environment, including the prevailing cultural learning norms that may be quite foreign to them. One Australian study has shown that international students, who generally do not have the same social support as their domestic counterparts, often find their studies confronting and are more likely to use dysfunctional coping techniques than other students.[9] In these circumstances, ensuring that such students are given a thoughtful orientation program that helps to prepare them for life as a student in the host country and that assists them with developing support mechanisms is particularly important.

Often central university administrations or residential colleges provide an orientation program for new international students that welcomes them to the university and city and helps with any issues that they might be having with things like visas, accommodation, taxation, understanding public transport and so forth. If that can be done at scale at university level, it is probably sensible that it be done in this way because many issues that international students face are common and can be most cheaply and efficiently resolved in this way. When the university or residential colleagues do not do this, however, the law school may want to give thought to whether such assistance can be provided there. Some practicalities that might seem obvious and straightforward to locals can take a lot of time and frustration for those new to the country.[10]

A nice additional touch in my city of Melbourne to make students feel welcome is a combined effort by the city, private partners and the universities in the state to host a welcome desk at the airport to greet new international students over the couple of weeks when they are most likely to arrive. The students receive a welcome pack with lots of practical information, as well as a friendly greeting and someone to ask for help if they are having difficulty in knowing how to deal with the transit system from the airport. That means that they feel welcome literally from the moment that they walk through customs.[11]

9 Nigar G. Khawaja and Jennifer Dempsey, A Comparison of International and Domestic Tertiary Students in Australia, 18 *Aust. J. Guidance & Counselling* 30 (2008).

10 See, e.g., Ernest R. Larkins, Coming to America: International Students Face a Labyrinth of Income Tax Issues, 15 *Conn. J. Int'l L.* 47 (2000).

11 For more information, *see* City of Melbourne, *Student Welcome Desk*, http://www.melbourne.vic.gov.au/CommunityServices/ForYouth/Pages/StudentWelcomeDesk.aspx.

However, at Melbourne Law School we have increasingly decided that the generic introduction to the university or city – important though it is – is insufficient and have worked towards having more detailed orientation programs for international students to supplement these. Our JD students generally have a several day orientation program that is quite rich in detail and information along with an intensively taught, small group subject for the first two weeks of the course that allows for students to develop a close relationship with one another and the teacher. We have therefore only added an additional one day at the start of the program for international students. For our Masters students, however, most of the domestic students are practising Australian lawyers who are studying part-time. We only host a half-day orientation for them on a weekend to fit with their busy schedules. We can also safely assume that, unlike the new JDs, the majority of them are familiar with the key legal research tools,[12] Australian conventions around legal writing and citation, and the conventions in Australian classrooms. International students may not be familiar with any of these.

In those circumstances, we have introduced a whole week orientation for new international students. This includes a cultural/social program that is law focused (visits to the court with talks by judges, visits to parliament and so forth) to help to develop an informal sense of Australian legal culture. It includes more hands-on training in areas such as legal research and writing, and an intellectual dimension with guest lecturers talking about their research.[13] Importantly, however, orientation for international students should include a clear articulation around cultural learning norms, which can differ significantly from country to country. This is something that we are still working on and is likely to continue to be a work in progress as we identify with each new batch of students their needs and areas of interest in one-to-one meetings with a professor as part of the orientation.

Articulating Cultural Learning Norms

One of the most valuable – but also most complex – aspects of studying in a foreign country is the cultural differences that are inherent in other systems. One of the difficulties is that, while many law schools will go to a great deal of trouble to outline the formal requirements around coursework, assessment and so forth, it can be difficult for us to reflect on the underlying cultural assumptions that play

12 For a discussion of the way in which the library and those involved in teaching legal research might need to rethink their practices for international students, *see* Prue Presser, Training the Trainers from Developing Countries: Issues for the Library, 28 *Int'l J. Legal Info*. 350 (2000).

13 For some useful information on the resources prepared for international students and the timetable of orientation, *see* Melbourne Law School, *Orientation – Melbourne Law Masters*, http://www.law.unimelb.edu.au/masters/current-students/orientation, accessed 9 December 2013.

out in our classrooms and beyond and to help those who are not native to the culture to understand these practices.

For example, international students and teachers who come to Melbourne Law School are often taken aback by the relatively informal culture that prevails in most Australian law schools. The overwhelming majority of students will call their teachers by their first name. There is no disrespect intended by it – it is simply the more informal and egalitarian nature of Australian society reflected in the classroom. Students used to a more formal learning culture (and that includes students from almost everywhere) can find it unsettling and unclear unless it is explained to them expressly. I always say to students that teachers will be happy to be called by their first names and will usually expect that, but if they feel uncomfortable they should feel free to use titles if they wish to. Similarly, I expressly warn our students who travel to other countries or are in correspondence with professors from countries where a more formal culture exists to be careful not to give inadvertent offence.

The nuances of cultural practices in the law school can trip up the unwary – everything from the clothing that is generally worn to the importance placed on punctuality to whether it is appropriate to give a gift to your teacher, can make an international student feel uncomfortable before even moving to the academic aspects of cultural difference. As a teacher, some of the most uncomfortable discussions that I had with international students were with those who came from a country in which giving gifts to a teacher was common and expected, whereas all but the most trivial gifts would be considered inappropriate in Australia. These conversations were embarrassing to both parties and could have been avoided by clearer communication. Communicating with current international students about the types of things that they found confronting or unexpected when they first arrived can be a good way to assess the type of issues that may need explicit mention.

The far more difficult and important elements of what type of student participation is required in the classroom, the type of assessment that will be required of students and the learning outcomes that are expected of them also require considerable thought and communication. Specific articulation of such academic norms can be beneficial to all students, but can be particularly valuable for students who may have come from very different academic systems.

One issue to be cautious about (and, again, this can be valuable for all students) is not simply falling back on terminology and shorthand that might seem obvious and clear to academic insiders but which is not helpful to international students. Arkoudis and Tran undertook a study of the way in which lecturers perceived themselves to be offering guidelines to students about the way in which their work would be assessed and compared this to the extent to which international students understood the assessment task. Several of the teachers involved were very thoughtful about the way in which they communicated their assessment criteria and believed that they had done a good job in doing so. By usual standards they indeed had done a far better job of giving detailed instructions than many teachers do. For the international students, however, the criteria were too general to be of much help. In interviews with students:

> [T]hey highlighted the need to unpack the meanings of such terms as 'clarity of topic or questions', 'understandings of terms', or 'coverage and relevance of literature'. In short, the lecturers might think they communicate their expectations of student academic writing clearly by providing them with the assessment criteria, but the students themselves actually desire far more specific explanations about the constructs of 'good writing' addressed in the criteria.[14]

Finally, it is important to be conscious that some students may need more assistance in reaching the desired outcome than others.[15] Students who have had little or no previous experience in classroom participation may need to have relatively safe and structured environments created for them to assist them in making the transition to vigorous in-class debate. In such cases it may not be sufficient to simply articulate the required expectations; rather, it will be important to also provide support and assistance to those who may require it. Such assistance might be specific to international students, particularly with respect to language support which looms large as an issue for international students who are not native speakers of the language of instruction.[16] However, some innovations to provide support for all students into the law school environment can be particularly beneficial to international students and other equity groups who may require more assistance in making the transition than some other groups.[17]

---

14 Sophie Arkoudis and Ly Tran, Writing Blah, Blah, Blah: Lecturers' Approaches and Challenges in Supporting International Students, 22 *Int'l J. Teaching and Learning in Higher Educ.* 169, 173 (2010).

15 For a thoughtful discussion of what this might require over several aspects of the Law School experience, *see* Mark E. Wojcik and Diane Penneys Edelman, Overcoming Challenges in the Global Classroom: Teaching Legal Research and Writing to International Law Students and Law Graduates, 3 *Legal Writing* 127 (1997).

16 It has increasingly become clear that simply reaching a certain level in a test of English proficiency does not mean that a student has a sufficiently sophisticated grasp of English so that no further support is required for the complex and challenging language requirements of law. See, e.g., Spanbauer, *supra* note 2, 413–21.

17 For example, in a peer mentoring program for first year students at the University of New South Wales Law School, international students were required to attend (and found the program very helpful) but all students were encouraged and permitted to do so. This can also reduce the possible stigma for international students of programs that assume that they are more likely to struggle than others are. See Dominic Fitzsimmons, Simon Kozlina and Prue Vines, Optimising the First Year Experience in Law: The Law Peer Tutor Program at the University of New South Wales, 16 *Legal Educ. Rev.* 99 (2006).

Being True to the Educational Mission of the Law School

One of the tempting responses to increased numbers of international students – particularly if those students provide essential financial support to the institution – is to deviate from the educational mission or usual standards of the law school. Whether through a desire to keep paying customers in the law school, or human sympathy for the struggles of international students, or uncertainty about the impact of cultural norms and fears of being labelled as insensitive (or actually being insensitive), it can be easy to give international students a leave pass from what is usually required. While domestic students might be pushed for questions in class or nominated to give presentations of group work, international students are left to volunteer if they want to be involved. Plagiarism, always a vexed issue in this context, is allowed to go on unchecked in some contexts or simply referred over and over for educational help rather than usual disciplinary action. Controversial topics are avoided in the classroom for fear of offending or insulting or blundering into culturally sensitive territory. At least this can be the response in some Western, common law classrooms.

This is the easy option, but is both self-defeating and short-sighted. First, it can create resentment and a lessening of the educational opportunities for domestic students. If they see international students being judged by a lower standard or getting away with behaviour that would not be allowed for them, this tends to reinforce the 'us and them' divide. Not unreasonably, it makes domestic students feel that they are being treated unfairly. If the classroom experience is changed in a way that reduces the challenge and intellectual boundary pushing for everyone to accommodate international students, both sets of students will have a lesser international education as a result.

While such an approach might make international students feel better in the short term, it also robs them of the full benefits of an education system other than their own. If they come from an education system where students do not challenge the teacher or discuss key issues in class, then being facilitated to do so is an important educational experience. If they come from a system where they are used to just putting up their hands and having their questions answered by teachers in class, then experiencing a system where the teacher simply lectures and students have to work out whatever they do not initially understand by themselves is a different type of learning experience. If they have never been required to memorize materials then the rote learning required in some classes might well be challenging and assist them to develop a new skill. It might well be appropriate to change teaching methods and curriculum in response to deeper thinking and understanding about what makes a rich educational experience – including by looking to models overseas – but we should not simply water down what we do and why we do it because it might be confronting for international students.

This is even the case to some extent with the required language skills. Carole Silver, in an examination of why internationally trained lawyers come to study in the United States notes that one of the key reasons given by graduate students is a desire to prove their competency in English (and, in some cases, to improve this competency).[18] While it is not reasonable to expect someone who is a non-native speaker to be as fluent in either written or spoken English as a native speaker, if the language standards are relaxed too much, the qualification will cease over time to have the currency that makes it valuable to the graduates.

That is not to say that international students will not need some understanding and additional assistance, particularly during a transitional phase. But it is much more satisfactory and in the long term interests of all students to work very clearly and in detail through issues. In a case such as plagiarism, such support might include offering assistance, particularly in early essay writing to help distinguish between referencing/paraphrasing and plagiarism, and potentially even allowing the first instance of non-egregious plagiarism to be used as a teaching experience. Ultimately, however, the same disciplinary and educational standards have to apply to everyone.

There are, however, clearly implications for the curriculum in having international students in the classroom (or, indeed, in trying to develop a more globalized curriculum for domestic students). There has been a great deal of thought already put in to how the curriculum and teaching methods might be developed to make them more internationally oriented and the details of this are not repeated here.[19] What is clear, however, is that teachers need to be conscious of the fact that, in multi-national classrooms, students will not necessarily share an understanding of history, politics and culture that is critical to fully understanding the law. As Professor Brostoff puts it in the context of the United States:

> International law students studying in United States law schools, regardless of their fluency in English, will be most successful when they can begin to feel comfortable with the context of US law. Helping students begin to understand the context, and not just the text or language of US law, requires that teachers of

---

18 Carole Silver, Internationalizing US Legal Education: A Report on the Education of Transnational Lawyers, 14 *Cardozo J. Int'l & Comp. L.* 143 (2006).

19 Quite a number of these have focused on the importance of internationalizing the law curriculum for the benefit of both international and domestic students. For a small sample, see Afshin A-Khavari, The Opportunities and Possibilities for Internationalizing the Curriculum of Law Schools in Australia 16 *Legal Educ. Rev.* 75 (2006); Vai Io Lo, Before Competition and Beyond Complacency – The Internationalisation of Legal Education in Australia, 22 *Legal Educ. Rev.* 1 (2012); Helena Whalen-Bridge, The Reluctant Comparativist: Teaching Common Law Reasoning to Civil Law Students and the Future of Comparative Legal Skills, 58 *J. Legal Educ.* 364 (2008); Teresa Kissane Brostoff, Using Culture in the Classroom: Enhancing Learning for International Law Students, 15 *Mich. St. J. Int'l L.* 557 (2007); David Barker, Beyond Australia and the Pacific Rim: Challenges for the Internationalization of Australian Legal Education, 21 *Penn St. Int'l L. Rev.* 75 (2003); Steven Freeland, Grace Li and Angus Young, Crossing the Language and Cultural Divide – The Challenges of Educating Asian Law Students in a Globalizing World, 14 *Legal Educ. Rev.* 219 (2004).

> international students understand the legal and educational contexts from which the students come.[20]

The complexity of undertaking such a task well should not be underestimated, particularly in a classroom that is made up of students from a wide variety of different legal and political backgrounds and whose legal systems may vary enormously.

Encouraging Meaningful Interactions between International and Domestic Students

One of the reasons that students choose to leave their home country and study elsewhere is to get to know and, hopefully, create friendships and bonds with students from other countries, particularly the host country. Domestic students should see – but often fail to – that creating friendships and understanding with students from other countries also offers enormous intellectual, cultural and personal opportunities for them. Sadly, students who are keen to embrace the opportunities to travel and study overseas, in part to meet new people, can fail to see the opportunities for cross cultural friendships awaiting them in their own classrooms.[21]

So all too often, students clump themselves into groups where they feel safe, comfortable and normal. It is entirely understandable that they seek peers who speak the same native language, understand the same cultural norms and who can provide a social network that is familiar and comforting. Domestic students with existing networks and forms of social support can be indifferent to the needs of international students or perceive those students as self-ghettoizing with no interest in reaching out. International students can form into nationality groups which may appear exclusive and self-contained from the outside and fail to make meaningful connections with others.[22]

So what can be done to encourage real and meaningful interactions between students from different cultures and between international students and people from the host country more generally? This is not easy to answer. One possible answer is to mandate group work of various kinds – moots, joint papers, clinical

---

20 Brostoff, *supra* note 19, at 557 (citation omitted).

21 The issue becomes a step more complicated in systems, such as those in place in many US law schools, where international Masters students sit in classes with predominantly United States national JD students who have been together since first-year: see Silver, *supra* note 18, at 168–70.

22 One of the key recommendations from a recent report to the Australian government on international students was to make a priority of enabling meaningful engagements between international and Australian students. International Education Advisory Council 'Australia – Educating Globally' (February 2013) 47, recommendation C3.

work or presentations. At Melbourne Law School, we do this in several subjects in first year, both for credit and not for credit assignments. The syndicate groups, as we call them, are required to work together across the semester. They are created by the student office on a random basis, rather than allowing friends to select one another. The international students are deliberately spread across groups. Sometimes it works very well. The group members become friends or at least spend time learning to work together in respectful ways which lead to meaningful interactions. Sometimes it does not go as well with students finding that cultural differences make working together difficult. We have learnt that we need to teach more explicitly how to work in a group, including building inter-cultural teams. We need to help students understand that learning to work with people from different cultural backgrounds is a valuable life and professional skill.

Of course, it is not only in the classroom or formal curriculum that these interactions can take place. We have a mentor program for all first year JD students which teams the students up with alumni who work in a field that is similar to the one that the student aspires to work in. This is valuable for all students, but provides additional support for international students in understanding Australian life, culture and employment practices. We extended the program to international students in the LLM last year.

Finally, it is important to recognize the vital role of student groups – law societies, journals, law comedy productions, social justice groups and so forth. Obviously those groups are independent, but encouragement from the faculty leadership to consider how they can reach out to international students can be valuable. We had an interesting student driven change some years back from having an International Law Students Society, which was made up exclusively of overseas students, to a Global Law Students Association, the focus of which is to assist students who wish to work or study overseas after graduation. Both international and domestic students make up the membership and leadership. In this refocusing, the society becomes a resource for all students with the networks, connections and language skills of the international students being used as a valuable resource for Australian and international students alike.

Similarly, particularly when faculty financial support is involved, student groups need to be encouraged to think about a range of activities that will include students from a variety of backgrounds. Social events at which alcohol plays a prominent part will always be part of student life in some countries, but expanding the range of activities on offer helps to ensure that all students feel that their interests are being met. While these needs may be catered for in part by the formation of smaller student groups aimed at people from particular ethnic, racial or religious groups, it is also critical that the societies that represent the whole student body are conscious of the needs of international students. Student groups do not always think about issues such as catering with an eye to the religious or cultural differences that exist within the law school, and the school administration can play a valuable role in simply assisting student groups to be conscious of the choices that they make and to think through how to be more inclusive when that is appropriate.

Career Pathways

With the market for graduate lawyers shrinking in many countries and many students taking on study overseas for motives that are often linked to career advancement, it is critical that the services and advice offered to law students include information tailored to international students.

For some international students, their aim is to obtain work and – ultimately – a migration outcome in the host country. For them, the regular programs run by many law schools outlining the local options for careers covers much of what they need to know. However, there will be issues (particularly around work visas) that will exist for them that do not exist for domestic students. In countries where informal networks or word of mouth may be important in securing positions, international students without a local network may need additional support (such as a formal mentoring scheme) to assist them in finding a position. They may also need to be given honest and realistic counsel about the difficulties facing international students seeking legal employment in a competitive market.[23] There will be a limited amount that any law school will be able to do towards assisting with the final aim of permanent immigration, but there may at least be some capacity to bring in genuine experts for advice and to warn students away from some of the more exploitative and dishonest agents in the migration market.

For other international students, their ultimate aim is to return to their home country or to a country other than their host country. (This may or may not be after a period of time working in the host country; particularly when such work is required for admission to practice.[24]) For such students, the regular careers advice and programs offered by a law school may be of limited value – although there might well be some international opportunities offered in that program. It will be impossible for any law school to provide comprehensive information about the opportunities available everywhere. However, even some simple steps such as gathering information about admission to practice in key jurisdictions and working with appropriate neighbouring jurisdictions to have one's degree recognized for practice by them can send a clear message of support. It may be important for students seeking admission in other jurisdictions to have aspects of their degrees explained or justified before admissions bodies and such students should be given clear advice about where to go to obtain the necessary documentation for this purpose.

---

23 For an outline of the real challenges facing international graduates, particularly those without very high level English skills, in obtaining such work in the United States, *see* Carole Silver, States Side Story: Career Paths of International LLM Students, or 'I Like to be in America', 80 *Fordham L. Rev.* 2383 (2012).

24 Programs that allow graduates to qualify to practise in the country in which they study (often then becoming dual qualified in their home and the host country) are very attractive to many graduates: see Silver, *supra* note 18, 165–67.

Conclusion

International students can provide numerous benefits to law schools and the appetite for international study appears to be undiminished. However, if law schools are to deal ethically with the students who often pay a considerable amount to travel internationally and undertake further study, it is not enough to simply slot international students into existing programs and hope for the best. Law schools need a strategy for engaging international students in a way that enhances and enriches both their learning experience and the experiences of domestic students. When done well, the educational benefits to all involved are significant.

International study can sometimes be dealt with as a purely recruitment based series of issues with the assumption that once international students are through the door they require nothing more than a map of the city and a bit of language support.[25] Instead, a significant international student population should cause us to re-examine each element of what we do from marketing through to careers and alumni development. Much of what is relevant to a high quality education for domestic students will be equally relevant for international students (and we must be sure that we do not lose those elements that originally attracted international students out of a desire to make their path easier). However, other aspects will require some modification or rethinking.

There is increased competition for international students, including the relatively new phenomenon of countries which are traditional exporters of students increasingly improving their education system to encourage students from other countries to come to them. So called 'South–South' transfers are likely to be a growing part of the international student market and may put pressure on the traditional Western law schools that have assumed that they are and will remain the chosen destination for most of those interested in international study. However, as countries such as China grow in importance, it is becoming more commonplace to see students from all over the world, including Western law schools, looking to complete their education with a degree from a leading university in such countries.

In such fluid circumstances, all law schools which wish to continue to attract international students will need to consider the best ways in which to create a valuable and meaningful experience for them; one that builds upon, but extends, the learning traditions of the home university. No doubt there are many useful examples from various law schools that could act as an example, but it is also critical to ensure that there are opportunities to listen directly to the voice of international students.[26] International students who are admitted into foreign law schools are usually intelligent, reflective and capable of articulating their needs and interests if given an opportunity to do so. They may, however, need to be

25 Lo, *supra* note 19, 36.

26 In some cases this may be informal but regular but in other cases it might be part of systematic research: see, e.g., Elizabeth Stevens et al, Equity, Diversity and Student Engagement in a Law School – A Case Study Approach, 16 *Legal Educ. Rev.* 1 (2006).

invited to share their views quite explicitly, particularly when they come from cultures in which deference to authority is important. It is just as important to hear from the student who has had a wonderful experience to help to understand what has worked in practice, as it is to hear from those who have criticism or even a profoundly unhappy experience.

There will always be limits – including constraints around both people and finance – which mean that it is not always possible to do everything that might ideally be done for international students.[27] However, working in partnership with international students themselves, we can at least work on understanding the needs, ambitions and concerns of this important cohort and try to ensure that their presence in our classrooms is enriching for everyone.

---

27 An LLM program at University of Technology Sydney Law School in Australia, for example, that taught an LLM program in Mandarin, had some real success but required substantial resources, including bi-lingual academic and support staff: see Freeland, Li and Young, Crossing the Language and Cultural Divide – The Challenges of Educating Asian Law Students in a Globalising World, 14 *Legal Educ. Rev.* 219, 233–36 (2004).

Chapter 5

Doctrine, Perspectives, and Skills for Global Practice

Simon Chesterman[1]

Legal education has always been influenced by the tension between being an academic pursuit and a professional qualification.[2] Different jurisdictions historically resolved these tensions in their own way, though most tend to hedge: requiring a professional qualification administered by the local guild (a bar exam or a pupillage) as well as a degree in order to practice law. Only a few allow lawyers to practice with only a degree, as various Latin American jurisdictions do, or with only a professional certification – such as a handful of US states[3] and, until recently, Japan.[4]

How one thinks of the purpose of legal education will naturally have consequences for how one teaches. If law is primarily vocational training for lawyers, that will tend to encourage practice-oriented classes that focus on issues that may arise in a future career. If law is intended to be an academic discipline and encompass a broader liberal education, this may encourage a more theoretical approach.

---

1 Dean and Professor, National University of Singapore Faculty of Law. This chapter draws heavily on material first published as Simon Chesterman, 'Doctrine, Perspectives, and Skills for Global Practice', in William van Caenegem and Mary Hiscock (eds), *The Internationalisation of Legal Education: The Future Practice of Law* (Cheltenham: Edward Elgar, 2014). Permission to reproduce the relevant sections is gratefully acknowledged.

2 See, e.g., Lauren Carasik, 'Renaissance or Retrenchment: Legal Education at a Crossroads' (2011) 44 *Indiana L. Rev.* 735, 738–44.

3 Note that the requirement to attend law school in most other states is a comparatively recent phenomenon. In 1922, no state required a law degree as a condition of admission to practice and law school was seen by many as an unnecessary delay in a legal career. Alberto Bernabe-Riefkohl, 'Tomorrow's Law Schools: Globalization and Legal Education' (1995) 32 *San Diego L. Rev.* 137.

4 See generally Gerald Paul McAlinn, 'Reforming the System of Legal Education: A Call for Bold Leadership and Self-governance' (2001) 2 *Asian-Pac. L. & Pol'y J.* 15; Setsuo Miyazawa, 'The Politics of Judicial Reform in Japan: The Rule of Law at Last?' (2001) 2 *Asian-Pac. L. & Pol'y J.* 89; Yoshiharu Kawabata, 'The Reform of Legal Education and Training in Japan: Problems and Prospects' (2002) 43 *S. Tex. L. Rev.* 419; Masako Kamiya, 'Structural and Institutional Arrangements of Legal Education: Japan' (2006) 24 *Wis. Int'l L.J.* 153.

Few law schools admit to being in the former category, but the efforts of almost all to aspire to the latter have led to grave economic problems in legal education in the US in particular. American Bar Association (ABA) accreditation requirements and the pressure to rank highly in the *US News & World Report* have pushed law schools into behaviour that distorts their activities away from education, raising tuition costs while lowering the quality of what they offer students. From 1987 to 2009, law school tuition at public institutions rose from \$2,400 per year to \$18,500; at private law schools, tuition went from \$8,900 to \$35,750.[5]

Such a bubble is possible in part because of the irrational exuberance of law students, who see lucrative careers at the end of a Juris Doctor (JD) programme. That bubble appears to have burst: in 2011, only 55 per cent of US law graduates had found full-time legal jobs nine months after graduation.[6] Indeed, a small group of law students now appear to be using their degree primarily for the purpose of suing their *almae matres* for misrepresentation as to their job prospects – though all five such cases to date have been thrown out.[7]

Things are not quite so bad in the rest of the common law world, but the US provides a cautionary tale as to what happens when one ignores the market, or focuses on only one aspect of it.

One area in which legal academia has been more sensitive to market concerns is in the response to globalization. The driving force was largely the profession, with changes in the way law is practised driving changes in the way it is taught. The past century saw legal education evolve through paradigms that can be broadly described as international, transnational, and now global.[8] Internationalization saw the world as an archipelago of jurisdictions, with a small number of lawyers involved in mediating disputes between jurisdictions or determining which jurisdiction applied; transnationalization saw the world as a patchwork, with greater need for familiarity across jurisdictions and hence a growth in exchanges and collaborations; globalization is now seeing the world as a web in more ways than one, with lawyers needing to be comfortable in multiple jurisdictions and dealing with new regulatory regimes that do not fall neatly into domestic or international paradigms.[9]

---

5 Brian Z. Tamanaha, *Failing Law Schools* (University of Chicago Press 2012). See also Judith S. Kaye, 'A Chief Judge's After-Life: Reflections on Educating Lawyers Today' (2012) 45 *Indiana L. Rev.* 291.

6 Karen Sloan, 'ABA: Only 55 Per cent of Law Grads Found Full-Time Law Jobs', *National L.J.*, 18 June 2012.

7 Ashley Post, 'Judge Dismisses Suits Against John Marshall, Kent', *Inside Counsel*, 13 November 2012.

8 T. Alexander Aleinikoff, 'Remarks on the Globalization of the American Law School' (2007) 101 *Proc. Am. Soc'y Int'l L.* 184. See also Simon Chesterman, 'The Globalisation of Legal Education' (2008) 2008 *Sing. J.L.S.* 58.

9 Simon Chesterman, 'Globalization Rules: Accountability, Power, and the Prospects for Global Administrative Law' (2008) 14 *Global Governance* 39.

Globalization has seen the need for harmonization between different regimes, though this is not the same as homogenization. The world may be a little smaller and flatter, but it is still complex. The challenges posed are in some senses new, but in reality legal education has always been – or should always have been – about preparing our graduates for a changing and dynamic world. As many law professors have patiently explained to employers, there is limited utility in cramming our students full of substantive law so that they can be 'practice-ready' the day after graduating.

The problem is that the law changes. We therefore need to give our students the tools not just to practice on day one but also in year ten, skills that will support them through the varied career paths of modern law graduates.

So what is a conscientious law school to do? Based on the context that I have outlined – the tension between professional and academic goals, the impact of globalization on that profession, and the need to be nimble and flexible in the application of their skills – I tend to think in terms of baskets of goals.

A modern legal education thus comprises academic and professional components, each complementing the other. It should provide graduates with:

a. *doctrine* – a sound understanding of general principles and doctrine;
b. *perspectives* – an appreciation of the contexts in which the law operates (historical, theoretical, cross-cultural, cross-disciplinary, or global); and
c. *skills* – the development of professional skills, including legal research, analysis, reasoning, writing, mooting and advocacy, negotiation and dispute resolution, as well as professional ethics.[10]

Where it is taught as a standalone undergraduate degree, as it is in Singapore, the Bachelor of Laws degree should also develop *general academic skills*, including the ability to think critically, to adopt interdisciplinary approaches to problem-solving, and to communicate with others clearly and effectively.

If we can achieve all this, then we as law professors will have done our job and our students will have got their money's worth.

Doctrine

In terms of doctrine, there is value to the orthodoxy of a law degree. Even if not required by the local guild or accrediting body, it would be odd if a graduate from a law school in the common law world had not studied the basics of criminal law, the law of obligations (torts and contracts), public law, and property. Others might

---

10 Note that no subject will fit solely into one of these categories. A course examining the civil law, for example, would necessarily embrace not only different doctrines but different methods and theoretical assumptions.

add company law, equity, ethics, and evidence to the substantive law requirements. More recently, claims have been made for public international law and conflicts.

The pedagogical challenge here is to work out what is *essential* for all students and what is *desirable*. Foundational subjects are those upon which others are built, or which lay the bedrock for an understanding of the law. They should not simply be an administrative convenience based on the simplicity of everyone doing the same courses to earn the same degree.

We can think of this in terms of *what* subjects are compulsory, *why* we make them compulsory, but also *how* we teach them.

What

What should be the core curriculum at a modern law school? The answer, of course, is 'it depends'.

At the National University of Singapore (NUS) Faculty of Law, what we term the "core curriculum" takes up approximately 55 per cent of the whole degree. This is slightly higher than the proportion at US and Canadian schools where it tends to be between 30 per cent and 40 per cent, but lower than many English and Australian schools where it tends to be around 60 per cent. Indian schools have a significantly higher proportion at around 70 per cent to over 80 per cent. At the second law school in Singapore, Singapore Management University (SMU), the proportion is just over 70 per cent.

It should be noted that the Australian schools and the Indian schools run double-degree programmes over five years and SMU has a significant proportion of non-law compulsories. Although NUS runs double-degree law programmes over five years as well, this is done on a very selective basis.

As indicated earlier, it is hard to imagine a credible lawyer who has never studied at least criminal law, the law of obligations (torts and contracts), public law, and property. Beyond that, however, compulsory subjects need strong justifications. As I will describe later, there is a case for courses that develop perspectives and skills, though it is far from self-evident that all students should follow exactly the same path.

Why

A better question, then, is to examine why certain subjects are made compulsory and to be clear about those reasons.

Some of the variation between law schools is due to capacity, but it is also a function of our attitude towards our students. US students are older, to be sure, and come with an undergraduate degree. But they are also consumers keen to customize their educational experience. Even where it is an undergraduate degree, law is still being studied by adults. My own view is that we should treat them as such and pare down the compulsory subjects to the absolute minimum. Rather than having only two types of subjects – compulsory and optional – a middle path is possible whereby students are required to choose from baskets of subjects. These might be organized by subject type (for example, my loose categorization of doctrine, perspectives, and skills) or field of specialization (for example, commercial, public and international, intellectual property, and so on).

Different law schools might adopt different approaches based on the expected qualities of their graduates.

How

Once the core doctrinal (and perhaps skills and perspectives) subjects are identified, there are still interesting questions about how they should be taught.

Criminal law, for example, is taught throughout most of the common law world by starting with homicide, perhaps followed by other assaults – in particular sexual assault. Though important, such crimes are relatively rare. As Kris Gledhill has pointed out, it is unlikely that the considered view of every criminal law lecturer around the world is that murder and rape are the best way to teach criminal law. A more probable explanation is that we teach that way because that is how we ourselves were taught.[11]

Given that the practice of criminal law in general, and prosecuting or defending alleged murderers and rapists in particular, is a somewhat specialized field, one could imagine other ways of teaching criminal law. For example, at a law school that primarily produces corporate lawyers, one could imagine teaching criminal law in significant part through white-collar crime.

As indicated earlier, different law schools might approach these questions in their own way. Such considered differentiation is distinct from inertia, however, and merely continuing what has been done in the past.

Perspectives

Having said a little about doctrine, let me turn to the question of perspectives: what we might think of as an appreciation of the *contexts* within which the law operates.

Legal pedagogy must be intellectually rigorous in its own right, but it must also respond to the changing demands of practice. For the NUS Faculty of Law, it is understood that we need to continue to produce lawyers who can provide the full range of services required in Singapore, though this increasingly includes cross-border work requiring an understanding of the civil law of neighbouring countries. It may also involve aspects of Islamic law.

An important consideration, then, is how we can include additional critical and comparative perspectives, encouraging students to take subjects that consider the many Asian legal traditions in more depth and develop a deeper understanding of

11 Kris Gledhill, 'The Teaching of Criminal Law: Are We Stuck in a Timewarp?' (National University of Singapore Faculty of Law, 6 September 2011).

civil law jurisdictions in particular. Our graduates should be known not only for their intellectual abilities, their professional skills, their ability to analyse problems and communicate answers, but also for their sensitivity to the context within which they operate. The goal need not be total affinity with the other jurisdictions. But one threshold might be ensuring that students know enough about another jurisdiction that they can quickly grasp what is different.

Perspectives should not merely be instrumental, however. In addition to cross-cultural understanding, a competent lawyer should have a basic grasp of the historical evolution of a legal system and some theoretical tools that help him or her understand how and why it changes. And given the nature of legal practice today, a lawyer should be able to cross not just geographical but also disciplinary boundaries. No client walks into a lawyer's office and says 'I have a contract law problem'. He or she just has a problem. It might be contract or property law, but it might also be a business problem, or there may be a political dimension.

In some jurisdictions like Australia, the double-degree structure ensures that no law student graduates solely with a law degree. In jurisdictions like Singapore and the UK, it may be up to the law school to ensure some kind of breadth on the part of the student.

Skills

Lastly, let me turn to skills.

Most law schools now have programmes that train students in basic legal research, analysis, reasoning, and writing. Most also provide opportunities for mooting, and an increasing number of law schools offer opportunities to practise negotiation and dispute resolution skills. The incorporation of skills elements has drawn heavily on the experience of medical schools, though typically with nothing like the rigour and empirically-grounded research that goes into the medicine curriculum.[12]

Loosely grouped under the skills heading, it may be helpful to say something about three areas that have seen some development in recent years: clinical programmes, ethics, and pro bono work.

Clinical Programmes

A relatively recent development at NUS Law is the introduction of a clinical programme.[13] Built as a natural extension to our Legal Skills Programme, the pilot module provides students with an opportunity to develop their legal skills in context,

12 Jennifer S. Bard, ''Practicing Medicine and Studying Law': How Medical Schools Used to Have the Same Problems We Do and What We Can Learn from Their Efforts to Solve Them' (2011) 10 *Seattle J. for Social Justice* 135.

13 Cf. Margaret Martin Barry, 'Practice Ready: Are We There Yet?' (2012) 32 *Boston College Third World L.J.* 247.

to acquire new skills for legal practice, and to make significant contributions to enhancing the provision of legal services to the community. Students work under the close supervision of practising lawyers to assist in live cases.

The present module has a strong pro bono emphasis, but we are exploring the development of a 'corporate clinic' to complement this. The faculty is also looking into other ways to expand the opportunities in this area, though clinical programmes are necessarily labour-intensive given the levels of supervision required.[14]

Ethics

The teaching of Legal Ethics also raises particular issues, with an argument that teaching Legal Ethics as a standalone course might send the wrong message.

A different approach is to teach Legal Ethics pervasively through the curriculum, with components in various courses and periodic opportunities for discussion about ethical concerns that arise in the practice of law.[15] Legal Ethics is currently covered in the first year as a topic within the Singapore Legal System and also touched on in other modules; one suggestion is to significantly increase (and concentrate) coverage of Legal Ethics in the first year.

Again, this could usefully draw on the experience of medical schools, where ethics now tends to be taught in a more contextual manner spread through the curriculum and clinical practice, rather than as a 'theoretical' standalone subject.[16]

Pro Bono Work

A third area of particular note is the move to increase opportunities to engage in pro bono work.

There is a rich tradition of pro bono work among staff and students at NUS Law. Students have initiated and organized pro bono activities at the Law Faculty, and now many opportunities are available through voluntary groups such as the Pro Bono Group and the Criminal Justice Club. Pro bono has also become an important part of the orientation programme for new students, and students have worked with individual law professors and gone overseas to work with international nongovernmental organizations (NGOs).

Students engaging in pro bono activities over the years have had an opportunity to get "real world" experience in the practice of law and see firsthand the important

14 Peter A. Joy, 'The Cost of Clinical Legal Education' (2012) 32 *Boston College Third World L.J.* 309.

15 See generally Kieran Tranter, Lillian Corbin, and Michael Robertson (eds), *The Ethics Project in Legal Education* (Routledge, 2010).

16 See, e.g., A.C. Molewijk et al., 'Teaching Ethics in the Clinic: The Theory and Practice of Moral Case Deliberation' (2008) 34(2) *J. of Medical Ethics* 120; J.A. Carrese et al., 'Everyday Ethics in Internal Medicine Resident Clinic: An Opportunity to Teach' (2011) 45(7) *Medical Education* 712.

role a lawyer plays in helping an individual. In addition to developing professional skills, pro bono work can help students identify an area of law in which they wish to practice – and expose students to the non-pecuniary aspects of the profession that may help to sustain a long and satisfying career.[17]

All law students should have an opportunity to see why access to justice is important. The vast majority of experience in the area of pro bono at NUS Law has been positive. But it has been confined to a minority of students. We are therefore planning to make a minimum of pro bono work mandatory for all Bachelor of Laws degree (LLB) students. This decision raises the issues of how to maintain the tradition of student leadership and ensure that all students are exposed to pro bono. One model is to cultivate a student–faculty partnership to ensure continued student involvement and commit resources to expand placements in projects that support the community and are challenging for students.

In terms of the larger goal, which is ensuring that lawyers recognize their own responsibilities to society and contribute to the public good, it is far from clear that mandating pro bono work at law school makes much difference in the medium term. Rather, support within the profession in the form of pro bono contributions being recognized as billable hours and having institutional support in a firm tends to have more impact.[18]

Conclusion

A legal education must aspire to do far more than teach a student what the law is. Though there is, of necessity, a certain body of doctrinal knowledge that must be imparted, we would not be doing our job if we did not equip our graduates with skills that will last them a lifetime. At the same time, we should also help our students to develop perspectives that enable them to see the logic behind the law, the factors that shape it, and the way it might be perceived from other cultures and traditions.

---

17 See Margaret Meriwether Cordray, 'Expanding Pro Bono's Role in Legal Education' (2011) 48 *Idaho L. Rev.* 29.

18 Deborah L. Rhode, *Pro Bono in Principle and in Practice: Public Service and the Professions* (Stanford University Press 2005); Robert Granfield, 'The Meaning of Pro Bono: Institutional Variations in Professional Obligations among Lawyers' (2007) 41(1) *Law & Society Rev.* 113. See further Richard Grimes, 'Why (and How) Do Pro Bono Work in Law Schools?' (2008) 6(1) *J. of Commonwealth Law and Legal Education* 27; Leonore F. Carpenter, '"We're Not Running a Charity Here": Rethinking Public Interest Lawyers' Relationships with Bottom-Line-Driven Pro Bono Programs' (2010) 29 *Buffalo Public Interest L.J.* 37; Douglas L. Colbert, 'Clinical Professors' Professional Responsibility: Preparing Law Students to Embrace Pro Bono' (2011) 18 *Georgetown J. on Poverty Law & Policy* 309; Nancy Morawetz, 'Counterbalancing Distorted Incentives in Supreme Court Pro Bono Practice: Recommendations for the New Supreme Court Pro Bono Bar and Public Interest Practice Communities' (2011) 86 *N.Y.U. L. Rev.* 131.

It will not always be possible to ensure that our students are able to provide ready answers to the problems that the globalized practice of law throws at them. But my modest hope is that, if the education we impart is effective, they will at least be asking the right questions.

Chapter 6
Cultivating High-Quality Internationalized Legal Talents under Legal Globalization

Liu Xiaohong[1]

With the accelerated process of economic globalization, legal globalization has become the centre of debates among the legal academia all over the world. In August 2013, the State Council approved the establishment of a Pilot Free Trade Zone in Shanghai; this is a big step that China has taken to adapt to global economic development which requires more high-quality internationalized legal talents. We believe that to keep pace with the legal globalization, legal educators should further update their knowledge, broaden their horizons, optimize the mode of cultivating talents and enhance the communications and cooperation with other countries. Meanwhile, it is also necessary to strengthen the training of internationalized legal talents to meet the requirements of our time, China's social reform and systematic transformation.

The Background of the Cultivation

The Deepening of Legal Globalization

Due to the inexorable development of economic globalization, social changes along with collisions and development of new thoughts and theories are unavoidable, among which is the idea of legal globalization. In the 1980s, legal globalization received extensive attention worldwide; many experts in our country also began to conduct research, trying to find ways to cope with it. For example, some experts believe that legal globalization is a process through which law will be no longer be restricted to nations, but to the whole world as a universal law; it is also a process through which the concepts, principals and rules within different nations are assimilated. However, some other experts argue that legal globalization doesn't necessarily mean the elimination of legal differences. According to these experts, rather than an isolated and close system, legal globalization underlines the equal relationship between the universal legal system and other legal systems. Some

1 Professor, Vice President of East China University of Political Science and Law.

other similar theories are: legal globalization will not lead to the elimination of the legal individualities or nationalities of different countries; legal globalization does not exclude diversity; legal globalization is not a mode that all legal systems have to adopt. Despite all the different focuses in these theories, there's one thing for sure – legal globalization is inevitable as the result of economic globalization and the globalization of public affairs. According to Jiang Ping, a well-known Chinese law expert, the trend of legal globalization is irresistible. To keep pace with this trend, legal educators should "act according to circumstances", guide students with scientific outlook, and optimize the training mode, mechanism, methodology and content in order to cultivate legal professionals who can adapt to the needs of our society.

On August 22 2013, Shanghai's Pilot Free Trade Zone was established, billed as a major step for financial reforms and economic experimentation. According to the latest statement by the Chinese Government, four current laws will not be valid in the Shanghai Pilot Free Trade Zone. Against this scenario, it is clear that high-quality internationalized legal talents are required to take part in setting up rules and regulations for the operation and management of the new zone, modifying regulations and policies that are imperfect for the zone and providing a professional legal service to the multinational companies in the zone. That is to say, the urgent requirement of cultivating high-quality internationalized legal talents is triggered by the establishment of Shanghai's Pilot Free Trade Zone. And acting on circumstance, East China University of Political Science and Law (ECUPL) established the ECUPL Institute of China Free Trade Zone Law to meet the urgent requirements.

The Aim of Higher Education in Our Country and Connotation Construction

Higher education has developed rapidly in China during the past few years. It has been largely expanded and has developed into the stage of popularization. In 2011, there were 2,049 higher education institutions in total in China, with 23.08 million college students, among whom over 620,000 were law majors. Meanwhile, there is a growing concern about the quality of higher education, requiring teaching assessment in higher education institutions and the improvement of education quality.

In this context, China's Ministry of Education announced two policies, one after another, in 2007, aimed at deepening the reform of higher education and enhancing the quality of education: "On the Implementation of Undergraduate Education Quality and Reform" and "On Further Deepening the Reform of Undergraduate Education and Comprehensively Improving the Education Quality". In 2010, "Long-term and Medium-term Education Reform and Development Scheme" (2010–20) further pointed out that "higher education institutions should comprehensively improve the quality of education, talents training, scientific research and overall level of social services in order to achieve the goal of establishing a group of world-class higher education institutions with features and superior education qualities." In 2012, after the Ministry of Education released "On Comprehensively Improving the Higher Education Quality", the Ministry of Finance and Ministry of Education jointly issued "On Improving the Innovative Skills in Higher Education Institutions" and some other documents, further stressing the importance of innovative ability training and the quality of talents' training. This is to say, connation construction has played a key role in the further development of higher education in our country.

The Initiation of the Cultivation Plan for Outstanding Legal Talents

At present there are more than 600 law schools in China with approximately 160,000 legal graduates in 2011 who have already become the pivotal force in promoting China's strategy of administrating the country by law enforcement. Nevertheless, some problems still exist in China's legal education, which are mainly reflected in the structural surplus of legal students and the severe shortage of the legal talents who are competent in practicing international legal affairs with internationalized perspectives and thorough knowledge of international rules and regulations.

Obviously, such a situation cannot satisfy the social demand for the legal talents in the process of legal globalization. In order to deepen the reform of legal education and improve the quality of the legal talent cultivation, China's Ministry of Education and the Central Political and Judiciary Commission jointly carried out the cultivation plan for outstanding legal talents. By the end of 2011, 58 training and educational bases for practical and interdisciplinary legal talents, 22 bases for foreign legal talents and 12 bases in the west and rural areas for grass-root legal talents had been established, with an innovative training mode to meet the need of high-quality legal talents. This not only gives rise to new requirements for legal education, but also brings some opportunities for the development of legal education.

Analysing the Connotation of Cultivating High-Quality Internationalized Legal Talents

Defining Training Levels

China's legal education system consists of popular higher legal education, adult legal education and vocational legal education varied in different training channels, forms and levels. In terms of the training level, it can be classified into vocational education, undergraduate education and graduate education. Considering the fact that China has already entered the phase of popularization in higher education, the goals of college education in China have gradually evolved into general education, quality education and basic education. Therefore, the education of internationalized legal talents should be defined as graduate education. According to the current educational system in China, the talents on this level would be cultivated mainly by the ordinary higher education institutions.

Defining Education Type

There are mainly two types of targeted talents in legal cultivation: one is the talent with a career orientation of legal education and the research of legal theory and practice. Such talents need to systematically study law and related theories, master research methods and skills and acquire the abilities of logic reasoning and theory innovating. In China, the traditional graduate education is mainly aimed at cultivating such type of talents. Another type is the practical talent with career orientation of legal application and practicing. Such talents are required to obtain a superior professional legal quality with extensive knowledge of law and other related disciplines; they should also be skilled in legal practice, familiar with legal processes and procedures, and competent in practicing law and innovating. From our perspective, there is no hierarchy between the research type and the practical type. The importance lies in the understanding of core requirements of talents' cultivation and the key indicators of the talent quality. The science of law itself is a discipline emphasizing on practice, the value of which is mainly reflected in its function of regulating social relationship, peoples' behaviors and social orders. Without the platform of social practice, the science of law will lose its vitality. In this case, cultivating high-quality practical legal talents is much more significant. According to what has been discussed above, the undergraduate education should be carried out on the basis of the enhancing of general graduate education, with equal emphasis on professional degree and academic degree. In terms of graduate education, legal professional (practical) training should be strengthened. For the doctoral education, a legal degree system should be established as soon as possible to cultivate interdisciplinary elite talents (practical) who are capable of coping with complicated legal affairs to meet modern society's demand for academic innovation and complex legal practice.

Defining Talents' Overall Quality

We believe that high-quality internationalized legal talents should obtain a good humanistic quality, solid legal expertise and practicing skills; they are also required to be proficient in related international rules, fluent in foreign languages and capable of providing legal services covering foreign affairs. In terms of standardizing talents' cultivation, there are three criteria, which are basic qualities, professional accomplishment and occupational accomplishment. The basic qualities refer to the possession of higher accomplishment of social sciences and humanities, the ability to process and analyse information, communications ability, the ability to handle public relations and international communications ability; professional accomplishment refers to the possession of solid legal knowledge, practicing skills, legal reasoning and research ability, as well as the competence of solving complex theoretical and practical issues with professional knowledge and practicing law in foreign languages; occupational accomplishment refers to the belief in law, the sense of social responsibility, a combined knowledge of economy management and other related subjects as well as good professional morality.

Key Issues in Cultivating High-Quality Legal Talents

To nurture high-quality legal talents, the following key issues should be better addressed:

The Issue between Elite Education and Mass Education

Consensus has already been reached that the law education in China is moving from elite education to mass education. There are more than 630 law institutions, which have 760,000 students majoring in law, including 460,000 undergraduates. Both the prestigious universities and the vocational schools share almost the same talents' training goal, teaching plan, course contents and so on. However, the diverse market demands talents with different types of education in law. In this sense, elite education still plays a very important role in that it can cultivate and develop personality for individual students and better prepare them for their future career.

The Issue between Application-Oriented Talents and Research-Oriented Talents

Agreement has now been reached that law education in China should follow a career-oriented road. However, two defects exist in the professionalization of Chinese law education: first, there are calls for training in judicial ethics. Judges, prosecutors and lawyers unarmed with judicial ethics are dangerous. There is a connection between judicial corruption and shortage of professional ethics education. Second, there is a shortage in professional techniques. Law-practitioners are unable to adjust to the requirement of their jobs without sufficient techniques. Hence these two defects lead us to reflect on the relationship between application-oriented talents and research-oriented talents.

The Issue between Globalization and Localization

The issue between globalization and localization is like the two sides of a coin. Localization does not exclude globalization. China has a profound history and diverse culture. It is critical for Chinese law students to maintain their cultural diversity.

Methods of Internationalized Legal Talents' Cultivation

Perfecting the Training Mechanism

When it comes to training sections, the training of internationalized legal talents can be divided into three stages, namely the stage of basic theoretical studying, the stage of vocational training and the stage of professional practice. In the first stage, students are required to grasp the basic knowledge of law and related theories; in the second stage, students would accept skill trainings such as defences and trials; in the third stage, students would be required to apply knowledge to practice, focusing on practical exercise of legal affairs. It is worth noting that the three stages, particularly the latter two, can be overlapping.

For training methods, "dual tutorial mechanism" would be adopted. In doing so, students would be divided into different groups according to their interests and professional backgrounds. Each group would be assigned to tutors (with certain practical experience). Meanwhile, senior legal practitioners (judges, prosecutors, lawyers and so on) would be introduced as practical instructors to improve the one-to-one teaching mode. In order to facilitate the cooperation with foreign higher education institutions, exchange programs of teachers and students, and a credit transfer and accumulation system would also be established. After the completion of undergraduate courses, students would be expected to go abroad for one year's study or internship which would help improve their practical skills and the ability to deal with international legal affairs. Additionally, cooperation on graduate programs and doctoral programs could also be established.

With regard to teaching methods, priority should be given to case studies, seminars and free discussions, accompanied by moot court and arbitral court and other court practices. Legal educators should also adopt new teaching methods such as a clinical legal teaching mode to strengthen students' practical ability to apply theories to work.

Optimizing the Curriculum

The first stage of optimizing the curriculum would be to introduce cross-disciplinary courses. Following the principle of refining legal knowledge and basic theories, the proportion of cross-disciplinary courses that are gradually formed and shaped by economic, social and scientific–technological development should be raised, adapting to the need of judicial practice; At the same time, the proportion of compulsory courses could be relatively lowered to provide students with a wider range of selective courses which would help them shape their development according to their own conditions and social needs.

The second stage of optimizing the curriculum would be to increase the gravity of practical courses. In addition to core legal professional courses, more practical courses should be incorporated into the curriculum. The practical curriculum should include experimental courses of law, legal skills and technique training courses, such as forensics, negotiations science, science of evidence, the trial science, forensic science and so on. Forensic science, for instance, has great significance for cultivating well-trained practitioners. In our country's current judicial practice, 30–40 per cent of the cases will involve issues of scientific technologies and other specific issues, such as disability rating evaluation, death cause identification, mental illness identification, paternity testing, judicial accounting appraisal, computer forensics and so on. The legal issues mentioned above cannot be determined merely by logic reasoning or judges' intuitions; under such circumstances, scientific technology and expertise are required. Although there are professional forensic institutions and personnel responsible for such issues, judges, lawyers and other legal practitioners should acquire basic skills and qualities of knowing how to identify specific issues in legal processing, what methods should be applied, how to audit and evaluate the scientific feasibility objectivity and accuracy of expert opinions, as well as how to obtain cross-examination results, attestation and admitted evidences.

The third stage would be to introduce internationalized courses. With the introduction of top-notch curriculums from other foreign universities, students can enjoy international educational resources in the domestic setting, resulting in broadened and internationalized perspectives. Meanwhile, in order to promote communications between teachers and students and optimize teaching methods, well-known legal experts from other countries would be invited to give lectures.

Strengthening Quality Control

Great importance should be attached to quality control issues in the process of cultivating high-quality internationalized legal talents. Participation in the international education certification and assessment process needs to be considered in order to bring this program more in line with international practice. The assessment could start from regional institutions such as the Asia–Pacific Quality Network (APQN). The third-party evaluation agencies could be established during the progress of improving the overall quality of higher education and thus enhancing the effectiveness of social media. The recently published "Undergraduate Teaching Quality Report", which has responded to the social needs of the higher education quality, may further require a specified assessment for different disciplines and majors. By strengthening quality control, social intermediary agencies will perform their researching, consultative, evaluative and directive functions to build connections between universities, government and society, thus the required information from the government as well as all levels of society could be delivered effectively. In the meantime, feedback and requests from higher education institutions will also be delivered to the government. News media, as the most popular media, is low in cost and highly accepted by society, schools, parents and students. Therefore, it is necessary to make full use of the importance of news media among the comprehensive improvement of higher education.

Reforming Graduate Admission Policy

The process of cultivating internationalized legal talents should be closely connected with economic and social development requirements and focus on those students with economic, financial, science and engineering, medical and foreign language knowledge background. Students should be required to obtain bachelor's degrees or higher with certain work experience to guarantee the quality of talent training; for entrance examinations, the proportions of comprehensive capability tests should be increased. With regards to admissions policy, higher education institutions should adopt their independent recruitment and admission principles and criteria, carry out experimental training programs and gradually improve them in the future. Colleges which are authorized to carry out bachelor–master combined programs and bachelor–master–doctor combined programs can take advantage of the resources to form their own features in order to achieve the talent training goals; or cooperate closely with the governmental organizations, enterprises and institutions and adopt the "order mode" to meet the urgent social needs of internationalized legal talents.

Experience of Cultivating High-Quality Internationalized Legal Talents

The Target of Cultivating High-Quality Internationalized Legal Talents

Our university aims to cultivate high-quality and cross-disciplinary internationalized legal talents with special proficiency in international economics, management, international finance and trade, admiralty and maritime, international investment and other areas for relevant international organizations and our legislative, judicial, law enforcement, legal services, and financial institutions and foreign trade agencies. Training will focus on international financial law, international shipping law, international economic law and the international commercial law.

The Features of Cultivating High-Quality Internationalized Legal Talents

Trial Implementation of Bachelor–Master Combined Program Although it is easier to carry out the training at graduate level, in order to achieve the goal of training internationalized legal talents, our school has initiated the program at undergraduate level and has given absolute priority to it. The bachelor–master combined program enables the effective implementation of our training philosophy and scheme, and aims to accomplish the expected objectives with concentrated resources.

Joint Degree Programs Based on the different training goals and mechanisms of different talents, our school carries out training programs of different types. After three and a half years' undergraduate study, students with outstanding performance are selected to participate in overseas education and practice. After graduation, students can also apply to study abroad for about one year, pursuing advanced legal education or a foreign LLM (Master of Law) degree.

Strengthen Students' Ability to Communicate Cross-Culturally We believe that internationalized legal talents should obtain cross-cultural communication skills, therefore students are sent abroad for at least one semester's study or internship after finishing the main law courses. With a better proficiency in legal English, and familiarity with foreign legal environment, students are thus fully prepared for foreign legal affairs in the future. In addition, students with outstanding performance in English also attend language courses in Japanese, German and French to hone their linguistic skills, which will play an important role in breaking language obstacles and increasing communications with these countries.

Introducing Featured Course Modules We have set up a "Perspective of Law" course to create a "foreign-related International Law module, foreign-related legal affairs, finance and trade module, finance and legal practice, the shipping trade module, shipping law practice" crossed-training module teaching mode. International course modules include those courses taught in English, partner-school's programs, bilingual courses and so on. Practice course modules include lawyers' practice, trial practice, prosecutors' cases and legal clinic courses. The live broadcasting of introduced international modules gives students a direct in-class perception.

Carrying Out an Elite Talent Management Model Relevant institutions will be established to cultivate elites in teaching management mode. A Dual Tutorial Mechanism will be applied to give students academic and practical guidance and training instructions provided by both professional and practical teachers. These tutors will also counsel students in course study, essay writing and research training; give instructions on academic planning and study planning and assist them in achieving high-level accomplishment in the training program. A strict quality control mechanism and elimination system will also be established with specific policies according to the different characteristics of foreign classes.

Legal globalization makes it necessary to boost international communications and will ultimately affect the conduct of legal education. The cultivation of high-quality internationalized legal talents is not only inseparable from national and regional inter-institutional cooperation and support, but also inseparable from the reform and exploration of law schools. We hope that we could learn from other foreign law schools in this respect, and that it will play a positive role in promoting the quality of legal education in our university.

PART II
Shifts in Teaching Philosophies and Methods

Chapter 7
The Values Dimension of Legal Education: Educating for Justice and Service

Paul Redmond[1]

Introduction

These are difficult times for legal education, particularly for its project of nurturing the profession's public character and values. The research literature points to the stifling effect of academic legal education upon student justice orientation; the current external forces reshaping legal education also militate against student idealism and prosocial professional aspiration. This chapter looks at these challenges for legal educators and some means to confront them.

Globalisation has weakened the authority of states in favour of markets. It has profoundly affected legal education as it has much else in economy, society and culture. Globalisation has lowered boundaries between states, untethered enterprises from their home state and generated what might be called "non-state normativity" – the sharing of norm-creation authority with a wide range of non-state actors, grounded in new power constellations, especially those involving business, and in expertise grounded authority rather than legitimacy derived from democratic mandate or sovereign authority.[2] This shared authority is expressed through multi-lateral framework agreements, codes of conduct and a wide range of other soft law instruments having normative effect in the global economy and social ordering. In the realm of legal services and education, visible expressions include

1 Emeritus Professor, Faculty of Law, University of New South Wales; Sir Gerard Brennan Professor, Faculty of Law, University of Technology, Sydney. This chapter draws upon material prepared by the author to guide implementation of a standard on ethics and professional responsibility: see Maxine Evers, Leanne Houston and Paul Redmond, *Good Practice Guide (Bachelor of Laws), Ethics and Professional Responsibility (Threshold Learning Outcome 2)* (Australian Learning and Teaching Council, 2011). It also develops ideas and recommendations for Hong Kong made in Paul Redmond and Christopher Roper, *Legal Education and Training in Hong Kong: Preliminary Review, Report of the Consultants* (The Steering Committee on the Review of Legal Education and Training in Hong Kong, 2001), chap. 14.

2 Peer Zumbansen, "What lies Before, Behind and Beneath a Case? Five Minutes on Transnational Lawyering and the Consequences for Legal Education" in Shauna Van Praagh and Helge Dedek (eds), *Stateless Law: Evolving Boundaries of a Discipline* (Ashgate, 2015); available at SSRN: http://ssrn.com/abstract=2370428.

the internationalisation of law school curricula,[3] increasing self-identification as "global law schools",[4] and the adoption by law firms of global practice structures that cross national borders and serve a globalised corporate clientele with greatly increased firm size relative to national and locally oriented firms.[5]

More significantly perhaps for legal education is an ideological shift, a "globalisation of the mind", under which "markets trump politics; law's mission is to make the world safe for markets; and, finally, the best kind of law is law which … disables the state's capacity for regulatory intervention".[6] Notions of law as an instrument of social justice give way in the rise of market ideology that accepts the primacy of markets and law's limited role as their curators. This rise shapes attitudes on the part of law teachers – the ascendancy of the "law and economics" movement in the North American legal academy is an example. The change in thinking is even more apparent among law students, burdened with increased educational debt, a bleaker employment market and uncertain career prospects as legal services markets are fundamentally restructured under globalisation and the economic viability of traditional practice structures appear less certain. This is a time of "existential crisis for law schools", in the United States but elsewhere also, and of increasing student cynicism as to law's purpose and capacity as an instrument for social welfare and amelioration.[7] It must be acknowledged, however, that student altruism endures; its nurture and growth is an important responsibility for law schools.

Law, it is widely said in reviews and statements of objectives of legal education, is a public profession and its practitioners assume responsibilities of a public character. Thus, it is said that law's connection with justice, and its role in distributing power and rights, and calling the exercise of each to account, means that its professional practice is more firmly impressed with the claims of the public interest and service than many other callings. This chapter argues for an explicit values dimension in legal education that focuses on the relation between law, justice and morality, and promotes an ethic of service in professional work. This may seem counter-intuitive in view of the myriad contemporary changes that make the present intellectual mood and legal and financial culture inhospitable to such an objective. This chapter argues, however, that these pressures strengthen, rather

---

3 See Michael Coper, "Ten Elements of the Internationalisation of Legal Education"; available at SSRN: http://ssrn.com/abstract=22268485.

4 See Harry W. Arthurs, "Law and Learning in an Era of Globalization" (2009) 10 *German Law Journal* 629 at 630–31.

5 See Kath Hall, "Educating Global Lawyers" (2013) 5 *Drexel Law Review* 391.

6 Arthurs, n. 4, at 631–32.

7 Lincoln Caplan, "An existential crisis for law schools", *New York Times*, July 14, 2012 <http://www.nytimes.com/2012/07/15/opinion/sunday/an-existential-crisis-for-law-schools.html> (accessed 28/01/2014); Kim Economides, "Cynical Legal Studies" in Jeremy Cooper & Louise G Trubek (eds), *Educating for Justice: Social Values and Legal Education* (Ashgate, Dartmouth, 1997), 26.

than weaken, the case for an explicit values dimension centred on promotion of justice and professional service in the public interest, including in the interest of those upon whom the law bears most harshly.

A social contract underlies each profession's privileges, an implicit contract between the profession and society that links the licence (or liberties) extended to its practitioners to a particular social mandate or function.[8] Lawyers perform multiple roles, not only as advocates of clients' interests but also a public role as officers of the court where they assume collective and individual responsibilities for the justice system's operation in securing rights. This latter role is properly seen as a form of social regulation and there is an inevitable tension between lawyers' client advocacy roles and these social regulatory functions.[9] Outside litigation contexts, they also perform roles as architects and regulators of social relations through transactional and counselling roles. This role duality is expressed consistently in official statements of professional responsibility so that the discharge of the ethical–social function is said to represent "the central moral tradition of lawyering".[10]

There are many values advanced by the profession of law and integral to its character and social function. Concern here is primarily with a sub-set of these professional values – the professional obligation to promote justice (including access to legal services) and the professional ethic of collective and individual service in the public interest. Other professional values such as those relating to competence, personal honesty and integrity, and ethical conduct are beyond the present scope, not because they are less important but because they raise distinct issues in elaboration of the particular content of the obligation and because there are in place norms and sanctions explicitly directed at securing respect for these values.

The next part of the chapter examines official statements of the public character of the legal profession and lawyers' public responsibilities; the following part examines implications for legal education and evidence of the negative effects of legal education upon student values and justice consciousness; after that we examine options for integration of justice consciousness and an ethic of service into legal education programs. The final part provides concluding observations.

8 William M. Sullivan et al., *Educating Lawyers: Preparation for the Profession of Law* (John Wiley & Sons, Inc., 2007) (Carnegie Report), 21, 30.

9 Sullivan et al., n. 8, 82.

10 Roger Cramton, "On Giving Meaning to 'Professionalism'" in *Teaching and Learning Professionalism, Symposium Proceedings* (Chicago: American Bar Association, 1997), 18, cited in Sullivan et al., n. 8, 140.

The Public Character and Responsibilities of the Legal Profession

The literature on the professional responsibilities of lawyers has long stressed their responsibilities to promote the cause of justice and an ethic of professional service. Thus, Roscoe Pound wrote that the defining quality of all professions is that their primary purpose is "[p]ursuit of the learned art in the spirit of a public service".[11] Alfred Reed, in his classic study of the development of legal education in the United States 90 years ago, wrote that "[p]racticing lawyers do not merely render to the community a social service, which the community is interested in having them render well. They are part of the governing mechanism of the state. Their functions are in a broad sense political. ... [The public nature of the legal profession springs] fundamentally from the fact ... that private individuals cannot secure justice without the aid of a special professional order to represent and to advise them. To this end lawyers were instituted, as a body of public servants, essential for the maintenance of private rights".[12] The preamble to the American Bar Association's Model Rules of Professional Conduct commences with the statement that a lawyer is "an officer of the legal system and a public citizen who has a special responsibility for the quality of justice".

Official reviews of legal education have repeatedly asserted the public character and public responsibilities of the legal profession and the importance of nurturing those values during legal education. Consider two foundational reviews during the 1990s. In the United States, the MacCrate Report, prepared by a task force appointed by the American Bar Association, cited "striving to promote justice, fairness, and morality" as one of four "fundamental values of the profession".[13] The MacCrate Report also emphasised the profession's responsibility to ensure that adequate legal services are available to those unable to afford them.[14] In the United Kingdom, the Lord Chancellor's Advisory Committee on Legal Education and Conduct (ACLEC) defined "legal values" as "commitment to the rule of law, to justice, fairness and high ethical standards, to acquiring and improving professional skills, to representing clients without fear or favour, to promoting equality of opportunity, and to ensuring that adequate legal services are provided to those who cannot afford to pay for them".[15]

---

11 Roscoe Pound, *The Lawyer from Antiquity to Modern Times* (West Publishing Co., St Paul Minn, 1953), 5.

12 A.Z. Reed, *Training for the Public Profession of the Law* (Updike, New York, 1921), 3.

13 American Bar Association, Section on Legal Education and Admissions to the Bar, *Legal Education and Professional Development – An Educational Continuum* (Chicago, 1992), 140–41.

14 American Bar Association, n. 13, Value § 2.2; see also *2013–2014 ABA Standards and Rules of Procedure for Approval of Law Schools*, Standards 3.01, 3.02.

15 Lord Chancellor's Advisory Committee on Legal Education and Conduct, *First Report on Legal Education and Training* (London, 1996), para. 2.4.

The English and United States formulations are not in radically different terms. Each is directed to values formation at the law school stage. A simple typology of the personal attributes, ethical capacities and values to be developed during legal education emerges:

- *ethical sensitivity*: the ability to recognise and resolve ethical dilemmas that arise in professional work;
- *legal values for which the profession has a particular responsibility*: for example, "a commitment to the rule of law, to justice [and] fairness" (ACLEC) and "striving to promote justice, fairness and morality" (MacCrate); and
- *social responsibility for the provision of legal services*: "to ensuring that adequate legal services are provided for those who cannot afford to pay for them" (ACLEC); "the provision of competent representation" (MacCrate).[16]

Implications for Legal Education:
Responsibility for Promotion of Justice Orientation and Service Ethic

To law schools then falls the responsibility of inculcating the "social responsibility which rests upon a public profession".[17] This responsibility calls on law schools to impress on students that law is closely related to the pursuit of justice with individual and collective responsibilities to place professional skills at the service of justice and fellow citizens. Law schools do not discharge their responsibilities merely by imparting academic proficiency: "the lawyer's task is ultimately concerned with justice and … any legal teaching that ignores justice has missed most of its point".[18]

16 In Australia, threshold learning outcomes for law degrees provide that graduates will demonstrate "an ability to recognise and reflect upon the professional responsibilities of lawyers in promoting justice and in service to the community": Australian Learning and Teaching Council, *Bachelor of Laws, Academic Standards Statement* (Learning and Teaching Academic Standards Project, 2010), 10 (TLO 2(c)); a similar statement applies for the Juris Doctor degree. The statements have been incorporated into *The CALD Standards for Australian Law Schools* adopted by the Council of Australian Law Deans. The *CALD Standards* also provide that the curriculum should seek to develop "awareness of and sensitivity to, and, so far as is practicable, internalisation of, the values that underpin the principles of ethical conduct, professional responsibility, and community service" (sect. 2.3.3).

17 Harlan F. Stone, "The Public Influence of the Bar" (1934) 48 *Harvard Law Review* 1, 14.

18 Max Radin, "The Education of a Lawyer" (1937) 25 *California Law Review* 676, 688 quoted in Tamara Walsh, "Putting Justice Back Into Legal Education" (2008) 17 *Legal Education Review* 119; Brainerd Currie identified as the pre-eminent duty of a law school "to help its students to understand the significance of the lifework they have undertaken" and,

The reality is, however, problematic. In the United States, the Carnegie Foundation's *Educating Lawyers* report in 2007 spoke of the need to "engage the moral imagination of students as they move towards professional practice [and] insofar as they fail to make systematic efforts to educate towards a central moral tradition of lawyering, legal education may inadvertently contribute to the demoralisation of the legal profession and its loss of a moral compass".[19] The Carnegie Report recommended that legal education be restructured to integrate three distinct apprenticeships: an apprenticeship of cognition (legal analysis or conceptual knowledge), performance (practical legal knowledge and skill) and an apprenticeship of values that leads to the formation of professional identity. The report recommended that this integration be achieved by supplementing what it saw as the present narrow focus on legal analytical skills with increased clinical experience and work in public interest settings.[20]

The Carnegie Report also criticised what it saw as the segregation of legal and moral issues in US legal education, "forced decontextualisation" that develops legal analytical skills abstracted from the personal experience and perspective of the human actors involved. A tacit message is conveyed that the justice dimension or merits of the case are irrelevant or mere matters of policy, expressed by a student saying "when I took criminal law, I started to think of it in technical terms and stopped looking at the human side"; another student quoted in the report accused law schools of creating people "who are smart without a purpose".[21]

Legality, morality and justice are not, of course, the same and differences between them require explication. Legal rules may work injustice. However, keeping the justice of a case outcome in the classroom conversation, in the domain of relevance and concern as the case is discussed, allowing students to interrogate their justice intuitions, and doing so pervasively, across the whole of the curriculum, helping them develop a vocabulary to discuss morality, ethics and justice in relation to law – these are essential to the nurture of legal values and ideals.

The responsibility cast upon law schools poses a particular challenge for them. The research literature in the United States reveals a disturbing body of evidence of the negative effect of legal education in which a cynical, game-oriented consciousness replaces student idealism and social justice commitment.[22]

---

quoting Oliver Wendell Holmes, "to live greatly in the law": Brainerd Currie, "Reflections on the course in the legal profession" (1969) 22 *Journal of Legal Education* 49, 55, 56.

19 Sullivan et al., n. 8, 140.

20 Sullivan et al., n. 8, 12–14, 145–61.

21 Sullivan et al., n. 8, 141, 142.

22 See Christine Parker, "What Do They Learn When They Learn Legal Ethics?" (2001) 12 *Legal Education Review* 175, 180–81, citing Susan Daicoff, "Lawyer, Know Thyself: A Review of Empirical Research on Attorney Attributes Bearing on Professionalism" (1997) 46 *The American University Law Review* 1337 at 1405–06; Howard S Erlanger, Charles R Epp, Mia Cahill & Kathleen M Haines, "Law Student Idealism and Job Choice: Some

The transformation of students with public interest career ambitions goals into graduates moving to private practice is but part of the picture. On the other hand, a student from Loyola University New Orleans also found his clinical experience with victims of Hurricane Katrina transformative in a reverse sense: "[y]ou know, the first thing I lost in law school was the reason that I came. This [experience] will help me get back on track".[23] This is not wholly an US phenomenon. In England Kim Economides has tracked the "rise of cynical legal studies".[24] In Australia, Tamara Walsh's empirical study of law students at the University of Queensland found that "most students did not explicitly state that their desire to use the law to achieve social justice outcomes, or to engage in public interest practice [nominated as the main reason for entering law school by 24 per cent of respondents, the largest group], had diminished over the course of their legal studies".[25] Anecdotal evidence among Australian law teachers, however, suggests that its legal education programs reflect trends evident elsewhere.

Some Modalities for Promoting Justice Consciousness and Service Ethic during Legal Education

Legal educators inevitably model values of professional conduct and purpose to students, in their daily, quotidian functions as teachers, colleagues and mentors. They are powerful, if unconscious, exemplars. Even when law teachers think they are merely teaching law, they are inevitably communicating much more, consciously or unconsciously modelling appropriate behaviour and values: "by the very act of teaching, law teachers embody lawyering and the conduct of legal professionals. We create images of law and lawyering when we teach doctrine through cases and hypotheticals".[26] Law teachers inevitably give students implicit messages about appropriate ways of acting and the values of the practice of law: "[f]or better or worse, the law school years constitute a powerful moral apprenticeship, whether or not this is intentional. Law schools play an important part in shaping their students' values, habits of mind, perceptions, and interpretations

---

New Data on an Old Question" (1996) 30 *Law & Society Rev* 851; Andrew Goldsmith, "Warning: Law School Can Endanger Your Health!" (1995) 21 *Monash University Law Review* 272; Robert Granfield, *Making Elite Lawyers: Visions of Law at Harvard and Beyond* (New York: Routledge, 1992); Robert V Stover, *Making It and Breaking It: The Fate of Public Interest Commitment During Law School* (Urbana: University of Illinois Press, 1989); see also Adrienne Stone, "Women, Law School and Student Commitment to the Public Interest" in Cooper and Trubek, n. 7, 74.

23 William P Quigley, "Letter to a Law Student Interested in Social Justice" (2007) 1 *DePaul Journal of Social Justice* 7, 8.

24 Economides, n. 7.

25 Walsh, n. 18, 133, 131.

26 Carrie Menkel-Meadow, "Can a Law Teacher Avoid Teaching Legal Ethics?" (1991) 41 *Journal of Legal Education* 3, 3.

of their legal world; their understanding of their roles and responsibilities as lawyers; and the criteria by which they define and evaluate professional success".[27] The values modelled shape students' professional lives and their future social contribution: we need therefore to model values with deliberation and judgment. How are we to provide in legal education a "powerful experience of the best sense of what it means to take up a profession"?[28]

Measures to promote justice consciousness and service ethic may be divided into curricular initiatives and those of a programmatic or extra-curricular nature.

Curricular Initiatives

Dedicated Subjects on Concepts of Justice and Access to Justice Many argue that the academic curriculum needs to enable students to think seriously and rigorously about the concept of justice and its relation to law, the legal system and the rule of law.[29] This study might be pursued in a dedicated subject, pervasively throughout the curriculum or in both forms. If introductory subjects provide a foundational view of different conceptions or theories of justice, they may introduce a dialogue that continues across the curriculum on law's relation to justice.[30] Other scholars argue the need for a similar curricular treatment of issues around access to justice including an understanding of how the law affects those who cannot afford its protection.[31]

Law School Clinical Legal Experience and Experiential Instruction Outside a Law School Clinic In United States law schools, the primary means of promoting a justice and service ethic is through the offering of clinical legal experience. Although virtually every United States law school offers one or more clinical programs, it is estimated that only one in three US law students takes a clinical experience course.[32] In Australia, where resource and other constraints limit the creation of law school clinics, that proportion is likely to be much lower. However, several Australian law schools complement clinical legal education, or compensate for its absence, by offering opportunities for supervised clinical experience in an external clinic or other forms of experiential learning involving

27 Sullivan et al., n. 8, 169; cf. Parker, n. 22, 175, 176.

28 Sullivan et al., n. 8, 30.

29 See, for example, John M Breen, "The Air in the Balloon: Further Notes on Catholic and Jesuit Identity in Legal Education" (2007) 43 *Gonzaga Law Review* 41.

30 The study of jurisprudence may also be a suitable vehicle for examining legal ideals and values, and law's relation to justice and morality: see Seow Hon Tan, "Teaching Legal Ideals Through Jurisprudence" (2009) 43 *The Law Teacher* 14.

31 Deborah L. Rhode, "Professional Regulation and Public Service: An Unfinished Agenda" in Scott L Cummings (ed.), *The Paradox of Professionalism: Lawyers and the Possibility of Justice* (Cambridge, Cambridge University Press, 2011), 153.

32 Breen, n. 29, 43.

personal exposure to the reality of law and justice. In all forms attention is given to developing the ability to reflect ethically on the experience, such as through the use of reflective journals.

The evidence of student experience of clinical education is very positive as the New Orleans example quoted above indicates. The experience of contact with and taking supervised responsibility, however minor and briefly, for real clients and their problems touches student attitudes. David Nicolson provides empirical evidence that "a clinical experience may encourage the development of an attitude of ethical professionalism [and that] combining ethical teaching with live-client clinics, particularly extra-curricular clinics with a social justice orientation, may enable law schools to positively influence the development of students' moral character ... at least in evidencing factors conducive to character development, such as the influence of role models, the experiencing of moral crises, and feelings of satisfaction and regret accompanying clinic experiences."[33] Studies also point to the positive influence of clinical experience upon the moral reasoning of student participants.[34] Describing the exposure to the Australian law school clinic that students in a large compulsory ethics course were given, Christine Parker wrote: "Scratch the surface of these cynical, world-weary law students with one client interview session, and we find that most of them regain some enthusiasm and idealism. They entered the [Kingsford Legal Centre conducted by the University of New South Wales] nervous – out of their comfort zone. They came out with a new sense of commitment to client contact, at least, and for some a better understanding of disadvantage and justice issues".[35]

Exposure to clinical experience in such settings, even in the form of a single interview session with real clients, is one of the most effective correctives for cynicism and the erosion of justice and service ideals. It is difficult to overstate "the affective experience of sympathy for a disadvantaged client in a clinical setting" as a means of conveying to students the possibilities and responsibilities of legal practice.[36] The Carnegie Report considered that "much of the humanizing and inspiring aspects of the law have always resided in actual contact with clients and their needs".[37] David Chavkin goes further to argue that "experience is the *only* teacher".[38] Certainly, the first professional experience appears to have a shaping influence on the formation of professional values. If a student's first experience of

33 David Nicolson, "Learning in Justice: Ethical Education in an Extra-Curricular Law Clinic" in Michael Robertson et al. (eds), *The Ethics Project in Legal Education* (Routledge, London and New York, 2011) 171, 172, 183.

34 Nicolson, n. 33, 174.

35 Parker, n. 22, 193.

36 Breen, n. 29, 52.

37 Sullivan et al., n. 8, 33.

38 David F. Chavkin, "Experience is the Only Teacher: Bringing Practice to the Teaching of Ethics" in Robertson et al, n 33, 52; Lorne Sossin, "Experience the Future of Legal Education", available at SSRN: http://ssrn.com/abstract=2337521.

legal practice is in a public interest setting or otherwise puts into practice idealistic conceptions of legal work and service, this has a powerful influence in nurturing idealism and justice orientation in later professional choices.[39]

The Use of Case Studies of Professional Work, Simulations and Interactive Discussions The Carnegie Report advocated the use of the "well-elaborated case studies of professional work [that] engage the moral imagination of students as they move towards professional practice" that medical, business and engineering schools employ so widely.[40] There is evidence of the successful use of such methods in Australian instruction in professional responsibility.[41] Tamara Walsh advocates greater use of role-play or simulations as tools to give students a sense of the reality of legal practice.[42]

Extra-Curricular Means to Promote Justice and Service Commitment

Law school initiatives to promote justice and commitment to community service in professional practice need not be confined to curricular or for-credit programs. Indeed, the scope for extra-curricular programs is extremely broad.

Volunteer Clinical Legal Exposure and Other Experiential Learning The beneficial influence on student values of practical experience in a community legal centre or other public interest setting has been noted above. These benefits are not confined to law school clinics or formal externship programs. Indeed, Nicolson's study showing positive influence on the development of students' moral character was conducted on students in an extra-curricular social justice clinic setting.[43] Other studies show that students whose idealism was maintained through law studies were those who had direct experience of public interest or community legal service during their studies or who retained earlier links to such organisations.[44] Parker writes that this "suggests that one of the most important things law schools could do to educate law students to be ethical and socially aware lawyers is to encourage public interest subcultures within the law school".[45]

These initiatives and the provision of clinical experience need not, therefore, be confined to for-credit laws school clinic and externship programs. Strong models exist of voluntary programs offering supervised clinical experience in service settings. Pro Bono Students Canada offers what is perhaps the most developed

39 Adrian Evans, "Client Group Activism and Student Moral Development in Clinical Legal Education" (1999) 10 *Legal Education Review* 179, 182, 199; Stover, n. 22, 109.

40 Sullivan et al., n. 8.

41 Parker, n. 22.

42 Walsh, n. 18, 141.

43 Nicolson, n. 33.

44 Stover, n. 22, 109.

45 Parker, n. 22, 192.

program of law student volunteer opportunities – a national program with chapters in all 21 Canadian law schools under which 1,600 students serve 400 organisations providing professional legal assistance to vulnerable populations and individuals.[46] Several Australian law schools have established programs that encourage and assist students to find voluntary placements in legal practice settings with public interest or community service missions.[47] At least one law school encourages its students from the earliest stage of their studies to seek volunteer opportunities in non-legal as well as legal service settings for the beneficial affective experience of engagement with those in need.[48] As we have seen, these early experiences are powerful influences on the values expressed in later legal practice.[49]

Reflections on Law and Social Justice

Other programmatic initiatives support a culture in the law school student community of concern for justice and of the value of a service orientation in professional work, formally embedded in a structure of reflection and study as well as a commitment to action. These include visiting speaker programs exploring concepts of justice, contemporary social justice issues, understanding of the rule of law and other topics that extend the formal curriculum outside the classroom. Instances operate at most law schools, often under the aegis of the law student society or conducted by the faculty in partnership with the society.

Conclusion

The challenge for legal education is to develop in students *both* legal technique and a sense of social purpose. The two goals need be kept in balance; neither is sufficient alone. Karl Llewellyn put it graphically: "[t]echnique without ideals is a menace; ideals without technique are a mess".[50] Similarly, the Chief Justice of the High Court of Australia warns: "[a] law graduate without a sense of the different conceptions of justice and its relationship to the rule of law goes into the world

---

46 See < http://www.probonostudents.ca> (accessed 11/09/2015).

47 See, for example, the University of Queensland Pro Bono Centre <http://www.law.uq.edu.au/uq-pro-bono-centre> (accessed 11/09/2015).

48 See the Brennan Justice and Leadership Program at the University of Technology, Sydney <http://www.uts.edu.au/future-students/law/beyond-classroom/brennan-justice-and-leadership-program> (accessed 11/09/2015).

49 Evans, n. 39, 182, 199.

50 Quoted in William Twining, *Karl Llewellyn and the Realist Movement* (London, Weidenfeld and Nicholson, 1973), 116.

with a patch over one eye. A law graduate with a keen sense of justice, whose knowledge of the law and legal skills are inadequate, is a danger to the public".[51]

Is the nurturing of justice consciousness and an ethic of professional service a Sisyphean task? Certainly, this project is endless and perhaps difficult, but it is not futile. If a law school encourages its students to reflect on their future professional role, to examine the role of law and its relationship to justice, to internalise and live out the proclaimed values of the profession, their education will enable them to "make their own the profession's possibilities for a useful and fulfilling life".[52] This is a worthy enterprise.

51 Hon Robert French AC, "Legal Education in Australia – A Never Ending Story", Australasian Law Teachers' Association Conference, 4 July 2011, 4.

52 Sullivan et al., n. 8, 85.

Chapter 8

Critique, Philosophy, and the Legally-Trained Citizen's Role in Working towards Just Institutions

Seow Hon Tan[1]

Introduction: The Special Responsibility of Legally-Trained Citizens

Much recent discussion on the future of legal education has centered on preparing law students to be lawyers in a globalised world,[2] teaching students skills necessary for legal practice, or equipping them in relation to client management.[3] Some law schools brand themselves as "international" or "global",[4] or require students to have a measure of familiarity with systems of law or judicial principles beyond domestic law.[5] While understanding the transnational dimension of law

1 Associate Professor and Associate Dean (Research), School of Law, Singapore Management University; Advocate and Solicitor (Singapore); LLB (National University of Singapore); LLM SJD (Harvard University). I am grateful for the invitation of Chinese University of Hong Kong to speak at the Law Deans' Summit in 2013. Also, I thank Mr Chua Wei Yuan for his assistance in locating some of the material used in this chapter.

2 Rosalie Jukier, Transnationalizing the legal curriculum, 56 *J. Legal Educ.* 172 (2006); Sebastien Lebel-Grenier, What is a transnational legal education?, 56 *J. Legal Educ.* 190 (2006); Jan Klabbers, Legal education in the balance: Accommodating flexibility, 56 *J. Legal Educ.* 196 (2006); Andras Jakab, Dilemmas of legal education, 57 *J. Legal Educ.* 253, 256 (2007).

3 David Dryden Henningsen and Ioanna Cionea, The role of comforting skill and professional competence in the attorney-client relationship, 57 *J. Legal Educ.* 530 (2007); Austin Sarat, Lawyers and clients: Putting professional service on the agenda of legal education, 41 *J. Legal Educ.* 43 1991. See, also, the detailed study commissioned by the American Bar Association in 1992: Report of the Task Force on Law Schools and the Profession (also known as the MacCrate Report), discussed in Jonathan Rose, The MacCrate Report's restatement of legal education, 44 *J. Legal Educ.* 548 (1994).

4 See, for example, National University of Singapore, which brands itself as "Asia's Global Law School" (http://law.nus.edu.sg/, accessed 28 April 2014).

5 See, for example, National Taiwan University's College of Law, the website of which states that "the undergraduate students of the department are required to study domestic and global judicial principles" (http://www.ntpu.edu.tw/english/colleges.php, accessed 28 April 2014).

and being prepared to function within a legal climate that is no longer primarily local are important aims of legal education, the role of legal education in shaping the lawyer's understanding of the foundational ideals of law has received, in comparison, short shrift. A concern with the foundational ideals of law might be seen as the special province of those who desire to work in areas such as transitional justice or international human rights. This state of unconcern with the foundational ideals of the legal system might have arisen from the dominant view of the amoral ethical role of lawyers. On such a view of professionalism, the lawyer is called to suspend her moral judgment of her client's case in order to facilitate the client's full access to whatever the law allows, however abhorrent the result engendered by the law might be in some cases. Such a view of professionalism stems from a contested understanding of the purpose of the legal system and the lawyer's role within it, though the question of the purpose of legal system may not be explicitly the subject of much discussion in a pluralist world where any discussion of values is likely to be contentious.[6]

Law has immense potential to transform society. By giving or refusing to give its stamp of approval on particular private economic arrangements, it changes economic relations; by denying or upholding the freedom of individuals from governmental interference in particular spheres of life, it permits governmental regulation of particular conduct or ensures that individual choices are respected. In view of the transformative potential of law, I argue that legally-trained citizens who have had the privilege of legal education have a special responsibility to work towards just institutions in their capacities as practitioners and as specially empowered citizens in the public square. The recognition of this special responsibility is seen, for example, in the mission statement of an East Asian law school, which suggests that it "aims to nurture the potentials of its students in the study of the principles and practice of law, to set up a fair and just society, and to improve legal structures of the country".[7] Even as much ink has been, and continues to be, spilt over what justice and fairness entail, law schools should not ignore such an educational mission. It is regrettable that such statements are not more often seen in the mission statements of law schools.

To prepare students to fulfill such a special responsibility, the inculcation of the ability to think critically about the law and ask whether it has been employed in service of salutary ideals is necessary. Students must begin to develop a habit of asking what the foundational ideals of the legal system in which they find themselves are or ought to be, and what it means to play their parts in working towards just institutions in the society in which they live.

---

6 Compare this to a time when a particular tradition, such as natural law theory, held sway, when assumptions in legal education were in line with it. (Mark Warren Bailey, Early legal education in the United States: Natural law theory and law as a moral science, 48 *J. Legal Educ.* 311, 353 (1998).

7 See http://www.ntpu.edu.tw/english/colleges.php, accessed 28 April 2014.

This chapter examines how the intentional teaching of critique through legal philosophy can shape the future lawyer's and legally-trained citizen's capacities to work towards just institutions. Four aspects of the teaching of critique through legal philosophy are significant. First, through the comparative study of schools of jurisprudence, students should be directed to examine whether law is connected to foundational ideals. Second, legal philosophical readings should be related to current issues to demonstrate the relevance of philosophy to day-to-day controversies in the public square. Third, the Socratic elenchus and dialectic should be more effectively employed to get students to think about fundamental assumptions behind their views on various theoretical issues and whether they are coherent and stand up to rational scrutiny. Fourth, students should be exposed to the challenges that critical legal studies (CLS) makes of traditional jurisprudence. CLS suggests that legal reasoning is not distinct from ideological reasoning, that law is not necessarily legitimate or justified, and that conflicting interests underlie legal doctrines. While CLS might not be the endpoint of choice for every individual, having worked through its challenges of traditional jurisprudence and assessed its claims would enable one to hold one's opinions knowing they have been tried and tested and stand up to rational scrutiny. My approach in this chapter is to provide, in the next four parts, concrete examples of how these aspects of the teaching of critique are emphasised and employed in two courses that I teach at the Singapore Management University. The first is a mandatory module called "Legal Theory & Philosophy" (LTP). The second is an upper year elective called "Jurisprudence: Modern and Critical Theories of Law" (JURIS).

Studying Schools of Jurisprudence

Some detractors think that if the aim of law schools is to produce legal practitioners, teaching jurisprudence is not useful unless it is demonstrated to be directly practically relevant to legal practice. But the view that producing practitioners is the main aim of law schools is disputed. It may be argued that law schools should also seek to produce "cultivated lawyers"[8] who are knowledgeable about the world they live in. Some argue that law professors should ask normative questions about the law as "they have a larger obligation, one that includes the probing of love and justice as well as the development of civic virtue and a sense of public duty".[9] Learning jurisprudence is valuable for its tendency to bring about the sensitivity to values and an understanding of the character and structure of law.[10] The ability

8 Jakab, *supra* note 2, at 255. See, also, Thomas D. Morgan, Teaching students for the 21st century, 36 *J. Legal Educ.* 285, 288 (1986).

9 Roger C. Cramton, Beyond the ordinary religion, 37 *J. Legal Educ.* 509, 510 (1987).

10 Thomas Huff, A heresy in the ordinary religion: Jurisprudence in the first curriculum, 36 *J. Legal Educ.* 108, 115–16 (1986).

for critical thinking may also be imparted through jurisprudence. But mention critique in the context of jurisprudence and one tends to think of CLS. If one must categorise broadly the jurisprudential theories, the divide may be readily seen as being between traditional schools of jurisprudence such as legal positivism, natural law theory, and Ronald Dworkin's theory of law, on the one hand, and critical theories such as American legal realism and CLS on the other. The former set does not explicitly treat law as politics, while the latter does. The teaching of critique in the context of schools of jurisprudence is not, however, limited to exploring how critical theories expose problems with traditional schools of jurisprudence. It extends to the critique of the critical theories. As it is in the elective, JURIS, that I teach about the different schools of jurisprudence, I shall describe how critique features in that course.

The theories of John Austin, HLA Hart, Hans Kelsen, Ronald Dworkin, John Finnis, Karl Llewellyn, and Roberto Unger are covered in JURIS through a selection of primary material. Each perspective of law is presented in the best light possible: this may be best done from its point of view, as what is best varies according to sometimes unspoken fundamental assumptions denied by other theories of law. Such assumptions are unpacked, and thereafter, each theory is challenged by reference to other theories not sharing the same assumptions. This provides the opportunity of critique that also sets the student thinking about her own fundamental assumptions linked to her broader worldview which inclines her to a particular theory of law. Critical schools of jurisprudence are taught in the same manner. They stem from fundamental assumptions that are contentious from the points of view of traditional theorists and may be challenged by them. The constant comparison through the unpacking of fundamental assumptions encourages students not to treat the theories as disparate, or dealing with similar questions at cross-purposes, or dealing with altogether different questions. It highlights opposing positions on fundamental questions so that students in touch with the diametric opposition better understand the repercussions of each view. I shall give two illustrations to elucidate how such comparison is done.

My first illustration relates to the debate between legal positivism and natural law theory. Some view this debate as occurring at cross-purposes and regard the former as dealing with what law is while the latter as addressing the question of what law ought to be.[11] Positivists assert that there is no necessary connection between laws and morals. Austin writes that "[t]he existence of law is one thing; its merit or demerit is another".[12] Hart notes: "[I]t is in no sense a necessary truth that laws reproduce or satisfy certain demands of morality, though in fact they

11 See the discussion in Lloyd Weinreb, The natural law tradition, 36 *J. Legal Educ.* 501 (1986).

12 J. Austin, *The Province of Jurisprudence Determined* 184 (H.L.A. Hart edn, Hackett Publishing rep. 1998).

have often done so."[13] Kelsen joins the positivists in suggesting that legal norms may have any kind of content.[14] Some positivists acknowledge a contingent connection between law and morality; for example, morals often influence the law, and a legal system that expects to command the respect of its addressees must rest upon the addressees' sense of obligation or a conviction of its moral value.[15] Natural law theory suggests that there is a necessary connection between law and morality – that laws posited by human authorities must conform to universal principles which stem from an objective conception of human nature,[16] God's law,[17] the law of reason, or morality.[18] In spite of what appears to be a clearly opposing claim, some maintain that the debate occurs at cross-purposes. They think that natural law theory's assertion of a necessary connection between law and morality does not impinge on the validity of laws. It is merely aspirational. Thus, where manifestly unjust laws are concerned, for some natural law theorists, if the law fails to be what it ought to be, it remains legally valid.[19] Such a view that the legal status of unjust laws is only a subordinate concern of natural law theory,[20] which serves only as a prescription for good law, has perhaps led to suggestions that it is possible to integrate[21] legal positivism and natural law theory. This view takes legal positivism and natural law theory to address the same question of law's connection with morality, but in different spheres – legal positivism explores the

---

13 H.L.A. Hart, *The Concept of Law* 185–86 (Clarendon Press, 2nd edn, 1994) (1961).

14 Hans Kelsen, *The Pure Theory of Law* 198–99 (The Lawbook Exchange 2002, 2009).

15 Hart, *supra* note 13 at 185 and 202–03.

16 The Stoics, for example, had an elaborate conception of nature. See A.A. Long, *Hellenistic Philosophy* 147–78 (University of California Press, 2nd edn, 1986) (1974).

17 Blackstone writes:

This law of nature, being co-eval with mankind and dictated by God Himself, is of course superior to any other. It is binding over all the globe, in all countries, and at all times: no human laws are of any validity, if contrary to this; and such of them as are valid derive all their force, and all their authority, mediately or immediately, from this original. (William Blackstone, *Commentaries* Book I, section 2, 41 (1765).)

There may be theories of law which lay claim to a necessary connection between laws and morals which are not, strictly speaking, "natural law theory", defined in this manner. These may refer, for example, to a system of universal principles that are neither ontological, nor linked to God's law. Whether such a system is viable is another question. This is how Alexy frames the debate in Robert Alexy, *The Argument from Injustice: A Reply to Legal Positivism* (Bonnie Litschewski Paulson and Stanley L. Paulson trans., Clarendon Press 2002) (1994).

18 *The Oxford Handbook of Jurisprudence & Philosophy of Law* 5–8 (Jules Coleman and Scott Shapiro eds, Oxford University Press 2002).

19 This is Finnis's interpretation of Aquinas and natural law theory in John Finnis, *Natural Law and Natural Rights* 351–68 (Clarendon Press 1993) (1980).

20 *Id.* at 351.

21 Harold Berman, Towards an integrative jurisprudence: Politics, morality and history, 76 *Cal L. Rev.* 779–801 (1988).

connection for legally valid laws, while natural law theory explores the connection for good or sound laws, which remain legally valid even if they fail to be good or sound. Others suggest that natural law theory does not merely explicate what law *ought to be*. It is also a theory about what law *is*: law *is* what conforms to an objective law or to reason.[22] This latter view reveals the cutting edge of natural law theory: Hart says that the rule of recognition *may* incorporate moral criteria, but these natural law theorists, in direct contradiction, suggest any test of law *must* incorporate such criteria.

The point of exploring such different perspectives of the age-old debate between legal positivism and natural law theory is to highlight one perspective that there is a real conflict between two primary schools of jurisprudence on a fundamental question of the nature of law (and its validity). Law students taking the alternative view that there is no real conflict might end up unthinkingly accepting, for all practical purposes in their practice of law, what is in fact the positivistic view that "law is law", and think that aspirational standards are the concern of legislators. They might not strive to make laws that are morally salutary, when they might have contributed to law's content if they had viewed law as necessarily connected to morality when litigating a case on a point of law. Or they might not resist heinous laws.

Law in fact becomes the power phenomenon that positivistic theories such as Austin's view of laws as sovereign commands render them. Even while students pay lip service to natural law theory in the sphere of justification, natural law theory is given short shrift and lacks true bite where it counts – when officials of the legal system who have sworn to uphold the law have a valid legal and not just moral duty to refuse to uphold what is in fact a legally invalid law on account of its manifest injustice,[23] and when legal practitioners help officials determine their legal duties through arguments about what counts as law.

Understanding whether law is a power phenomenon or is connected with morality affects other areas of legal doctrine. For example, the law student studying the law of contracts would be concerned with ethical issues such as what to do in relation to a client who wants to drive a hard bargain, what the client should be encouraged to disclose, and so on.[24] The answer to the ethical questions would be influenced by an understanding of the foundations of contract law, which is in turn informed by a general understanding of the foundation of law.

My second illustration concerns a fruitful way of teaching theories which do not on their face address the same questions. The questions may be reframed to highlight points of convergence in the theories or contending positions on similar topics (which compels students to the choice amongst different theories).

22 See, for example, Radbruch's view, recounted in the Hart–Fuller debate (H.L.A. Hart, Positivism and the separation of law and morals (1958) 71 *Harv. L. Rev.* 593 at 616–17).

23 Alexy, *supra* note 17.

24 Scott J. Burnham, Teaching legal ethics in contracts, 41 *J. Legal Educ.* 105 (1991).

For example, Dworkin's true community in *Law's Empire*[25] can be compared with Finnis's common good, the set of conditions necessary to help individuals secure the seven basic values of human flourishing.[26] While Dworkin does not address the question of human flourishing, does his idea of the true community as one in which laws regard each individual with equal concern and flow from a more general sense of responsibility to all in the community result in laws with substantively similar content as Finnis's laws in the focal sense which facilitate and structure an individual's pursuit of the basic values of human flourishing in Finnis's community? In turn, how vastly different are such legal frameworks from Unger's self-revisable structure of government which increases what he terms the "negative capability" of individuals,[27] that in Unger's view best allows the individual to achieve true freedom and "a place … in the world"?[28] Another example relates to the different views of adjudication. Dworkin suggests that the ideal judge Hercules must view law as a seamless web and endeavor to find an interpretation of law that best fits and justifies legal practice.[29] In contrast, American legal realists think that legal rules are under-determinative and techniques of treating precedents give judges the leeway to find a legal rule to justify a decision they prefer for reasons unrelated to the rules.[30] CLS scholars take the view that law is politics further than the American legal realists by suggesting that even if there is order in the legal material, such order facilitates the entrenchment of the interests of the ruling classes and should be resisted by adjudicators.[31] Duncan Kennedy suggests that the judge should aid in re-imagining an altruistic order,[32] while Unger proposes that adjudicators engage in "purposive analogical reasoning" which acknowledges no systematic closure but instead develops the disharmonies in law in a manner that facilitates the ideal of a free people.[33] While such views reflect vastly different visions of adjudication, students need the help of the teacher to be able to inter-relate the theories. In addition to directly engaging the comparison in class, examination questions may also be set to require students to explain problems

25 Ronald Dworkin, *Law's Empire* 211–15 (Fontana Press 1986).

26 Finnis, *supra* note 19, at 154–56.

27 Roberto Mangabeira Unger, *The Critical Legal Studies Movement* 48 and 94 (Harvard University Press, 1983, 1986).

28 Roberto Mangabeira Unger, *The Self-Awakened: Pragmatism Unbound* 13 (Harvard University Press 2009). This chapter is not an appropriate forum to discuss the ideas in detail. See *id.* and Roberto Mangabeira Unger, *Passion: An Essay on Personality* (Free Press 1984).

29 Ronald Dworkin, *Taking Rights Seriously* 115–17 (Duckworth 1977).

30 Karl N. Llewellyn, *The Theory of Rules c. VII* (Frederick Shauer ed., University of Chicago Press, 2011).

31 Unger, *supra* note 27, c.1.

32 Duncan Kennedy, Form and Substance in Private Law Adjudication, 89 *Harv.L.Rev.* 1685, 1778 (1976).

33 Roberto Mangabeira Unger, *What Should Legal Analysis Become?* 114–16 (Verso 1996).

with a particular view of adjudication from the perspective of another theorist's view. For example, is the view that the judge is able to determine the rights of parties even when no settled rule disposes of the case[34] a sham? This involves a critique of Dworkin's claims from the perspectives of American legal realists and CLS, and a defense of Dworkin's view through a rebuttal of their critiques.

Throughout, students are encouraged not to see the theories as unrelated, which they might if the debates are seen to be at cross-purposes or there is no point of convergence of the theories, which are seen to address wholly different questions. The objective is for students to discover and elucidate their own theory of law, which may even involve a wholesale rejection of all the theories, or an adoption of what turns out to be a hybrid of some of these theories.

Philosophy in the Public Square

Getting pragmatic Asian students in a professional school to be interested in philosophical abstractions and concepts and to persevere in readings they regard as immensely difficult, last-century, and sometimes dry and boring is an uphill task. Anecdotally, it appears that a significant proportion of the students have set their minds on embarking on private legal practice. A legal philosophy course, especially if mandated by law school, can empower law students to participate in working towards just institutions and law in future. Students may be sensitised to contentious values in legal institutions, which they can play a part in transforming.

In the mandatory course for third and fourth year law students, LTP, I explore jurisprudential issues thematically. We begin by asking what law is and how, as a form of monopolisation of coercive force, it is different from the arbitrary exercise of power. Must law be justified? What is the legitimate basis of law in a postmodern, pluralist society? Is the restriction of the liberty of an individual to engage in immoral conduct justifiable given that we do not share the same moral values? Are unjust laws law? Is justice always done when rules are followed? How do judges decide cases? Can a good lawyer be a good person? Taking off from a conventional view of law as a purposive enterprise regulating human conduct, we go on to consider the meaning and significance of underlying ideals such as formality, justice, morality, liberty, and rationality. We also explore critical perspectives that challenge conventional views of law. Along the way, we engage the most intractable debates in the public square as familiar contexts for them to think about philosophical issues. Each classical reading is paired with contemporary illustrations to demonstrate to the students that it is still relevant today. This is especially important as Singaporeans are not predisposed to thinking philosophically – a state of affairs that sometimes leads to the impoverishment of debates over important legislative or public policy decisions. For instance, when the issue of legalisation of casino gambling in Singapore was hotly debated years ago

34 Dworkin, *supra* note 29, at 81.

in Parliament and in the public square, the debate centered on whether economic benefits outweighed social costs and whether Singaporeans could be trusted to act responsibly[35] or needed the government to take paternalistic measures to protect them from excessive gambling in casinos. Classic jurisprudential debates, such as the Hart–Devlin debate over the enforcement of morality[36] and Finnis's idea of human flourishing in the form of seven basic values,[37] could have informed the decision of the government but were not raised in parliamentary debates. While teaching the classic jurisprudential debates, I highlight to students what different concerns might have arisen if members of Parliament were familiar with these debates. As society at large is not accustomed to thinking beyond the narrow confines of consequentialist or utilitarian arguments, introducing other issues expands and empowers students to think about what it means for them to flourish and how law is implicated in that. As one commentator notes, "while we cannot and should not try to impose a particular view of thriving on others, we can and should at least avoid using our bully pulpit to narrow their souls."[38]

To give students the incentive to take what they learn in class beyond the classroom, I award students marks for contribution in public square debates through readers' letters to the newspapers. In the last few years, students have been very actively contributing to letters to the local newspapers, many of which have been published. In some public debates in the newspapers, letters came solely from students in my courses. A sample of their contributions include:

- in relation to a case on whether a constitutional provision gave the prime minister the discretion not to call for a by-election when one of the seats in Parliament was vacated, a student wrote to the press to discuss the manner in which rules should be interpreted, whether there should be a reference to the principles embedded in the legal institutions and material, as Dworkin proposes for interpretation;[39]
- on the role of law, students wrote about whether laws should be made for the resolution of disputes amongst neighbors;[40]

---

35 Sing, *Parliamentary Debates*, vol. 77, col. 2725ff. (Apr. 19, 2004) (Minister of State for Trade and Industry, Dr Vivian Balakrishnan) (Oral answers to questions, Setting up of casino); Sing., *Parliamentary Debates*, vol. 80, col. 54ff. (Apr. 18, 2005) (Ministerial statement, Proposal to develop integrated resorts).

36 H.L.A. Hart, *Law, Liberty, and Morality* (Stanford University Press 1963); Patrick Devlin, *The Enforcement of Morals* (Oxford University Press 1965).

37 Finnis, *supra* note 19.

38 Sherman J. Clark, Neoclassical public virtues: Towards an aretaic theory of law-making (and law teaching) in *Law, Virtue and Justice* 81, 98 (Amalia Amaya and Ho Hock Lai eds, Hart Publishing, 2013).

39 Do we look beyond legal obligation?, *Today*, March 2, 2012; Dworkin, *supra* note 29, at 101–5.

40 Legal framework may help neighborliness, *The Straits Times*, September 14, 2012; Law not proxy for morality but it can shape moral opinion, *Today*, September 14,

- in relation to a public series of conversations known as the Singapore Conversation which was spearheaded by the government to discern the direction for Singapore's future, a student wrote about what John Finnis's view on human flourishing suggested;[41]
- a student applied the jurisprudential debate on the proper basis of criminal laws to laws prohibiting suicide;[42]
- students considered whether religion has a role in public decisions;[43] and
- students considered if steps should be taken to ban or block the online extramarital dating website Ashley Madison.[44]

There are many benefits of encouraging student participation in the public square. First, students are sensitised to jurisprudential issues as they read the news. Second, they have an opportunity to apply what they learn to current issues and make a difference in the real world. Third, they are empowered as they stand up for what they believe in. Fourth, their arguments are scrutinised by their peers and the public, not just the marker of an examination, and in time, they learn what the weaknesses of their arguments are. Fifth, they make a special contribution to the education of the general public. While it might be cynically thought that students would write for the sake of grades and thereafter return to their indifferent selves, some students continued to write after they graduated from the course.

In LTP, research papers have also been set on the justifiability of the Singapore Government's decision to legalise casino gambling, whether euthanasia and physician-assisted suicide should be permitted, whether there is a right to civil disobedience, and whether organ trade amongst living persons should be legalised. These assignment questions, alongside the public square participation, allow students to apply old classic jurisprudential writings such as the Hart–Devlin

---

2012; Code of conduct for constituencies?, *Today*, September 18, 2012; Diversity calls for 'more facilitative laws', *Today*, September 18, 2012.

41 Role of law in helping people thrive, *The Straits Times*, March 19, 2013; Finnis, *supra* note 19.

42 Don't let suicide become an offence against society, *Today*, February 21, 2013; Defence of moral standards not good reason for keeping suicide laws, *Today*, February 23, 2013; Consider the costs of suicide, *Today*, March 1, 2013.

43 Defining the scope of religious views in public debate, *The Straits Times*, October 23, 2012; Religiously motivated views have a place in secular space, *The Straits Times*, October 22, 2012.

44 Extramarital dating site: Society has right to enforce public morality, *Today*, October 28, 2013; Distinguish the act from the opportunity for adultery, *Today*, October 30, 2013; Ban on extramarital dating site would just be a paper tiger, *Today*, October 30, 2013; Law may be ineffective but this doesn't justify inaction, *Today*, November 1, 2013; Majority consensus or not, Ashley Madison ban justified, *Today*, November 13, 2013.

debate[45] and Martin Luther King Jr'.s *Letter from Birmingham Jail*[46] to the world they live in.

The Socratic Method

Unfortunately, perhaps in part because of the movie, *Paper Chase*, featuring the inimitable Professor Kingsfield in the setting of Harvard Law School, the Socratic method has had a bad name. In real life, it has been associated with abusive teaching.[47] As one student put it, "I learned that the Socratic method of teaching meant I would be driven into a corner by my professors' endless questions in response to my black-letter answers."[48] I would like to suggest that the Socratic method means more than "an intensive interrogation of professor-selected students into the doctrinal logic of a legal case".[49] It is not synonymous with cross-examination or embarrassment of students. Though it is commonly thought that the Socratic method features dominantly[50] in the teaching of law, this is not necessarily so of the Socratic method properly understood. The infamous scene of Professor Kingsfield interrogating his student Hart about the case of *Hawkins v. McGee*[51] is hardly representative of the method.

It should be remembered that the Socratic method in its origins was used to promote a concern for justice.[52] It encompasses the elenchus and the dialectic, which were the methods by which Socrates discoursed with his interlocutors. According to the *Cambridge Encyclopaedia of Philosophy*, the elenchus involves getting one's interlocutor to realise that "what he thinks he knows is inconsistent with his other opinions".[53] The dialectic involves an "argument conducted by question and answer, resting on an opponent's concessions, and aiming at refuting the opponent by deriving contradictory consequences".[54] The basic idea of both is to get an interlocutor to realise that a theory she puts forth contradicts with other theses she endorses, for example, in stemming from contradictory premises, such

45 *Supra* note 36.

46 See http://www.africa.upenn.edu/Articles_Gen/Letter_Birmingham.html, accessed 28 April 2014.

47 James P. Rowles, Towards balancing the goals of legal education, 31 *J. Legal Educ.* 375, 375 (1981–82).

48 Margaret F. Uhlig, The making of a lawyer, 38 *J. Legal Educ.* 611, 612 (1988).

49 Edward Rubin, Curricular stress, 60 *J. Legal Educ.* 110, 114 (2010–11).

50 Nira Hativa, Teaching large law classes well, 50 *J. Legal Educ.* 95, 103 (2000).

51 84 N.H. 114, 146 A. 641 (N.H. 1929).

52 Mary Jewell, Teaching law ethically: Is it possible?, 8 *Dalhousie L.J.* 474, 485–86 (1984).

53 *The Cambridge Dictionary of Philosophy* 257 (Robert Audi ed., Cambridge University Press, 2nd edn, 1999).

54 *Id.* at 232–33.

that the theory must be revised. It encourages one's interlocutor to revise her views if there is no integrity in the set of assumptions or views she holds.

Each student tends to be inclined to a theory of law because of her particular worldview, which includes opinions on matters such as whether there is an objective morality. If the person is a moral skeptic, for example, the person would be more inclined to CLS and legal positivism. As an illustration of how the elenchus and the dialectic might be employed, I might find out the student's preferred theory of law, as well as her positions on unrelated legal issues that engage morally intractable debates, such as whether abortion should be allowed. If the assumptions behind two opinions – the first, on the theory of law, and the second, on the specific legal issue – are unpacked, the assumptions might turn out to be contradictory. For example, the student is a moral skeptic on the first, and a moral realist on the second. If so, one of the opinions has to be abandoned or revised. In this process, the student picks up the importance of consistency in analysis. Sometimes, too, just leading the student to unpack more specific implications of a general view that the student bandies without much critical thought helps the student revise the general view if the student realises that she does not really hold that view after all. For example, students commonly speak of their belief that "morality is a social construct". Using the Socratic method, I might lead them to explain what they mean, whether, for example, they are of the view that social consensus binds everyone. In turn, what is needed to establish social consensus, and why is such significance attached to social consensus? For some students, it might come down to their belief that every person has equal dignity, and hence each person's view counts aggregatively to constitute a common morality. This belief about equal dignity might be embraced as absolute, and not as a social construct, thus suggesting that the student does not really believe in morality as a social construct, but in the absolute moral value of equal dignity.

Legal philosophy offers an especially good context to learn analytical skills because philosophical arguments, as contrasted with polemical arguments which defend particular positions, require students to develop a sustained argument and consider different positions before arriving at a conclusion from "plausible premises".[55] I encourage students to treat the exercise of determining their opinions differently from a debate, and to consider arguments and counter-arguments before arriving at their opinions. This is also reflected in my marking, which rewards students for being able to recognise counter-arguments, and places far less emphasis on the actual conclusion of the students.

It has been observed in relation to doctrinal law courses that something as run-of-the-mill to law professors as issue spotting[56] needs to be explicitly dealt

55 Claire Grant, On writing: The essay in jurisprudence, 58 *J. Legal Educ.* 351, 353 (2008).

56 Deborah Zalesne and David Nadyomey, Why don't they get it?: Academic intelligence and the under-prepared student as "other", 61 *J. Legal Educ.* 264, 278–79 (2011–12).

with and taught to the students through a check list, as not all students have the "academic intelligence" to pick up for themselves the skill of issue spotting. One critic defines "academic intelligence" as "a student's actual level of academic preparation, i.e., a student's readiness or ability to engage productively with an academic environment and to benefit from that interaction".[57] Someone with academic intelligence "will have strong reading comprehension, writing, and study skills, be able to take effective notes in class, outline, and manage their time – in other words, the skills that determine, ultimately, who will be successful in law school".[58] It might not be obvious to average students going through legal doctrines in class that they are expected to pick up legal reasoning skills, as their performance in examinations suggest.[59] A similar problem in my view exists in relation to philosophical issues arising in law: while it ought to have been obvious that we should ensure that our various opinions on different issues do not stem from contradictory assumptions, students are not conscious of such problems with the opinions they hold until they are forced to unpack their views in class. Thus, the use of the elenchus and the dialectic are particularly effectively in leading them to rethink incoherent or inconsistent views.

Critical Legal Studies

Despite what has been said to be the decline of the CLS school, a shift towards market-oriented methodology, and an acceptance of the reproduction of hierarchies in the global market,[60] I argue that CLS has much to offer in terms of training critical thinking and helping law students become empowered citizens and lawyers. While Professor Roberto Unger said in his Tanner Lectures on Religion[61] that he is a sympathetic unbeliever in relation to religion, I consider myself a sympathetic unbeliever in relation to CLS. Many aims and methods of CLS are admirable and a necessary part of any thinking about law even if I do not agree with its fundamental assumptions or in treating the aims and methods as the be all and end all of legal thought.

Whether CLS has lost its gloss globally, as I anecdotally surveyed my students, I confirmed that they knew very little, if anything at all, about it (though, to be fair, they knew little about other legal theories too). I am not sure it was otherwise in the heyday of CLS. Some law students learnt of it only in their upper years in the mandatory LTP course; others heard of critical views, not in the context of law but

57 *Id.* at 264.

58 *Id.* at 266.

59 *Id.* at 271.

60 Daria Roithmayr, A dangerous supplement, 55 *J. Legal Educ.* 80, 81–82 (2005).

61 Roberto Unger, *The Future of Religion and the Religion of the Future*, available on http://www.law.harvard.edu/faculty/unger/philosophy.php, accessed 28 April 2014.

in the context of cultural studies, where they were introduced to the idea of social constructs or society as an artefact.

I suggest that three sets of factors have contributed to the cool reception towards CLS in Singapore. The first set of factors concerns legal education in Singapore. Legal education is private practice-oriented, with a focus on helping students master the legal doctrines and skills essential for practice. This is an understandable aim given that the nation is small. Law schools, as professional schools, are expected to serve the profession and the community. Perhaps there is also a dearth of doctrinal teachers teaching private law who are actively researching in legal theory, let alone critical theory. The second set of factors relates to Singapore as a society in which the prevailing social attitude is conservative. As an Asian society, deference towards, and respect of, authority are valued. The community is more important that the individual. Some might in the past have equated a questioning of established laws and institutions with a challenge (in bad faith) of governmental authority, instead of a good faith attempt to work towards fairness and justice in law. Furthermore, many Singaporeans were for a long time politically apathetic though this seems to have changed in the latest general[62] and presidential[63] elections during which the use of social media was instrumental in fostering a critical questioning atmosphere. Ordinary citizens actively turned into political commentators on blogs, Facebook, and Twitter.[64] The third set of factors accounting for the slow take up of CLS is perhaps internal to CLS. As a school of jurisprudence that is disruptive of whatever is established, it may be opposed by those who are most versed with it and in a privileged position to be able to harness it for transformative purposes as they want to keep the system going. It also demands too much personal engagement from people who are far too comfortable with their lives to push for change or otherwise too lazy to step out of their comfort zone, especially in a materialistic society.

There are several ways I employ CLS in LTP and JURIS to help law students reflect on their special responsibility to work towards just institutions, whether as lawyers or legally-trained citizens.

The first reading I prescribe in LTP is an excerpt from Duncan Kennedy's *Legal Education and the Reproduction of Hierarchy*.[65] I use it to set the tone for the rest of the course. Students are encouraged to think about the manner in which legal education has constructed boundaries of law and whether legal reasoning is different from political or ideological reasoning. This is important given that some

62 This took place in 2011.

63 This took place in 2012.

64 See, for example, Singapore PM promises "strategic shift" to protect city state's success, *Financial Times*, August 18, 2013: "Yet the government is contending with a vibrant social media where criticism of policy is aired openly. That was a big factor in the PAP's worst general election result in 2011, a performance that it will be hoping not to repeat at the next poll in 2016."

65 NYU Press, new edn, 2007.

empirical studies by critical sociologists suggest that law schools play a part in producing students who uncritically accept the economic and political status quo, the entrenchment of which is aided by law.[66]

The themes of CLS cannot be fully engaged in this chapter. Three lessons, reflecting a concern with social justice that is characteristic of the American leftist tradition, are particularly important for students who "try to make a difference in the quality of our private and public lives".[67] I shall briefly mention them. The first is the idea that law is politics. More specifically, legal doctrines and the boundaries of law are not necessary or inevitable. Law as it stands may reflect the ideology of a class, and may not be legitimate or justified. When we treat the law as our first port of call, and are content to make our claims within the law, we accept its negotiation of interests without question. We should be more vigilant to ask if the law we plead in the courts as binding on parties is fair or just. Lawyers should see each private dispute before the court as an opportunity for the law to be transformed. This is ballast against what has been critiqued as the private litigation focus of the first year curriculum where the "overwhelming message is that real law and real lawyers maintain the status quo by resolving disputes between private parties".[68] The second important lesson of CLS is its recognition that we are products of our contexts. We need to transcend our contexts. Crits are vigilant to expose conflicting interests underlying the law and reveal how law entrenches power relations and masks the protection of particular interests. Such delegitimation of the law can serve a constructive outcome of enabling us to see more possibilities for our lives regulated by the law. The third valuable lesson is Unger's recognition that the individual has an identity that is not defined by social hierarchy or context.[69] Thus, he advocates context-smashing with a view to bringing about a world in which we can relate to one another as more than mere bearers of rights.

There are insurmountable problems, however, with the premises of CLS.

First, while the context-transcendent narrative is attractive, if we are products of context, how can we be sure that we have successfully transcended context, and not merely spoken from within our context? There seems to be a possibility that CLS is merely a reaction to existing philosophies as CLS is negatively defined – being a rebellion against existing structures and social conservatism. Unger gives a modernist restatement of the Christian romantic image of man in one of his earlier works but rejects Christianity. He is attracted to the Christian view of man as an end in himself and as more than a product of context. The view Unger rejects, while not acceptable to atheists and those of other religions, and not

---

66 Robert Granfield, *Making Elite Lawyers* (Routledge 1992). Compare with J.D. Droddy and C. Scott Peters, The effect of law school on political attitudes, 53 *J. Legal Educ.* 33 (2003).

67 Gene R. Nichol, *Law's Disengaged Left*, 50 *J. Legal Educ.* 547, 549 (2000).

68 Rubin, *supra* note 49, at 110.

69 Unger, *supra* note 28.

attractive to agnostics, does not suffer from the logical problem of every discovery being context-dependent: the personal God of Christianity is an external personal power that is capable of speaking to man from a situation outside of man's context. Moreover, man is not merely a product of context because worth is conferred upon him by a personal God who creates him.

The second problem with CLS is whether anything concrete can come out of the view that everything is contingent. In its belief in the importance of smashing one's context, is it not obliged to smash even the context that emerges out of any constructive programs it implements? If everything, including its own outcomes, must be smashed, this results in a problem that is best articulated in these words:

> There are progressions in which the last step is *sui generis* – incommensurable with the others – and in which to go the whole way is to undo all the labour of your previous journey … you cannot go on "explaining away" forever. You will have explained explanation itself away. You cannot go on "seeing through" things forever. The whole point of seeing through something is to see something through it. It is good that the window should be transparent, because the street or garden beyond it is opaque. How if you saw through the garden too? It is no use trying to "see through" first principles. If you see through everything, then everything is transparent. But a wholly transparent world is an invisible world. To "see through" all things is the same as not to see.[70]

The third problem is the attitudinal change that CLS seems to require but cannot bring about. Unger, in an earlier work, wrote:

> The program of radical democracy has a more troubled relation to the strengthening and cleansing of solidarity. The fulfilment of its proposals does not ensure us of coexisting in peace. *It does not take away our hearts of stone and give us hearts of flesh.* But it does enable us to live out more fully the tense, ambiguous, ennobling connection between solidarity and empowerment, between the experience of mutual acceptance and the development of our faculties, between our longing for one another and our efforts to find particular expressions for the impulse within us that rebels against all particularity. What more could we ask of society than a better chance to be both great and sweet?[71] (*emphasis mine*)

While no attribution is made in the text, the italicised words are quoted from the prophet Ezekiel in the Bible, whose exact words, speaking on behalf of God, are: "I will give you a new heart and put a new spirit within you; and I will remove the heart of stone from your flesh and give you a heart of flesh."[72] Unger's reference

70 C.S. Lewis, *The Abolition of Man* 48 (Fount 1978).

71 Roberto Mangabeira Unger, *Politics: The Central Texts* 436 (Verso 1997).

72 Ezekiel 36:26, *New American Standard Bible.*

acknowledges that the CLS effort falls short of what would be possible if a context-transcendent power was available to effect our true transformation.

In spite of these problems with CLS, its value lies in teaching us to question things we take as given or necessary or incapable of revision, and encourages us to re-imagine possibilities of law. As a commentator notes:

> (E)ven though one might not find Unger's arguments persuasive in the final analysis, his signal contribution must surely be the spirit that lies behind his work, which spirit must not be underestimated – not least because, despite the apparently obvious point that things ought to be perceived as capable of being better, the fact of the matter is this: that apart from a few remarkable individuals, most labour under the illusion that they are powerless to work a greater good in society at large, not realising that that 'greater good' lies not in a final decisive victory as such but, rather, a continuous and committed effort to try to alter what we sincerely feel requires change.[73]

It is this spirit of continually and constantly working for just institutions that the teaching of critical thinking through CLS can foster in the future lawyer and legally-trained citizen.

The Special Contribution of the Lawyer and the Legally-Trained Citizen

Of late, the legal community in Singapore has been encouraging more pro bono commitment. Students in the two law schools in Singapore are now required to perform 20 hours of pro bono service before graduation.[74] Commentators have long spoken of public service as an obligation[75] of lawyers. While doing pro bono work is salutary, it still falls short of the "Jeffersonian vision of legal education", which was for lawyers, through learning broad political theory and moral philosophy, amongst others, to develop into virtuous leaders who place public interest above private interests.[76] How far law schools have moved from such a vision is seen from how we have had to critique legal education for fostering an unhealthy form of "thinking like a lawyer". Anything other than "the cognitive, rational, and analytical" is devalued, leading students to perceive that the ethical

73 Andrew Phang, Roberto Unger and the politics of transformation in an Asian context, *TSAR* 472, 495–96 (1997).

74 See http://www.sile.edu.sg/pro-bono-programme, accessed 28 April 2014.

75 Lucie E. White, Pro bono or Partnership? Rethinking lawyers' public service obligations for a new millennium, 50 *J. Legal Educ.* 134 (2000).

76 Davison M. Douglas, The Jeffersonian vision of legal education, 51 *J. Legal Educ.* 185 (2001).

and moral values they cherish must be given up if they were to become good lawyer.[77] As one commentator notes:

> Many students enter law school with a strong sense of right and wrong. Over time, however, their professors teach these students to "think like a lawyer". Many times, there is no right answer and the answer is simply "it depends". It does not depend on whether the defendant committed the crime; more often than not it depends on who the judge is, the mandatory sentencing requirements imposed, whether the police preserved the evidence, or whether the key witness was secured by the state. These students must come to conclusions not because they believe something is right or fair or just but because it is "what the law says". Law students are trained to ignore their heart and to go with their head in all situations. They are taught that there are no real "right" answers. The right answer is determined by who can make the best argument. This can lead to cognitive dissonance for law students and result in their losing the passion and purpose that originally brought them to law school.[78]

On a personal level, promoting critical legal thinking through the methods identified in this chapter enables students to find out who they really are and work through the relation between their fundamental beliefs and legal doctrines. The constant examination of beliefs through the Socratic elenchus and dialectic forces each student to abandon those beliefs that do not stand up to rational scrutiny or which stem from contradictory assumptions that the student cannot endorse alongside other beliefs. Exposure to the challenges of CLS makes each student conscious of legal doctrines which are not legitimate or justified. They are empowered to lead examined lives instead of practising law thinking it to be netural and justified and being found in the end to have served particular interest groups.

On a public level in their capacity as lawyers, students are better able to harness the transformative potential of law when they realise how it is occasionally being employed to serve factional interests, and seek a revision of what is not fair.

A public lawyer may question the constitutionality of legislation in good faith, to ensure that constitutionally guaranteed rights are protected.[79] In Singapore, such

---

77 Daisy Hurst Floyd, We can do more, 60 *J. Legal Educ.* 129, 131 (2010–11).

78 Ben Gibson, How law students can cope: A law student's view, 60 *J. Legal Educ.* 140, 142 (2010–11).

79 When the Minister of Law was asked in an interview if people were challenging the government more these days, he acknowledged that an application for judicial review was a right that the people had, and "where it is fair or where it is properly applied for, is a matter for the courts". (*Shanmugam: 'No country wants to send anyone to death'* at http://www.singapolitics.sg/supperclub/shanmugam-no-country-wants-send-anyone-death, accessed 28 April 2014.)

challenges[80] have been made, though none has been successful at the appellate level.[81] There is nothing sinister about this, though, as it may be the case that all the challenges failed because the legislation in question was well thought through and constitutional.

A private lawyer might be less accepting of current legal doctrines and seek to develop less dominant counter-principles in areas of law. In contract law, Unger notes that the dominant principles respect the idea of contract as promise, with its emphasis on the freedom of the parties to enter into contracts, while less dominant counter-principles value fairness and prevent the subversion of communal aspects of social life and limit the enforcement of contracts that otherwise may seem to have been freely entered into.[82] These counter-principles are seen as exceptional and as generating ad hoc qualifications to the dominant principles, but Unger suggests they may be generative of a different body of rules.[83] A private lawyer who endorses Unger's view might push for the courts to apply existing, or create, exceptions to general rules while litigating a contract dispute on a point of law, without viewing those exceptions as applying only in the exceptional instances. This might lead, for example, to the recognition of more categories of factors which vitiate a contract, beyond the cases in which parties could be seen as not having freely entered into a contract, to cases in which the courts respect a more general idea of fair bargain. Or a more general expansive general principle (in this case, of inequality of bargaining powers) might be discovered to underlie the existing categories of factors, as Lord Denning M.R. proposed in *Lloyd's Bank Ltd. v. Bundy*.[84] The more recent works of some academics in contract law which

---

80 See, for example, some recent cases: *Nguyen Tuong Van v. PP* [2004] SGCA 47 and *Yong Vui Kong v. PP* [2010] SGCA 20 (whether the mandatory death penalty under the Misuse of Drugs Act (Cap 185, 2001 rev. edn) violated the constitutional guarantee of equality under Art 12 of the Constitution of the Republic of Singapore (1985 rev. edn, 1999 Reprint) (hereafter, "the Singapore Constitution") or the right not to be deprived of life or personal liberty save in accordance with law under Art 9 of the Singapore Constitution); *Lim Meng Suang and another v. AG* [2013] SGHC 73 (whether section 377A of the Penal Code (Cap 224, 2008 rev. edn) violated Article 12 of the Singapore Constitution); and *Ramalingam Ravinthran v. AG* [2012] SGCA 2 (whether the exercise of prosecutorial discretion to charge two persons involved in the same criminal enterprise with two different offences, one capital and the other non-capital, violated Art 12 of the Singapore Constitution).

81 The challenge of Section 37 of the Prevention of Corruption Act (Cap 241, 1993 rev. edn) succeeded at the High Court level in *PP v. Taw Cheng Kong* [1998] SGHC 10, but was overturned by the Court of Appeal [1998] SGCA 38.

82 Unger, *supra* note 27, at 60–75.

83 *Id.* at 75.

84 [1975] Q.B. 326. The need for his proposal was doubted in *National Westminster Bank plc v. Morgan* [1985] A.C. 686.

emphasise the doctrine of good faith and the idea of reasonable expectations of the parties provide other examples for developments in such a direction.[85]

On a public level in their capacity as legally-trained citizens, students might realise they can impact public decisions and law-making with their special contribution of legal philosophical knowledge. I hope that students, having sampled the relevance of legal philosophy to current issues, continue to contribute as citizens in future debates.

In terms of educating future lawyers to these ends, what does one make of the fact that the nature of law and its purpose are contentious? Does it mean that, in a postmodern pluralist world, it would be unfair to teach any particular view about the nature of law as true? The reality is that a teacher cannot help but model some ideas, even in doctrinal classes.[86] To refuse to explicate on values underlying the law might be to create an impression that the law is value-neutral or the work of a lawyer is amoral. In spite of the existence of contending viewpoints, if educators focus on fostering critical thinking in the manner that has been described in this chapter, students remain free to choose their own viewpoint. It has been suggested that a legal system represents a "society's attempt to institutionalize justice".[87] Its success hinges on its key players – lawyers[88] – who help to shape the vision of what justice demands and refine the workings of justice in concrete ways. It is in their formative years that we as educators help to sensitise them to their future roles.

---

85 See, for example, Roger Brownsword, *Contract Law: Themes for the Twenty-First Century* (Oxford University Press, 2nd edn, 2006).

86 Carrie Menkel-Meadow, Can a law teacher avoid teaching legal ethics?, 41 *J. Legal Educ.* 3 (1991).

87 Ian Johnstone and Mary Patricia Treuthart, Doing the right thing: An overview of teaching professional responsibility, 41 *J. Legal Educ.* 75, 78 (1991).

88 *Id.*

Chapter 9

Rethinking Teaching, Learning and Assessment in the Twenty-First Century Law Curriculum

Rick Glofcheski[1]

Introduction

For much of the past decade, legal education as provided by university law schools has been under review and criticism in many places in the common law world. A major review has just been completed in the UK.[2] Only a few years ago two large-scale studies in the US[3] were conducted. Another, undertaken by the American Bar Association, is currently in production.[4] And we should not overlook the 2001 Redmond–Roper Report,[5] which reviewed and made recommendations on all stages of legal education here in Hong Kong.[6]

---

1 Faculty of Law, University of Hong Kong.

2 *Legal Education and Training Review* (LETR) 2013 – a joint project of the Solicitors Regulation Authority (SRA), the Bar Standards Board (BSB) and ILEX Professional Standards (IPS), available at http://letr.org.uk/ (accessed February 22, 2014).

3 William Sullivan, Anne Colby, Judith Wegner, Lloyd Bond and Lee Shulman, *Educating Lawyers: Preparation for the Profession of Law* (2007) (the '*Carnegie Report*') (summary available at http://www.carnegiefoundation.org/publications/educating-lawyers-preparation-profession-law, accessed February 22, 2014); Roy Stuckey et al., *Best Practices for Legal Education: A Vision and a Road Map* (2007) Clinical Legal Education Association (executive summary available at http://www.cleaweb.org/Resources/Documents/best_practices-cover.pdf, accessed February 22, 2014).

4 *ABA Task Force on the Future of Legal Education*. The draft report and recommendations can be found at http://www.americanbar.org/groups/professional_responsibility/taskforceonthefuturelegaleducation.html (accessed February 22, 2014).

5 *Legal Education and Training in Hong Kong: Preliminary Review* (2001), often referred to as the "Redmond-Roper Report", available at http://www.hklawsoc.org.hk/pub_e/news/societyupdates/20010813a.asp (accessed March 10, 2014).

6 According to *Legal Week*, another review is about to take place in Hong Kong. See e.g. http://www.legalweek.com/legal-week/news/2266957/hong-kong-aims-to-simplify-local-qualification-system-amid-fierce-competition-for-places (accessed March 10, 2014). See also http://www.ntu.ac.uk/apps/news/150407–15/Team_of_experts_to_prepare_report_into_possible_changes_to_Hong_Kongs_lega.aspx (accessed March 10, 2014).

These studies are just a representative sample.[7] Criticizing legal education is nothing new.[8]

There are multiple stakeholders in legal education, and the factors that might trigger the need or perceived need for a legal education review are many, including political. They are usually driven, at least in part if not in the main, by a perception that there is a gap between academic achievement and professional requirements, that legal education is not fit for purpose.[9] It is not uncommon to hear complaints from the profession that graduates have not been properly prepared for lawyering work.[10] One observation that can be made is that although most of these reviews are concerned to some degree with issues of fitness for purpose, rarely do they examine the tools for learning that predominate in the law school curriculum. The focus is on larger, institutional issues.

Resistance to Change

It is not the present intention to attempt an analysis or even a summary of the various legal education reviews, but rather to observe not only that these studies have taken place with such frequency, but that they are still taking place. Of course, it is healthy for legal education systems to be subject to evaluation and criticism. Evaluation and criticism is very much in the spirit of education itself. On the other hand, what if anything becomes of these reviews? Has legal education changed in any significant way in response to them? According to Sally Kift, a leading Australian legal education scholar, it has not:

---

7 Citations to more than a dozen other legal education reviews in the US, UK, Australia and Canada can be found in Sally Kift, "21st Century Climate for Change: Curriculum Design for Quality Learning Engagement in Law" (2008) 18 *Legal Education Review* 1, notes 24–27 (hereafter, "Kift").

8 See e.g. Karl Llewellyn, "On What is Wrong with so-called Legal Education" (1935) 35 *Columbia Law Review*, 651; and Duncan Kennedy, "Legal Education and the Reproduction of Hierarchy" (1982) 32 *Journal of Legal Education* 591: "Law teachers teach lawyering skills in a way that 'almost completely mystifies them for almost all students'" (at 596).

9 A concern expressed by the authors of *Best Practices for Legal Education*: "Most law schools are not committed to preparing students for practice … most law school graduates are not as prepared for law practice as they could be and should be". See Stuckey et al (note 3 above) at 7–10.

10 It was this very issue that to a large degree motivated a recent wholesale legal curriculum renewal undertaken at three Australian universities (Queensland University of Technology, Griffith University and the University of Western Australia). See *Curriculum Renewal in Legal Education* (2013) available at http://eprints.qut.edu.au/64249/1/Final_Report%5B1%5D.pdf (accessed February 22, 2014).

> … if Professor Langdell walked into a contemporary law school in the US or Australia … he would feel right at home. Although the elective programs at modern law schools have expanded enormously and become ever more specialized, and clinical electives are now available, the nature of the core curriculum, the dominance of doctrine, and the basic approach to pedagogy have changed very little.[11]

James Moliterno, an American professional legal education scholar, put it more wryly:

> The profession seems to repeat the same question in response to every crisis: How can we stay even more the same than we already are?[12]

To be fair, some change has taken place. Clinical legal education, an initiative pioneered in the US in the 1960s is now offered in many forward-thinking law schools around the world, whether for credit or on a voluntary basis, in the form of live-client, internship and simulation.[13] Many law schools, other than the most traditional, offer electives that are assessed entirely by research paper. Some law schools offer courses that include, as part of the assessed work, group projects that can vary from the familiar moot course exercise to the production of legal documentary videos. Most law schools have a compulsory moot exercise, and the possibility of entering inter-school moot competitions. Although not a legal education initiative as such, most law schools provide for the opportunity to study part of the degree overseas. Others provide the opportunity to study law in tandem with another discipline. Legal education has not completely ossified.

---

11 Sally Kift, *First Year Renewal to Engage Learners in Law*, 7th Pacific Rim First Year in Higher Education Conference (2003). The reference to Professor Langdell is to Christopher Columbus Langdell, a nineteenth century American jurist and Harvard University Professor, often credited with pioneering the case method for teaching and learning law. Speaking of the current American experience, A Benjamin Spencer is largely in agreement: "the contemporary law school remains remarkably Langdellian in its design as a three-year system in which doctrinal knowledge and legal analytical abilities are transmitted to students mostly via a traditional or modified case-dialogue approach …": see Spencer, "The Law School Critique in Historical Perspective" (2002) 69 *Washington & Lee Law Review* 1949.

12 James Moliterno, "The Future of Legal Education Reform", (2013) 40 *Pepperdine Law Review* 423 at 423.

13 The University of Hong Kong offers the possibility of taking clinical legal education for course credit – see http://www.law.hku.hk/syllabuses/LLB_2013_14.pdf at p. 31. Both the University of Hong Kong and the Chinese University of Hong Kong offer law students the opportunity to participate in legal advice programmes – see e.g. http://www.law.hku.hk/ccpl/cons/clep/ and http://www.hkrac.org/what-you-can-do/training/ (both sites accessed February 22, 2014).

However, these initiatives work at the periphery, and in the main, most law schools have been resistant to serious change.[14] The central components of the law curriculum have remained largely the same, in particular the pre-eminence of legal doctrine, the teaching and learning of law through appellate judgments, the lecture format and the use of heavily weighted examinations as the assessment method.[15] There are many possible reasons for this state of affairs, among them: influence of the profession, the members of which are comfortable with the conventional methods; large intakes and few teachers, requiring large class sizes that prevent in-class engagement and inhibit teacher supervision and assessment of more activity-based learning; student resistance to learning that is not related to the assessment;[16] student expectations for teacher-centred learning; student preference for predictable and familiar assessment formats; and student preference for surface and passive learning.[17] To this list could be added teacher and institutional apathy. Law teachers do not want to think about teaching when "it is going perfectly well" – or at least when no one is complaining to them about it. It is a well-known phenomenon that university teachers, lacking formal training in teaching and learning, teach in the way they were taught by their own teachers. Teachers of law are likely to model their teaching on the teacher they recall as their best law school teacher. This is not surprising, nor is it necessarily to be criticized. Moreover, career trajectory is driven by research achievements and not teaching success, and these inevitably dictate priorities, a position supported by the institution. All of these factors may contribute to a law school culture of – why fix it if it's not broken?[18]

---

14 Perhaps this is not terribly surprising in an intellectual milieu that is as steeped in tradition as law. Its essential *modus operandi* looks to the past (precedent) for wisdom.

15 The authors of the *Carnegie Report* remarked in the second of its five Key Observations that "compared to other professional fields, which often employ multiple forms of teaching through a more prolonged socialization process, legal pedagogy is remarkably uniform across variations in schools and student bodies" (see *Carnegie Report*, note 3 above).

16 Many law teachers will have "experienced the sound of pens dropping and the silent but perceptible click of minds switching off when some theoretical or critical question is raised and sometimes even a hostility or impatience that time is being wasted" – see Charles Sampford and David Wood, 'Theoretical Dimensions of Legal Education' in John Goldring, Charles Sampford, and Ralph Simmonds (eds) *New Foundations in Legal Education* (Sydney: Cavendish Publishing, 1998), p. 116.

17 A survey of law students conducted at the University of Hong Kong in 2006 (Tai et al., *How Law Students Learn*) revealed a preference for passive and surface learning in lectures and tutorials over activity-based learning, because they more closely reflected the assessment process. Moots, debates, presentations and the like require time and effort, and because they do not feature on the summative assessment, normally a heavily weighted final examination, students are not interested in them as learning activities.

18 For a discussion of yet other obstacles to change, see Richard Johnstone and Sumitra Vignaendra, *Learning Outcomes and Curriculum Development in Law*, a report commissioned

Elsewhere in higher education, there is a more palpable interest in the student learning experience, out of which has grown a considerable body of scholarship that has informed the way that learning and teaching is designed. Emphasis has shifted from teacher-centred to student-centred learning. It is now widely accepted that learning should be outcomes-based, requiring the formulation and articulation of learning outcomes suitable to the discipline. Generic outcomes have also been identified: life-long learning skills, independent learning skills and the ability to solve ill-defined problems. Learning should be constructively aligned, meaning that the learning activities and assessment should be aligned with the learning outcomes in a way that ensures the learner who engages in the learning activities and is assessed on them will achieve the intended learning outcomes.[19] Learning should be authentic, as close as possible to real-world scenarios. Learning should allow student transition to post-graduation life and work. Hence, learning should not be reproductive, suitable only for satisfying the examiners. Multiple modes of learning should be employed, not only to reflect and anticipate real-world experiences but to ensure that all students can learn in ways that take account of differences in learners' characteristics. For the same reason, multiple modes of assessment should be used. It is now widely acknowledged that the method of assessment has a powerful influence on learning behaviour.[20] Assessment should be carefully designed to ensure that students learn the right kinds of things in the right kinds of ways and that the learning is sustainable, available to students after graduation.

In the meantime, there has been a global movement in higher education toward accountability systems, to ensure the acquisition of graduate attributes and more meaningful learning that imbue ethical and community values and an awareness of and sensitivity to community problems and needs.[21]

---

by the Australian Universities Teaching Committee (2003), chapter 13, available at http://www.cald.asn.au/docs/AUTC_2003_Johnstone-Vignaendra.pdf (accessed February 22, 2014).

19 Constructive alignment as an educational imperative was embraced by the recent *Legal Education and Training Review* (note 2 above) at 4.122 – see http://letr.org.uk/the-report/chapter-4/robust-learning-and-assessment-approaches/index.html.

20 Assessment has been identified as possibly the single most important influence on student learning, directing students' to organize their learning on topics likely to be examined and the modes of examination to be used. See e.g. Paul Ramsden, *Learning to Teach in Higher Education* (London: Routledge, 1992); Chris Rust, "The impact of assessment on student learning" (2002) 3 *Active Learning in Higher Education*, 145–58; Karen Scouller and Michael Prosser, "Students' experiences in studying for multiple choice question examinations" (1994) 19 *Higher Education*, 267–79; and Gordon Joughin, *Assessment, Learning and Judgment in Higher Education: A Critical Review* (Dordrecht: Springer, 2009).

21 Teaching quality and accountability are now enforced through audits conducted by quality assurance bodies. In Hong Kong an audit was conducted in 2009, and another is planned for 2015. For the most recent audit of the University of Hong Kong see http://www.ugc.edu.hk/eng/qac/publication/report/hku200911e.pdf (accessed February 22, 2014).

Aside from isolated pockets of classroom innovators and the minority of law teachers interested in improving the learning opportunities of their students,[22] there is little evidence that law schools have taken notice of much of this, leaving the impression that learning law is separate and somehow different from learning other disciplines in higher education. The world has changed, but legal education has not changed much. Yet the continuation of the main forms of law teaching and assessment have never been explained or justified according to accepted theories of learning or instructional design.

How Law is Taught and Learned

At the risk of some over-simplification, let us consider the typical learning experience in a law school today. A law course typically consists of a course syllabus, a case reading list, lectures, and in the UK model, small group tutorials. Law is learned through the reading of cases and/or case extracts, and the reading of other teacher-assigned materials such as journal articles and extracts. Students learn legal principles as derived from case law and legislation. They attend classes in which the teacher subjects the cases to critical analysis, in order to expose contradictions, and students play a small, often passive, role. Undergraduate learning of law is knowledge-based – only to a very limited degree is it skills-based. It is largely passive, with little or no activity-based learning. This is a model premised on the notion of knowledge transfer: the lecturer transmits knowledge[23] which students are required to master and reproduce on final examinations.[24]

---

22 Evidence of such interest by law teachers can be seen in the papers published in legal education journals such as the UK-based *Law Teacher*, and the Australia-based *Legal Education Review*, as well as in the annual conferences of bodies such as the UK-based Association of Law Teachers and the Australia Law Teachers Association. For a list of legal education reform initiatives in US law schools spurred by the Carnegie Report, see Sara Rankin, "Tired of Talking: A Call for Clear Strategies for Legal Education Reform: Moving Beyond the Discussion of Good Ideas to the Real Transformation of Law Schools" (2011) 10 *Seattle Journal for Social Justice* 11 at notes 6–11. Notwithstanding these efforts, Rankin concludes that legal education "essentially remains unchanged" (at 18).

23 What Biggs and Tang explain as declarative or content propositional knowledge, what teachers "declare" in lectures. It is to be distinguished from functioning knowledge, which involves the ability to do something with knowledge. See John Biggs and Catherine Tang, *Teaching for Quality Learning at University* (London: McGraw-Hill, 2007 (3rd edn)) at 72–73.

24 This description is consistent with the findings of Karen Clegg, who conducted a study on the teaching and learning of law for the UK Centre for Legal Education: "There is consistent evidence from all the institutions to suggest that traditional tutorial, seminar and lecture formats dominate in law teaching. In some cases credible explanations are given for this approach, i.e. lectures are perceived to be a sensible way of communicating

The main (perhaps the only) expected learning outcome is the mastering of legal knowledge and the ability to solve legal problems through issue-identification and legal reasoning. That is, it is hoped that, on being presented with a legal problem (for instance in the form of the client's narrative) or a case for appeal consideration, the student will have the ability to identify the legal issues that arise, and the legal principles and reasoning that would be applied by a judge hearing the case. Although there can be no doubt that it is vital that law graduates master the skill of legal analysis, if it is the sole learning outcome of legal education, one might well wonder whether three or four years of study are required for this purpose.

Learning and Assessment

An arguably under-developed and under-utilized area in law school pedagogy is assessment.[25] In the law schools, assessment is seen as summative. That is, it is viewed as an instrument for measuring and accrediting student learning achievement, often with a ranking attached. Too little attention is paid to its other potential functions. It would be worrying if measurement of learning achievement was the only function, because most law teachers will admit to doubts about the reliability of grading law examination questions in the form of essays or open-ended fictional narratives.[26] A little reflection on how students are motivated in learning soon leads to some alternative approaches to assessment that can transform assessment into an educational moment.[27] There is now a considerable literature on assessment that envisions a more powerful, more enabling role for assessment in higher education. Assessment is now viewed as

basic legal facts to student numbers exceeding 200. However, when exploring with staff how analysis, evaluation and reflection are developed the data reveals a lack of alignment between intended learning outcomes, teaching and assessment methods". See *Playing Safe: Learning and Teaching in Undergraduate Law*, UK Centre for Legal Education, 2004, p. 5, available at http://www.ukcle.ac.uk/projects/past-projects/ncle/ (accessed April 22, 2014).

25 Of the five Key Observations in the *Carnegie Report*, the two of immediate relevance are: "Law Schools Rely Heavily on One Way of Teaching to Accomplish the Socialization Process"; and "Assessment of Student Learning Remains Underdeveloped".

26 For an early study demonstrating this unreliability see Benjamin Wood, "Measurement of Law School Work" (1950) 24 *Columbia Law Review* 230.

27 Implicitly acknowledged in the recent Legal Education and Training Review (2013) at 4.122 – see http://letr.org.uk/the-report/chapter-4/robust-learning-and-assessment-approaches/index.html (accessed February 22, 2014).

having a formative function.[28] For many, assessment *for* learning has displaced assessment *of* learning.[29]

It is well-known that assessment is an important, if not *the* most important factor driving student learning behaviour in formal education. Intuitively we know this to be true, and in any case it is well-supported in the literature.[30] Certainly it is true in higher education, where the stakes are high, or at least students perceive them to be higher than at earlier levels of formal education. This means, stating it simply, that students will strive to become good at whatever it is that the teachers require of them in the assessment. This is particularly true of law students, who – again at the risk of over-simplification – we know to be practical and arguably more goal-oriented than other students.[31]

This insight means that, to advance student learning so that it is meaningful and sustainable, law school assessments should be designed strategically. To say the least, it suggests the need for diverse forms of assessment, in order to account for the diversity of learning outcomes required of a law graduate. Assessment

28 Royce Sadler, "Formative Assessment and the Design of Instructional Systems" (1989) 18 *Instructional Science* 119–44; David Boud, "Sustainable Assessment: Rethinking Assessment for the Learning Society" (2000) 22 *Studies in Continuing Education*, 2, 151–67; Graham Gibbs, "How Assessment Frames Student Learning" in Cordelia Bryan and Karen Clegg (eds), *Innovative Assessment in Higher Education* (Abingdon, Oxon: Routledge, 2006) at 23–36; David Boud and Nancy Falchikov, *Rethinking Assessment in Higher Education: Learning for the Longer Term* (Abingdon, Oxon: Routledge, 2007). For another important resource see www.assessmentfutures.com.

29 David Boud, "How Can Practise Reshape Assessment" in Gordon Joughin, *Assessment, Learning and Judgment in Higher Education: a Critical Review* (Dordrecht: Springer, 2009), pp. 35–36; see generally Peter Knight (ed.), *Assessment for Learning in Higher Education* (London: Kogan Page, 1995).

30 "Students learn what they think they will be tested on" (Biggs and Tang, note 23 above). "From our students' point of view, assessment defines the actual curriculum" (Paul Ramsden, *Learning to Teach in Higher Education* (New York: Routledge, 2003, 2nd edn). Motivated students are cue-seekers, listening for clues dropped by the teacher, or seeking advice from the teacher's past students, to work out what is really going on in the course and in the assessment – see C.M.L. Miller and Malcolm Parlett, *Up to the Mark: A Study of the Examination Game* (Guildford: Society for Research into Higher Education, 1974). Students follow their own curriculum, derived from their understanding of the assessment – see Benson Snyder, *The Hidden Curriculum* (New York: Alfred A. Knopf, 1973). This has also been described as a "strategic approach" to learning – see Noel Entwistle and Paul Ramsden, *Understanding Student Learning* (London: Croom Helm, 1983). In the legal education context see Erik Driessen and Cees Van der Vleuten, "Matching Student Assessment to Problem-based Learning: Lessons from Experience in a Law Faculty" (2000) 22 *Studies in Continuing Education* 235.

31 This is not to say that there are no other drivers of law students' learning. Intellectual curiosity is certainly a factor, particularly for switched-on, highly motivated learners, those most likely to become law professors. But this does not account for the majority of law students.

tasks should capture an appropriate amount of study time and effort, and these efforts should not be concentrated at the end of the course but should be distributed evenly throughout, to ensure students do not defer their efforts until the very end.[32] It also suggests the need for relevant learning assessments – that is, relevant to law graduate attributes and the kind of work law graduates are expected to undertake. It requires that teachers and course coordinators plan and design the assessment as a first priority in the curriculum, rather than as a last-minute add-on. There are other features to a well-designed assessment strategy, not all of which can be explored here.[33]

At this point it will be instructive to consider another dimension of higher education learning theory: constructive alignment.[34] Although law students will surely be motivated to work when an assessment is looming, law teachers need to find ways to motivate students throughout the semester. This requires that the learning activities law students are asked to do be aligned not only to learning outcomes and the achievement of graduate attributes, but also to the assessment. That is, the learning activities will reflect and build into what is required in the assessment. Assuming that students are aware, even broadly, of this alignment, they are more likely to be motivated to attend to these learning tasks throughout the semester.

Against this, let us consider how law students are typically assessed. Learning in law school, particularly in the foundational courses, is predominantly measured according to a single instrument. In the foundational courses, it is measured largely through end-of-course, time-limited, unseen in-hall examinations.[35] Examination questions typically consist of teacher-designed, fictional narratives as learning and assessment problems.[36] The narrative usually consists of a compressed sequence

---

32 See e.g. Graham Gibbs (note 28 above).

33 For instance, assessment tasks should capture an appropriate amount of study time and effort, and these efforts should not be concentrated at the end of the course but should be distributed evenly throughout – see e.g. Graham Gibbs (note 28 above). For other considerations to be taken into account in a sound assessment strategy, see e.g. Sally Brown and Phil Race, "Using Effective Assessment to Promote Learning", in Lynne Hunt and Denise Chalmers (eds) *University Teaching in Focus: A Learning-centred Approach* (Sydney: Australian Council for Educational Research and Routledge, 2012), pp. 74–91.

34 See Biggs and Tang (note 23 above) pp. 50–54.

35 A survey conducted by the author in 2011 and sent to a list of tort law teachers in five common law jurisdictions revealed that all of them (22) assessed by way of unseen final examination, and that, on average the assessment weight of the final examinations was 70 per cent of the course. These findings are broadly consistent with those of Karen Clegg in her UKCLE study – see note 24 above p. 27.

36 The same 2011 survey revealed that for almost all of them (18/22) the final examination consisted mainly if not exclusively of fictional problems designed by the teacher in a way to achieve coverage of the issues taught on the course. Thirteen respondents reported that there was limited or no choice of question in the examination. Twelve of 21 respondents who answered the question about the nature of the problems used acknowledged that their examination questions consisted of exaggerated fact patterns

of unfortunate events that befall a central character.[37] An objective in this design is to achieve course content coverage.[38] Taken separately, the events in the narrative may be the sort of things that might occur in life, but in the aggregate, as a sequence of events usually happening to the same character, it is most certainly not realistic or believable. The unreality of the situation is often exacerbated by the tendency of law teachers to ascribe strange-sounding names to the central characters, presumably in an attempt to inject humour into the examination experience. This innocent gesture may however have the effect of reinforcing the overall impression that what is being presented is not real, is very much a contrivance, a sort of puzzle or brain-teaser, often producing student effort that is directed as much at trying to figure out what is going on in the teacher's mind as it is to a serious and focused evaluation of the legal issues at stake. It is generally accepted that the teacher has a pre-conceived solution in mind, against which student analysis is assessed. The student is aware of this format from an early stage, and naturally, works toward mastering it. In this model there is a very serious risk that students will be distracted from learning in the right way, while trying to learn the ropes of this artificial format. It is thus not surprising how often we hear law graduates remark that they find little or no relation between how they studied and what they learned in law school, and what is required in the practice of law.

Given that the hypothetical narrative problem is the predominant means of assessment, the question naturally arises as to whether it is the best or even an appropriate means of assessment. This is an important question, given the impact it will have on student learning behaviour. It is probably fair to say with some degree of certainty that in the post-graduation world of work, one thing graduates will not be called upon to do is to solve improbable, artificial hypothetical narratives of the sort that law students are being assessed on.[39]

This observation brings to mind another well-established precept of learning theory. Students learn by doing rather than listening. Listening produces a very low

---

not likely to happen. The survey has obvious limitations, but suggests that in terms of assessment, not a lot has changed in tort law over the last five or more decades.

37 There are variations to this kind of question, including advocacy-oriented questions that invite a more deliberate construction of complex arguments. A well-known variation is to ask the student to compose a legal judgment to decide the case, with reasons in support.

38 In the 2011 survey, 22 of 22 respondents agreed that this was a feature of the assessment design.

39 An Australian law student expressed the conundrum thus: "I would like to see more practical assessments. I've done like three essays this semester and it's stupid, it's pointless. You're not going to do an essay when you work. The type of questions that they ask to assess that valuable content, they weren't good enough. They weren't real life enough. We talk about all this practical side of thing which is really important but if we go through our assessments, the majority of them are essays or exams and for … well no, majority are 'hypotheticals' and exams, you don't need legal research skills that much so you have all the information in your textbook pretty much" – from *Curriculum Renewal in Legal Education* (note 10 above) p. 58.

level of learning.[40] If listening and reading are the primary learning activities, and are what students are assessed on, the learning gain is not likely to be substantial. Indeed, listening and reading are very likely to encourage short-term reproductive learning habits rather than more sustainable learning. There is little in such a format that would encourage the development of deep learning, or independent and life-long learning skills.

The problem can be traced in part to the predominant teaching and learning method: the lecture (or in the Anglo–Hong Kong model, the lecture/tutorial). The lecture, as conventionally practised, is likely to encourage passive learning, discouraging interrogation and critique.[41] For this reason, practice in classroom legal education must move beyond a model that emphasizes knowledge transmission, to one that encourages knowledge discovery and creation, in order to position law students for life after graduation. Learning and assessment activities must be designed to free the learner to develop creative and independent learning habits. What is required is a more activity-based approach to curriculum design, one that engages students in learning activities that aim for a multiplicity of learning outcomes that capture the sorts of attributes that law graduates are expected to possess. Although the learning of law should not be dictated by the profession, it should nonetheless bear some resemblance to what lawyers are expected to do on entering the profession. The law curriculum must be designed so that, in addition to reading and listening, students are required to *do* things. Deep learning can take place only if students engage with the material. Engagement requires doing something.[42] Listening is not enough. And of course, students must be assessed on these activities, in order to ensure that they are motivated and learn to do them well. This requires the introduction of more task-based assessments.

Authentic Learning and Assessment

The shortfall can also be addressed through adoption of more authentic learning and assessment strategies and materials. Authentic learning and assessment has tremendous advantages over the current, dominant model of legal education. Some forms of more authentic assessment are already in use, in particular in the senior years, where take-home research essays and examinations are common, and where clinical courses and experiential learning activities, such as court visit reports and other field trips, are assigned. However, it is important that the right kind of assessment be used in the foundational year courses, to avoid encouraging

40 Fergus Craik and Robert Lockhart, "Levels of Processing: A Framework for Memory Research" (1972) 11 *Journal of Verbal Learning and Verbal Behaviour*, 671–84.

41 Margaret Thornton and Lucinda Shannon, "Selling the Dream: Law School Branding and the Illusion of Choice" (2013) 23 *Legal Education Review* 249 at 268.

42 See generally Phil Race, *Making Learning Happen: A Guide for Post-compulsory Education* (Sage, 2010).

the wrong sorts of learning habits early on or, to put it more positively, in order to use the assessment strategically, to encourage more desirable learning habits and to ensure the achievement of the desired learning outcomes.

There is a rich abundance of scholarship on authentic learning and assessment, far too much to do justice to in a short chapter.[43] It is important that both the learning activities and the assessment be authentic.[44] Some of the salient features of authentic learning and assessment can be summarized:

- Instructors design activities for their students that match as nearly as possible the real-world tasks of professionals in the field.[45]
- The tasks students undertake should be complex, ambiguous and multifaceted in nature, requiring sustained investigation.[46]
- Learning and assessment tasks should have clear goals and real-world relevance, requiring production of knowledge rather than reproduction.
- Authentic tasks generally involve learning by doing, are ill-defined and are completed over a longer period of time.
- Authentic learning focuses on real-world, complex problems and their solutions.[47]
- In authentic assessment, the cognitive demands (the thinking required) are similar to those that starting professionals might be confronted with in their working life.[48]

---

43 For a useful starting point see Anthony Herrington and Jan Herrington (eds), *Authentic Learning Environments in Higher Education* (Hershey, PA: Information Science Publishing, 2006).

44 For an introduction to authentic learning in higher education and its possible application to the social sciences, see Fiona Borthwick et al, "Applying Authentic Learning to Social Science: A Learning Design for an Inter-disciplinary Sociology Subject" (2007) 2 *Journal of Learning Design* 1. For a discussion of authentic assessment in the teaching of undergraduate law, see Caroline Hart et al., "The Real Deal: Using Authentic Assessment to Promote Student Engagement in the First and Second Years of a Regional Law Program", (2011) 21 *Legal Education Review* 97.

45 The tasks should be "engaging and worthy problems or questions of importance, in which students must use knowledge to fashion performances effectively and creatively. The tasks are either replicas of or analogous to the kinds of problems faced by adult citizens and consumers or professionals in the field": Grant Wiggins, *Assessing Student Performance* (San Francisco: Jossey-Bass, 1993), p. 229.

46 Marilyn Lombardi, "Approaches that Work: How Authentic Learning is Transforming Higher Education", Educause Learning Initiative Paper No. 5, 2007, available at http://net.educause.edu/ir/library/pdf/eli3013.pdf (accessed February 22, 2014).

47 Marilyn Lombardi, "Authentic Learning for the 21st Century", (2007) *ELI Paper 1*: 2007, available at http://net.educause.edu/ir/library/pdf/ELI3009.pdf (accessed February 22, 2014).

48 John Savery and Thomas Duffy, "Problem Based Learning: An Instructional Model and its Constructivist Framework" in Brent Gale Wilson (ed.), *Constructivist Learning Environments* (Englewood Cliffs, NJ; Educational Technology Publications, 1995).

It can be observed that the creation of authentic learning environments is likely to be more labour-intensive than in the conventional model of law teaching. This is certainly true of clinical programmes, whether live-client or simulated, as well as internships and the like. This is because an authentic learning environment requires "doing" rather than merely reading or listening, and this may very well require supervision in varying degrees. But with some imagination, authenticity can be introduced that need not be much more labour-intensive or expensive – perhaps not more expensive at all.

Authentic learning involves instructional design, and a rethinking of current teaching and learning materials. Authentic assessment should of course be aligned to authentic learning environments and activities.[49] Knowledge of doctrinal law is crucial, so we cannot do without case reading and problem-solving exercises. The examination format continues to provide a practical, not to say familiar, tool by which this can be done, one that is not too radical for professional accrediting bodies. But the challenge is to do this more authentically. This chapter concludes with a suggestion as to how that might be done in the context of final examinations.

A Proposal

Assuming the continued use of final examinations for summative assessment purposes,[50] probably unavoidable in large group classes,[51] both the content and the format of examinations must be revisited. As a first step, the teacher-invented

49 Judith TM Gulikers, Theo J Bastiaens and Paul A. Kirschner, "Defining Authentic Assessment: Five Dimensions of Authenticity", in Anton Havnes and Liz McDowell, *Balancing Dilemmas in Assessment and Learning in Contemporary Education* (New York: Routledge, 2008).

50 This chapter should not be understood as an argument in favour of their retention. Indeed, many objections can be raised to the almost universal use of timed, in-hall final examinations in law, in particular, that legal analysis and advice should be formulated carefully and with reflection, certainly not in the haste required by the conventional examination format. For those who are interested, a thorough critique of the law examination tradition has been provided – see Philip Kissam, "Law School Examinations" (1989) 42 *Vanderbilt Law Review* 433. See also Janet Motley, "A Foolish Consistency: The Law School Exam" (1985–86) 10 *Nova Law Journal* 723; and Norman Redlich and Steve Friedland, "Challenging Tradition: Using Objective Questions in Law School Examinations" (1991–92) *41 DePaul Law Review* 143. More recently, the authors of *Best Practices in Legal Education* had this to say: "the end-of-the-semester essay exam is an inadequate method for assessing student learning … [that] is neither valid, nor reliable, nor fair". See Stuckey et al. (note 3 above) at 207–63.

51 In-hall, against-the-clock final examinations have been rightly criticized for their emphasis on mere recall and reproduction, but Phil Race also offers some arguments for the retention of examinations: they can be "one of the more time-efficient and cost-effective methods of assessment, where it is fairly easy to achieve fairness and reliability, and with the added bonus that plagiarism or cheating cause less headaches to markers than in many

hypothetical narrative should be discarded as an assessment tool, no less than as a learning tool. If problem-solving is considered to be an important legal education learning outcome (an uncontroversial position this writer would support), then the problems require a new design model to achieve authenticity. Authenticity cannot be invented. Authentic sources must be identified.

One way to achieve authenticity is through the use, as assessment questions, of verbatim news reports taken from the local news media. Another way is through the use of the statement of facts of judgments taken from the local courts. The former are to be preferred because, written by non-lawyers, news reports contain more uncertainties. The statement of facts provided by a judge is obviously expertly prepared from a legal perspective. It is also important that the sources of the material be local, in order to ensure student familiarity with, and immersion in, the sorts of legally-charged events that happen in one's community.

News reports provide a particularly appropriate form of authentic learning material. The material is realistic and relevant to the community. It is readily available. Original material is constantly being generated. The material is generally complex, requiring multiple perspectives in analysis, including social policy. Social policy is something hard for a student to take seriously in the conventional, teacher-invented, improbable hypothetical exam question scenario. It is vital that law student learning not become distanced from the social and human dimension in legal disputes.[52] The material in a news report is often factually incomplete, thereby mimicking a realistic professional scenario. Its authenticity and relevance can foster a more serious approach to analysis and can help develop the habit of identifying issues in unflagged situations. The use of news reports fosters good reading habits, and an awareness of the community and social policy issues. It requires students to make connections between their learning of legal doctrine and the kinds of problems that are occurring in the world around them. There is no concern about plagiarism – the reports are original and not likely the subject of professional legal analysis available from web-based or other sources. The use of news reports requires original thinking on the part of students. News reports are not invented by the teacher, not owned by the teacher, and the teacher has no claim to the correct answer. Indeed, the problem-solving process is a shared one, teacher and students working together.

Of course, the proposal is not in any way a fully authentic assessment experience. That could only be achieved if, for instance, the students were

---

other forms of assessment" – see Phil Race, *The Lecturer's Toolkit:* (London: Routledge, 2006 (3rd edn)).

52 A concern expressed by the authors of the *Carnegie Report* in the third of its five Key Observations (see *Carnegie Report*, note 2 above). On this point Robin West has written about the danger of legal education squeezing out of law students the moral and social sensibility that motivated students to come to law school in the first place – see Robin West, *Teaching Law: Justice, Politics, and the Demands of Professionalism* (New York: Cambridge University Press, 2014) at 46.

required not only to analyse the legal issues as reported in the news story but to actually provide legal advice to at least one of the parties concerned, an obviously impractical proposition. This sort of thing could be done in a clinical setting, for instance in a live-client clinical advice course, or in an internship. But such learning environments, although more authentic, are expensive and labour-intensive, and are not practical for large groups of students. The proposal here is more modest, and less costly, while achieving a significantly increased degree of authenticity.[53] This is not an argument in support of the retention of final examinations in law, though examinations, if appropriately designed, may still have a role to play.

Ideally, such examinations should not be conducted under closed-book conditions. That is because the closed-book format does not reflect the world-of-work realities.

More controversial is whether the examination should be in-hall or take-home, and strictly timed or allow more than a few hours to complete. A practical problem here is not so much that of plagiarism of professional work or web-based material as it is the sharing of work among students. If the learning outcomes emphasize the production of individual work, the in-hall timed examination format should be retained. If not, the assessment format might benefit from a change to one that permits collaboration within a small, named group of students in a take-home examination format. This format, after all, more closely replicates the environment in post-university professional life.

There are other possible permutations of these suggestions that can be suited for a particular course and particular circumstances and learning outcomes. The key point is that whatever assessment mechanism is chosen, relevant and sustainable learning should be a key consideration, so that students are able to make connections between their academic learning and the world in which they live, and in which they are about to work. This change in orientation has the potential to produce learning gains that go far beyond those likely to be achieved in the conventional legal education model still practised around the common law world.

Conclusion

The pedagogical conventions of legal education are deeply embedded. Law teachers continue these conventions because they are familiar with them and perhaps also because they feel that their own careers were served well enough by them. Today there is growing evidence of an increased awareness that conventional teaching and learning practices may not be suited for the learning outcomes that most law teachers would agree are the goals of a modern, practical and relevant legal education. The multitude of legal education reviews demonstrates if nothing

---

53 At any rate, as David Boud says, authentic contexts "need not necessarily involve students being placed in external work settings, but involve the greater use of features of authentic contexts to frame assessment tasks". See Boud, note 29 above, p. 40.

else a recognition that conventional methods are deficient. Nonetheless, it remains a challenge to win the hearts and minds of legal educators and to persuade them to a more reflective and outcomes-oriented approach to their teaching and learning design. It is hoped that suggestions proposed in this chapter may go at least some way in taking up that challenge.

Chapter 10

The Unfulfilled Promise of Law Schools to Prepare Students for the Practice of Law: An Empirical Study Demonstrating the Effectiveness of General Law School Curriculum in Preparing Lawyers for the Practice of Law[1]

John Sonsteng[2] with Leigha Lattner,[3] Emily Parks[4] and David Camarotto[5]

Introduction

Four studies conducted over 38 years demonstrate that lawyers perceive themselves as increasingly more prepared to effectively practice law upon graduation from law school. However, two Minnesota studies – one in 1997–99 and the other in 2013 – demonstrate that law schools provide only a small portion of the preparation necessary for lawyers to practice law. Law schools do not offer a curriculum that trains law students to effectively use their law degrees for the practice in the current legal practice system, in non-law professions, or for the changing future of legal practices. Before the advent of the United States' law schools in the late 1800s, attorneys learned their trade through their own experience, often as apprentices or through work-related experience. An analysis of the sources of legal training based on the 1997–99 and 2013 Minnesota studies show that, in spite of the enormous amount of money and effort spent on formal legal education,

1 Portions of this chapter were previously published in John Sonsteng with Donna Ward et al., *A Legal Education Renaissance: A Practical Approach for the Twenty-First Century* (2008), and John Sonsteng with David Camarotto, *Minnesota Lawyers Evaluate Law Schools, Training and Job Satisfaction*, 26 *Wm. Mitchell L. Rev.* 327 (2000).

2 Professor of Law, William Mitchell College of Law, St. Paul, Minnesota, United States.

3 BA University of St. Thomas; JD William Mitchell College of Law, 2014.

4 BA Macalester College; JD candidate, William Mitchell College of Law, 2015.

5 BA St. John's University; JD William Mitchell College of Law, 2000.

two sources of a lawyer's training – a lawyer's law-related work while in law school and the lawyer's own experience – remain by far the most significant.

Following the publication of the results of the first Minnesota study in 2000,[6] along with all of the criticism of legal education and suggestions for reform,[7] we naively assumed that there would be significant change and improvement in legal education. The evidence seemed obvious, and the criticisms of legal education were substantial. The MacCrate Report in 1992 set the tone. The Carnegie Report in 2007 added support for change. However, the results of the 2013 Minnesota study demonstrate that systemic changes in the delivery of legal education have not occurred.

The study of law is becoming increasingly expensive.[8] Law graduates have substantial debt from law school and undergraduate loans.[9] The number of jobs available in law practice is decreasing and most law graduates practice in a solo practitioner or in a small firm.[10] Law schools are recruiting students from a diverse, yet shrinking pool of applicants.[11] The wide variety of learning styles possessed by this diverse group makes it difficult for professors to reach a significant proportion of law students.[12]

The legal education system has not made systemic improvement to make a legal education more relevant. That law schools are not doing what is necessary to prepare students to practice law but leaves it up to each lawyer to obtain their own training just like they always have.

From 1975 to 2013, four studies have analyzed the effectiveness of a general law school curriculum in preparing students to practice effectively in the legal profession.

---

6 See John Sonsteng with David Camarotto, Minnesota Lawyers Evaluate Law Schools, Training and Job Satisfaction, 26 *Wm. Mitchell L. Rev.* 327 (2000).

7 See, e.g., John Sonsteng with Donna Ward et al., *A Legal Education Renaissance: A Practical Approach for the Twenty-First Century* (2008).

8 Tuition Three Times Faster than Inflation, but Some Schools Buck the Trend, *Nat'l Jurist* (February 22, 2012), http://www.nationaljurist.com/content/tuition-three-times-faster-inflation-some-schools-buck-trend (last visited August 20, 2015).

9 Which Law School Graduates Have the Most Debt?, *US News & World Rep.* (March 22, 2012), http://www.usnews.com/education/best-graduate-schools/the-short-list-grad-school/articles/2012/03/22/10-law-schools-that-lead-to-the-most-debt (accessed May 21, 2014).

10 Why Attending Law School is the Worst Career Decision You'll Ever Make, *Forbes* (June 26, 2012), http://www.forbes.com/sites/jmaureenhenderson/2012/06/26/why-attending-law-school-is-the-worst-career-decision-youll-ever-make (last visited August 20, 2015).

11 See, e.g., *Statistics*, ABA, http://www.americanbar.org/groups/legal_education/resources/statistics.html (accessed May 21, 2014).

12 Harold Pashler et al., Learning Styles: Concepts and Evidence, 9 *Psychol. Sci. Pub. Int.* 105, 105 (2008).

1975–76: Zemans and Rosenblum

Frances Kahn Zemans and Victor G. Rosenblum conducted a study from 1975 to 1976 on the legal profession that was published in 1981 by the American Bar Foundation.[13] Zemans and Rosenblum sought a better understanding of how law school education affects the professional development of lawyers.[14] The survey asked lawyers about the relative importance of selected skills and areas of knowledge important to the practice of law;[15] the law school's contribution to these skills and areas of knowledge, showing how prepared the lawyers were after law school;[16] and the effectiveness of teaching the skills and areas of knowledge in law school.[17] The importance score was the mean response on a five-point scale, with one being the most important and five of the lowest importance.[18]

1991–92: Garth and Martin

Fifteen years later, from 1991 to 1992, Bryant G. Garth and Joanne Martin conducted a series of four surveys.[19] First, Garth and Martin sought to compare their survey to the earlier Zemans and Rosenblum survey and to measure any of the changes that had occurred since the late 1970s.[20] Thus, this study repeated portions of the Zemans and Rosenblum study to survey many of the same skills.[21]

---

13 See Frances Kahn Zemans and Victor G. Rosenblum, *The Making of a Public Profession* (1981).

14 *Id.* at xiii.

15 The 1975–76 Zemans and Rosenblum study surveyed the "importance" of lawyering skills, similar to the skills in both the survey of Minnesota lawyers and the 1991–92 Garth and Martin survey, including: ability to understand and interpret opinions, regulations, and statutes; drafting legal documents; knowledge of substantive law; legal research; fact gathering; effective oral expression; letter writing; instilling others' confidence in you; negotiating; and knowledge of procedural law. Each score of "importance" was based on the mean of the responses. The responses rated each skill on a five-point scale; one for highest importance to five for lowest importance. See *id.* at 123–28.

16 See *id.* at 135–50.

17 See *id.* at 140–50.

18 See *id.* at 125 tbl. 6.1.

19 The Garth and Martin study consisted of four surveys and sample groups. See Bryant G. Garth and Joanne Martin, Law Schools and the Construction of Competence, 43 *J. Legal Educ.* 469, 471–72 (1993). The first survey, which was conducted by telephone, targeted hiring partners in all firms in Chicago that had a minimum of five partners. *Id.* at 471. The second survey was aimed at practising lawyers in Chicago who had been admitted to the bar between 1986 and 1991; the "young Chicago lawyers". *Id.* Surveys were mailed to a random sample of 1,500 attorneys and over 50 per cent of the attorneys responded. *Id.* The final two surveys were outside the large urban context and were sent to two samples in Missouri. *Id.* at 472. These two surveys were similar to the survey of the "young Chicago lawyers". *Id.*

20 *Id.* at 471.

21 *Id.*

The survey of "young Chicago lawyers"[22] by Garth and Martin asked the lawyers to rank the "importance" of 17 legal skills and areas of knowledge.[23] The Garth and Martin survey, like the Zemans and Rosenblum survey, was based on a five-point scale with one being "extremely important" and five being "not important at all".[24] Second, Garth and Martin sought to update the list of surveyed legal skills by including parts of the MacCrate Report list.[25] Third, Garth and Martin sought to probe the lawyers about their ability to obtain and keep clients.[26]

1997–99 and 2013: Minnesota Studies – Sonsteng

In 1997–99 and 2013, the Minnesota Studies undertook to determine to what extent law schools provided Minnesota lawyers consistent training in important legal practice and law practice management skill areas.[27] The legal practice skills surveyed are the same 17 that were used in the Garth and Martin survey,[28] which Garth and Martin had expanded upon from the MacCrate Report.[29] The list of practice management skills was taken from the *Lawyer's Handbook*.[30]

Minnesota lawyers were surveyed between October 17, 1997 and August 12, 1998 and again between August 10, 1999 and September 30, 1999.[31] The most recent survey was conducted between May 29, 2013 and August 9, 2013.[32]

22 "Young Chicago lawyers" was defined as lawyers who were admitted to the bar between 1986 and 1991. *Id.* at 471; see also *id.* at 473 tbl. 1.

23 See *id.* at 473 tbl.1. These same skills were used in the Minnesota studies.

24 *Id.* at 472.

25 See *id.* at 471.

26 See *id.*

27 See *infra* Appendix C (survey instrument).

28 See American Bar Association Legal Education and Professional Development – an Educational Continuum: Report of the Task Force on Law Schools and the Profession: Narrowing the Gap 138–40 (1992) [hereinafter MacCrate Report].

29 See *id.* at 138–40.

30 See generally Austin G. Anderson et. al. (eds), *The Lawyer's Handbook: How to Effectively, Efficiently and Profitably Manage Your Law Firm* (3rd edn 1992) [hereinafter *The Lawyer's Handbook*].

31 Of the 726 Minnesota attorneys in the 1999 survey, 288 respondents (39.7%) attended William Mitchell College of Law, 165 respondents (22.7%) attended the University of Minnesota Law School, 96 respondents attended Hamline University College of Law (13.2%), and 177 respondents (24.4%) attended other law schools. Of the 1,042 respondents who completed the 1997–98 survey, 354 (41.4%) graduated from William Mitchell, 264 (30.9%) graduated from the University of Minnesota, and 50 (5.9%) graduated from Hamline University and the remainder attended law schools throughout the country.

32 Of the 1,108 Minnesota attorneys who responded to the 2013 survey, 503 respondents (45.4%) attended William Mitchell, 131 respondents (11.8%) attended the University of Minnesota, 166 respondents attended Hamline University (15.0%), 83 respondents (7.5%) attended University of Saint Thomas Law School, and 190 respondents (17.1%) attended law schools outside of Minnesota. Thirty-five respondents (3.2%) did not respond.

The Minnesota survey instrument was designed to study how well prepared Minnesota lawyers felt after law school in 17 legal practice skills and nine management skills.[33] The lawyers were also asked to what extent Minnesota lawyers perceived those skills to be important and from what sources they received those skills.[34]

The 1992 MacCrate Report[35] identified 10 fundamental lawyering skills:

1. problem solving;
2. legal analysis and reasoning;
3. legal research;
4. factual investigation;
5. communication;
6. counseling;
7. negotiation;
8. litigation and alternative dispute resolution procedures;
9. organization and management of legal work;
10. recognizing and resolving ethical dilemmas.[36]

The Minnesota studies follow the Garth and Martin surveys, which expanded the number of lawyering skills set out in the MacCrate Report and surveyed the following 17 areas:

1. ability to diagnose and plan solutions for legal problems;
2. ability in legal analysis and reasoning;
3. knowledge of substantive law;
4. knowledge of procedural law;
5. library legal research;
6. computer legal research;
7. factual gathering;
8. oral communication;

---

607 respondents (54.8%) were women, 501 respondents (45.2%) were men.

The 2013 survey was sent to Minnesota attorneys who passed the Minnesota bar in the past 10 years. 96 respondents (8.7%) were admitted in 2012, 100 respondents (9.0%) in 2011, 118 respondents (10.6%) in 2010, 110 respondents (9.9%) in 2009, 120 respondents (10.8%) in 2008, 129 respondents (11.6%) in 2007, 111 respondents (10%) in 2006, 87 respondents (7.9%) in 2006, 87 respondents (7.9%) in 2005, 95 respondents (8.6%) in 2004, 94 respondents (8.5%) in 2003, 9 respondents (.8%) in 2002, 3 respondents (.3%) in 2001, 4 respondents (0.4%) in 2000, 20 respondents (1.8%) from earlier than 2000, and 11 respondents (1%) did not enter a legible response.

33 See *infra* Appendix C (survey instrument).

34 There were no significant differences among the law schools identified in the two Minnesota surveys.

35 See MacCrate Report, *supra* note 28.

36 *Id.* at 138–40.

9. written communication;
10. counseling;
11. instilling others' confidence in you;
12. ability to obtain and keep clients;
13. negotiation;
14. understanding and conducting litigation;
15. organization and management of legal work;
16. sensitivity to professional ethical concerns;
17. drafting legal documents.[37]

All surveys from 1975–2013 asked the respondents:

1. to rank the importance of each legal practice skill;
2. to rank the extent they perceived they were prepared for the practice of law in each legal skill.[38]

The 1997–99, and 2013 Minnesota studies also asked respondents:

1. Which of the practice skills could be learned in law school?
2. What was the source of training in each of the skills?

The 1997–99 and 2013 Minnesota studies analyzed nine additional law practice management skills:

1. fee arrangements, pricing, billing;
2. human resources, hiring, support staff;
3. capitalization, investment;
4. project and time management, efficiency;
5. planning, resource allocation, budgeting;
6. market, client development;
7. technology, computers, communications;
8. governance, decision-making, long-range strategic planning;
9. interpersonal communications, staff relations.[39]

Respondents were asked to rank the importance and their perceptions of preparedness for each management skill, as well as whether they believed those

37 See Garth and Martin, *supra* note 19, at 472–73. Garth and Martin surveyed practicing lawyers in Chicago, Illinois. See *id.* at 471. The sample of the survey consisted of all firms in Chicago that had a minimum of five partners. *Id.*

38 None of the surveys asked participants to respond to the question: "To what extent did your legal education prepare you to use your law degree in non-law-related fields?"

39 See generally *The Lawyer's Handbook*, *supra* note 30 (providing additional information on the relevant management skills).

skills could be learned in law school. Respondents were asked to name their top three sources of training for each legal practice skill and each management skill.

Survey participants were asked to rank the three main sources of their training from a list of 15 sources.

Summary Findings[40]

The survey results demonstrate gaps in legal education and why law schools should revise their missions, curriculum, and teaching and learning methods to meet the needs of the law school and the profession to provide sufficient training and learning opportunities and become relevant for the present and future.

1. The 2013 respondents perceived themselves to be better prepared than earlier respondents in legal practice skills[41] and in law practice management skills[42] than the respondents in the earlier survey.
2. Nearly all of the legal practice and law practice management skills were perceived as important.[43]
3. The legal practice and law practice management skills could be learned in law school.[44]
4. Only five sources of training in the legal practice skills and were ranked as one of the top three sources of training in both the 1997–99 and 2013 surveys. For both legal practice skills and law practice management skills, respondents were asked to choose the top three sources of their training from the following list of 15 sources:

Top Five Sources

- General law school curriculum;
- law-related work experience in summers or during academic year;
- own experience;
- observation of other lawyers;
- advice from other lawyers.

Other Sources

- Moot court/other competitions;
- continuing legal education courses;

---

40 The summary findings are based on an analysis of the tables found in Appendix A.

41 See *infra* Tables 10.2, 10.4.

42 See *infra* Tables 10.6, 10.8.

43 See *infra* Tables 10.1, 10.3, 10.5, 10.8.

44 See *infra* Tables 10.3, 10.4, 10.7, 10.8.

- training by another school;
- legal practice simulations in law school;
- law review experience;
- client contacts through law school clinics;
- observation of non-lawyers;
- advice from non-lawyers;
- training by product or service vendors;
- other.[45]

1. The same sources were named as the "top five" sources of legal practice and law practice management skills in the 1997–99 and 2013 survey.[46]
2. Law school legal practice simulations and law school clinics play a small but increasing role in legal education.[47]
3. All 17 legal practice skills and all nine law practice management skills were perceived by attorneys as important to their practice of the law and a significant number of attorneys believe these subjects could be taught successfully in law school.[48]

Legal Practice Skills

Importance of Legal Practice Skills

Minnesota attorneys were asked to rate the importance of the legal practice skills on a scale of one (not at all important) to seven (very important). A skill was considered "important" if it received a score of five, six, or seven.[49] More than 69 per cent of the respondents perceive the 17 legal practice skills as important to the practice of law. However, in the 2013 survey only 28.5 per cent of the respondents perceived library legal research to be important.

45 See *infra* Tables 10.10A–Q.

46 See *infra* Tables 10.12A–I.

47 See *infra* Tables 10.10A–Q, 10.12A–I.

48 See *infra* Tables 10.3, 10.4, 10.7, 10.8.

49 For the purposes of this comparison, the "percentage important" includes the responses of "extremely important" and "important", i.e., the responses of one and two on a five-point scale of importance for the Zemans and Rosenblum study and the Garth and Martin survey. The "percentage important" in the survey of Minnesota lawyers consisted of the rankings of five through seven, the rankings of "important" to "very important".

Table 10.1 Legal practice skills: changes in perceptions of importance over time

Legal Practice Skills	*Zemans–Rosenblum 1975–76*[1]	*Garth–Martin 1986–91*[2]	*Minnesota Lawyers 1997–99*	*Minnesota Lawyers 2013*
Ability to diagnose and plan for legal problems	*	81.5	97.9	96.1
Ability in legal analysis and legal reasoning	86.6	90.9	97.5	96.8
Written communication	*	96.3	97.2	97.4
Oral communication	87.4	97.6	96.8	96.0
Instilling others' confidence in you	88.6	90.5	92.0	89.0
Negotiation	78.9	73.4	90.0	86.2
Sensitivity to professional and ethical concerns	*	68.9	86.4	85.4
Fact gathering	93.0	71.6	85.9	86.6
Drafting legal documents	74.2	84.9	85.8	91.0
Organization and management of legal work	*	75.4	85.0	85.2
Counseling	*	62.0	82.6	86.4
Ability to obtain and keep clients	*	54.0	80.2	80.4
Knowledge of procedural law	62.9	67.8	79.6	80.2
Knowledge of the substantive law	90.1	83.0	79.1	79.4
Computer legal research	*	34.9	76.6	87.1
Library legal research	80.6	59.8	69.1	28.5
Understanding and conducting litigation	*	62.2	69.0	71.5

Notes: [1]See Zemans and Rosenblum, supra note 13, at 125 tbl. 6.1. Legal skills not specifically surveyed by the 1975–76 Zemans-Rosenblum study are noted by a *. [2]See Garth and Martin, supra note 19, at 473 tbl. 1.

Perception of Preparedness in Legal Practice Skills

The 1975–76 Zemans and Rosenblum study asked respondents whether they learned specific lawyering skills and areas of knowledge.[50] The responses were tallied in a "Yes" or "No" format.[51] The 1991–92 survey of young Chicago lawyers by Garth and Martin also asked their respondent lawyers the same question, whether the 17 skills or areas of knowledge were "learned essentially through law school",[52] in the same format. The Minnesota surveys asked the same question, asking "how prepared" the lawyer was immediately after law school.[53]

A comparison of all the 1975–2013 surveys demonstrates the changes in how prepared lawyers perceived themselves to be in the 17 legal practice skills immediately after law school.

In both the 1999 and 2013 Minnesota studies, attorneys were asked to rate on a scale of one to seven how well they thought law school prepared them in that skill. As Table 10.4 shows, most of the 1999 and 2013 survey respondents felt most prepared immediately after law school for "legal analysis and legal reasoning" (1999: 85 per cent, 2013: 84.3 per cent). Respondents perceived themselves to be least prepared immediately after law school for the "ability to obtain and keep clients" (1999: 13.2 per cent, 2013: 10 per cent). In nine of the 17 legal practice skills, less than 50 per cent of 1999 and 2013 survey respondents felt that they were well prepared immediately after law school.

50 See Zemans and Rosenblum, *supra* note 13, at 135–50.

51 See *id.* at 222 app. 1.

52 See Garth and Martin, *supra* note 19, at 479 tbl. 4.

53 For the purposes of this analysis, the percentage of "Yes's" from the Zemans and Rosenblum and the Garth and Martin surveys were compared to the rankings of five through seven in the study of Minnesota lawyers ("prepared" to "very well prepared").

Table 10.2 Legal practice skills: changes in perceptions of preparedness over time

Legal Practice Skills	*Zemans–Rosenblum 1975–76*	*Garth–Martin 1986–91*	*Minnesota Lawyers 1997–99*	*Minnesota Lawyers 2013*
Ability to diagnose and plan for legal problems	*	33.0	54.9	58.3
Ability in legal analysis and legal reasoning	77.0	71.0	85.0	84.3
Drafting legal documents	11.0	18.0	33.2	45.0
Knowledge of the substantive law	79.0	81.0	61.9	57.1
Library legal research	75.0	83.0	83.7	59.1
Computer legal research	*	66.0	76.0	81.7
Fact gathering	16.0	10.0	37.5	49.8
Oral communication	15.0	6.0	69.3	72.7
Written communication	*	27.0	81.1	78.6
Counseling	*	1.0	28.6	39.1
Instilling others' confidence in you	4.0	4.0	37.7	42.0
Negotiation	2.0	9.0	29.9	43.6
Knowledge of procedural law	50.0	53.0	49.0	45.6
Understanding and conducting litigation	*	11.0	25.7	28.7
Organization and management of legal work	*	4.0	20.5	30.7
Ability to obtain and keep clients	*	2.0	13.2	10.0
Sensitivity to professional and ethical concerns	*	74.0	68.2	50.0

Whether Legal Practice Skills Can Be Learned in Law School

Minnesota lawyers were asked whether they believed the identified legal skills could be learned in law school. Respondents answered "Yes" or "No".

In both the 1999 and 2013 studies, respondents believed that a majority of the legal practice skills could be learned in law school. Of the respondents, 70 per cent or more of believed that 14 of the 17 legal practice skills could be learned in law school. The three skills that less than 70 per cent of respondents believed could be learned in law school were:

- instilling others' confidence in you (1999: 54.7 per cent, 2013: 35 per cent);
- organization and management of legal work (1999: 65.1 per cent, 2013: 58.7 per cent);
- ability to obtain and keep clients.

Table 10.3 Legal practice skills: importance, preparedness and ability to learn in law school

Legal Practice Skills	**Percent Perceiving:**					
	Importance		*Preparedness*		*Skill can be learned in law school*	
	1997	**2013**	**1997**	**2013**	**1997**	**2013**
Ability to diagnose and plan solutions for legal problems	97.9	96.1	54.9	58.3	90.5	90.7
Ability in legal analysis and legal reasoning	97.9	96.8	85.0	84.3	97.7	99.4
Written communication	97.2	97.4	81.1	78.6	95.0	96.4
Oral communication	96.8	96.0	69.3	72.7	85.6	88.9
Instilling others' confidence in you	92.0	89.0	37.7	54.7	35.0	54.7
Negotiation	90.0	86.2	29.9	43.6	85.2	86.8
Sensitivity to professional and ethical concerns	86.4	85.4	68.2	50.0	95.9	95.8
Fact gathering	85.9	86.6	37.5	49.8	78.7	80.9
Drafting legal documents	85.8	91.0	33.2	45.0	94.1	96.2
Organization and management of legal work	85.0	85.2	20.5	30.7	58.7	65.7
Counseling	82.5	86.4	28.6	39.1	70.0	74.7
Ability to obtain and keep clients	80.2	80.4	13.2	10.0	32.7	47.4
Knowledge of procedural law	79.6	80.2	49.0	45.5	97.5	96.4
Knowledge of substantive law	79.1	79.4	61.9	51.7	95.3	95.2
Computer legal research	76.6	87.1	76.0	81.7	99.7	99.6
Library legal research	69.1	29.5	83.7	59.1	100	99.3
Understanding and conducting litigation	69.0	71.5	25.7	28.7	81.4	81.1

Table 10.4 Legal practice skills: whether skills can be learned in school

Legal Practice Skills	Skill can be learned in law school	
	1997–99	2013
Ability to diagnose and plan solutions for legal problems	90.5	90.7
Ability in legal analysis and legal reasoning	97.7	99.4
Written communication	95.0	96.4
Oral communication	85.6	88.9
Instilling others' confidence in you	35.0	54.7
Negotiation	85.2	86.8
Sensitivity to professional and ethical concerns	95.9	95.8
Fact gathering	78.7	80.9
Drafting legal documents	94.1	96.2
Organization and management of legal work	58.7	68.7
Counseling	70.0	74.7
Ability to obtain and keep clients	32.7	47.4
Knowledge of procedural law	97.5	96.4
Knowledge of the substantive law	95.3	95.2
Computer legal research	99.7	99.6
Library legal research	100	99.3
Understanding and conducting litigation	81.3	81.9

Importance of Law Practice Management Skills

The 1997–99 and 2013 surveys of Minnesota attorneys in practice 10 years or less also asked about respondents' perceptions of the importance to their practice of a number of management skills. The management skills were:

1. project and time management, efficiency;
2. interpersonal communications, staff relations;
3. technology, computers, communications;
4. market, client development;
5. governance, decision-making, long-range strategic planning;
6. planning, resource allocation, budgeting;
7. fee arrangements, pricing, billing;
8. human resources, hiring, support staff;
9. capitalization, investment.[54]

54 See generally *The Lawyer's Handbook, supra* note 30 (providing additional information on the relevant management skills).

Table 10.5 Law practice management skills: importance

Law Practice Management Skills	Importance	
	1997–99	2013
Project and time management, efficiency	91.9	91.0
Interpersonal communications, staff relations	91.6	81.5
Technology, computers, communications	81.9	80.4
Marketing, client development	69.7	67.9
Governance, decision-making, long-range strategic planning	61.9	62.7
Planning, resource allocation, budgeting	61.2	67.5
Fee arrangements, pricing, billing	59.2	64.0
Human resources, hiring, support staff	57.8	49.0
Capitalization, investment	29.9	32.7

Perceptions of Preparedness in Law Practice Management Skills

Respondents were asked how well prepared they perceived themselves to be upon graduation from law school to practice management skills.

Table 10.6 Law practice management skills: perceived preparedness

Law Practice Management Skills	Preparedness	
	1997–99	2013
Project and time management, efficiency	31.9	40.3
Interpersonal communications, staff relations	42.1	39.6
Technology, computers, communications	50.3	53.4
Marketing, client development	7.9	10.2
Governance, decision-making, long-range strategic planning	13.3	13.4
Planning, resource allocation, budgeting	12.8	13.7
Fee arrangements, pricing, billing	6.3	9.0
Human resources, hiring, support staff	10.2	8.9
Capitalization, investment	3.1	4.0

Whether Law Practice Management Skills Can Be Learned in Law School

Table 10.7 Law practice management skills: whether skills can be learned in schools

Law Practice Management Skills	This skill can be learned in law school	
	1997–99	2013
Project and time management, efficiency	77.3	81.8
Interpersonal communications, staff relations	51.9	58.6
Technology, computers, communications	94.0	88.2
Marketing, client development	67.7	72.1
Governance, decision-making, long-range strategic planning	57.5	62.2
Planning, resource allocation, budgeting	64.6	70.4
Fee arrangements, pricing, billing	73.0	76.0
Human resources, hiring, support staff	49.0	54.7
Capitalization, investment	53.7	56.7

Table 10.8 Law practice management skills: importance, preparedness and ability to learn in law school

Law Practice Management Skills	Percent Perceiving					
	Importance		*Preparedness*		*Skill can be learned in law school*	
	1997–99	2013	1997–99	2013	1997–99	2013
Project and time management, efficiency	91.1	91.9	31.9	40.3	77.3	81.8
Interpersonal communications, staff relations	91.6	81.5	42.1	39.6	51.9	58.6
Technology, computers, communications	81.9	80.4	50.3	52.4	94.0	88.2
Marketing, client development	69.7	67.9	7.9	10.2	67.7	72.1
Governance, decision-making, long-range strategic planning	61.9	62.7	13.3	13.4	57.5	62.2
Planning, resource allocation, budgeting	61.2	67.5	12.8	13.7	64.6	70.4
Fee arrangements, pricing, billing	59.2	64.0	6.3	9.0	73.0	76.0
Human resources, hiring, support staff	57.8	49.0	10.2	8.9	49.0	54.7
Capitalization, investment	29.9	32.7	3.1	4.0	53.7	56.7

Summary of the Sources of Legal Practice Skills Training

In the 1997–99 and 2013 Minnesota surveys, attorneys were asked to select up to three sources that most led to their development in each of the 17 legal practice skills.[55] The goal of these surveys was to determine the extent to which law schools provided training in these skill areas, and to what extent lawyers received their training from other sources.[56]

Table 10.9 Rank of sources for legal practice skills training

Source of Training	Rank		
	First	*Second*	*Third*
Law school curriculum	6 times	1 time	4 times
Own experience	6 times	2 times	7 times
Law-related work while in school	3 times	6 times	2 times
Observing other lawyers	1 time	5 times	3 times
Advice from others	1 time	2 times	

Legal Practice Skills:
Identified Sources of Legal Practice Skills Training of Minnesota Lawyers[57]

In the 1997–99 and 2013 Minnesota surveys, attorneys were asked to identify the three most important sources of training for each of the 17 legal practice skills.[58] The following tables identify the top three sources of training for each skill, along with the percentage of survey participants who selected them. The tables also include selection percentages for the five law school-specific sources of training: law school curriculum, legal practice simulations, law school clinics, law review, and moot court/competitions.

55 See *infra* Appendix A.
56 See *supra* text accompanying note 45 for a full list of the 15 sources of training.
57 See *infra* Appendix A for complete tables.
58 See *supra* text accompanying note 37.

Table 10.10a Ability to diagnose and plan for legal problems

Top Three			
1997–99	*%*	*2013*	*%*
1. Law-related work experience	53.5	1. Law-related work experience	63.7
2. Own experience	52.2	2. Own experience	46.0
3. Law school curriculum	51.2	3. Law school curriculum	44.3
Law School-Related Sources of Training			
1997–99	*%*	*2013*	*%*
Law school curriculum	51.2	Law school curriculum	44.3
Legal practice simulations	20.2	Legal practice simulations	26.6
Law school clinics	8.5	Law school clinics	16.9
Law review	1.0	Law review	1.0
Moot court/competitions	9.8	Moot court/competitions	7.7

Table 10.10b Ability in legal analysis and legal reasoning

Top Three			
1997–99	*%*	*2013*	*%*
1. Law school curriculum	88.2	1. Law school curriculum	88.3
2. Law-related work experience	54.0	2. Law-related work experience	57.5
3. Own experience	38.3	3. Own experience	30.2
Law School-Related Sources of Training			
1997–99	*%*	*2013*	*%*
Law school curriculum	88.2	Law school curriculum	88.3
Legal practice simulations	14.5	Legal practice simulations	20.4
Law school clinics	3.8	Law school clinics	8.2
Law review	9.4	Law review	9.3
Moot court/competitions	17.6	Moot court/competitions	16.5

Table 10.10c Drafting legal documents

Top Three			
1997–99	%	*2013*	%
1. Law-related work experience	59.8	1. Law-related work experience	60.3
2. Own experience	41.0	2. Law school curriculum	43.5
3. Law school curriculum	39.4	3. Own experience	36.7
Law School-Related Sources of Training			
1997–99	%	*2013*	%
Law school curriculum	39.4	Law school curriculum	43.5
Legal practice simulations	18.5	Legal practice simulations	24.6
Law school clinics	5.4	Law school clinics	8.7
Law review	4.0	Law review	3.9
Moot court/competitions	9.5	Moot court/competitions	12.0

Table 10.10d Knowledge of the substantive law

Top Three			
1997–99	%	*2013*	%
1. Law school curriculum	91.8	1. Law school curriculum	84.7
2. Law-related work experience	51.5	2. Law-related work experience	52.4
3. Own experience	35.1	3. Own experience	33.2
Law School-Related Sources of Training			
2013	%	*1997–99*	%
Law school curriculum	84.7	Law school curriculum	91.8
Legal practice simulations	9.2	Legal practice simulations	5.3
Law school clinics	5.9	Law school clinics	2.9
Law review	4.0	Law review	4.6
Moot court/competitions	5.2	Moot court/competitions	7.3

Table 10.10e Library legal research

Top Three			
1997–99	%	*2013*	%
1. Law school curriculum	93.7	1. Law school curriculum	93.4
2. Law-related work experience	52.1	2. Law-related work experience	22.2
3. Own experience	34.4	3. Own experience	20.2
Law School-Related Sources of Training			
1997–99	%	*2013*	%
Law school curriculum	93.7	Law school curriculum	93.4
Legal practice simulations	8.5	Legal practice simulations	13.8
Law school clinics	1.2	Law school clinics	0.5
Law review	16.5	Law review	17.9
Moot court/competitions	15.4	Moot court/competitions	9.0

Table 10.10f Computer legal research

Top Three			
1997–99	%	*2013*	%
1. Law school curriculum	84.4	1. Law school curriculum	84.6
2. Law-related work	43.6	2. Law-related work	45.0
3. Own experience	40.4	3. Own experience	36.3
Law School-Related Sources of Training			
1997–99	%	*2013*	%
Law school curriculum	84.4	Law school curriculum	84.6
Legal practice simulations	6.6	Legal practice simulations	11.4
Law school clinics	0.8	Law school clinics	1.3
Law review	15.3	Law review	17.4
Moot court/competitions	10.8	Moot court/competitions	11.1

Table 10.10g Fact gathering

Top Three			
1997–99	%	*2013*	%
1. Own experience	63.0	1. Own experience	55.7
2. Law-related work experience	44.6	2. Law-related work experience	53.2
3. Observe other lawyers	34.7	3. Observe other lawyers	36.3
Law School-Related Sources of Training			
1997–99	%	*2013*	%
Law school curriculum	25.9	Law school curriculum	28.2
Legal practice simulations	12.9	Legal practice simulations	15.8
Law school clinics	8.8	Law school clinics	15.4
Law review	2.0	Law review	0.7
Moot court/competitions	5.3	Moot court/competitions	6.6

Table 10.10h Oral communication

Top Three			
1997–99	%	*2013*	%
1. Own experience	69.7	1. Own experience	58.8
2. Law school curriculum	36.9	2. Observe other lawyers	39.3
3. Observe other lawyers	32.7	3. Law school curriculum	34.2
Law School-Related Sources of Training			
1997–99	%	*2013*	%
Law school curriculum	36.9	Law school curriculum	34.2
Legal practice simulations	17.3	Legal practice simulations	25.3
Law school clinics	4.9	Law school clinics	12.6
Law review	1.2	Law review	0.8
Moot court/competitions	25.6	Moot court/competitions	27.8

Table 10.10i Written communication

Top Three			
1997–99	%	*2013*	%
1. Law school curriculum	65.8	1. Law school curriculum	66.0
2. Own experience	56.9	2. Law-related work experience	49.4
3. Law-related work experience	42.9	3. Own experience	44.5
Law School-Related Sources of Training			
1997–99	%	*2013*	%
Law school curriculum	65.8	Law school curriculum	66.0
Legal practice simulations	9.8	Legal practice simulations	19.9
Law school clinics	3.3	Law school clinics	7.1
Law review	14.6	Law review	14.4
Moot court/competitions	17.2	Moot court/competitions	16.6

Table 10.10j Counseling

Top Three			
1997–99	%	*2013*	%
1. Own experience	63.1	1. Own experience	52.8
2. Observe other lawyers	46.6	2. Observe other lawyers	49.6
3. Advice from other lawyers	31.6	3. Law-related work experience	36.0
Law School-Related Sources of Training			
1997–99	%	*2013*	%
Law school curriculum	17.2	Law school curriculum	19.7
Legal practice simulations	13.2	Legal practice simulations	16.6
Law school clinics	10.0	Law school clinics	19.5
Law review	0.8	Law review	0.1
Moot court/competitions	3.9	Moot court/competitions	2.9

Table 10.10k Instilling others' confidence in you

Top Three			
1997–99	%	*2013*	%
1. Own experience	80.4	1. Own experience	69.7
2. Observe other lawyers	40.1	2. Observe other lawyers	43.4
3. Advice from other lawyers	27.4	3. Advice from other lawyers	33.9
Law School-Related Sources of Training			
1997–99	%	*2013*	%
Law school curriculum	7.8	Law school curriculum	6.8
Legal practice simulations	4.3	Legal practice simulations	7.5
Law school clinics	6.1	Law school clinics	13.4
Law review	2.0	Law review	1.4
Moot court/competitions	2.7	Moot court/competitions	4.5

Table 10.10l Negotiation

Top Three			
1997–99	%	*2013*	%
1. Own experience	65.5	1. Own experience	50.5
2. Observe other lawyers	47.6	2. Observe other lawyers	45.6
3. Advice from other lawyers	28.5	3. Law school curriculum	34.4
Law School-Related Sources of Training			
1997–99	%	*2013*	%
Law school curriculum	26.3	Law school curriculum	34.4
Legal practice simulations	15.7	Legal practice simulations	24.0
Law school clinics	4.9	Law school clinics	6.8
Law review	0.8	Law review	0.0
Moot court/competitions	4.5	Moot court/competitions	6.1

Table 10.10m Knowledge of procedural law

Top Three			
1997–99	*%*	*2013*	*%*
1. Law school curriculum	82.5	1. Law school curriculum	78.1
2. Law-related work experience	44.9	2. Law-related work experience	50.5
3. Own experience	36.6	3. Own experience	32.6
Law School-Related Sources of Training			
1997–99	*%*	*2013*	*%*
Law school curriculum	82.5	Law school curriculum	78.1
Legal practice simulations	8.6	Legal practice simulations	14.1
Law school clinics	3.8	Law school clinics	6.9
Law review	1.2	Law review	0.5
Moot court/competitions	5.5	Moot court/competitions	5.8

Table 10.10n Understanding and conducting litigation

Top Three			
1997–99	*%*	*2013*	*%*
1. Law-related work experience	44.2	1. Law-related work experience	47.1
2. Observe other lawyers	43.7	2. Observe other lawyers	44.7
3. Law school curriculum	39.8	3. Law school curriculum	36.1
Law School-Related Sources of Training			
1997–99	*%*	*2013*	*%*
Law school curriculum	39.8	Law school curriculum	36.1
Legal practice simulations	18.6	Legal practice simulations	23.2
Law school clinics	4.9	Law school clinics	7.6
Law review	0.5	Law review	0.0
Moot court/competitions	6.1	Moot court/competitions	7.6

Table 10.10o Organization and management of legal work

Top Three			
1997–99	%	*2013*	%
1. Own experience	63.1	1. Own experience	60.2
2. Observe other lawyers	46.1	2. Law-related work experience	46.0
3. Advice from other lawyers	41.2	3. Observe other lawyers	45.5
Law School-Related Sources of Training			
1997–99	%	*2013*	%
Law school curriculum	11.1	Law school curriculum	12.1
Legal practice simulations	7.4	Legal practice simulations	9.3
Law school clinics	5.3	Law school clinics	8.5
Law review	0.7	Law review	1.2
Moot court/competitions	2.0	Moot court/competitions	1.4

Table 10.10p Ability to obtain and keep clients

Top Three			
1997–99	%	*2013*	%
1. Own experience	60.3	1. Observe other lawyers	55.7
2. Observe other lawyers	55.7	2. Advice from other lawyers	55.1
3. Advice from other lawyers	50.9	3. Own experience	53.9
Law School-Related Sources of Training			
1997–99	%	*2013*	%
Law school curriculum	6.1	Law school curriculum	3.9
Legal practice simulations	3.2	Legal practice simulations	3.2
Law school clinics	3.9	Law school clinics	5.8
Law review	0.4	Law review	0.0
Moot court/competitions	0.0	Moot court/competitions	0.0

Table 10.10q Sensitivity to professional ethical concerns

Top Three			
1997–99	*%*	*2013*	*%*
1. Law school curriculum	84.5	1. Law school curriculum	86.8
2. Own experience	39.0	2. Advice from other lawyers	34.2
3. Advice from other lawyers	31.0	3. Own experience	32.2
Law School-Related Sources of Training			
1997–99	*%*	*2013*	*%*
Law school curriculum	84.5	Law school curriculum	86.8
Legal practice simulations	4.1	Legal practice simulations	6.1
Law school clinics	1.1	Law school clinics	4.9
Law review	0.6	Law review	0.5
Moot court/competitions	1.4	Moot court/competitions	0.8

Summary of the Sources of Law Practice Management Skills

The 1997–99 and 2013 Minnesota surveys asked the respondents to identify up to three sources that most led to their development of each of the 14 law practice management skills. The goal of the surveys was to determine the extent to which law schools provided training in these skill areas and the extent to which lawyers received their training from other sources. Only five out of 15 sources were identified as sources of training.[59]

Table 10.11 Rank of sources for law practice management training

Source of Training	**Rank**		
	First	*Second*	*Third*
Law school curriculum	–	1 time	–
Own experience	8 times	1 time	–
Law-related work while in school	–	–	2 times
Observing other lawyers	–	2 times	5 times
Advice from others	1 time	times	2 times

59 See *supra* text accompanying note 45 for a full list of the 15 sources of training.

Law Practice Management Skills: Identified Sources of Law Practice Management Skills of Minnesota Lawyers[60]

In the 1997–99 and 2013 Minnesota surveys, attorneys were asked to identify the three most important sources of training for each of the 14 law practice management skills.[61] The following tables identify the top three sources of training for each skill, along with the percentage of survey participants who selected them. The tables also include selection percentages for the five law school-specific sources of training: law school curriculum, legal practice simulations, law school clinics, law review, and moot court/competitions.

Table 10.12a Fee arrangements, pricing, billing

Top Three			
1997–99	*%*	*2013*	*%*
1. Advice from other lawyers	61.5	1. Advice from other lawyers	55.0
2. Own experience	55.1	2. Own experience	51.4
3. Observe other lawyers	52.1	3. Observe other lawyers	49.5
Law School Training			
1997–99	*%*	*2013*	*%*
Law school curriculum	4.3	Law school curriculum	7.9
Legal practice simulations	3.9	Legal practice simulations	5.3
Law school clinics	1.2	Law school clinics	2.0
Law review	0.4	Law review	0.0
Moot court/competitions	0.3	Moot court/competitions	0.3

60 See *infra* Appendix A for complete tables.

61 See *supra* text accompanying note 37.

Table 10.12b Human resources, hiring, support staff

Top Three			
1997–99	*%*	*2013*	*%*
1. Own experience	74.7	1. Own experience	64.3
2. Observe other lawyers	42.4	2. Observe other lawyers	41.9
3. Advice from other lawyers	37.9	3. Advice from other lawyers	40.0
Law School Training			
1997–99	*%*	*2013*	*%*
Law school curriculum	0.6	Law school curriculum	1.8
Legal practice simulations	0.0	Legal practice simulations	0.7
Law school clinics	1.1	Law school clinics	0.9
Law review	0.0	Law review	0.0
Moot court/competitions	0.3	Moot court/competitions	0.1

Table 10.12c Capitalization, investment

Top Three			
1997–99	*%*	*2013*	*%*
1. Own experience	64.7	1. Own experience	60.0
2. Advice from other lawyers	41.9	2. Advice from other lawyers	43.7
3. Observe other lawyers	33.2	3. Observe other lawyers	36.6
Law School Training			
1997–99	*%*	*2013*	*%*
Law school curriculum	1.2	Law school curriculum	2.3
Legal practice simulations	0.9	Legal practice simulations	1.0
Law school clinics	0.7	Law school clinics	0.3
Law review	0.0	Law review	0.0
Moot court/competitions	0.0	Moot court/competitions	0.2

Table 10.12d Project and time management, efficiency

Top Three			
1997–99	%	*2013*	%
1. Own experience	78.5	1. Own experience	69.5
2. Observe other lawyers	37.4	2. Law-related work experience	36.2
3. Advice from other lawyers	36.7	3. Advice from other lawyers	34.5
Law School Training			
1997–99	%	*2013*	%
Law school curriculum	16.9	Law school curriculum	23.0
Legal practice simulations	4.5	Legal practice simulations	9.5
Law school clinics	2.6	Law school clinics	5.0
Law review	3.1	Law review	4.6
Moot court/competitions	2.4	Moot court/competitions	3.1

Table 10.12e Planning, resource allocation, budgeting

Top Three			
1997–99	%	*2013*	%
1. Own experience	72.7	1. Own experience	68.3
2. Advice from other lawyers	42.5	2. Advice from other lawyers	41.3
3. Observe other lawyers	37.3	3. Observe other lawyers	39.0
Law School Training			
1997–99	%	*2013*	%
Law school curriculum	6.25	Law school curriculum	7.1
Legal practice simulations	2.1	Legal practice simulations	3.5
Law school clinics	1.7	Law school clinics	1.7
Law review	1.4	Law review	1.2
Moot court/competitions	1.1	Moot court/competitions	1.3

Table 10.12f Marketing, client development

Top Three			
1997–99	%	*2013*	%
1. Own experience	62.0	1. Own experience	58.8
2. Advice from other lawyers	58.8	2. Advice from other lawyers	54.6
3. Observe other lawyers	57.6	3. Observe other lawyers	53.1
Law School Training			
1997–99	%	*2013*	%
Law school curriculum	2.0	Law school curriculum	3.9
Legal practice simulations	0.8	Legal practice simulations	1.0
Law school clinics	1.0	Law school clinics	1.0
Law review	0.4	Law review	0.1
Moot court/competitions	0.4	Moot court/competitions	0.0

Table 10.12g Technology, computers, communications

Top Three			
1997–99	%	*2013*	%
1. Own experience	69.3	1. Own experience	74.1
2. Law school curriculum	49.8	2. Law school curriculum	41.0
3. Law-related work experience	28.1	3. Law-related work experience	30.2
Law School Training			
1997–99	%	*2013*	%
Law school curriculum	49.8	Law school curriculum	41.0
Legal practice simulations	3.8	Legal practice simulations	6.0
Law school clinics	2.3	Law school clinics	1.5
Law review	4.5	Law review	3.3
Moot court/competitions	2.7	Moot court/competitions	1.7

Table 10.12h Governance, decision-making, long-range strategic planning

Top Three			
1997–99	%	*2013*	%
1. Own experience	69.3	1. Own experience	74.1
2. Advice from other lawyers	43.1	2. Advice from other lawyers	41.0
3. Observe other lawyers	40.7	3. Observe other lawyers	30.2
Law School Training			
1997–99	%	*2013*	%
Law school curriculum	3.9	Law school curriculum	41.0
Legal practice simulations	0.8	Legal practice simulations	6.0
Law school clinics	0.9	Law school clinics	1.5
Law review	1.4	Law review	3.3
Moot court/competitions	0.4	Moot court/competitions	1.7

Table 10.12i Interpersonal communications, staff relations

Top Three			
1997–99	%	*2013*	%
1. Own experience	86.8	1. Own experience	81.7
2. Observe other lawyers	39.2	2. Observe other lawyers	40.8
3. Advice from other lawyers	27.6	3. Advice from other lawyers	27.4
Law School Training			
1997–99	%	*2013*	%
Law school curriculum	4.3	Law school curriculum	5.0
Legal practice simulations	1.5	Legal practice simulations	2.4
Law school clinics	4	Law school clinics	3.9
Law review	2.8	Law review	1.2
Moot court/competitions	1.5	Moot court/competitions	1.5

Appendix A: Identified Sources of Legal Practice Skills Training – Full Tables Showing Results of the 1997–99 and 2013 Surveys

Table 10.13a Ability to diagnose and plan for legal problems

	1997–99	2013
Source of Skill: Law School Training:		
Law school curriculum	51.15	44.3
Legal practice simulations	20.15	26.6
Law school clinics	8.5	16.9
Law review	1.0	1.0
Moot court/competitions	9.8	7.7
Source of Skill: Non-Law School Training:		
Own experience	52.2	46.0
Law-related work experience	53.5	63.7
Advice from other lawyers	34.3	34.8
Observe other lawyers	34.8	37.3
CLE courses	10.3	6.7
Advice from non-lawyers	1.6	0.2
Observe non-lawyers	1.7	1.0
Training at other school	1.2	0.5
Training by vendors	0.0	0.2
Other	2.0	2.5

Table 10.13b Ability in legal analysis and legal reasoning

	1997–99	2013
Source of Skill: Law School Training:		
Law school curriculum	88.2	88.3
Legal practice simulations	14.5	20.4
Law school clinics	3.8	8.2
Law review	9.4	9.3
Moot court/competitions	17.6	16.5
Source of Skill: Non-Law School Training:		
Own experience	38.3	30.2
Law-related work experience	54.0	57.5
Advice from other lawyers	20.5	20.6
Observe other lawyers	19.5	22.6
CLE courses	7.0	4.1
Advice from non-lawyers	0.5	0.1
Observe non-lawyers	0.3	0.3
Training at other school	2.3	0.7
Training by vendors	0.0	0.1
Other	1.7	2.0

Table 10.13c Drafting legal documents

	1997–99	2013
Source of Skill: Law School Training:		
Law school curriculum	39.4	43.5
Legal practice simulations	18.5	24.6
Law school clinics	5.4	8.7
Law review	4	3.9
Moot court/competitions	9.5	12.0
Source of Skill: Non-Law School Training:		
Own experience	41.0	36.7
Law-related work experience	59.8	60.3
Advice from other lawyers	36.3	33.2
Observe other lawyers	29.9	29.2
CLE courses	15.6	9.4
Advice from non-lawyers	1.3	0.5
Observe non-lawyers	0.6	0.6
Training at other school	0.5	0.7
Training by vendors	0.3	1.1
Other	3.7	2.8

Table 10.13d Knowledge of the substantive law

	1997–99	2013
Source of Skill: Law School Training:		
Law school curriculum	91.8	84.7
Legal practice simulations	5.3	9.2
Law school clinics	2.9	5.9
Law review	4.6	4.0
Moot court/competitions	7.3	5.2
Source of Skill: Non-Law School Training:		
Own experience	35.1	33.2
Law-related work experience	51.5	52.4
Advice from other lawyers	21.9	21.0
Observe other lawyers	8.9	13.5
CLE courses	38.3	28.9
Advice from non-lawyers	0.0	0.0
Observe non-lawyers	0.5	0.1
Training at other school	0.8	0.7
Training by vendors	0.7	1.7
Other	3.3	3.3

Table 10.13e Library legal research

	1997–99	2013
Source of Skill: Law School Training:		
Law school curriculum	93.7	93.4
Legal practice simulations	8.5	13.8
Law school clinics	1.2	0.5
Law review	16.5	17.9
Moot court/competitions	15.4	9
Source of Skill: Non-Law School Training:		
Own experience	34.4	20.2
Law-related work experience	52.1	22.2
Advice from other lawyers	7.6	3.5
Observe other lawyers	2.6	1.3
CLE courses	2.1	1.7
Advice from non-lawyers	2.6	1.3
Observe non-lawyers	0.7	0.8
Training at other school	1.3	1.5
Training by vendors	5.5	5.8
Other	2.3	2.8

Table 10.13f Computer legal research

	1997–99	2013
Source of Skill: Law School Training:		
Law school curriculum	84.4	84.6
Legal practice simulations	6.6	11.4
Law school clinics	0.8	1.3
Law review	15.3	17.4
Moot court/competitions	10.8	11.1
Source of Skill: Non-Law School Training:		
Own experience	40.4	36.3
Law-related work experience	43.6	45.0
Advice from other lawyers	5.9	5.7
Observe other lawyers	2.7	2.7
CLE courses	6.0	2.8
Advice from non-lawyers	3.0	1.0
Observe non-lawyers	0.8	0.1
Training at other school	0.8	1.5
Training by vendors	26.8	25.9
Other	2.2	3.3

Table 10.13g Fact gathering

	1997–99	2013
Source of Skill: Law School Training:		
Law school curriculum	25.9	28.2
Legal practice simulations	12.9	15.8
Law school clinics	8.8	15.4
Law review	2.0	0.7
Moot court/competitions	5.3	6.6
Source of Skill: Non-Law School Training:		
Own experience	63.0	55.7
Law-related work experience	44.6	53.2
Advice from other lawyers	30.8	29.7
Observe other lawyers	34.7	36.3
CLE courses	4.4	2.4
Advice from non-lawyers	2.9	2.4
Observe non-lawyers	3.3	3.7
Training at other school	1.6	0.8
Training by vendors	0.0	0.4
Other	2.1	2.0

Table 10.13h Oral communication

	1997–99	2013
Source of Skill: Law School Training:		
Law school curriculum	36.9	34.2
Legal practice simulations	17.3	25.3
Law school clinics	4.9	12.6
Law review	1.2	0.8
Moot court/competitions	25.6	27.8
Source of Skill: Non-Law School Training:		
Own experience	69.7	58.8
Law-related work experience	30.4	33.8
Advice from other lawyers	14.8	14.2
Observe other lawyers	32.7	39.3
CLE courses	2.35	1.3
Advice from non-lawyers	3.75	2.5
Observe non-lawyers	3.35	5.5
Training at other school	8.6	5.0
Training by vendors	0.2	0.4
Other	1.65	2.2

Table 10.13i Written communication

	1997–99	2013
Source of Skill: Law School Training:		
Law school curriculum	65.8	66.0
Legal practice simulations	9.8	19.9
Law school clinics	3.3	7.1
Law review	14.6	14.4
Moot court/competitions	17.2	16.6
Source of Skill: Non-Law School Training:		
Own experience	56.9	44.5
Law-related work experience	42.9	49.4
Advice from other lawyers	19.0	23.2
Observe other lawyers	20.4	24.0
CLE courses	3.6	1.7
Advice from non-lawyers	1.6	1.5
Observe non-lawyers	1.3	2.3
Training at other school	11.1	5.0
Training by vendors	0.2	0.5
Other	2.0	2.8

Table 10.13j Counseling

	1997–99	2013
Source of Skill: Law School Training:		
Law school curriculum	17.2	19.7
Legal practice simulations	13.2	16.6
Law school clinics	10.0	19.5
Law review	0.7	0.1
Moot court/competitions	3.9	2.9
Source of Skill: Non-Law School Training:		
Own experience	63.1	52.8
Law-related work experience	28.5	36.0
Advice from other lawyers	31.6	31.5
Observe other lawyers	46.6	49.6
CLE courses	3.6	2.1
Advice from non-lawyers	3.3	2.7
Observe non-lawyers	6.3	6.1
Training at other school	2.6	1.4
Training by vendors	0.4	0.1
Other	1.8	1.7

Table 10.13k Instilling others' confidence in you

	1997–99	2013
Source of Skill: Law School Training:		
Law school curriculum	7.8	6.8
Legal practice simulations	4.3	7.5
Law school clinics	6.1	13.4
Law review	2.0	1.4
Moot court/competitions	2.7	4.5
Source of Skill: Non-Law School Training:		
Own experience	80.4	69.7
Law-related work experience	25.3	31.5
Advice from other lawyers	27.4	33.9
Observe other lawyers	40.1	43.4
CLE courses	2.3	2.3
Advice from non-lawyers	5.2	7.4
Observe non-lawyers	6.5	8.9
Training at other school	2.8	1.6
Training by vendors	0.4	0.1
Other	2.0	2.5

Table 10.13l Negotiation

	1997–99	2013
Source of Skill: Law School Training:		
Law school curriculum	26.25	34.4
Legal practice simulations	15.7	24.0
Law school clinics	4.9	6.8
Law review	0.8	0.0
Moot court/competitions	4.5	6.1
Source of Skill: Non-Law School Training:		
Own experience	65.45	50.5
Law-related work experience	24.45	30.3
Advice from other lawyers	28.5	27.7
Observe other lawyers	47.6	45.6
CLE courses	9.55	5.3
Advice from non-lawyers	1.9	2.4
Observe non-lawyers	7.05	6.7
Training at other school	3.2	2.2
Training by vendors	0.5	0.4
Other	2.15	1.9

Table 10.13m Knowledge of procedural law

	1997–99	2013
Source of Skill: Law School Training:		
Law school curriculum	82.5	78.1
Legal practice simulations	8.6	14.1
Law school clinics	3.8	6.9
Law review	1.2	0.5
Moot court/competitions	5.5	5.8
Source of Skill: Non-Law School Training:		
Own experience	36.6	32.6
Law-related work experience	44.9	50.5
Advice from other lawyers	25.6	25.4
Observe other lawyers	18.0	19.2
CLE courses	14.2	11.9
Advice from non-lawyers	1.2	0.5
Observe non-lawyers	0.6	0.5
Training at other school	0.6	0.6
Training by vendors	0.7	0.7
Other	3.0	2.1

Table 10.13n Understanding and conducting litigation

	1997–99	2013
Source of Skill: Law School Training:		
Law school curriculum	39.8	36.1
Legal practice simulations	18.6	23.2
Law school clinics	4.9	7.6
Law review	0.5	0.0
Moot court/competitions	6.1	7.6
Source of Skill: Non-Law School Training:		
Own experience	38.1	32.2
Law-related work experience	44.2	47.1
Advice from other lawyers	37.3	33.1
Observe other lawyers	43.7	44.7
CLE courses	10.0	7.5
Advice from non-lawyers	0.7	0.6
Observe non-lawyers	0.7	1.1
Training at other school	0.9	0.7
Training by vendors	0.3	0.4
Other	1.6	2.3

Table 10.13o Organization and management of legal work

	1997–99	2013
Source of Skill: Law School Training:		
Law school curriculum	11.1	12.1
Legal practice simulations	7.4	9.3
Law school clinics	5.3	8.5
Law review	0.7	1.2
Moot court/competitions	2.0	1.4
Source of Skill: Non-Law School Training:		
Own experience	63.1	60.2
Law-related work experience	38.0	46.0
Advice from other lawyers	41.2	41.1
Observe other lawyers	46.1	45.5
CLE courses	4.6	4.9
Advice from non-lawyers	3.0	2.2
Observe non-lawyers	2.2	2.8
Training at other school	1.0	1.3
Training by vendors	0.9	1.0
Other	2.7	2.2

Table 10.13p Ability to obtain and keep clients

	1997–99	2013
Source of Skill: Law School Training:		
Law school curriculum	6.1	3.9
Legal practice simulations	3.2	3.2
Law school clinics	3.9	5.8
Law review	0.4	0.0
Moot court/competitions	0.0	0.0
Source of Skill: Non-Law School Training:		
Own experience	60.3	53.9
Law-related work experience	20.4	26.4
Advice from other lawyers	50.9	55.1
Observe other lawyers	55.7	55.7
CLE courses	3.2	5.7
Advice from non-lawyers	4.6	6.9
Observe non-lawyers	4.1	4.7
Training at other school	0.9	0.4
Training by vendors	0.7	0.8
Other	1.7	4.4

Table 10.13q Sensitivity to professional ethical concerns

	1997–99	2013
Source of Skill: Law School Training:		
Law school curriculum	84.5	86.8
Legal practice simulations	4.1	6.1
Law school clinics	1.1	4.9
Law review	0.6	0.5
Moot court/competitions	1.4	0.8
Source of Skill: Non-Law School Training:		
Own experience	39.0	32.2
Law-related work experience	24.7	26.5
Advice from other lawyers	31.0	34.2
Observe other lawyers	25.0	22.6
CLE courses	24.0	21.3
Advice from non-lawyers	0.9	0.7
Observe non-lawyers	1.6	0.5
Training at other school	1.1	0.7
Training by vendors	0.0	0.9
Other	1.7	1.0

Appendix B: Identified Sources of Law Practice Management Skills Training – Full Tables Showing Results of the 1997–99 and 2013 Surveys

Table 10.14a Fee arrangements, pricing, billing

	1997–99	2013
Source of Skill: Law School Training		
Law school curriculum	4.3	7.9
Legal practice simulations	3.9	5.3
Law school clinics	1.2	2.0
Law review	0.4	0.0
Moot court/competitions	0.3	0.3
Source of Skill: Non-Law School Training:		
Own experience	55.1	51.4
Law-related work experience	29.0	28.8
Advice from other lawyers	61.5	55.0
Observe other lawyers	52.1	49.5
CLE courses	5.2	8.3
Advice from non-lawyers	4.3	3.2
Observe non-lawyers	2.8	2.0
Training at other school	0.7	0.3
Training by vendors	1.1	1.0
Other	1.6	6.1

Table 10.14b Human resources, hiring, support staff

	1997–99	2013
Source of Skill: Law School Training:		
Law school curriculum	0.6	1.8
Legal practice simulations	0.0	0.7
Law school clinics	1.1	0.9
Law review	0.0	0.0
Moot court/competitions	0.3	0.1
Source of Skill: Non-Law School Training:		
Own experience	74.7	64.3
Law-related work experience	20.3	23.9
Advice from other lawyers	37.9	40.0
Observe other lawyers	42.4	41.9
CLE courses	2.4	3.0
Advice from non-lawyers	15.3	11.1
Observe non-lawyers	9.3	11.8
Training at other school	4.55	1.5
Training by vendors	0.8	0.6
Other	2.0	5.3

Table 10.14c Capitalization, investment, budgeting

	1997–99	2013
Source of Skill: Law School Training:		
Law school curriculum	1.2	2.3
Legal practice simulations	0.9	1.0
Law school clinics	0.7	0.3
Law review	0.0	0.0
Moot court/competitions	0.0	0.2
Source of Skill: Non-Law School Training:		
Own experience	64.7	60.0
Law-related work experience	12.0	15.5
Advice from other lawyers	41.9	43.7
Observe other lawyers	33.2	36.6
CLE courses	2.5	4.4
Advice from non-lawyers	17.1	15.2
Observe non-lawyers	6.2	7.4
Training at other school	4.7	1.8
Training by vendors	1.8	0.8
Other	1.3	9.0

Table 10.14d Project and time management, efficiency

	1997–99	2013
Source of Skill: Law School Training:		
Law school curriculum	16.9	23.0
Legal practice simulations	4.5	9.5
Law school clinics	2.6	5.0
Law review	3.1	4.6
Moot court/competitions	2.4	3.1
Source of Skill: Non-Law School Training:		
Own experience	78.5	69.5
Law-related work experience	30.5	36.2
Advice from other lawyers	36.7	34.5
Observe other lawyers	37.4	33.2
CLE courses	4.7	4.8
Advice from non-lawyers	4.2	7.1
Observe non-lawyers	4.2	5.9
Training at other school	4.0	2.1
Training by vendors	1.2	1.5
Other	1.0	2.8

Table 10.14e Planning, resource allocation, budgeting

	1997–99	2013
Source of Skill: Law School Training:		
Law school curriculum	6.3	7.1
Legal practice simulations	2.1	3.5
Law school clinics	1.7	1.7
Law review	1.4	1.2
Moot court/competitions	1.1	1.3
Source of Skill: Non-Law School Training:		
Own experience	72.7	68.3
Law-related work experience	18.8	23.3
Advice from other lawyers	42.5	41.3
Observe other lawyers	37.3	39.0
CLE courses	2.8	3.2
Advice from non-lawyers	9.6	9.9
Observe non-lawyers	7.3	5.4
Training at other school	3.8	1.0
Training by vendors	1.9	0.6
Other	1.5	3.5

Table 10.14f Marketing, client development

	1997–99	2013
Source of Skill: Law School Training:		
Law school curriculum	2.0	3.9
Legal practice simulations	0.8	1.0
Law school clinics	1.0	1.0
Law review	0.4	0.1
Moot court/competitions	0.4	0.0
Source of Skill: Non-Law School Training:		
Own experience	62.0	58.8
Law-related work experience	15.9	21.0
Advice from other lawyers	58.8	54.6
Observe other lawyers	57.6	53.1
CLE courses	5.1	8.8
Advice from non-lawyers	11.9	11.9
Observe non-lawyers	7.6	7.5
Training at other school	3.7	1.5
Training by vendors	1.1	1.6
Other	1.1	5.3

Table 10.14g Technology, computers, communications

	1997–99	2013
Source of Skill: Law School Training:		
Law school curriculum	49.8	41.0
Legal practice simulations	3.8	6.0
Law school clinics	2.3	1.5
Law review	4.5	3.3
Moot court/competitions	2.7	1.7
Source of Skill: Non-Law School Training:		
Own experience	69.3	74.1
Law-related work experience	28.1	30.2
Advice from other lawyers	11.4	16.7
Observe other lawyers	12.1	11.3
CLE courses	7.8	6.5
Advice from non-lawyers	12	11.9
Observe non-lawyers	4.2	4.3
Training at other school	6.8	3.3
Training by vendors	24.5	15.6
Other	1.8	2.1

Table 10.14h Governance, decision-making, long-range strategic planning

	1997–99	2013
Source of Skill: Law School Training:		
Law school curriculum	3.9	7.2
Legal practice simulations	0.8	2.2
Law school clinics	0.9	0.9
Law review	1.4	0.3
Moot court/competitions	0.4	0.6
Source of Skill: Non-Law School Training:		
Own experience	69.3	65.7
Law-related work experience	14.2	19.1
Advice from other lawyers	43.1	44.6
Observe other lawyers	40.7	40.1
CLE courses	1.8	4.0
Advice from non-lawyers	11.9	12.5
Observe non-lawyers	8.3	8.2
Training at other school	4.5	1.8
Training by vendors	1.2	0.7
Other	2.2	5.7

Table 10.14i Interpersonal communications, staff relations

	1997–99	2013
Source of Skill: Law School Training:		
Law school curriculum	4.3	5.0
Legal practice simulations	1.5	2.4
Law school clinics	4.0	3.9
Law review	2.8	1.2
Moot court/competitions	1.5	1.5
Source of Skill: Non-Law School Training:		
Own experience	86.8	81.7
Law-related work experience	22.0	26.6
Advice from other lawyers	27.6	27.4
Observe other lawyers	39.2	40.8
CLE courses	2.0	1.9
Advice from non-lawyers	11.8	10.1
Observe non-lawyers	11.7	14.5
Training at other school	5.5	3.1
Training by vendors	0.4	0.5
Other	1.7	2.7

Appendix C: Survey Instrument

Letter to Minnesota Lawyers

Dear Colleague:

William Mitchell College of Law is conducting a survey to help the school identify additions and improvements to its curriculum that best meet the needs of its students and the practicing bar. This survey, a follow-up to the original 1999/2000 study, focuses on attorneys listed with the Minnesota State Bar Association that have been in practice since 2000. We would appreciate your participation in this 10-minute survey. In order that the results truly represent the thinking and attitudes of this segment of Minnesota lawyers, it is important that each questionnaire be completed.

Here is a link to the survey: http://www.surveymonkey.com/s.aspx?sm=XEqJM1nFmBPCEkdIBkRfsQ_3d_3d.

Please note: This link is uniquely tied to this survey and your email address. Please do not forward this message.

We can assure you complete confidentiality. The questionnaire has an identification number for statistical purposes only. Your name will never be placed on the questionnaire or identified with any results.

You may receive a summary of our results by emailing me with a request.

We would be glad to answer any questions you might have. Please contact me at john.sonsteng@wmitchell.edu or at (651) 290–6324. You may also contact my assistant, Jennifer Miller, at jennifer.miller@wmitchell.edu or at (651) 290–6314.

Thank you for your participation.

Sincerely,
Professor John Sonsteng
Project Director

Link to Survey

http://www.surveymonkey.com/s.aspx?sm=XEqJM1nFmBPCEkdIBkRfsQ_3d_3d

Chapter 11

Integrating the Idea of Global Governance and International Collaboration into Law School Education

Shi Yan'an[1]

We all feel that we are now living in an age of globalization and network, in which the scope of our activities and the ways of advocating our interests and rights are becoming more internationalized, whether individually or collectively. In the meantime, the conflicts and disputes accompanying this are more complicated and severe. Many of them are transnational legal issues that need to be resolved by multinational negotiation and coordination. In the past decades, the international community has set up some legal mechanisms on global governance, yet up to now, these mechanisms have been in the primary stage in managing and resolving international disputes and cannot keep pace with the current trend of globalization. As a result, many international disputes have resorted to violence instead of utilizing legal procedures. It's a shared dream of all lawyers to establish a reasonable legal order under which all disputes are resolved by the rule of law. To realize this dream, we, legal educators, are required to advocate the spirit of internationalism, to bring in the idea of global governance and international cooperation into daily education, to cultivate an intense awareness of global concerns and to encourage them to analyze and resolve these problems with legal thinking.

Legal education in law schools, the features of which are systematically teaching, academically dominating and ideologically guiding, and students being evaluated by a degree system, is the main force of legal education. As a part of modern college education, education in law schools certainly assumes all of its obligations of creating knowledge, leading culture and constructing the future. What the society will be depends on what kind of talents we are now training. We are indeed constructing the social governance structure by qualifying our students with a broad view, a spirit of the humanity and a sense of social responsibility. These young pioneers will dominate global governance in years to come, with their global vision, their persistent pursuit of rule of law and their deep love to others and the world. We can expect that the next generation will embrace a bright future.

1 Vice Dean, School of Law, Renmin University of China.

However, unfortunately, the spirit of humanism is waning in current law school education. Law schools have somewhat transformed into a factory-line that will take working-hours, cost and market into consideration, which inevitably generates many "law craftsmen", most of whom only regard their knowledge of law as a means of making a living, with importance placed on social responsibilities and obligations. The law students are not to blame, rather the existing education mode under which teachers are merely passing on the techniques of law, barely touching on the enlightenment of humanistic spirit. With the law schools transforming into such icy processing workshops isolated from humanistic concern, what can we expect from them?

View and philosophy determine goal and objective. Legal educators need to firstly open their minds to include global governance into law school education, that is, to extend their sight from mainly focused domestically to abroad and internationally, to bring in the latest legal ideas and practices from overseas as well as worldwide focused issues into everyday teaching. This will inspire students to learn on their own to meet the needs of globalization and to devote themselves to global governance practice. Secondly, legal educators need to transform teaching approaches and methods by integrating the idea of global governance into legal education. We shall impart to students the approaches and patterns of global governance and possible ways to get involved other than simply tell them what the international community has done and what it is about to do. To live up to that, an indispensible part is to recruit both domestic and international theorists and practitioners into law school faculties.

It's true that nowadays law school education places more emphasis on internationalization, and the proportion of international law courses has been increased. However, even so, global concerns have still not become a main part of classrooms teaching or law students' thinking. Law school education, as a whole, is more interested in developed areas and industries, with a lack of enthusiasm about under-developed regions. Although in some sense, courses on human rights law can help students to pay attention to the welfare of ethnic minorities, vulnerable groups and people living in the bottom of society as well as those from the under-developed countries and regions, these courses are still dominated by the values oriented from some particular culture, which inevitably ignores the gaps on human rights recognition due to cultural differences. Hence such courses can do little more than just stuff students with some illusory theories and concepts, other than providing students with sufficient approaches to practise human rights law. As a result, law students know little about the real world and they can only discuss the problems of human rights and development based on their imagination.

One of the essential links in integrating the idea of global governance into law schools' daily education is to acquaint the students with the global issues, such as famine, environment problems, war, human trafficking, smuggling, transnational corruption, distribution of water resources, anti-disaster, epidemic prevention, food safety, economic crisis, multinational corporations, human rights and so on, and to include them in regular teaching. These problems affect the interests of millions of people, and apparently cannot be resolved by the legal system of one or two states, nor controlled by any superpower. Currently, in the process of resolving these issues, there is no concept of "global interest", while national interest, especially the interest of superpowers, has always been given priority, without taking the interest of small nations and groups into full consideration. Wars launched in the name of human rights and democracy by some countries have actually caused tremendous damage to civilians, which in fact is the result of ignoring the interest of vulnerable groups. From this perspective, many measures that are used to deal with global disputes are problems themselves, or create more problems.

To resolve global issues, cross-cultural, multicultural and even beyond-cultural studies are required. In this sense, we shall treat different civilizations, traditional values and social governance experiences as backgrounds and realities with a multicultural perspective when integrating the idea of global governance into law school education. We all acknowledge the importance of respecting different social traditions and values. However, in legal practice, groups that stick to certain traditions in a particular society are often forced into a disadvantaged position because of cultural difference. As for law students who are trained for future social governance, it is of great significance for them to acknowledge the concept of multiculture and to seek universal values out of different civilizations. Idioms such as "to seek common ground while reserving differences" and "agreeing to disagree" which reflect the wisdom of ancient sages of China are still worth sticking to and practising. To act is harder than to know. It is difficult to qualify our students with the ability to truly face, with experience and respect, cultures and traditions they are not familiar with. Acquainting students with an abstract concept is easy but making it their acting guideline is difficult. The latter requires integrating more international communications and cooperation into law school education, both among the students and the professors.

We believe that international communication and academic cooperation will help students to have a better understanding of different cultures as well as the diversified doctrine and practice of law. For future global governance, how to know about, get along with, accept and even integrate with others is the critical part. An essential keyword of the traditional Chinese culture is "benevolence". Confucius said: "Benevolence means to love people." The word "love", as a verb, is a kind of behaviour, a kind of practice, starting with respecting others and leading up to a harmonious world. Today, "loving people" means to treat others as the same free human as ourselves out of our rationality and desire for harmony, rather than to put them above ourselves just out of fear or humbleness or to love them out of sympathy as someone inferior. "Loving people" means to combine self-freedom with the respect for others, and to view all social disputes as well as legal issues caused by it with an inclination to goodness. It's true that, in some cases, loving others does not always reward you the same love from them, however, sincere love does bring hearts closer, and gradually eliminates the estrangement caused by prejudice and historical reasons. Law schools educate social governors and the hearts of benevolence is the internal power that encourages them to lead the future society to peace and prosperity.

It seems quite necessary for us to reconsider the orientation of "students' training" in law school education. Is it being transformed into a processing machine that only outputs law craftsmen for the legal service market? This doubt does not come out of nowhere. As we can see, in the legal service market, disputes and conflicts are regarded by lawyers as resources which they can make good use of for their own benefits and, for some of them, creating disputes is far more profitable than resolving them. Can it contribute to social harmony, justice and equality? It's now necessary for us to rethink whether the current legal service market is functioning as the "positive energy" in society, what the relationship between law school education and gloomy legal practice is, and how many law students have given away or are giving away their doctrine as a lawyer? If the answer is negative or pessimistic, we really ought to re-examine whether law school education has deviated from the course it is supposed to take.

No matter whether we view current law school education optimistically or pessimistically, we all need to reflect with longing. As the economic crisis goes on, some law schools are worried about enrolment and some are anxious about the employment prospects of their graduates. In fact, when looking into the future, what we should worry about or reflect upon is how to face the challenges that are coming along. If the aim of law school education is social and even global governance, all we need now is to have a clear outline of what to do in the future by reflecting on what we have done in the past. Certainly, we all look to the future of law school education over the next 10 or 20 years, which reflects the future of society, as an opportunity to design and plan what lawyers could or should do. In this respect, the burden is on law schools to set up a dispute resolution mechanism based in law and to eliminate violence as a means of solution. Our horizon must change from domestic-oriented to global-based, or in other words, our local and domestic vision must be integrated with a global one.

We all know what "future" means to law school education in China and the challenges imposed on it by globalization. Since its renaissance in 1978, legal education in China has experienced a dramatic development over the past 35 years, yet it is confronted with various developing issues as well as the risk of hard-landing and the current crisis. However, it still benefits from globalization, just like the Chinese economy. Nowadays, those who graduated from the well-known law schools all over the world or those who have been there as visiting scholars have become the backbone of the law schools in China. The increasing amount of exchange programs enable students to learn more about the legal systems and cultures of other nations or regions, and to communicate with their peers. However, just like the Chinese economy, law school education in China is still facing various increasingly conspicuous issues. With respect to globalization, law school education in China is still in its early stage, and hasn't come up with any influential resolutions to the global legal concerns yet.

In the past decades, Renmin University of China Law School has been committed to becoming internationalized and it is no exaggeration to say that our law school has played a leading role in the internationalization of law schools in mainland China. So far we have nine foreign faculty members in our law school, and we have signed bilateral agreements on students exchange programs, double degree education and cooperation in academic research with more than 50 well-known law schools worldwide. We provide diverse opportunities for our students to go abroad to open their minds. Every year, there are more than 60 students who will have the chance to go abroad as exchange students for a semester or a year, or to obtain a degree from famous worldwide universities. Also, each year, a number of students will take a three to six-month internship at the European Court of Human Rights, the World Intellectual Property Organization, the United Nations Headquarters, the United Nations Office on Drugs and Crime, foreign law firms as well as other institutions. Every year during the summer, nearly 80 law school students from China go overseas to participate in various summer programs. Student delegations from our law school have participated in various international moot court competitions overseas, and have won an impressive array of awards. Additionally, through hosting top forums – such as the International Forum for Law School Deans and Jurists, the China–US Law School Deans' Forum, the China–Australia Forum for Law School Deans, the China–Africa Forum for Law School Deans – cooperation and communication on law education with foreign law schools is greatly enhanced. Meanwhile, in the academic field, the "Geneva–Harvard–RUC–Sydney" Symposium, the UK–China Conference on Public Law, as well as other academic seminars, co-hosted by our law school and top law schools overseas, have also helped to deepen the exchange and cooperation between Chinese and foreign law schools. As for self-construction within our law school, we have set up an affiliate Asia–Pacific Institute of Law to promote the legal education and communication in Asia–Pacific regions. In spite of the above efforts and achievements, the internationalization of our law school is still in a very early stage due to its limited time, lack of talents, experience and funds, and is confronted with various problems, which in turn warn us to review the current pattern and mechanism of internationalization. One basic objective of law schools is to cultivate talents that adapt to the trend of globalization, have a global vision and could contribute to the common welfare of the world. To achieve it, Renmin University of China Law School sincerely wishes to establish good relations of cooperation with other law schools, so as to cultivate the legal talents needed by the future.

Chapter 12

Navigating E-Spaces in Legal Education and Legal Practice

Rita Shackel[1]

Introduction

This chapter explores the use of e-spaces[2] and information technology[3] as an important tool for teaching and learning in legal education. *E-learning* is a broad concept and is inclusive of teaching and learning strategies that utilise a wide range of electronic, information and technological media and tools, often in combination with one another including the Internet, video, audio, intranet and computer-based platforms. E-based learning can take varied shapes and forms and may be asynchronous or synchronous in format and delivery. Indeed a single definition of e-learning is difficult to advance despite its extensive usage. In part, this is because the subject is in constant change and is evolving, but arguably also because 'different understandings of e-learning are conditioned by particular professional approaches and interests'[4] and shaped by the particular discipline, focus of study and specific learning objectives.

This chapter argues that in the context of legal education, not only does the e-medium provide a fertile ground for active, student-led and collaborative learning – learning styles which typically characterise deep and quality learning experiences – but importantly e-learning spaces also represent a powerful key intermediate between law school and the new realities of professional work in an e-based legal services market and e-age of legal practice.

1 Rita Shackel, Associate Professor, Sydney Law School.

2 E-spaces are defined broadly here to include electronically-based spaces. It includes the Internet but also extends to spaces created by other forms of technology such as television, video and audio recordings.

3 Information technology is broadly defined here to include all forms of technology used to create, store, use, manipulate, exchange and retrieve information in all its various forms. Information technology extends beyond the use of computers and includes other forms of telecommunications.

4 Albert Sangra, Dimitrios Vlachopoulos and Nati Cabrera, 'Building an Inclusive Definition of E-Learning: An Approach to the Conceptual Framework', *The International Review of Research in Open and Distance Learning* 13 (2012).

Many law schools around the world are currently confronting various challenges including: fierce market competition, increased pressure from students and employers for a practice-ready graduate, and close scrutiny of law school curricula from professional and regulatory bodies with a thrust towards redevelopment and the innovation of legal education.[5] The American Bar Association (ABA) Task Force on the Future of Legal Education, for example, in its Draft Report published in September 2013,[6] made several recommendations for reform of legal education in the United States, recognising in particular the need for:

- greater heterogeneity in law schools and in programs that deliver law-related education;
- emphasis on the delivery of value to students in law schools and in law-related education;
- clear acknowledgment that law schools exist to teach people to provide law-related services; and
- greater innovation in law schools and programs that deliver law-related education.

These recommendations arguably are at least in part, fuelled by and reflect a growing sentiment manifest in various professional quarters, that law school programs and law curricula are in the moment orphaned from the professional roots and practice origins from which legal education is derived. Moreover, there is a growing sentiment that the learning outcomes of legal study need to become more congruent and be better aligned with the needs of the modern day legal profession and the actual exigencies and realities of a contemporary legal services marketplace; namely a marketplace that is rapidly being reshaped by new technologies and e-based platforms for communication, information exchange, professional engagement and business activities.

Thus against this backdrop, and at a moment which might well represent a key inflection point in the evolution of legal education and legal professional training on a global scale, the need to examine the role of e-media as a potentially transformative tool in legal education and in the professional training of lawyers is timely.

---

5 See, for example, American Bar Association Taskforce on the Future of Legal Education.

6 American Bar Association Taskforce on the Future of Legal Education, *Draft Report and Recommendations*, September 20, 2013, accessed October 1, 2013, http://www.americanbar.org/content/dam/aba/administrative/professional_responsibility/taskforcecomments/task_force_on_legaleducation_draft_report_september2013.authcheckdam.pdf.

What is the Purpose of Law School?

The very purpose of legal education is a key question that must be considered at the outset of any discussion about reform of law curricula, legal educational program design and the pedagogy of legal instruction. The ABA Task Force (2013) on the Future of Legal Education has noted wide disagreement about the purpose of law schools:[7]

> … a commonly stated purpose of law schools is to train lawyers, but there is no consensus about what this means. It matters, for example, whether one takes a view of lawyers as just (or at least primarily) deliverers of technical services requiring a certain skill or expertise, or as persons who are broad-based problem solvers and societal leaders. Different views about what it means to 'train lawyers' yield different views about curricula; different views about faculty; and different emphases regarding services to students.

Most law schools would acknowledge they play a fundamental role in educating the next generation of lawyers but increasingly law schools are also catering for students who see law as a generalist degree that creates pathways for graduate entry into careers such as politics, international relations, economics, finance, accounting and public policy. Indeed, legal training

> can also be extremely valuable – not just because law graduates have a grasp of a large body of rules and regulations, but for the intellectual rigour, the clarity of analysis, the precision with language, the facility for critical thought, the capacity for intensive research, and the confidence in public speaking that a good degree in law should build and provide.[8]

However, the demand for law as a generalist degree may at times be seen to inadvertently dilute the professional focus of legal education. For example, as a teacher of a mandatory legal professional responsibility core unit of study in the Bachelor of Laws (LLB) and Juris Doctor (JD) programs at Sydney Law School, I am regularly challenged by some of my students who feel that studying the ethics of lawyering is not an effective use of their time at law school as they do not intend to practise law. This sentiment, at least in part, is impelled by a substance-driven view of legal education. Of course, the value of such study extends to beyond just those students who must, because of admission requirements, understand the ethical obligations and duties of a lawyer; its value lies in understanding and encouraging deep and reflexive thinking on a range of ethical issues relevant to

7 Ibid., 13.

8 Richard Susskind, *Tomorrow's Lawyers: An Introduction to Your Future* (Oxford: Oxford University Press, 2013), PDF e-book, chap. 13, 3–4.

professional work in many spheres beyond legal practice and the insight and self-awareness that such reflection is capable of precipitating.

Undoubtedly individual law schools have learning outcomes and graduate attributes consistent with their particular school's mission, institutional values and philosophy, and the local legal professional context. The learning objectives of a law school are inextricably linked to the pedagogy of its law curricula. A school for example that seeks to develop its students' capacity for critical argumentation will adopt teaching and learning strategies that promote development of such skills and which create learning spaces that promote opportunities for students to gain experience in analytical approaches. Similarly a law school that views social justice as a priority or legal policy analysis as a core competency in legal education, will facilitate learning experiences for its students that enable a deep, holistic and real-world analysis of law, economics and politics, and may for example seek to achieve this by providing opportunities for students to participate in legal clinics or undertake relevant legal placements or internships with a practical orientation. However, irrespective of the particular emphasis or priorities that individual schools identify and articulate, surely, as a legal education provider, every law school in providing programs towards a professional qualification and where relevant accreditation as a lawyer, must have as one of its fundamental concerns, the skilling up and employability of its legal graduates. However, in reality 'little space in the curriculum is typically devoted specifically to preparing students to pursue and compete for jobs [and transition into the legal profession]. Rather, it is generally delegated to a non-academic unit of the law school'.[9] This approach to legal education is likely a factor contributing to the schism we are currently witnessing between the law school experience and transition into and practise as a legal professional.

Evidence suggests that current market forces increasingly will require that law schools: (i) align curricula with its key function as a legal education provider and the training of lawyers; and (ii) adapt programs or practices to meet the demands of the marketplace and the pressures of business competition.[10] This is not to say that the traditional learning objectives of legal education, such as high order critical thinking and analysis, are to be supplanted by such practice-oriented priorities. To the contrary, the challenge for law schools is to develop curricula that effectively merge rigorous academic learning objectives with the acquisition of the knowledge and skills demanded of modern legal professionals.

If this view is correct and law schools cannot resist market considerations and pressures, then law school curricula must transition consistent with the needs and realities of the current legal services marketplace. Returning then to the modern law school's role in ensuring its graduates' employability, in the current legal services market and considering the likely needs of future legal

9 American Bar Association Taskforce on the Future of Legal Education, *Draft Report and Recommendations*, 13.

10 Ibid.

professionals, a key element of graduate employability seems to be the capacity to navigate the e-technology which is visibly transforming modern day legal practice and a graduate's capacity to understand and respond to the professional and ethical challenges that this new and still rapidly evolving e-terrain throws up for the modern lawyer. In other words, not only do law curricula need to dovetail to a greater extent with the practising branches of the legal profession[11] moving into the future, but law school must prepare 'the next generation of lawyers to be more flexible, team-based, hybrid professionals, who are able to transcend legal boundaries, speak the language of the boardroom, and are motivated [and capable] to draw on techniques of modern management and information technology'.[12]

If legal education is to effectively harness the opportunity to leverage law student experience of, and learning in legal technology, then inevitably it is law teachers that must lead the way and carve out appropriate learning spaces and create appropriate pathways within law curricula for such learning to occur. Goodenough (2013) suggests this may pose a challenge for the legal academy noting that:

> A technology-driven revolution is overturning how America practices law, runs its government, and dispenses justice, and the revolution has so far gone almost completely unnoticed by the people who teach aspiring lawyers. This has to change.[13]

In a similar vein Susskind (2013) argues:

> In many law schools, the law is taught as it was in the 1970s, by professors who have little insight into or interest in the changing legal marketplace. Too often, scant attention is paid to phenomena such as globalization, commoditization, information technology, modern business management, risk assessment, decomposing and alternative sourcing.[14]

It is likely that legal academics around the world are struggling to bridge this disconnect between the technological realities of a rapidly developing 'e-lawyering' era and traditional law school curricula and pedagogy. As Goodenough (2013) challenges, 'teaching the technology of law is a subject that really does require its law trained teachers to master new ways of thinking, new realms of knowledge,

11 Susskind, *Tomorrow's Lawyers*, chap. 13, 4.

12 Ibid., chap. 13, 6.

13 Oliver R. Goodenough, 'Developing an E-Curriculum: Reflections on the Future of Legal Education and on the Importance of Digital Expertise', *Chicago-Kent Law Review* 88 (2013): 847.

14 Susskind, *Tomorrow's Lawyers*, chap. 13, 10.

Ibid., chap. 13, 6.

and new domains of performance'.[15] The technology of law as a scaffold to enliven curriculum reform in legal education is as Goodenough (2013) further argues justified for at least four reasons: (i) the widespread use of e-technology in practice; (ii) the power of technology in promoting access to justice and legal services; (iii) the need to evaluate the impact of technology on development of law and its processes; and (iv) the practical necessity for law graduates to understand, navigate and ultimately drive the use of technology and new e-spaces in legal work.[16]

This chapter has so far presented arguments for why law schools must reform law curricula in ways that seek to bridge the purpose of legal education with the realities of modern day legal practice, and in particular recognise that law as a profession is being transformed by information technology and an e-based marketplace. This chapter will next examine the impact of e-spaces and information technologies on the work that lawyers undertake and in the provision of legal services. It will argue that e-lawyering raises a suite of ethical and professional issues transfigured from those grounded in traditional legal practice. It will then examine how law curricula can harness legal technology as a tool not only for more effective teaching and learning in law, but also as a springboard for both enhancing the law student experience and as a vehicle for better preparing and equipping law students for the realities of an e-based legal marketplace and the professional challenges of 'e-lawyering'.

The Impact of E-Based Technologies on the Legal Services Marketplace and Challenges to Legal Professionalism

A great deal has been written over the past six or seven years about the impact of technology on legal practice.[17] As foreshadowed by Richard Susskind (2008) 'various existing and emerging technologies' have challenged the way in which lawyers work.[18] The Internet in particular is having a profound impact on lawyering and is both opening up new opportunities for legal practice and challenging some fundamentals of traditional legal professionalism.[19]

Susskind (2008) has described the Internet as not just a:

15 Goodenough, 'Developing an E-Curriculum', 860.

16 Ibid., 863.

17 See, for example, Tahlia Gordon, Rita Shackel and Steve Mark, 'Regulation of Legal Services in the E-World: a Need to Short Circuit Hot Spots in Ethics and Novel Practices?', *International Journal of the Legal Profession* 19 (2012); Richard Susskind, *The End of Lawyers?: Re-Thinking the Nature of Legal Services* (Oxford: Oxford University Press, 2008); Susskind, *Tomorrow's Lawyers.*

18 Susskind, *The End of Lawyers?*

19 Gordon, Shackel and Mark, 'Regulation of Legal Services in the E-World'.

> global network of networks, but also ... a technology infrastructure that supports three main utilities. The first is electronic mail, an application that has revolutionized the communication habits of hundreds of millions of people on our planet. The second is the Web, the world's largest information resource, which has transformed our information-seeking habits. The third is online community – with human beings connected to one another through the Internet, this gives rise to fundamental new ways for us to interact and collaborate with one another.[20]

Today the use of email, the World Wide Web and online communities are integral to the way legal information is shared and legal work performed. Email is a common mode of communication today between lawyers themselves, between lawyers and clients and third parties. Even confidential communications are as a matter of common practice typically exchanged via email. The Web is widely utilised as a portal for clients to access lawyers and the legal system, and is now a staple medium through which lawyers service clients and the marketplace. Online communities provide a platform for communication, production, collaboration, networking, community building, trading and exchange.[21] Online communities increasingly are shaping all manner of social relationships and professional domains and the law and legal practice are no exception. As described by Susskind (2013):

> There are over 2.2 billion Internet users, 800 million subscribers to Facebook, 3.5 billion email accounts, 1 million kilometres of sub-sea fibre-optic cables, more than 5 billion subscriptions to mobile phones, and, every two days, according to Google's Eric Schmidt, 'we create as much information as we did from the dawn of civilisation up until 2003'. Every two days, in fact, we create more than 5 quintillion (5×10^{18}) bytes of data.[22]

Moreover, as recently noted by Gordon, Shackel and Mark (2012):

> In the US alone, 2010 saw a 12.6 per cent growth in online retail sales reaching US$176.2 billion, despite a challenged economy. US eCommerce is expected to reach US$278.9 billion in 2015. Similar double digit growth is also expected in Western European markets. In Australia, online retail sales are projected to double from A$16.9 billion in 2009 to A$33.3 billion in 2015.[23]

Legal practice in cyberspace is also exploding and e-spaces and new information technologies have permanently reconfigured the structure of the legal profession and the provision of legal services. Virtual law practices and extra-jurisdictional

20 Susskind, *The End of Lawyers?*, chap. 3, 17.
21 Ibid., chap. 3, 17–18.
22 Susskind, *Tomorrow's Lawyers*, chap. 1, 11–12.
23 Gordon, Shackel and Mark, 'Regulation of Legal Services in the E-World', 55.

outsourcing are now firm landmarks in the new e-terrain, and social media and networking sites like Facebook, MySpace, Twitter, LinkedIn and blogging sites are tools well used, to both market and provide legal services.[24]

It is thus indisputable that information technologies and e-spaces have altered the contours of the administration of justice itself, the nature of the lawyer–client relationship, the way lawyers deliver legal services and how legal clients experience justice and interact with the law. Some common examples of e-lawyering and e-justice practices that have emerged and which now are well entrenched around the globe, with particular implications for increased access to justice, include courts increasingly automating their processes, for example adopting e-filing procedures; lawyers managing litigation and dispute resolution through e-mechanisms such as e-discovery; there has also been an explosion in the use of document assembly software products; and automated search and research processes.[25] It is unlikely that the e-wave and its impact on legal services and business more broadly will subside into the future. Susskind (2013) in his most recent book, *Tomorrow's Lawyers: An Introduction to Your Future*,[26] suggests that:

> … it might be time for lawyers to rethink some of their working practices. It is simply inconceivable that information technology will radically alter all corners of our economy and society and yet somehow legal work will be exempt from any change.
>
> It is exciting and yet disconcerting to contemplate that there is no finishing line for IT and the Internet.
>
> One key challenge for the legal profession, however, is to adopt new systems earlier; to identify and grasp the opportunities afforded by emerging technologies.
>
> We need, as lawyers, to be open-minded because we are living in an era of unprecedented technological change.

The pervasive use of new technologies and e-based spaces in the practice of law thus renders competence in technology an essential element of legal professional responsibility and the duties of a lawyer.[27] This is increasingly being recognised by professional bodies around the globe and reflected in formal statements made by such bodies. For example, the ABA House of Delegates in August 2012 approved the ABA's Commission on Ethics 2020 proposal to include direct reference to a lawyer's duty to maintain technological competence in the Comment to Rule 1.1. This Rule states that:

24 Ibid., 56.
25 Goodenough, 'Developing an E-Curriculum'.
26 Susskind, Tomorrow's Lawyers, chap. 1, 15–17.
27 Goodenough, 'Developing an E-Curriculum', 863.

> A lawyer shall provide competent representation to a client. Competent representation requires the legal knowledge, skill, thoroughness and preparation reasonably necessary for the representation.[28]

Comment [8] as approved by the House of Delegates[29] provides that:

> To maintain the requisite knowledge and skill, a lawyer should keep abreast of changes in the law and its practice, including the benefits and risks associated with relevant technology, engage in continuing study and education and comply with all continuing legal education requirements to which the lawyer is subject.

Similarly the Commentaries to the Canadian Bar Association Code of Professional Conduct (2009)[30] state that:

> 4. Competence involves more than an understanding of legal principles; it involves an adequate knowledge of the practice and procedures by which those principles can be effectively applied. To accomplish this, the lawyer should keep abreast of developments in all areas in which a lawyer practises. The lawyer should also develop and maintain a facility with advances in technology in areas in which the lawyer practises to maintain a level of competence that meets the standard reasonably expected of lawyers in similar circumstances.[31]

A lawyer's competence in the technology that today supports the legal services marketplace generally, and in specific areas of a lawyer's practice and legal work, is thus undeniably an essential dimension of a lawyer's professional responsibility. However, a lawyer's professional responsibility also necessitates that lawyers understand not only how relevant technology works but also how such technology may challenge lawyers' professional responsibilities – their duties to the court, to clients and to third parties. E-spaces increase the risk, for example, of inadvertent disclosure of confidential information, conflicts of interest, inadvertent communications or unintended professional relationships.[32] A competent lawyer

28 American Bar Association, *Model Rules of Professional Conduct*, Rule 1.1, accessed October 1, 2013, http://www.americanbar.org/groups/professional_responsibility/publications/model_rules_of_professional_conduct/model_rules_of_professional_conduct_table_of_contents.html.

29 American Bar Association House of Delegates, Resolution 105A, 'Approval of Commission's Recommendations.(Technology & Confidentiality)', August 6, 2012, accessed September 1, 2013, http://www.americanbar.org/content/dam/aba/administrative/ethics_2020/20120802_revised_resolution_105a.authcheckdam.pdf.

30 Canadian Bar Association, *Code of Professional Conduct*, accessed October 1, 2013, http://www.cba.org/CBA/activities/pdf/codeofconduct.pdf.

31 Ibid., chap. 2.

32 Gordon, Shackel and Mark, 'Regulation of Legal Services in the e-World'.

must thus be able to navigate both the *practical* and *ethical* contours of new technologies in conduct of legal work.

Therefore the next question that arises for consideration in our discussion, is whether law schools should be responsible for ensuring that law graduates have obtained at least a threshold level of competence in legal technology and understanding of the ethical challenges such media present. The New York Bar Association in its 2011 report of the Task Force on the Future of the Legal Profession concluded that law schools should play a greater role in training prospective lawyers about practical ways to use technology in legal work stating that:

> Law schools throughout the state should place greater emphasis on practical courses in various aspects of legal technology such as eDiscovery, document management technology, advanced online research, legal technology in the courtroom, and project management … law schools can better serve their students and the profession by offering instruction in a broader range of technological subjects and integrating such classes into the requirements for graduation.[33]

Whilst competence in legal technology is one thing, arguably, lawyers and particularly the lawyers of the future, will have to go beyond a threshold level of technological competency. As Susskind (2013) challenges, lawyers must '… innovate, to practise law in ways that we could not have done in the past'.[34] The challenge then for law schools and law teachers is to ensure that the foundations for such innovation are laid down as a core part of legal education, with a view not only to ensuring that law graduates are competent to navigate the future e-landscape of legal practice but to *innovate* it, shape its contours and to do so in a way that meets the needs of the market and also ensures that public confidence in the administration of justice and in the legal profession is preserved and that legal professional responsibility and ethical decision-making in legal practice is not eroded but rather remains a concrete cornerstone of lawyering, even in the new e-world and e-based marketplace.

The next section of this chapter thus considers how e-based technologies can be utilised as a tool for teaching law so as to meet the needs of law graduates, the legal profession, the legal services marketplace and the interests of the administration of justice.

---

33 New York State Bar Association, *Report of the Taskforce on the Future of the Legal Profession*, April 2, 2011, accessed October 1, 2013, http://www.nysba.org/WorkArea/DownloadAsset.aspx?id=26691, 99.

34 Susskind, *Tomorrow's Lawyers*, chap. 1, 18.

E-based Technologies as a Tool for Teaching and Learning in Law

Drawing in part on the discussion above, it is clear that utilising e-based technologies in legal education serves at least three primary goals: (i) e-based technologies provide a medium to enable active, student-engaged and collaborative learning as a pathway to quality in experience and education; (ii) provides students with the opportunity to develop understanding of and skills in using the technology that is shaping the legal services marketplace; and (iii) provides students with an opportunity to reflect upon and experience first-hand some of the professional and ethical challenges thrown up by e-based technologies.

In consideration of how e-based technologies can serve learning in law and fulfil the role of legal education, we must first ask: *What are the opportunities for the use of e-technologies within the law curricula?* Secondly: *How do these opportunities enable student learning and enhance the law school experience for students?* And thirdly: *How does the e-medium in legal education bridge the gap between law as an academic focus and preparation of students for the realities of legal practice?*

Much has been written about the pedagogical value of 'flipped' or 'blended learning' in higher education[35] including specifically within the law curricula.[36] Flipped or blended learning[37] is a teaching strategy that utilises online or electronic modes of teaching in conjunction with traditional face-to-face classroom-based modes of teaching. For example, teachers can provide material to students online and create channels for student learning in a myriad of ways such as using podcasts, webinars, videos, blogs or online discussion boards including in conjunction with one another in varied ways. These learning activities are coupled or 'blended' with face-to-face modes of teaching and learning. The study of law creates many rich opportunities for blended learning, for example, learning activities outside of the classroom supported by various forms of e-media can be used to help students develop research, statutory interpretation, case analysis and critical thinking skills. Classroom time can then be freed up and devoted to other key learning activities, such as problem questions, moots, and classroom discussion or debates that create opportunities for students to share the knowledge and skills they have acquired outside the classroom and further build upon, extend and refine such knowledge, understanding and skills, in collaboration and with guidance from their peers and teacher.

---

35 See, for example, US Department of Education, Office of Planning, Evaluation, and Policy Development, *Evaluation of Evidence-Based Practices in Online Learning: A Meta-Analysis and Review of Online Learning Studies* (Washington, D.C., 2010).

36 Sarah Lambert and Chris Brewer, '1st, 2nd and 3rd Generation Implementations of an eLearning Design: Re-use from Postgraduate Law to Block/online Engineering Course', *Journal of Learning Design* 2 (2007).

37 Mark Stubbs, Ian Martin and Lewis Endlar, 'The Structuration of Blended Learning: Putting Holistic Design Principles into Practice', *British Journal of Educational Technology* 37 (2006).

E-based learning thus can be seen to encourage flexible and independent student learning and facilitates individualised, student-driven learning by permitting students to work at their own pace outside of the classroom, when and how they find most productive. The e-learning space creates a cradle for students to explore and engage with new information and knowledge. This effectively flips the traditional teacher–student dynamic from teacher-centred to student-centred. The teacher is effectively ousted from 'sage on the stage'[38] to the role of a facilitator in student learning. The classroom thus becomes a forum for engaging students in active, collaborative and problem-based learning activities and providing students with targeted formative feedback. Research suggests that flipped or blended learning is as effective, and in some settings, even more effective for adult learners, compared to teaching that is entirely classroom-based.[39] For the adult learner e-based learning opens up spaces for collaborative and shared learning experiences which arguably do not only deepen the student's learning experience but simultaneously creates pathways for sustainable communities of learning in the educational setting which can also be extended into professional spaces. Given the increased importance of connectivity, networking and community building in the e-landscape of legal practice and business, this collateral benefit of e-based learning is not to be underestimated and indeed should be actively cultivated within the law school setting.

Importantly also, e-learning provides law students with first-hand experience of the e-medium. This creates an important opportunity for students to also explore and navigate the ethical contours and dynamics of e-communication and e-spaces. E-lawyering throws up many ethical challenges for the modern lawyer that extend beyond the duty of competence into duties of confidentiality and security, supervision, conflicts of interest, the nature of lawyer–client relationships and the risk of inadvertent or inappropriate communications.[40] As students navigate and utilise e-learning tools and platforms, many of the same challenges will present themselves in the course of students accessing, communicating and producing information as part of their learning journey. This provides students with an invaluable opportunity to become sensitised to these ethical realities of e-spaces outside of the social spaces that students are already likely to be familiar with, and confront such issues within the context and parameters of professional engagement and exchange.

The use of e-based teaching and learning strategies offers law teachers fertile ground for providing students with a deep, quality and positive learning experience at law school, and one that can help law students attain the substantive

38 Alison King, 'From Sage on the Stage to Guide on the Side', *College Teaching* 41 (1993).

39 Lambert and Brewer, '1st, 2nd and 3rd Generation Implementations of an eLearning Design'.

40 See generally Gordon, Shackel and Mark, 'Regulation of Legal Services in the E-World'.

knowledge needed for successful modern day legal practice, sensitise students to the ethical challenges of e-lawyering, obtain the skills necessary to navigate legal technology and additionally can create opportunities for students to build long-lasting relationships that can be taken forward into the professional context. In this way e-learning can be a vehicle for planting various seeds during the law school years, which can over time, be harvested by graduates as they transition into the legal profession and which they can draw upon as they navigate the contours of the e-terrain that now sustains legal practice and the legal services marketplace.

The benefits of e-based learning in legal education have been clearly outlined in the discussion above, this however is not to suggest or ignore the challenges that information technologies and blended modes of learning present to law schools and law teachers. Apart from the potential resource implications (both in terms of time and money) that such learning strategies give rise to, e-media also potentially raise ethical issues for the law school teacher, these include that e-based learning activities and asynchronous modes of learning are arguably more open to abuse by students, for example, through inappropriate student collusion, recycling of student materials/answers, plagiarism and there is also the risk that some students may flounder rather than thrive in such a flexible learning environment. Ultimately, however, it is the role of the law teacher to shape such activities in ways that offer students sufficient structure in their learning and at the same time minimise such risks and pitfalls. Indeed it is well recognised that e-learning strategies are not only labour intensive for teachers but demand a high level of expertise and technical proficiency on the part of the teacher. This of itself may also be an important factor that ultimately helps bridge the gap between law school and the legal profession. As Susskind (2013) suggests '[i]nvolving practitioners in the delivery of ... courses would be good, both to give students insight into evolving experience in the market and to encourage cross-fertilisation between the academic and practising branches of the profession'.[41]

Conclusion

This chapter has argued that the time is ripe for law schools and law teachers to strategically review and redevelop curricula and adopt teaching and learning strategies that fulfil the fundamental purpose of legal education – the training of our future lawyers – but at the same time continue to provide an academic education for its students that is rigorous and which instils the foundations for life-long professional learning and development, reflexive thinking and ethical decision-making and practice. Law schools must recognise and respond to the needs of a modern legal profession and to the realities of legal practice and a legal services marketplace that has been transformed and which continues to be shaped by e-spaces and new information technologies. Law schools must redevelop and

41 Susskind, *Tomorrow's Lawyers*, chap. 13, 10.

deliver curricula that provide students with a legal education that recognises that many of its graduates will not only be the lawyers of the future but will be pioneers in navigating new terrain in e-lawyering. As legal academics we have a duty to rise to this challenge and meet the needs of our students, our profession and of the administration of justice.

PART III
International Experiences

Chapter 13

The Case of the Common Law in European Legal Education

Avrom Sherr[1]

The journey across the Channel Tunnel may not be far, but the distance that divides systems based on the Napoleonic code from the precedential basis of the Common Law is considerable. The Common Law countries of Europe suffer an extra set of difficulties in relation to European legal education. Not only do they need to contemplate, consider and discuss the development, integration and harmonisation of European law (issues which other European countries also face); they have the additional difficulty of absorbing the approach of a different juridical family and legal culture. The adjustment involved in trying to keep up with massive political change in the growing coverage of the European Union is exacerbated by the absence of a set of shared assumptions that exist between jurisdictions from the same juridical family. The UK can seriously wonder whether the Common Law approach will have a long term future in Europe, or whether it will be subsumed within the Civil Law culture of its European colleagues.

But, the European context is not the only operating factor. Europe itself must do business internationally and with multi-national companies. The importance of the United States of America in international trade and the effect this will have on modes of transaction and legal culture should not be ignored. Americanisation includes a strengthening of Common Law approach. The nature of this effect though, may not be politically channelled through the Common Law members of the European Union, but will be felt across all countries, through transactional rather than political impetus. But, in the same way that the effect of the United States constitution was to be transported strongly through interstate trade rather than politics in the early days of American federalism, the power of commerce may still prove stronger than that of policy.[2]

So, what may be learned from the case of the Common Law in European legal education, given this background? This chapter will concentrate on three issues:

---

1 Professor, Director 2004–2012, Institute of Advanced Legal Studies, University of London, England.

2 See e.g. K. Karst, Judicial Review and the Channel Tunnel in 1980 *Southern California Law Review*, vol. 53, 402–785.

1. The English and Welsh model of legal education, training and qualification.
2. The impact of the Common Law/Civil Law families divide on European law and legal education.
3. The impact of changing legal professions and professionalism on future legal education across Europe.

Although the collection of these items ranges across a wide set of issues, each issue may be instructed in terms of the Common Law tradition and its place in European legal education.

"Il Modello Inglese"

In an essay published by the Faculty of Law at the University of Genoa in 1996 I elucidated the theoretical division between two traditional approaches to legal education, the apprenticeship model and the educational model, as two different models of professional "formation".[3]

Table 13.1 Approaches to legal education

Apprenticeship Model	Eduational Model
Practice	Theory
Reality	Concepts and Ideas
Sitting at the feet of …	Abstraction
Inheriting the mantle of the Priesthood	A formative approach

The assumptions which underlie each of the above models are fairly clear. However, the reality of legal education turns out to be very different. Apprenticeship is supposed to provide a full understanding of what is involved in legal practice. As a system of training the new profession it ought to give, like a set of courses in a formalised training structure, a full range of understanding of the world of practice. However, the venues in which apprenticeship takes place both for solicitors and barristers in England and Wales are now heavily specialised firms and chambers with little capacity to provide the full range of real practice which would be an ideal introduction to the law.[4] Solicitors' practices which provide apprenticeship training (the training contract) are largely orientated

3 I am indebted to Margot Horspool for the original conception of these different models. See also the range of these across Europe as set out in *International Journal for the legal Profession*, vol. 2, no. 1 (1995) Special Issue Legal Education and Training in Europe.

4 See e.g. A. Sherr, Professional and Legal Training in 1992 *Journal of Law and Society*, 163–74.

towards company and commercial work, or are involved in the "high street" work of conveyancing and legal aid family and crime. There is now very little crossover between these two groupings. Training in practice now therefore means training in a very particular sort of specialised practice. The ability of lawyers to move to other areas of practice at a later date is considerably undermined by this massively specialised form of training.

The type of firms and chambers who are prepared to take on trainees are also usually quite special. They need to be large enough to support the new bureaucracy of the training contract and they will also as a result, be quite involved in managing their practices as a business enterprise, with a level of standardisation of work in order to provide efficiency. The management of a business enterprise does not always go well, hand in hand, with effective training. Some trainees complain of being overworked in some repetitive task areas. Some complain of long hours and a strong expectation to pull their weight as money earners from the beginning.[5]

Apprenticeship is also supposed to provide reality, as compared with a more formal educational approach, dealing with clients and others directly and the vicissitudes of real life. However, trainees in large organisations are often kept at some distance from clients. Their work is devolved down to them and deskilled. They often do not understand the nature of transactions or litigation in which they are involved, because the tasks they carry out and the role they fulfil are such a small part only of the whole process.[6]

In the traditional model of the apprenticeship relationship, the apprentice would "sit at the feet of" his or her "master" or "mistress" who would initiate the apprentice into the secrets of the trade. They would be imbued with the fire of experience and they would receive, individually, the professional tradition on a one-to-one basis. Now, in order to avoid the uncertainties of a poor apprenticeship, the system of training is much more formalised. There is rarely an individual-to-individual relationship. Trainees move from "seat" to "seat" in different departments of a larger enterprise and they miss out on the fire of enthusiasm which could be handed from generation to generation in the old system. They would also traditionally have inherited "the mantle of the priesthood" and then moved into the position of their "master" when their master retired or died. The liklihood of job inheritance is now quite small. Although, in some firms they do intend to take on trainees who will move into partnership, this progression is much more of a corporate style of movement than an individualistic right of passage. Nowadays, it is unlikely that apprenticeship in any occupation can be considered to be a job for life.[7]

5 Richard Moorhead and Fiona Boyle Quality of Life and Trainee Solicitors: A Survey, 1995 *International Journal of the Legal Profession*, 217–51.

6 See e.g. A. Sherr *Client Care for Lawyers*, Sweet & Maxwell, London 1999, 138–47.

7 M. Galanter and T. Palay *The Tournament of Lawyers – The Transformation of the Big Law Firm*, Chicago University Press, Chicago 1991; M. Galanter and W. Henderson, The Elastic Tournament: A Second Transformation of the Big Law Firm in 2008 *Stanford Law Review*, vol. 60, no. 6.

Over in the educational model is the system of formation which is more usually to be found as the exclusive model both in parts of Europe, and in the United States. The assumptions underlying this model are that it presents a stronger, more basic, theoretical approach to the study of law. Unfortunately, in England and Wales, we find our undergraduate programme to include increasingly "black letter" law, providing considerable amounts of doctrinal information to be learned and regurgitated. The subjects are often limited to a fairly narrow "core" which is partly dictated by the profession. There is little jurisprudence in the sense of "legal theory" and very little comparative law. There is very little study of the system and how it works or of any higher theory or social science doctrine. In some subjects, where the pressure of more and more material has been greatest, teachers have been forced to analyse their subject area more into concepts and ideas rather than sheer knowledge. But, often this conceptualisation has not occurred. Courses tend to be so packed with cases and statutes that there is little time within the three years of the undergraduate law degree for abstract thought and reflection. In general the examination method still applies and the form of the examination tends to dictate the method of teaching and the approach and culture of the students.

The three years within formal education is intended to provide a formative period for students, during which they can develop both emotionally and intellectually. This issue is especially important in relation to their ethical and moral development.[8] But, our students do not now treat this period in any idealised fashion. They consider the degree merely to be a stepping stone to take them forward to their goal. Examination results are therefore the only outcomes which matter.

Apart from changes in the social culture of education generally and legal education in particular, there have been both regulatory and bureaucratic changes in the systems for monitoring education in England, Wales and Scotland. The Higher Education Funding Councils organise a Research Excellence Framework (REF) and the Quality Assurance Agency for Higher Education organises an assessment of the quality of teaching and teaching systems. Both of these have the tendency towards the formalisation and standardisation of research and teaching approaches.

Coupled with the Institute for Teaching and Learning in Higher Education, these have produced an important advantage in relation to higher education establishments which previously fell below the norm. However, there are serious negative effects also possible for those establishments which did not previously need bureaucratic intervention or formalisation in order to achieve, or operate at, a high standard in relation both to research and teaching. Such interventions are clearly aimed at a mass system of higher education, organised to include institutions and students which would not previously have considered degree status. In general, law degree authorised institutions have tended to deal with faculty and staff motivated towards objectives beyond the mere label of an

8 Lord Chancellor's Advisory Committee on Legal Education and Conduct, First Report on Legal Education and Training, 1996, 55–72.

undergraduate degree. Disciplines such as law and medicine may benefit less from these interventions than others. But, the effect of such educational policy will be felt across all sectors and disciplines.

The largest changes within legal education for the profession have occurred at an even later stage through the development of vocational professional courses, formal elements of training within apprenticeship (as mentioned above) and the Continuing Professional Development (CPD) of lifelong learning.

In summary, the informality and variability of apprenticeship is considerably controlled within a structured and formalised system for solicitors (and further changes are about to take place through the Solicitors Regulation Authority[9]), although less so for barristers, and this reduces some of the major advantages of an apprentice system. However, it does strengthen individual areas of poor performance within that system which would otherwise have fallen below an acceptable norm. The educational model is now perceived by students and utilised by society more pragmatically than as a stage of development and maturity. It is a product-orientated period aiming to achieve the narrower objectives of securing a qualification, and preparing students for some elements of practice. Formalisation and bureaucratisation of higher education are also beginning to standardise legal education. This may raise the standard of lower achieving institutions but will limit diversity. The Common Law approach to legal education can therefore provide some interesting comparison for the rest of Europe. As we move to harmonisation of qualifications such issues will need careful attention.

Common Law at the Suit of Civil Law or the Harmonisation of the Two

The educational aspects of handling European law may be separated from the issues relating to the distinctions between national legal systems and the new law of Europe. But, for the Common Law countries there is a separate and much greater problem of the harmonisation, merger, or take-over of Common Law jurisprudence by the Civil Law jurisprudence of most countries in Europe. Although this is seen as the problem of England, Wales, Scotland and Ireland it is undoubtedly a problem, in relation to harmonisation, for the other European countries to contend with, as well.

This raises a much considered but undecided set of issues about the precise distinctions between the Civil and Common Law. It is an issue with cultural, theoretical, political, sociological and economic, as well as legal, dimensions. It is very much a "big issue" which has vexed jurists for some time. Many, including in particular Mirjan Damaska,[10] have endeavoured to explain the fundamental differences in the two systems, approaches, philosophies, cultures and histories

9 http://www.sra.org.uk/sra/policy/training-for-tomorrow/work-streams.page.

10 See e.g. Mirjan R. Damaska, *The Faces of Justice and State Authority: A Comparative Approach to the Legal Process*, Yale University Press, New Haven CT, 1986.

and so on. It seems clear that the overall comparisons defy a simplistic analysis on an intellectual plain. The politics of Europe are rather more obvious, but they still defy rational solutions as can be seen in the negotiation processes involved in agreeing all the major treaties of the Common Market, European Economic Community and European Union. Although the politics may be more obvious, they are less certain in their outcome.

With an uncertain intellectual base, and a set of unclear political results, it is difficult to know how to handle the legal educational aspects of the Common Law–Civil Law divide. Europe has done rather well in producing the Erasmus and Socrates programmes, providing both student and faculty exchanges across the members of the European Union. Professor Fenge's work on the effect of these programmes provides interesting evidence of the degree of awareness of European issues, involvement in European exchange and study of European law. This author's own intuitive research among students who have come across from mainland Europe on these programmes, or English students who have gone to other countries in Europe suggests that this method of exchange may not be sufficient by itself to produce the necessary analysis of distinctions between Common Law and Civil Law systems. Such students, and indeed staff, who have been involved in these exchanges, note only the complexity of the comparisons between the different systems. Although we have therefore produced a group of exchange students and staff who are to some extent "super Europeans" with some real understanding of both Civil and Common Law approaches, ultimate analysis of fundamental difference which intellectually will be necessary for real harmonisation still defies easy achievement.

It is suggested that, like the inbreeding of the evolutionary process, more widespread integration will be achieved through continuing this dual learning approach. But integration and true harmonisation are quite different processes with a rather different outcome. The two systems may continue to live happily side by side, but European law will have a more long term effect on trying to bring them closer together.

The disciplines of comparative law and the insights they allow is somehow not sufficient for the fast moving process of Europeanisation. Comparativists are tested quite strongly by the political nature of this process and what can be achieved in unpicking differences over a short period of time.

One instance, showing the complexity of any analysis relates to the effect of the European Money Laundering Directive on legal professions across Europe. The Law Societies of the Common Law jurisdictions of Europe, England and Wales, Scotland and Ireland signed up to the first Money Laundering Directive, incorporating into their own ethical rules of conduct a total obedience to the aims of the Money Laundering Directive, which were then largely pointed at banks and other financial institutions. It would appear that these presented "a good example" of public interest in fighting crime.

The position taken by the Common Law jurisdictions contrasts strongly with the opposite position taken by most of the Civil Law countries of Europe, apart from the Netherlands. Most Civil Law countries considered the principles of lawyer–client confidentiality and of privilege to be essential elements in championing liberty against the shadow of the over powerful state.

This position appeared to be a stark contrast and difficult discussions were held in Brussels on how to harmonise the total opposition of principle. However, on a closer inspection of the reality of practice it became clear that legal professionals in the Common Law countries were not in fact reporting their clients, or even potential clients to the (then) National Criminal Investigation Service where there was any question of money laundering, or doubts about the identity of potential clients or of the provenance of funds. In the Common Law tradition, although the rules were clearly stated in the rule book they were politely, if hypocritically, ignored and ways were found around the reporting obligations which appeared to be present. In reality therefore the differences of principle turned out to be similarities of practice, thus proving that any work in this area must consider a number of different levels, both of reality and of principle in producing a complete analysis of where differences occur and where problems arise.

Changes in the Legal Professions of Common Law Europe and the Effect of these Changes on Legal Education

Borrowing, as they do, from the experience of the United States, the Common Law legal professions of Europe have been ahead of the Civil Law jurisdictions in changes in structure, organisation, work and specialisation. These changes can be summarised as a move towards industrialisation and deprofessionalisation. These professional changes ought to change considerably the structure, nature and education and training needs of the legal professions of the future.

Elsewhere[11] I have discussed the effect of these changes on current work practices. It is now necessary to consider how legal education and training should, or should not match up to the new paradigms of legal work. If legal education should react to the new legal profession and not serve its own, or separate, interests, how should legal education and training be organised for the future? Some possible changes in career paths for lawyers and in legal subject areas within the Common Law system need also to be addressed.

Among the new legal careers emerging are the "back office" drafts person, information officer/professional support lawyer, specialist technician, advocate, manager, client handler/manager/partner, strategist and risk manager.[12] In addition, for Common Law lawyers there may be some new legal concepts as

11 A. Sherr, *Superheroes and Slaves – Images of the New Legal Professional, Current Legal Problems*, Oxford University Press, Oxford, 1995.

12 Beyond Superheroes and Slaves: Educating the Lawyer for 2010 – Theory in Legal Education, Eds. Sugarman & Sherr, Editorial, Special Issue on Legal Education, *International Journal of the Legal Profession*, 2000.

subject classifications. These include relative need, risk, right, relationship, responsibility, remedy and quality of life. There may also be some new legal subject classifications including the state, the individual, the family, the corporate body, the trust, the environment, capacity and conflict. Although many of these are similar to areas of legal work currently covered, the argument is that the new classification will overall present a rather different picture for the evolution of both legal practice and legal education. Some of these areas are already better recognisable within Civil Law jurisdictions than within the Common Law, but some other elements may need further consideration as to how the impact of the changes in the law and the legal profession will be taken up within legal education.

Conclusion

The member countries of the European Union need a continuing, open awareness to differences in approach in legal education as well as in law of other member countries. There is a great deal we can still learn from each other. Student, teacher and practitioner exchange schemes are essential elements of this progressive development. Changes occur outside of the European Union context which will impact on the profession and legal education. These also must continue to be monitored so that we can understand and plan for the future in circumstances of growing harmonisation. A similar position might be of interest for Hong Kong in its relationship of legal systems with the Law of the PRC.

Chapter 14
The Challenge of Massive Open Online Courses (MOOCs) to Traditional Legal Education: The Australian Experience

Joellen Riley[1]

To MOOC or Not to MOOC?

Will the phenomenon of the 'Massive Open Online Course' or 'MOOC' – typified by the extensive program of courses offered by the US-based Coursera,[2] Udacity,[3] and EdX[4] – radically change the delivery of a legal education, in the way that it promises to revolutionise the delivery of computer science and business degrees?[5] I doubt it. While many potential candidates for enrolment in a MOOC in computer science, or in some fascinating humanities subject, may see value in education simply for education's sake, most potential candidates for a law degree are seeking an accredited qualification which will enable them to practise law. While an employer seeking to recruit a webmaster or computer programmer may be prepared to trust a candidate who has acquired knowledge through online study without obtaining formal credit, it is likely (at least for the foreseeable future) that employers of lawyers will want to employ people with degrees that qualify them for admission to practise. The most ambitious law students will certainly want to acquire those qualifications. So until it is possible to obtain an accredited law degree through MOOCs, 'real-time', in-person enrolment in law schools is

---

1 Dean and Professor of Labour Law, Sydney Law School, Australia.

2 See https://www.coursera.org/# (last accessed 20 September 2013). As at 20 September 2013, Coursera boasted 4,823,514 enrolled students (called 'Courserians'), and 447 separate courses offered by 87 partner organisations across the world. A number of the courses on offer relate to law.

3 See https://www.udacity.com/ (last accessed 20 September 2013).

4 See https://www.edx.org/ (last accessed 20 September 2013).

5 See for example plans by Georgia Institute of Technology to mass-market a computer science degree: Gabriel Kahn, 'The master of MOOC', *Australian Financial Review*, Monday 12 August 2013, p. 25.

likely to remain the norm. It will take a considerable revolution in the thinking of admission authorities to change this situation.

This is not to say that excellent MOOCs are not already available offering instruction in legal subjects. There are. See, for example, the course on Constitutional Law offered by Professor Akhil Reed Amar from Yale,[6] and the course on English Common Law: Structure and Principles offered by Professor Adam Gearey at the University of London.[7] Presently, these are not being offered for credit towards any formal legal qualification, and indeed there are insufficient offerings at present to cover anything like a full law curriculum. Nevertheless, I believe we can expect that over time the MOOC – and the digital revolution that has enabled this phenomenon – will influence the way we teach law, even in accredited law degree programs.[8]

This chapter presents a view from the perspective of a legal educator in Australia, and particularly in New South Wales, who must remain ever mindful of the stipulations of the Legal Profession Admission Board (LPAB) when contemplating even minor changes to curriculum or delivery of accredited law degrees such as the Bachelor of Laws (LLB), or the Juris Doctor (JD). But I imagine that many of my fellow deans around the region will share similar experiences in dealing with their own admission authorities.

New South Wales Admission Requirements

In order to be admitted to legal practice in New South Wales, a person must hold an LLB or JD from a university, or a Diploma of Law issued directly by the LPAB,[9] plus a diploma from an accredited 'practical legal training' provider.[10]

The LPAB guards the quality and content of accredited law programs particularly jealously. In the short time I have been dean of Sydney Law School[11] I have had two detailed 'please explain' letters from the LPAB about matters related to the content and delivery of the LLB/JD programs. One concerned the extent to which our degree programs provided adequate learning in statutory interpretation.

6 See https://www.coursera.org/#course/conlaw (last accessed 20 September 2013).

7 See https://www.coursera.org/#course/engcomlaw (last accessed 20 September 2013).

8 According to Richard Susskind, author of *Tomorrow's Lawyers: An Introduction to your Future*, Oxford University Press, 2013, and *The End of Lawyers? Rethinking the Nature of Legal Services*, Oxford University Press, 2008, the digital revolution will have a much more fundamental impact on the delivery of legal services more generally.

9 Teaching of the LPAB's own law qualification is managed by the Law Extension Committee, appointed by the Senate of the University of Sydney. The LPAB directly controls the curriculum and assessment requirements for the Diploma of Law course. See http://sydney.edu.au/lec/ (last accessed 20 September 2013) for more information on this program.

10 See http://www.lpab.lawlink.nsw.gov.au/lpab/legalprofession_req_admssn_lawyer.html (last accessed 20 September 2013) for admission requirements in NSW.

11 I assumed my current post on 2 January 2013.

The request for information stipulated that we should demonstrate not only how we teach, but also how we assess competency in statutory interpretation skills. The LPAB is concerned not only with course content, but with graduate outcomes. Every law school in New South Wales was required to respond to this request. We understand that the request for information is to be considered by the national Law Admissions Consultative Committee (LACC) in determining whether to recommend that accredited law schools should offer a stand-alone, special unit of study in statutory interpretation as part of the core curriculum. We are already required (for the purposes of accreditation) to demonstrate that our curriculum contains adequate coverage of what are known as the 'Priestley 11' topics,[12] and at our law school, this means that two-thirds of our overall degree program is comprised of compulsory units of study.[13] (We embed statutory interpretation in a number of these courses, and offer an advanced elective in Interpretation.)

The second request from the LPAB required a report on how our law school ensures that all candidates for an LLB or JD complete the equivalent of three years full-time study in academic law subjects (not including clinical legal training courses). The correspondence indicated that the LPAB preferred the view that three full-time years should be interpreted as three calendar years of full-time study. In our response to this enquiry we needed to explain the way that summer and winter schools fit into our programs of study. Particularly ambitious students who wish to complete their legal studies in less than three calendar years can (if they are diligent enough) complete one or two units of study over the December to February summer break, and they can also complete a single unit of study in the June–July winter break. Consistently using the summer and winter breaks to complete units can enable a candidate to complete the JD qualification in two and a half calendar years.

We believe that we provided a satisfactory answer to the LPAB's concerns, because we were able to demonstrate that a summer school unit of study involves precisely the same requirements – in terms of hours of face-to-face tuition, range of topics, volume of reading, and quantity and quality of assessment – as a unit of

12 The Legal Profession Admission Rules 2005, made under the *Legal Profession Admission Act 2004* (NSW) s 38, conform to the Uniform Admission Rules for Australian jurisdictions. See http://www1.lawcouncil.asn.au/LACC/images/pdfs/212390818_1_LACCUniformAdmissionRules2008.pdf (last accessed 23 September 2013). These rules include the requirement that an accredited law qualification must include coverage of the 11 topics, determined by the Law Admissions Consultative Committee chaired by Justice LJ (Bill) Priestley in 1992. Law schools must demonstrate that their compulsory curriculum covers these topics in order to secure and retain accreditation. The topics are: 1. Criminal Law and Procedure; 2. Torts; 3. Contracts; 4. Property; 5. Equity (including Trusts); 6. Company Law; 7. Administrative Law; 8. Federal and State Constitutional Law; 9. Civil Procedure; 10 Evidence; 11. Ethics and Professional Responsibility.

13 For the list of compulsory subjects in the Sydney Law School LLB course, see http://sydney.edu.au/law/cstudent/undergrad/docs_pdfs/2013_LLBUnitlist.pdf (last accessed 20 September 2013).

study taught during the regular semester. We were particularly mindful in making our responses that the admission authorities may harbour some suspicion of any kind of 'intensive' delivery of a law course. Conventional wisdom suggests that law is a complex discipline in which knowledge is absorbed gradually and skills are developed incrementally. Too intensive a format for class delivery challenges those assumptions, and provokes fears that graduates may be inadequately prepared for the rigours of practice.

Given this kind of scrutiny of our regular face-to-face teaching programs, I think the New South Wales admission authorities would look rather sceptically on any move to provide a legal education through a MOOC. MOOCs may look too much like a cut-price 'short cut' to a jealously guarded qualification. And of course there is no real advantage in a 'global' law degree provided by a MOOC, when each candidate needs a jurisdictionally specific legal education that meets the requirements for admission in a particular jurisdiction.[14] Nevertheless, law schools – and, dare I say, the admission authorities – will need to respond to the digital revolution, to see what advantage can be taken of the new capacity to provide legal education through online course delivery. After all, there is at least one 'distance education' law program in New South Wales already, delivered by the University of New England (UNE), located in northern rural New South Wales.[15] UNE has been successfully offering law degree by a distance education, supported by some residential schools, for decades.

What MOOCs Can and Can't Do

From scans of web sources,[16] and my conversations with academics in the United States, I understand that MOOCs can be either open and free (that is, students do not pay any charges to complete the program), or they can be offered for a fee. MOOCs can also take two formats: the MOOC based on the 'cognitive–behaviourist pedagogical model', sometimes referred to as an 'x-MOOC', and the 'c-MOOC', based on 'connectivism'.[17] These terms require some explanation. The first model is the one most familiar to legal educators: the MOOC provides a course outline and materials, and an author/ instructor who manages and presents the course. The author/instructor is the expert (hence the 'x-' prefix to 'MOOC'), who disseminates knowledge to the students. The

14 See, for example, the Priestley 11 requirements set out above at n. 12.

15 See http://www.une.edu.au/courses/2014/courses/BLAWS (last accessed 20 September 2013).

16 See the web pages for Coursera, Udacity and EdX at nn. 2, 3 and 4.

17 See C. Osvaldo Rodriguez, 'MOOCs and the AI-Stanford like Courses: Two Successful and Distinct Course Formats for Massive Open Online Courses', *European Journal of Open, Distance and E-Learning*, http://www.eurodl.org/?article=516 (last accessed 1 November 2013).

x-MOOC mimics the traditional class room, but uses online platforms for the teacher to deliver instruction. The c-MOOC, however, is a facilitated collective of participants, who define the content of the course themselves, as their interaction progresses. The c-MOOC is based on the philosophy that learners define their own path to knowledge. Their mutual engagement becomes an 'iterative process of search, practice and reflection'[18] as they work together, communicating through blogs, twitter and social media sites. This kind of MOOC is more like a student study group – though one in which the students themselves search out, select and share resources and so design their own programs of study. This second kind of MOOC is less likely to provide a threat to traditional law schools than the first kind, although it may provide a particularly valuable platform for collaboration among legal research students.

Free or Fee?

The Yale course in Constitutional Law noted above is available for free. What is the benefit to the institution of offering these courses for free? Many of the larger US schools are already well-funded by philanthropic bequests. They can afford to offer services without charging fees, and use these courses as a form of brand marketing.[19] The highly selective schools (like Yale) take very few 'real' students, and will always have a queue at the door of highly qualified students willing to pay for the benefit of a real-time, face-to-face student experience, so they can afford to participate in the Coursera experiment as 'good global citizens'. Even lesser known schools may decide that the costs of offering an online course are worth the potential benefit of gaining a global profile for the school, which may prove valuable as a way of recruiting international students. The institutions who participate on this basis will generally offer nothing more than a certificate acknowledging participation in an online course. They will not offer these courses for credit to any degree program. The courses provide a 'taster' for potential students, who may then take the step of seeking enrolment in the face-to-face degree program.

MOOCs can also provide a self-promotion platform for individual lecturers hungry to acquire international 'rock star' status, and to improve their own employment mobility.

---

18 Ibid.

19 The marketing value of a MOOC is noted as one of five advantages by the Robert McGuire, Editor of *Moocs News and Reviews*, in '5 Tactical Questions Higher Ed Administrators Should Be Asking About MOOCs', 18 July 2013. See http://moocnewsandreviews.com/5-tactical-questions-higher-ed-administrators-should-be-asking-about-moocs/ (last accessed 20 September 2013).

Courses for Credit

Some institutions do charge fees, and have even devised ways to assess students and provide grades to acknowledge completion of courses. One obvious concern for an institution purporting to charge fees for a course that offers a recognised qualification is guaranteeing quality of graduates. It is already hard for face-to-face learning institutions to prevent plagiarism and other forms of cheating. How much more challenging is this in an online environment? There are sophisticated means of identifying students (or so I am told[20]) by the way in which they type into a computer, so each student has a 'biometric digital signature' in the form of their characteristic typing patterns. Likewise, webcams can be used to monitor whether a student is alone when completing online assessment tasks, to ensure that students don't cheat by calling in expert assistance to help out as they are being examined. Evidently the feed from multiple webcams can be monitored by people paid for that task. This is the kind of work that can be 'offshored' to a jurisdiction with lower labour costs. (This is another 'advantage' of the global digital revolution – there are no boundaries to how far away one can locate a workforce for these kinds of supervision tasks.)

Even assuming that assessment challenges and the risk of cheating can be overcome, I suspect that we are a long way from being able to deliver accredited legal education through MOOCs. As discussed above, legal profession admission authorities jealously guard admission to the profession and are likely to be very reluctant to open admission to candidates whose qualifications have been gained entirely 'online'. This is especially so, given that there is little incentive in the currently tight market for legal services for the profession to widen access to entry.[21] The old protectionist voices are again calling for law schools to reduce enrolments to help stem a potential flood of unemployable graduates.[22] The entry of MOOCs into what is already thought to be an overcrowded 'market' for legal qualifications is unlikely to be welcomed by the profession. This does not mean, though, that we cannot learn a great deal from the success of the MOOC in other fields.

---

20 The author derived much of this information from a conversation with Professor Edward Rock of Penn State University. See also Simon Cooper, 'MOOCs: Disrupting the University or Business as Usual?' (2012/2013) *Arena Journal*, 39/40, 182–202 at 194 for an explanation of techniques for 'cheat-proofing' MOOC assessments.

21 See Leanne Mezrani 'Exclusive: Clerkship System Failing Grads', *Lawyers Weekly*, 20 September 2013 at 1.

22 See for example the views expressed in blog comments to the article by Elvira Naiman, 'It is the worst time in living history to be a law graduate, at http://www.lawyersweekly.com.au/news/it-is-the-worst-time-in-living-history-to-be-a-law (last accessed 23 September 2013).

How Might Law Schools Use MOOCs and Other Digital Platforms?

... As Marketing Tools

As many of the Coursera offerings show, an x-MOOC can provide a wonderful channel to showcase the strengths of a particular law school, and enliven student interest (particularly international student interest) in the school. A well-managed MOOC can profile engaging professors and fields of expertise. There is real scope for well-targeted MOOCs to be used to support international student recruitment efforts.

... To Relieve Some of the Pressure of Content Delivery

Is there a more substantial role for MOOCs is supporting the education of enrolled students? I think there can be. Something I have observed in the 20 years since I first undertook legal studies myself, is the accelerating expansion of the volume of legal materials that students need to master in the course of their studies. I am often called upon to act as an apologist in defending our current legal curriculum from criticism from the elder statesmen of our profession who studied law back in the 1960s and 1970s. These eminent professionals, many of them retired or retiring judges, frequently bemoan the demise of important subjects like Legal History and Roman Law from the compulsory law curriculum. In attempting to explain the shape of our current curriculum, I remind them of the huge expansion in the Australian legal system since the 1970s. When our elders were at law school, there was no trade practices or consumer protection legislation, and no *Family Law Act 1974 (Cth)*. Many of the current chapters in our corporations' legislation (dealing with the regulation of ever more complex securities markets) had not been written yet. Administrative law had not been reformed by the introduction of merits review according to new statutory regimes. The opening of national borders to increasing global trade had not introduced new kinds of legal problems. The immediately post-war generation presently retiring from the courts had yet to witness the explosion of interest in international humanitarian law. Environmental law was hardly imagined. Today there are so many fields of law commanding the attention of lawyers and current law students. It is no wonder that our curricula have become crowded, and in the clamour of many demands, students and teachers find it challenging to cover all aspects of the traditional core of subjects. In our law school Roman Law and topics in Legal History are still taught, but only as final year electives to relatively small classes.

This is where the MOOC – and the digital platforms upon which MOOCs are built – can assist the contemporary law school. In many ways, digital tools can supplement the more traditional forms of 'knowledge transfer' to free up more class time for interactive learning. Straight lecturing (which was never more than an oral presentation of what could be gleaned from a well-organised text book in any event) can be delivered in engaging online formats, so class time can be reserved for Q&A sessions, discussion, debate and problem solving. Of course, we will want to develop our own online programs tailored to the specific curriculum requirements of our own units of study. But it may also be possible to free-ride on some of the resources available through free MOOCs offered by other institutions, where those courses provide resources relevant to our own programs. Our own classrooms can be liberated from some of the pressure of content delivery, because genuine, real-time interaction is so much easier in a traditional classroom. Indeed one of the criticisms levelled at MOOCs has been that many courses are delivered in the most old-fashioned pedagogical manner, as one-way transmissions of expert information, without opportunity for real-time critical responses from students.[23]

... As Safe Places for Students to Practise

Digital platforms can also assist us to manage the frequent demands of contemporary students for more 'coaching' in how to write essays and answer legal problems, and more 'feedback' on their attempts at assessment tasks. We are constantly pestered for 'model answers' to exam questions. Online tools can be created to demonstrate techniques for constructing persuasive legal arguments, and for unpacking in logical sequence the relevant legal issues in a hypothetical problem. At Sydney Law School we have been developing these kinds of online resources as a generic tool box to be made available to all students to assist them in managing the assessment requirements for all their units of study.

Online assessment tools may also prove useful as formative assessment tasks even before they become reliable enough and sufficiently 'cheat-proof' to use for summative assessment. Formative assessment enables students to practise their skills without the risk of influencing their final grades. More practise allows students to become more confident in their skills, and may reduce students' temptation to procrastinate and claim 'special consideration' to defer submitting assignments and taking examinations.

... To Enable Time-Shifting of Class and Consultation Time, for the Time-Poor Student

A particular advantage of online tools is that they can be used at any time of the night or day. We are beginning to realise at Sydney Law School that there is no longer such a creature as a full-time law student. Most students hold down part-time jobs that require many more hours of work than typical student jobs in the past. Once upon a time (in a more highly regulated labour market), students might do some casual retail work on a Thursday evening or Saturday morning, or may wait tables at night. Now, the typical JD student will be doing 20 or more hours a week of professional or semi-professional work, using the skills and knowledge gained during their first degree. In Australia, it is increasingly rare for a university

23 See Cooper above n. 20 at 193.

to offer entry directly into a 'straight' law degree to recent school leavers. School leavers more commonly combine law with another discipline (arts/law; commerce/law; science/law, and even engineering/law are popular options) so by the time law students are coming near to the end of their legal studies they already have a qualification in another discipline. A degree in another discipline is mandatory for entry into JD programs. These kinds of students are juggling many responsibilities with their studies. They want greater flexibility in course delivery. Digital platforms for delivering essential course content, and providing formative assessment tasks for skills practice and knowledge testing, can assist them to manage their studies, notwithstanding the many other demands on their time.

At Sydney, we often use online discussion boards to deal with student questions after classes. A question posted online, for all to see the question and the answer, is an efficient and equitable way of dealing with follow up from classes. From the perspective of managing staff workloads, the task of attending the discussion board can be shared by a number of colleagues.

... *To Introduce International Talent to Local Classes*

Even 'real-time' digital tools and social media can enhance the delivery of a world-class legal education. As tools such as Skype improve, we may be able to make better use of technology to 'beam' in real-time input from overseas experts. At Sydney Law School we have offered a course in Comparative Constitutional Law which is taught by one of our own professors, Helen Irving, assisted via Skype by a professor from a US or Canadian law school. In this way, technology allows our students exposure to great minds from around the globe, without the expense of travel costs or inconvenience and discomfort for jet-lagged scholars. All you need is a classroom wired up for Skype with a sufficiently large projection screen.

Conclusion

The jurisdictionally specific nature of much of the law curriculum, and the requirement for law schools to meet the accreditation requirements of local admission authorities, is likely to mean that MOOCs will never take over the field of legal education. Not, at least, until the predictions of futurists like Richard Susskind[24] come to pass. It is difficult to see that happen in my lifetime, at least in New South Wales, which is governed by a relatively conservative legal profession. In-person enrolment in a face-to-face degree program is likely to remain the norm, and will always be preferred by elite institutions and the most ambitious and serious students. MOOCs may, however, provide a useful supplement to the many resources law teachers currently call upon to meet the challenges of providing a satisfying and engaging legal education for the student of the digital age.

---

24 See above n. 8.

Chapter 15

The Structure, Purposes and Methods of German Legal Education

Rainer Wernsmann[1]

Introduction

This chapter focuses on German legal education. It will first introduce the general structure of legal education in Germany, and then explain its purposes and methods, relating to ongoing criticism as well as evaluating the influence of globalization.

General Structure of German Legal Education

Law students need to acquire a certain level of high school degree, called the "Abitur", in order to pass the general university entrance conditions. Only public universities and their law faculties are allowed to offer general study of law in Germany. The only exceptions are the private owned Bucerius Law School in Hamburg and the EBS Law School in Wiesbaden. German legal education consists of recommended four and a half years of studies, majoring in a special field of law for two semesters.

Structure of German Law Faculties

Over 40 universities in Germany offer legal education, but they do not bear scintillating names such as law schools like Harvard, Yale or Oxford. There are, perhaps, two reasons for this. First, there are no admission exams for entrance to university in Germany; law faculties may only refuse admission to a student if they cannot provide the needed capacity. And, although recently law faculties have begun to specialize in and emphasize certain areas like legal language education, international or business focus in order to create a unique feature,

1 Professor Dr Rainer Wernsmann was Dean of the Law Faculty of the University of Passau, Germany (2012–14) and is now (since 2014) Vice President of the University of Passau. He holds the Chair of Constitutional and Administrative Law, particularly Finance Law and Tax Law. Special thanks to my research assistant, Florian Kühnlein, for the preparation of this chapter. It is based on the talk that was held on 26 October 2013 at the Chinese University of Hong Kong. The way of delivery has been retained.

legal education is more or less standardized across German universities.[2] Second, studying at public German universities is – apart from a small administrative fee – free for students and no tuition fees have to be paid. Thus, every student can afford to study at any law faculty he or she wants to attend. In 2007 several states introduced tuition fees in the amount of up to 500€ per semester. Today, almost seven years later, tuition fees have been abolished again and the attempt to establish them in Germany can be declared a failure due to the immense resistance among the population and the political difficulties in upholding them.

As of 2011, about 100,000 students were studying law at German universities, and 53% of this number were female.[3] The total number of students has increased constantly since 2008 at an average of 4% per year.[4] Moreover, approximately 10,000 students pass the Second State Examination every year.[5]

General Curriculum

German legal education consists of two parts: during the first stage, students are taught legal studies at university law faculties, studying a wide range of compulsory subjects, such as civil law, criminal law, public law, procedural law and the law of the European Union, plus an elective subject for specialization. After that, their legal education continues with a two-year professional training period, called "Referendariat" or apprenticeship.

Basic Studies

In addition to studying civil law, public law and criminal law, students learn about the historical, philosophical, social, economic and political fundamentals and basic principles of law. Throughout this period, students have to take final examinations at the end of a class. Those examinations are designed to control the individual's learning success. Passing the intermediate examination completes the basic studies.[6]

2 More about the current developments: Papier, Hans-Jürgen/Schröder, Meinhard, *Neue Juristische Wochenschrift* 2012, pp. 2860–64 (2862).

3 See https://www.destatis.de/DE/ZahlenFakten/Indikatoren/LangeReihen/Bildung/lrbil03.html?cms_gtp=152378_list%253D1&https=1 , accessed 17 August 2015.

4 See https://www.destatis.de/DE/ZahlenFakten/Indikatoren/LangeReihen/Bildung/lrbil03.html?cms_gtp=152378_list%253D2&https=1, accessed 17 August 2015.

5 See https://www.destatis.de/DE/Publikationen/Thematisch/BildungForschungKultur/Hochschulen/PruefungenHochschulen2110420117004.pdf?__blob=publicationFile, accessed 17 August 2015.

6 For more details and a critical analysis of the status quo: Hesse, Albrecht, *Zeitschrift für Rechtspolitik* 2002, pp. 232–33 (232).

Main Study Period

During the main study period, the knowledge acquired during the basic studies will be expanded and deepened, which will lay the foundation for the state exam preparation. At the same time, the training begins in an elective focal area, called "Schwerpunktbereich". For instance, the University of Passau offers classes in core legal areas such as tax law, international business law, media law or employment law, to name only a few.[7] The elective focal areas include a minimum of 16 hours and a maximum of 24 hours per week during two semesters, and conclude with the university legal examination which makes up 30% of the overall grade of the first legal exams. The remaining 70% is contributed by the state examination.

Preparation Period

During the preparation period, students deepen their knowledge and prepare intensively for the state examination. Students then take the first state examination, a state-wide organized set of exams that places emphasis on the students' academic and general knowledge of the law and covers the entire scope of the law.[8] During the state examination several comprehensive written exams and an oral exam must be completed. The exams are issued by the Ministry of Justice of each state in Germany. Each exam will be marked by two different examiners, a law professor and a practitioner (often a judge) who will not know the identity of the examinees, in order to ensure the result is as objective as possible. The German lawyer Max Friedlaender said about his state examination, which he took in 1898: "It was the fairest and most reasonable test that you could think of."[9] I think time has shown that this was a fairly true statement.

The Professional Training "Referendariat"

The First State Examination is followed by a two-year practical training period, the so-called "Referendariat". During this professional training, students, who are now called "Referendare", get practical instruction at a civil court, a criminal court or prosecutor's office, an administrative agency and in a law firm. The last stage of the professional training is optional and students can choose where to spend this time, for example at court, ministries, agencies, law firms, and so on. Students also attend classes taught by practitioners during this period. Reforms in

7 The author of this chapter offers tax law, financial law and budget law; for more information: http://www.jura.uni-passau.de/en/wernsmann.

8 § 5d I Deutsches Richtergesetz (German Law of Judiciary); § 16 I Bayerische Ausbildungs- und Prüfungsordnung für Juristen (Bavarian Education and Examination for Jurists Act).

9 Papier, Hans-Jürgen/Schröder, Meinhard, *Neue Juristische Wochenschrift* 2012, pp. 2860–64 (2863).

2002 emphasized the importance of practical training in lawyering skills such as negotiation, advocacy and legal advice.[10]

Students then must pass the Second State Examination, a comprehensive set of exams that place emphasis on practical legal skills. Upon successful passage, students are entitled to work in any legal profession and their legal education is officially finished. Certain jobs though, especially in public offices or at international law firms, require a certain grade in both exams, which only the best 10–15% of a class accomplish.

The Purposes and Methods of German Legal Education

German law students deal primarily with applicable law, its systematic and conceptual penetration and interpretation as well as its relationship to other areas of life such as politics, the economy and social structure. In contrast to other legal systems, the influence of case law is limited in German legal education because Germany has a civil law system. Since the legal system of Hong Kong is based on the common law system of England and Wales, the main difference between our two legal systems is that in Germany we generally base our legal decisions on abstract norms rather than established cases. Nevertheless, the influence of prior decisions of the Constitutional Court, called "Bundesverfassungsgericht", and the several Federal Courts is enormous for the daily application of law in Germany as well.

The primary goal of legal education in Germany is to be qualified as a judge and in particular to work in the legal profession, although in fact only a small percentage of successful graduates will actually become judges. The frame of legal education is regulated by the German Law of Judiciary. Law students are taught to deal with the often quite abstract formal way of thinking of the German legal system as well as the constantly changing life circumstances. In order to come to sound legal results, both always have to be taken into account and the reasons have to be balanced and evaluated in light of abstract norms.

A Critical View on German Legal Education

At German universities there are basically no admission restrictions for law students. This easy access to law faculties leads to high numbers of students in the early semesters. However, this also leads to numerous dropouts who sooner or later come to the conclusion that it would be better to go and devote themselves to other academic studies or those who have to leave due to poor examination results.

So students have to find out, in the first or in the first two semesters, whether law school suits them or not.

---

10 § 48 II Nr. 3 Bayerische Ausbildungs- und Prüfungsordnung für Juristen.

The multiplicity of students in mainstream subjects such as law leads to further problems. Although the number of students has mounted over the decades, as required by policy and economy, especially in subjects such as law, jobs for teaching staff and funds for library facilities have not increased at the same rate. Lectures with up to 800 participants in the compulsory courses of the first semesters, where there are no differentiation and specialization classes, are not uncommon. A reasonable professor–student ratio looks different to me. Through tutorials in smaller groups, in which students are trained in the solving of cases, universities try to counteract this deficiency. However, these events are not usually held by the professors themselves, but by scientific employees.

Since its inception, the German legal education system seems to be constantly addressing its actual and alleged weakness. Nonetheless, the basic orientation of the current system is sound.

In order to manage the wide subject area, the majority of German law students need private tutor services. These have a long tradition in Germany because universities themselves have not offered special training for the First State Examination at the end of the legal education for a long time. It is believed that tutors, called "Repetitors", were introduced into the Law School of Bologna in the thirteenth and fourteenth centuries, eventually becoming part of the German legal education system. As far back as the eighteenth century, the German poet Goethe took lessons from a private tutor. Tutors work for commercial and private companies. Compared to fairly large classes at German law faculties, private tutors can offer way smaller classes and, thus, react more to the needs and problems of their students.

Until recently, universities did not offer special refresher or focus classes to help students to prepare for the first state examination. However, this is beginning to change. Especially at the University of Passau the law faculty has established a unique one-year programme to prepare students for the first state examination. This course can easily compete with private tutor services and has the added advantage of being free.

The main problem with the system of the state examination is that the students have to know and be able to deal with the whole curriculum at the same time. Some argue that the quantity of material is simply too extensive and that it is more important to gain the ability to deal with unknown areas of law rather than providing voluminous detailed knowledge.

On the other hand, no area of law stands isolated in itself, but rather has connecting points with each other. Hence, our students have a broad knowledge of German law and not only "island knowledge" or a "knowledge bulimia". The negative side effect though is that our students have a lot of emotional and actual stress during the preparation period for the state examination. The study of law is very generalist whereas, later, specific knowledge will be required when employed in a legal role. But I believe that once you understand the system and the methods, one can always specialize, using those tools learned during legal studies.

The German legal education system is building a frame for every student and giving them the tools they need. But whatever picture the students then draw is up to their abilities, qualities, work ethic, inspiration and duration. Ultimately, the students are required to decide for themselves how they want to learn and what courses they wish to take, what kind of internships they want to do and where to focus their studies. Students must learn to be independent and self-organized. This freedom in self-organization must not cause students to feel alone or helpless. In this sense, universities should not give the students a fish, but should teach them how to fish.

Influences of Globalization

Ideas, companies and thus legal disputes go global, but nonetheless the law stays local.

Obviously, it is not enough these days for a lawyer to know about his or her own national law. Globalization and European integration has resulted in litigation becoming international. Hence, we have to teach our students not only national law, but also an understanding of worldwide developments as well as interdisciplinary and international aspects of law. The crucial legal skill will be the ability to analyze legal issues from a comparative perspective. But law is simply quite different from other scientific disciplines and remains at its core a national issue, although there are increasingly unified areas.

In order to cope with these international developments, German law faculties have introduced many foreign language education programmes. It is important to speak other languages fluently and to get an understanding for different cultures. In the legal world though, this is not enough. Therefore, the University of Passau has introduced a language programme that not only teaches the language but also looks at the basic legal concepts of that country.

Many countries in the world have a common law system. The German law system – a civil law system that is based on Roman law – is probably as far away on the legal spectrum from other systems as it is possible to be. But with most students taking at least foreign language classes in English, they learn the core legal principles of common law. At the University of Passau, students also have the opportunity to take part in the Bachelor of Laws (LLB) programme of the University of London, parallel to their German legal education.

As another component in preparing our students for international challenges, they are given the opportunity to participate in a variety of diverse exchange programmes around the world. With over 50 partner universities on all continents, we try to provide exchanges without tuition fees. Students from our partner universities and law schools also study at the University of Passau, which creates an international climate on campus. Our students can explore the legal world and foreign exchange students can learn what "Made in Germany" means. This personal exchange is important for our students, but also for us law professors.

At last, German law faculties are placing emphasis on international law and its impact on the German legal system. At the University of Passau, we have had an English-speaking Chair of Common Law since 2013. This is again an attempt to make students more comfortable with global matters, but also to establish a more international working atmosphere among the law faculty.

Conclusion

The major goal of German legal education is to produce the so-called "Einheitsjurist", which means that German law students receive a broad and general legal education. Although law is becoming more globalized and diversified, German law students can work on specified legal matters without losing the overall view of the law. I believe that this is a huge advantage, given the fact that lawyers have to deal more and more with multinational companies and legal matters which do not stop at national borders.

Being able to adapt to these constantly new circumstances and having the general legal tools to work with unknown legal matters, even from different jurisdictions, make German lawyers unique. Thus, German jurisprudents can be called "general experts".

Chapter 16
Reforming Taiwan's Legal Education in the Age of Globalization

Ming-Yan Shieh and Yen-Chia Chen

Introduction

Globalization has profound influences on legal education in many places around the world,[1] including Taiwan.[2] Alongside the expansion of globalization, fierce global competition, increasing cross-border interaction and cooperation, as well as growing external influences, have altered the landscape of the legal services market in many countries.[3] In order to prepare the new generation of legal professionals to compete in the international marketplace and to cope effectively with the challenges of legal practice in the globalization era, law schools around

1 Harry W. Arthurs, Law and Learning in an Era of Globalization, 10 *German L.J.* 629, 630–31 (2009); Thomas Chih-hsiung Chen, Legal Education Reform in Taiwan: Are Japan and Korea the Models?, 62 *J. Legal Educ.* 32, 64 (2012) [hereinafter Chen, Are Japan and Korea the Models?]; Charles R. Irish, Reflections of an Observer: The International Conference on Legal Education Reform, 24 *Wis. Int'l L.J.* 5, 14–15 (2006).

2 Simon Chesterman, The Evolution of Legal Education: Internationalization, Transnationalization, Globalization, 10 *German L.J.* 887, 887 (2009) (noting that "[t]he transformations driven by changes in the practice of the law, by the types of students pursuing degrees, and – somewhat belatedly – by research developments in the loosely defined area of 'global law' have radically changed the nature of legal education"); Chang-fa Lo, Driving an Ox Cart to Catch Up with the Space Shuttle: The Need for and Prospects of Legal Education Reform in Taiwan, 24 *Wis. Int'l L.J.* 41, 41 (2006) [hereinafter Lo, Driving an Ox Cart].

3 In an era of globalized economy, as Professor Carole Silver notes, "[e]vidence of internationalization is ubiquitous in the legal services market. Greater economic interaction among national actors … has stimulated growing interaction among nationally based lawyers and law firms". Carole Silver, Winners and Losers in the Globalization of Legal Services: Situating the Market for Foreign Lawyers, 45 *Va. J. Int'l L.* 897, 897 (2005). See also Irish, *supra* note 1, at 14–15.

the world have reinvented their curriculum, teaching and research.[4] So have law schools in Taiwan.[5]

In Taiwan, over the past few decades there have been a number of discussions and initiatives toward fundamental reforms of the legal education system.[6] Some legal education reform efforts made their way through while others ended in failure.[7] Today there is no agreement on the ideal of Taiwan's legal education system in the new century.[8] Neither have we figured out a one-shot total solution for the reform of our legal education system in an era of globalization.[9] However, the majority of legal professionals in Taiwan agree that there are problems in our antiquated legal education system.[10] The current legal education system in Taiwan has failed to produce legal professionals capable of meeting the needs of Taiwan's rapidly developing society and handling the challenges of severe competition in an era of a

---

4 Arthurs, *supra* note 1, at 630–31; Robert E. Lutz, Reforming Approaches to Educating Transnational Lawyers: Observations from America, 61 *J. Legal Educ.* 449, 452 (2012) (noting that "[g]lobalization is … a primary force behind curricular reforms that seek to prepare students to function as lawyers in a transnational legal world"); Chen, Are Japan and Korea the Models?, *supra* note 1, at 64; Lo, Driving an Ox Cart, *supra* note 2, at 71. *See also* Chesterman, *supra* note 2, at 886 (asserting that "the emergence of 'global law schools' will certainly be an elite phenomenon").

5 Joseph L. Pratt, The Two Gates of National Taiwan University School of Law, 19 *UCLA Pac. Basin L.J.* 131, 133 (2001); Chen, Are Japan and Korea the Models?, *supra* note 1, at 59–64.

6 Chen, Are Japan and Korea the Models?, *supra* note 1, at 48–51; Lo, Driving an Ox Cart, *supra* note 2, at 83.

7 For example, since Japan reformed its legal education in April 2004, there has been a fierce debate in Taiwan over whether Taiwan should follow in the footsteps of Japan and implement the legal education model in the United States to replace the current system in Taiwan. Chen, Are Japan and Korea the Models?, *supra* note 1, at 49; Lo, Driving an Ox Cart, *supra* note 2, at 83. Between 2005 and 2007, there were government initiatives that proposed to reform Taiwan's legal education by following the Japanese model. Nevertheless, these radical reform attempts eventually turned out to be failed efforts due to legal academia's resistance and the will of powerful politicians. Chen, Are Japan and Korea the Models?, *supra* note 1, at 48–51.

8 Chen, Are Japan and Korea the Models?, *supra* note 1, at 34 (citing 台灣各大學法律相關系所主管針對「國內法學教育變革」公聽會發表新聞稿)

[Press Release by Law School Deans in Taiwan regarding the Public Hearing on "Legal Education Reform" held on April 18, 2007], available at http:// justice.nccu.edu.tw/News/news_view.asp?id=155, accessed August 16, 2015.

9 Lo, Driving an Ox Cart, *supra* note 2, at 82–84.

10 Chen, Are Japan and Korea the Models?, *supra* note 1, at 34 (citing 台灣各大學法律相關系所主管針對「國內法學教育變革」公聽會發表新聞稿 [Press Release by Law School Deans in Taiwan regarding the Public Hearing on "Legal Education Reform" held on April 18, 2007], available at http:// justice.nccu.edu.tw/News/news_view.asp?id=155, accessed August 16, 2015).

globalized economy.[11] Fortunately, it is not too late. In every challenge to the status quo lies an opportunity to reshape the future legal education system in Taiwan.[12]

This chapter briefly reviews the current legal education system in Taiwan, the challenges it is facing, and efforts that have been carried out at National Taiwan University College of Law (NTU Law) to address the need for reforming the status quo. The second part of the chapter provides an overview of Taiwan's current legal education. This is followed by a discussion on the challenges facing Taiwan's antiquated legal education system and the needs for reform. Next, NTU Law's initiatives to address the aforementioned challenges and needs are presented. The chapter concludes with a call that all law schools in Taiwan take a greater role in reforming Taiwan's legal education and training the next generation of Taiwan's legal professionals to a better standard of competence.

Current Legal Education in Taiwan

Since the education reform movement in the 1990s of the last century, Taiwan's higher education has become a booming industry.[13] The expansion of the higher education system[14] has resulted in the growth of legal education and the growing number of law students[15] responding to this growth.[16] Over the past two decades,

11 Lo, Driving an Ox Cart, *supra* note 2, at 82; Chen, Are Japan and Korea the Models?, *supra* note 1, at 52.

12 In one of his newspaper articles, Professor C. Raj Kumar noted that "[g]lobalisation has posed multiple challenges to the future of legal education in India but it has provided an opportunity to challenge the status quo, which is an essential condition for seeking any reform". C. Raj Kumar, Op.-Ed., Globalisation and Legal Education, *The Hindu* (India), August 6, 2007, http://www.thehindu.com/todays-paper/tp-opinion/globalisation-and-legal-education/article1886307.ece, accessed August 16, 2015. We share the same view with Professor Kumar when looking at the challenges facing Taiwan's legal education system.

13 Critics argue that the education reform movement in Taiwan is a failed effort because the reform has made no substantial improvement in our higher education and neither has it reduced the gap between education goals and reality. A commentator alleges that the education reform movement has turned higher education in Taiwan into a fraud industry printing lots of junk diplomas. Hsiao-yun Lin (林曉雲), 20 years after the Educational Reform/"Even Monkeys Can Go to College", says a Professor at National Taiwan University (教改廿年／台大教授轟：連猴子都能上大學), *Liberty Times* [Taiwan], September 1, 2013, http://news.ltn.com.tw/news/life/paper/709909, accessed August 16, 2015.

14 Please refer to "Figure 16.1: Increase in number of universities in Taiwan (1994–2013)" in Appendix.

15 Please refer to "Figure 16.2: Increase in number of law graduates in past 20 years (undergraduate only)" in Appendix.

16 Lo, Driving an Ox Cart, *supra* note 2, at 50–51.

the number of law graduates in Taiwan has been multiplied to four times the number of 20 years ago.[17]

There have been a number of discussions and initiatives toward fundamental reforms of Taiwan's legal education over the past few decades.[18] Some attempted efforts of legal education reform ended in failure due to various reasons.[19] An exception to this observation is the implementation of the two-track model of legal education in recent years.[20]

In Taiwan, a four-year law major program offered at the undergraduate level has been the mainstream in the legal education system over the years.[21] Most people go to law school for four years and earn a bachelor of law degree upon graduation.[22] Those interested in pursuing advanced legal education may continue by enrolling in graduate programs such as the Master of Laws (LLM) program and the Doctor of Philosophy (PhD) in Law program.[23] In addition to the traditional track, over the past two decades some universities in Taiwan, with or without a traditional undergraduate law program, established graduate institutes for legal studies to admit

---

17 Chen, Are Japan and Korea the Models?, *supra* note 1, at 58–59 (citing Tay-Sheng Wang, The Development of Legal Education in Taiwan: An Analysis of the History of Law and Society, in *Legal Education in Asia: Globalization, Change and Contexts*, 141 (Stacey Steele and Kathryn Taylor eds, Routledge Press 2010). For instance, Figure 16.2 in Appendix shows that the number of undergraduate law students has increased two-fold in the past 18 years. Please refer to "Figure 16.2: Increase in number of law graduates in past 20 years (undergraduate only)" in Appendix.

18 Chen, Are Japan and Korea the Models?, *supra* note 1, at 48–51.

19 *Id.*; Lo, Driving an Ox Cart, *supra* note 2, at 83.

20 Chen, Are Japan and Korea the Models?, *supra* note 1, at 54; Lo, Driving an Ox Cart, *supra* note 2, at 55–56.

21 Hundgah Chiu and Jyh-pin Fa, *Taiwan's Legal System and Legal Profession* 13–14 (Maryland Occasional Papers/Reprints Series in Contemporary Asian Studies No. 5, 1994), *available at* http://digitalcommons.law.umaryland.edu/mscas/vol1994/iss5/1, accessed August 16, 2015; Shu-chin Grace Kuo, Rethinking the Masculine Character of the Legal Profession: A Case Study of Female Legal Professionals and Their Gendered Life in Taiwan, 13 *Am. U.J. Gender Soc. Pol'y & L.* 25, 38 (2005); Chih-Hsiung Chen, The Role of Practice in Legal Education: National Report for Taiwan, paper delivered at the 18th International Congress on Comparative Law, 4 (Jan. 12, 2012), http://ssrn.com/abstract=1984374, accessed August 16, 2015 [hereinafter Chen, Role of Practice]; Lo, Driving an Ox Cart, *supra* note 2, at 51; Chen, Are Japan and Korea the Models?, *supra* note 1, at 35; Pratt, *supra* note 5, at 148.

22 Kuo, *supra* note 21, at 38. However, some law schools in Taiwan require five years of study for their undergraduate law program. Chen, Role of Practice, *supra* note 21, at 10. For instance, students who enroll in the undergraduate law program offered at Soochow University School of Law must spend five years of study before obtaining a bachelor of law degree. Soochow University School of Law, Introduction of the School, Characteristics, http://webbuilder.scu.edu.tw/BUILDER/web_page.php?web=249&pid=6041, accessed January 17, 2014.

23 Kuo, *supra* note 21, at 39; Pratt, *supra* note 5, at 149.

students who do not hold a first degree in law.[24] For example, in 2004, NTU Law established the Graduate Institute of Interdisciplinary Legal Studies (科際整合法律學研究所, hereinafter GIILS) that admits non-law graduates "interested in pursuing collaborative legal education combined with other disciplines".[25] The implementation of the two-track model of legal education expands access to Taiwan's legal education system and results in developing a more diversified legal profession in Taiwan.[26]

Taiwan's legal education focuses on educating law students to generally understand some basic legal concepts and philosophical aspects of law.[27] Law schools offer many doctrinal courses in a number of different areas of law in order to help law students gain a basic understanding of the laws and legal system.[28] Conducting courses through giving lectures is the traditional and most preferable teaching method adopted by most law professors.[29] Many believe that

---

24 Lo, Driving an Ox Cart, *supra* note 2, at 54; Chen, Are Japan and Korea the Models?, *supra* note 1, at 52. In 1990, Soochow University School of Law launched the first graduate program of legal studies for non-law graduates in Taiwan. Soochow University School of Law, Introduction of the School, http://webbuilder.scu.edu.tw/BUILDER/web_page.php?web=70&pid=1441, accessed September 15, 2013; Lo, Driving an Ox Cart, *supra* note 2, at 42 fn.4; Pratt, *supra* note 5, at 166. Ten years later, with the same goal of promoting interdisciplinary education in law and technology, National Tsing Hua University and National Chiao Tung University separately established their graduate institutes for legal studies, namely "National Tsing Hua University Institute of Law for Science and Technology" and "National Chiao Tung University Institute of Technology Law". National Tsing Hua University Institute of Law for Science and Technology, Our Profile, http://www.lst.nthu.edu.tw/files/11–1176–3827.php, accessed September 14, 2013; National Chiao Tung University Institute of Technology Law, Introduction, http://www.itl.nctu.edu.tw/nctulaw/index_en.htm, accessed September 15, 2013. In 2004, National Chengchi University College of Law followed the foregoing law schools and established its Institute of Law and Inter-discipline to admit students without a bachelor degree or above in law. National Chengchi University College of Law, Institute of Law and Inter-discipline, About Us, http://www.interdisc-law.nccu.edu.tw/eindex.aspx, accessed January 17, 2014.

25 National Taiwan University College of Law, About GIILS, http://www.law.ntu.edu.tw/giilslaw/english/versec/aboutgiils_english.htm, accessed October 12, 2013.

26 Chen, Are Japan and Korea the Models?, *supra* note 1, at 51–52.

27 Lo, Driving an Ox Cart, *supra* note 2, at 57.

28 *Id.* at 57–58.

29 Kuan-Chun Chang, The Teaching of Law in the United States: Studies on the Case and Socratic Methods in Comparison with Traditional Taiwanese Pedagogy, 4 NAT'L TAIWAN U. L. REV. 1, 31 (2009); Kuo, *supra* note 21, at 38; Serge A. Martinez, Law Clinics in Taiwan: Can Clinical Legal Education Succeed in this Civil Law Jurisdiction with an Undergraduate Legal Education System?, 7 NAT'L TAIWAN U. L. REV. 343, 370 (2012); Lo, Driving an Ox Cart, *supra* note 2, at 62. In Taiwan, the Socratic method is not popular among most law professors because some believe that this method delays the instructor's delivery of knowledge, that such a teaching method will make students confused, or that it will not help students to receive knowledge systematically. *Id.* nn.116 and 118.

this lecture method helps law professors to deliver knowledge systematically and also helps students understand the law effectively in a short period of time.[30] As a consequence, it is not common to observe interaction between students and their professors in class.[31]

Law schools in Taiwan play a minor role in training practical skills of law students because Taiwan's legal education places its primary emphasis on doctrinal teaching rather than practical training.[32] Practical training is not a common feature in law school curriculum.[33] Many believe that law school is a place primarily focused on academic study and scholarship.[34] This divide is further reinforced by laws and traditions as practitioners are excluded from becoming a full-time law faculty member at any public university, and law faculty members at public universities are prohibited from practicing as full-time lawyers.[35] As a result, the historical approach to lawyer's practical training in Taiwan has been the half-year post-bar apprenticeship program that every bar examination passer must take before being licensed to practice.[36] On the other hand, those who pass the judicial examination received their practical training at the Academy for the Judiciary (司法官學院)[37] before serving as judges or prosecutors.[38]

---

30 Martinez, *supra* note 29, at 370; Lo, Driving an Ox Cart, *supra* note 2, at 62 n.117.

31 Chang, *supra* note 29, at 31; Lo, Driving an Ox Cart, *supra* note 2, at 62.

32 Kuo, *supra* note 21, at 38–39; Lo, Driving an Ox Cart, *supra* note 2, at 57; Martinez, *supra* note 29, at 343, 349.

33 Chen, Role of Practice, *supra* note 21, at 7. Some law schools in Taiwan offer students a few practical training courses and extra-curricular activities containing practice elements. For instance, moot court courses prepare students to participate in different international moot court competitions. Moreover, legal aid courses provide students with opportunities to offer pro bono legal services to those who need legal services while developing students' skills in legal practice and client counseling. *Id.* Nonetheless, these courses are not mandatory in most law schools and not all law students have the same opportunities to enroll in these courses or participate in these activities. In some law schools, it is possible that legal aid is not a course offered by the law school, but simply one of those extra-curricular activities for students.

34 *Id.* at 10; Martinez, *supra* note 29, at 376.

35 Martinez, *supra* note 29, at 376.

36 Chen, Role of Practice, *supra* note 21, at 6; Martinez, *supra* note 29, at 360.

37 The Academy for the Judiciary is a training institution administered by the Ministry of Justice and offers pre-job education for judges and prosecutors in Taiwan. The Academy was formerly known as the Judges and Prosecutors Training Institute (司法官訓練所) before the Ministry of Justice renamed it as the Academy for the Judiciary in 2013. Academy for the Judiciary, Ministry of Justice, History, http://www.tpi.moj.gov.tw/ct.asp?xItem=56464&CtNode=15109&mp=186, accessed January 12, 2014.

38 Article 2 of the Organization Act of the Academy for the Judiciary, Ministry of Justice (法務部司法官學院組織法) provides, "The Academy is charged with the following responsibilities:

1. Develop and train the personnel who have passed the judicial official examinations.
2. Train the judicial personnel from the Ministry of Justice.

The bar and judicial examinations have a strong influence upon the legal education system in Taiwan.[39] Some even note that Taiwan's legal education is driven more by the bar and judicial examinations than formal law schooling.[40] Most law students feel the pressure of the bar and judicial examinations shortly after attending law school.[41] In Taiwan, these examinations are challenging to law

---

3. Develop and train personnel other than those stipulated in the previous two paragraphs, per the approval by the Ministry of Justice.

4. Investigate, analyze and research on criminal issues at the national level and policies related to criminal justice.

Guidelines, plans and other matters related to the training stipulated in the first paragraph under this Article shall be determined by the Judges and Prosecutors Training Committee and implemented by the Academy.

The Committee shall consist of 15 members with the Chief Justice of the Supreme Court serving as the Chairperson and the Prosecutor General of the Supreme Prosecutors Office as the Vice Chairperson. The Chairperson, the Vice Chairperson of the Committee, and the President of the Academy are ex-officio committee members, and the remaining members are assigned as follows: two (2) members designated by the Executive Yuan, three (3) members designated by the Judicial Yuan, three (3) members designated by the Examination Yuan, two (2) members shall be attorneys at law and/or experts and scholars, and two (2) shall be impartial advocates for social justice. Both genders must be represented within the Committee; either gender must occupy no less than one-third (1/3) of the Committee seats. All Committee positions are without remuneration". Organization Act of the Academy for the Judiciary, Ministry of Justice, art. 2.

39 Pratt, *supra* note 5, at 153–55, 158–59. There was once a common saying around campus stating that "[a] legal education is a waste if you don't pass the examinations". *Id.* at 155.

40 *Id.* at 157–58. Unfortunately, the bar and judicial examinations are not perfect indicators of professional competence because these examinations "reward comprehensive knowledge of the law" rather than "measuring the capacity to make effective use of that knowledge". In other words, these examinations "mostly measure memorization skills". Irish, *supra* note 1, at 16. Professor Irish further pointed out that "[t]he combination of low pass rates and tests that do not measure professional competence means that young, smart Taiwanese ... may devote enormous time and energy learning information of limited utility to the actual practice of law, and for the great majority of them who are unsuccessful in their quests, the time and energy may be wasted. Those favored few who do pass the bar exams gain entry into the massively protected legal services industry, where they are able to enjoy a very profitable livelihood. However, their comfortable position does not exist because of their global competitiveness as legal professionals; it exists only because the legal services industries in Taiwan ... are effectively protected from foreign competition". *Id.*

41 Kuo, *supra* note 21, at 39; Pratt, *supra* note 5, at 153.

students due to the low passage rate[42] of the examinations.[43] As a consequence, many law students attend preparatory schools outside law schools for help on the preparation of the bar and judicial examinations.[44] Some call it the "double school phenomenon"[45] in Taiwan.[46] Drawbacks that come along with the pressure of bar examination preparation are that law students tend to devote little time to developing practical skills or prefer skipping courses of subjects not tested in the bar or judicial examinations.[47]

---

42 Mark E. Steiner, Cram Schooled, 24 *Wis. Int'l L.J.* 377, 383 (2006); Lo, Driving an Ox Cart, *supra* note 2, at 65 (noting that "the passage rates for the judicial and bar examinations [in Taiwan] are low compared to the rates in other countries"); Pratt, *supra* note 5, at 155–58; Irish, *supra* note 1, at 15. Please refer to "Table 16.1: Numbers of bar examinations applicants and passage rates in Taiwan (2005–12)" and "Table 16.2: Numbers of judicial examinations applicants and passage rates in Taiwan (2005–12)" in Appendix. Due to the low passage rate of the bar and judicial examinations, not all law school graduates pass the examinations upon graduation. In fact, most of them do not. Thus, it is hard to track and estimate exactly how many law school graduates end up practicing law while how many of them do not. Chen, Role of Practice, *supra* note 21, at 5.

43 Pratt, *supra* note 5, at 155–56.

44 Kuo, *supra* note 21, at 39; Lo, Driving an Ox Cart, *supra* note 2, at 69. A commentator noted that preparatory school is one of the three core components of Taiwan's legal education. Steiner, *supra* note 42, at 382–83.

45 The "double school phenomenon" is a term picked up from Japanese, describing that students attend formal schools while going to preparatory schools at the same time. Accordingly, the double school phenomenon in Japanese legal education refers to the phenomenon of law students going to law schools for legal education and also attending preparatory schools for bar examination preparation. The Justice System Reform Council, Recommendations of the Justice System Reform Council – For a Justice System to Support Japan in the 21st Century – (June 12, 2001) ch. III, pt. 2., 1, http://www.kantei.go.jp/foreign/judiciary/2001/0612report.html, accessed October 12, 2013.

46 Chen, Are Japan and Korea the Models?, *supra* note 1, at 40. Over the years, many have criticized the negative impact of the bar and judicial examinations on Taiwan's legal education. Unfortunately, changes made regarding these two examinations have remained typically slow for decades. Hwei-syin Chen (陳惠馨), Transparency and Innovation of the Judicial Examination & Selection System (透明度與司法人員考選制度之興革), 1:2 *Nat'l Elite* 42 (June 2005), available at http://wwwc.moex.gov.tw/main/Quarterly/wHandQuarterly_File.ashx?quarterly_id=18, accessed August 16, 2015. However, a commentator contended that it is the politics in legal academia, rather than the low passage rate of the bar and judicial examinations, that have resulted in the inefficiency in Taiwan's legal education system. Chen, Are Japan and Korea the Models?, *supra* note 1, at 34.

47 Irish, *supra* note 1, at 8 (noting that "[a] frequent complaint about legal education in civil law countries is that the students do not take their formal university training seriously. They do not buy the required texts, and they often do not attend their classes; when they do attend, they are unprepared and passive. The students in civil law countries spend more of their time in cram schools than in the formal university environment"); Pratt, *supra* note 5, at 158.

Challenges Facing Current System and the Need for Reform

Taiwan's legal education is in crisis. It is in crisis because the current legal education system is far from the ideal – a system capable of effectively producing quality and skilled legal professionals.[48] There is a need for reforming the legal education system in Taiwan because the current system fails to recognize the value and importance of practical training, and neither does it adequately respond to the trend of globalization.[49] Consequently, legal professionals trained in Taiwan's legal education system are incapable of meeting the changing needs of Taiwan's rapidly developing society,[50] and practicing in an increasingly global environment full of challenges and severe competition.[51]

The changing world in this globalization era is challenging Taiwan's legal education and legal professionals produced by this system.[52] There is an increasing demand in Taiwan's society for lawyers with capability to handle complex legal issues that are new to the people due to globalization.[53] In addition, globalization has resulted in fierce competition not only in Taiwan, but also in the global market.[54] "Legal education must be responsive to changes in the underlying society".[55] In order to train legal professionals capable of meeting the changing needs of Taiwan's rapidly developing society and practicing in an increasingly global environment full of challenges and severe competition, law schools in Taiwan must reinvent their curriculum, teaching and training for law students.[56]

The next issue is to identify the goals of the legal education reform.[57] Each of us will get some ideas about the goals of legal education reform if someone asks us about our expectation on legal professionals trained and produced by Taiwan's legal education system. Our answer to this question is clear. We want Taiwan's legal education to produce skilled professionals capable of meeting the society's changing

---

48 Chang, *supra* note 29, at 31; Lo, Driving an Ox Cart, *supra* note 2, at 74.

49 Chang-fa Lo, International Conference on Legal Education Reform: Reflections and Perspectives, 24 *Wis. Int'l L.J.* 1, 1 (2006) [hereinafter Lo, Reflections and Perspectives]; Lo, Driving an Ox Cart, *supra* note 2, at 77.

50 Lo, Driving an Ox Cart, *supra* note 2, at 83.

51 *Id.* at 43, 82.

52 Irish, *supra* note 1, at 14; Lo, Driving an Ox Cart, *supra* note 2, at 74.

53 Lo, Driving an Ox Cart, *supra* note 2, at 75–76.

54 Irish, *supra* note 1, at 14; Lo, Driving an Ox Cart, *supra* note 2, at 74.

55 Irish, *supra* note 1, at 14.

56 Chen, Are Japan and Korea the Models?, *supra* note 1, at 64; Lo, Driving an Ox Cart, *supra* note 2, at 71.

57 In Taiwan, some goals of legal education reform, for instance, are "including law students from more diverse backgrounds", "enhancing the competence of law school graduates to deal with international and transnational matters", and "narrowing the gap between theory and practice through clinical legal education". Chen, Are Japan and Korea the Models?, *supra* note 1, at 51.

needs.[58] We want our law graduates to become problem solvers with independent thinking.[59] We want our law schools to "foster students attentive to the society and humanity",[60] and train them to become open-minded leaders with far-sighted vision.[61]

Bridging the Gap: Initiatives at National Taiwan University College of Law

Over the past decade, NTU Law has devoted substantial effort in amending the law school's curriculum in order to enhance the professional competence of our students and graduates in an era of globalized economy. The initiatives launched at NTU Law are divided into three aspects, including "diversity", "practical training", and "global collaboration".

Diversity

In today's legal education, diversity matters.[62] The diversity of the law faculty and the student body is essential to the excellence of a law school.[63] The conventional wisdom believes that a diverse law school community offers law students a better legal education and a richer learning environment than a homogeneous one.[64] A diverse law school community is more likely to better prepare law students for practicing in a globally interconnected and increasingly culturally diverse world[65] because "skills needed in today's increasingly global marketplace can only be developed through exposure to widely diverse people, cultures, ideas, and viewpoints".[66]

NTU Law recognizes the value of diversity in society and embraces it in legal education because it is important for a law school to develop a community embracing various perspectives and reflecting different concerns of the society.[67] A law school, "the proving ground for legal learning and practice, cannot be effective in isolation from the individuals and institutions with which the law interacts"[68] since "[l]aw is an area in which effective analysis and advocacy

58 Lo, Driving an Ox Cart, *supra* note 2, at 84.

59 *Id.*

60 *Id.* at 77.

61 *Id.* at 84.

62 Cruz Reynoso and Cory Amron, Diversity in Legal Education: A Broader View, a Deeper Commitment, 52 *J. Legal Educ.* 491, 491 (2002).

63 Kevin R. Johnson, The Importance of Student and Faculty Diversity in Law Schools: One Dean's Perspective, 96 *Iowa L. Rev.* 1549, 1566 (2011).

64 *Id.* at 1552–53.

65 *Id.* at 1552.

66 Grutter v. Bollinger, 539 U.S. 306, 330 (2003).

67 Richard H. Sander, Class in American Legal Education, 88 *Denv. U. L. Rev.* 631, 631 (2010–2011).

68 Sweatt v. Painter, 339 U.S. 629, 634 (1950).

obviously require as deep an understanding as possible of various points of view on key legal issues and of the social and economic realities in which they arise".[69] Moreover, "[f]ew students, and no one who has practiced law would choose to study in an academic vacuum, removed from the interplay of ideas and the exchange of views with which the law is concerned".[70] Thus, over the years NTU Law has strived to promote diversity among the faculty and the student body.

Diversity in the law faculty contributes to a better legal education, and enriches law teaching and legal scholarship by bringing in different perspectives, life experiences and knowledge.[71] The NTU law faculty is composed of leading scholars and experienced legal professionals with diverse backgrounds.[72] Our faculty members not only received legal education in our motherland, but also pursued advanced legal education and obtained their Doctorates in many different countries, including civil law countries, common law jurisdictions, and countries with mixed legal systems.[73] Our diverse faculty is not only committed to providing our students with knowledge and skills they need to acquire in the globalization era, but is also capable of helping our students develop the ability to analyze legal issues from a comparative perspective.

A diverse student body has a significant effect on classes offered at law schools[74] because it makes "classroom discussion … livelier, more spirited, and simply more enlightening and interesting".[75] A diverse student body also benefits students by "better prepare[ing] students for an increasingly diverse workforce and society, and better prepare[ing] them as professionals".[76] NTU Law is committed to pursuing diversity of many different types in its student body. At NTU Law, the majority of the student body is composed of undergraduate law students enrolling in our law school after passing the University Entrance Examination. In addition, the GIILS admits non-law graduates interested in pursuing collaborative

---

69 Gary Orfield and Dean Whitla, Diversity and Legal Education: Student Experiences in Leading Law Schools, in *Diversity Challenged: Evidence on the Impact of Affirmative Action*, 147 (Gary Orfield ed., Harvard Educ. Publication Group 2001).

70 *Painter*, 339 U.S. at 634.

71 Johnson, *supra* note 63, at 1562–63, 1566.

72 The faculty's diverse educational background has long been viewed as a primary strength of NTU Law. Pratt, *supra* note 5, at 144–45.

73 By December of 2013, there were 73 faculty members at NTU Law, including 46 full-time faculty members and 27 adjunct faculty members. National Taiwan University College of Law, Homepage, http://www.law.ntu.edu.tw, accessed January 16, 2013. Among the 46 full-time faculty members, 20 faculty members obtained their doctorates in Germany, 11 of them graduated from law schools in the United States, 7 faculty members received their doctorates in Japan, 5 of them obtained their doctorates in the United Kingdom, 2 faculty members got their doctorate degrees from law schools in Taiwan, and 1 faculty member earned his doctorate degree in France. *Id.*

74 Chesterman, *supra* note 2, at 883.

75 *Bollinger*, 539 U.S. at 330.

76 *Id.*

legal education combined with other disciplines. This newly established system is expected to play a critical role in improving both the diversity and quality of Taiwan's legal profession.[77] Furthermore, we have international students from all over the world who study at NTU Law for degree[78] or non-degree programs.[79]

Practical Training

Practical training courses matter in legal education.[80] "[A]lthough the law is a highly learned profession, … it is an intensely practical one".[81] Nowadays law is considered a means rather than an end because it serves as a problem-solving tool in society. More and more law schools in different countries offer different practical training courses with inspired teaching to help students develop useful legal skills for future practice.[82]

In Taiwan, overemphasizing doctrinal teaching while ignoring the practical training of law students is one of the primary concerns driving the pressures to reform the legal education system.[83] Law schools in Taiwan should offer more practical training courses in legal curriculum because practical training is a critical component in legal education.[84] Offering practical training courses does not cost law schools a fortune.[85] Moreover, it is unrealistic to rely on the post-bar apprenticeship program to equip every soon-to-be lawyer with all the necessary skills since the legal practice part of the program is too short, not well-designed, and not every

77 Lo, Driving an Ox Cart, *supra* note 2, at 56.

78 International students may study in the undergraduate law program, the LLM program, or the PhD program at NTU Law. Information of these programs is available on the website of NTU Law via following links: (1) undergraduate law program: http://www.law.ntu.edu.tw/main.php?mod=custom_page&site_id=1&page_id=79, accessed August 17, 2015; (2) LLM. program: http://www.law.ntu.edu.tw/main.php?mod=custom_page&site_id=1&page_id=80, accessed August 17, 2015; and (3) PhD program: http://www.law.ntu.edu.tw/main.php?mod=custom_page&site_id=1&page_id=81, accessed August 17, 2015.

79 At NTU Law, non-degree programs available for international students are the exchange program and the summer program. Information of these programs is available on the website of NTU Law via following links: (1) exchange program: http://www.law.ntu.edu.tw/main.php?mod=custom_page&site_id=1&page_id=87, accessed August 17, 2015; and (2) summer program: http://www.law.ntu.edu.tw/main.php?mod=custom_page&site_id=1&page_id=94, accessed August 17, 2015.

80 A commentator said that producing lawyers through legal education without practical training courses is like teaching pilots how to fly a plane simply by reading flight theory in books, or like training physicians without having them see any patient before graduation. Martinez, *supra* note 29, at 377.

81 *Painter*, 339 U.S. at 634.

82 Lo, Driving an Ox Cart, *supra* note 2, at 61.

83 Irish, *supra* note 1, at 7.

84 Martinez, *supra* note 29, at 377; Chen, Role of Practice, *supra* note 21, at 10.

85 Chen, Role of Practice, *supra* note 21, at 10.

apprentice is guaranteed to receive quality skill training.[86] It takes time for young lawyers to acquire legal practice skills, but the last thing we want to see is for young lawyers to use their clients' cases as training to develop their legal practice skills.[87] Law schools should play a critical role in law students' practical training by offering more skill training courses in legal curriculum because this is the most effective and efficient way to prepare law students for future legal practice.[88]

In early 2013, NTU Law joined a long tradition of clinical education in law schools around the world[89] by including a law clinic course in the legal curriculum.[90] The core idea of introducing this law clinic course is to help students apply their doctrinal knowledge of law to legal practice and gain hands-on experience by exposing themselves to real world practice settings.[91] In the law clinic, students learn to practice law by acting in the role of lawyers under the close supervision of experts.[92] The student–teacher ratio of this course is five to one.[93] This ratio could be lower as we have a large counselor group composed of diverse and experienced legal experts, such as lawyers from prestigious law firms, prosecutors, and legal experts from non-governmental organizations.[94]

Practical training courses offered at NTU Law are more than just the law clinic.[95] We provide various advanced skill training courses which train students for roles like trial advocates, negotiators, in-house counselors and so on.[96] The purpose of offering these skill training courses, in short, is to enhance the professional

86 *Id.*; Martinez, *supra* note 29, at 361–62. In Professor Martinez's opinion, "[t]he apprenticeship has worked in the past – in a different set of professional circumstances – and it could still be a valuable way to introduce young lawyers to local practice. But it can no longer be relied on as the sole source of practical training for lawyers. Clinical education can help address the weaknesses in the apprenticeship model while serving as a tool to prepare Taiwanese lawyers for practice". *Id.* at 363.

87 Chen, Role of Practice, *supra* note 21, at 10.

88 Lo, Reflections and Perspectives, *supra* note 49, at 2; Martinez, *supra* note 29, at 363; Chen, Role of Practice, *supra* note 21, at 10.

89 Martinez, *supra* note 29, at 357–58.

90 Applying Doctrinal Learning to Practice – Introduction of the Law School's Practical Training Courses, *NTU Law Newsletter* (Nat'l Taiwan U. Coll. Law, Taipei, Taiwan), Autumn, 2013, no. 11, at 2–3, 10–11 [hereinafter *Applying Doctrinal Learning to Practice*].

91 *Id.* at 10; Martinez, *supra* note 29, at 347–48. According to Professor Martinez, "[a]n effective lawyer must combine client communication skills with doctrinal knowledge to understand the client's options under the law, understand how each option affects the client's individual situation and preferences, and put the client in a position to make the best possible decision about what to do". *Id.* at 350.

92 *Applying Doctrinal Learning to Practice*, *supra* note 90, at 10–11; Martinez, *supra* note 29, at 349–51.

93 *Applying Doctrinal Learning to Practice*, *supra* note 90, at 10.

94 *Id.* at 11.

95 *Id.* at 3.

96 In the academic year of 2013–2014, skill training courses offered at NTU Law include criminal trial practice, commercial dispute resolution, mergers and acquisitions

competence of our law students by equipping them with useful legal knowledge and skills they need for their future practice.[97]

Global Collaboration

Thanks to advances in technology and communications, nowadays "geographic proximity with one's legal advisors" is no longer essential.[98] Consequently, the demand for legal professionals with international legal competence is increasing under the impact of globalization.[99] Law schools around the world, including those in Taiwan, should address the need to produce globally competitive legal professionals who are "not only professionally competent within their own jurisdiction, but also in possession of the cultural sophistication to work with [other professionals] from markedly different legal and social environments".[100] In order to achieve this goal, law schools should "constantly reinvent themselves for facing the challenges of globalization through [international academic] exchange and collaboration program".[101] Moreover, law schools should encourage law students to participate in international academic exchanges in order to attain cultural sophistication through immersing themselves in environments with different cultures, history and world views of diverse people.[102]

---

practice, commercial legal practice, intellectual litigation practice, civil trial practice, labour and employment practice, and litigation documents drafting. *Id.*

97 *Id.* at 3–6; Martinez, *supra* note 29, at 359.

98 Irish, *supra* note 1, at 15.

99 *Id.* at 14–15.

100 *Id.* See also Chesterman, *supra* note 2, at 883 (alleging that "[t]o operate effectively in … a [globalization] world, individual lawyers need to be comfortable in multiple jurisdictions, often simultaneously"). Professor Irish contended that legal education systems failing to address this need "will see their graduates doing little more than carrying the briefcases of those better trained to deal with the complexities of a globalized economy". Irish, *supra* note 1, at 15.

101 C. Raj Kumar, Legal Education, Globalization, and Institutional Excellence: Challenges for the Rule of Law and Access to Justice in India, 20 *Ind. J. Global Legal Stud.* 221, 234 (2013). See also Chesterman, *supra* note 2, at 888 (maintaining that "faculties will seek ways to ensure that their graduates are both intellectually and culturally flexible, capable of adapting not merely to new laws but to new jurisdictions. Comparative and international subjects will receive greater emphasis, with comparative and international perspectives also being introduced to a wider range of subjects"). Nonetheless, Professor Kumar also noted that "token arrangements of collaboration may not be helpful to the institutions involved. There is a need to develop a shared understanding of the nature of exchange and collaborative programs being established for them to be effective and beneficial for all the parties concerned". Kumar, *supra* note 101, at 234.

102 Irish, *supra* note 1, at 15. *See also* Chesterman, *supra* note 2, at 887 (contending that "a truly global legal education requires … a genuine engagement with the people and the places that make up today's global profession"). According to Professor Chesterman,

In a globalization era, "the world [is] a web in more ways than one, with lawyers needing to be comfortable in multiple jurisdictions".[103] Legal professionals are no longer just talents in a particular jurisdiction, but should be viewed "as part of [a] global elite in a worldwide market for talent".[104] In order to enhance the professional competence of our students and expand international career prospects for our graduates in the global market, our faculty has strived to globalize the educational experience at NTU Law. Our ongoing global collaboration effort is to expand our law school's global network by entering into partnerships with law schools worldwide.[105] Our global collaboration effort aims to go "beyond the [typical] exchange model to integrate courses into a whole that is greater than the sum of its parts".[106] We believe that a close collaboration with law schools globally offers our students opportunities to combine their legal knowledge and skills with global perspectives, and therefore broadens their prospects and enhances their professional competence in an era of a globalized economy.

Conclusion

The legal landscape is ever expanding under the increasing trend toward globalization.[107] However, Taiwan's current legal education system does not adequately respond to the trend of globalization.[108] Neither does the current system effectively produce quality and skilled legal professionals capable of meeting the society's changing needs[109] and practicing in an increasingly global environment.[110] There is an urgent need to reform the current legal education system in Taiwan. It will take time to reform Taiwan's legal education, but there is no doubt that changes will be done.[111]

Law schools and law faculty, which play a critical role in educating and training future legal professionals, "are among the major guardians of the future of the [legal] profession and naturally tasked with the responsibility of developing a 'vision' for its future".[112] In order to enhance the international legal competence

"in the phenomenon of global legal education … it is essential for lawyers to be able to cope with diversity". *Id.* at 886.

103 Chesterman, *supra* note 2, at 877.

104 *Id.* at 883.

105 By January of 2014, NTU Law entered into partnerships with more than 50 law schools around the world.

106 Chesterman, *supra* note 2, at 885.

107 *Id.* at 887.

108 Lo, Reflections and Perspectives, *supra* note 49, at 1; Lo, Driving an Ox Cart, *supra* note 2, at 43, 61, 77.

109 Lo, Driving an Ox Cart, *supra* note 2, at 83.

110 *Id.* at 43, 82.

111 Chen, Are Japan and Korea the Models?, *supra* note 1, at 58.

112 Lutz, *supra* note 4, at 454.

of Taiwan's legal professionals in the globalization era, over the years NTU Law has devoted substantial effort to enrich the diversity of the law school community, reinvent the legal curriculum to embrace more practical training elements, and expand international academic partnerships globally. Nonetheless, this is simply the beginning of the legal education reform in Taiwan. There are still lots of things to be done in reforming Taiwan's legal education system.

The reform of Taiwan's legal education requires the joint effort of all law schools in Taiwan. NTU Law has taken the initiative, but the goal of reforming Taiwan's legal education cannot be reached without the participation of other law schools. We urge all law schools in Taiwan to take a greater role in reforming Taiwan's legal education and training the next generation of Taiwan's legal professionals to a better standard of competence. Every law student in Taiwan deserves a high quality legal education. It is our obligation to give them a better legal education through reforming the current system in Taiwan. Moreover, it is our obligation to help them achieve excellence in all facets of the legal profession. And last but not least, it is our obligation to better prepare them for practicing in an increasingly global market and a culturally diverse world.

Appendix

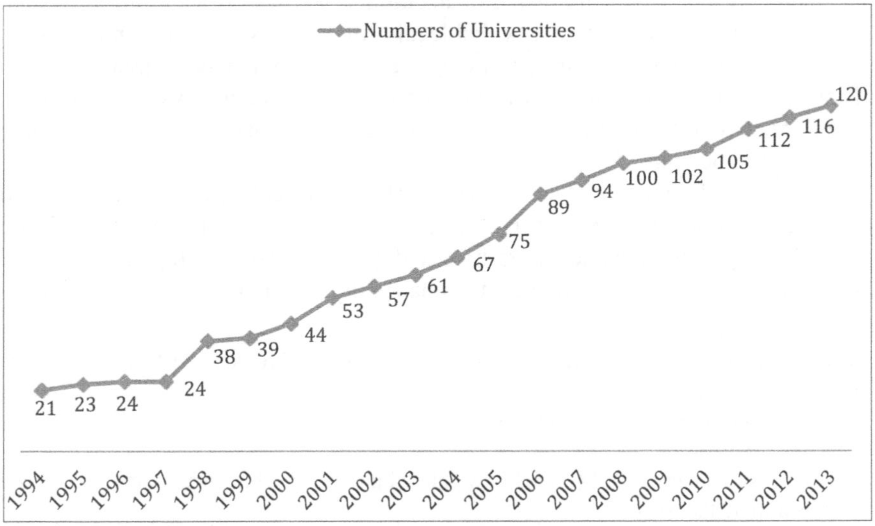

Figure 16.1 Increase in number of universities in Taiwan (1994–2013)[113]

113 Ms. Hsin-Yu Chiang (江心瑜), a lawyer in Taiwan and a graduate student at National Taiwan University College of Law, created this diagram based on the information provided in a statistics report "General Statistics of Colleges and Universities (Academic Years 1991–2012)" (大專校院概況表 (80–101 學年度)) published by the Department of Statistics, Ministry of Education in Taiwan. An excel file of this statistics report is available

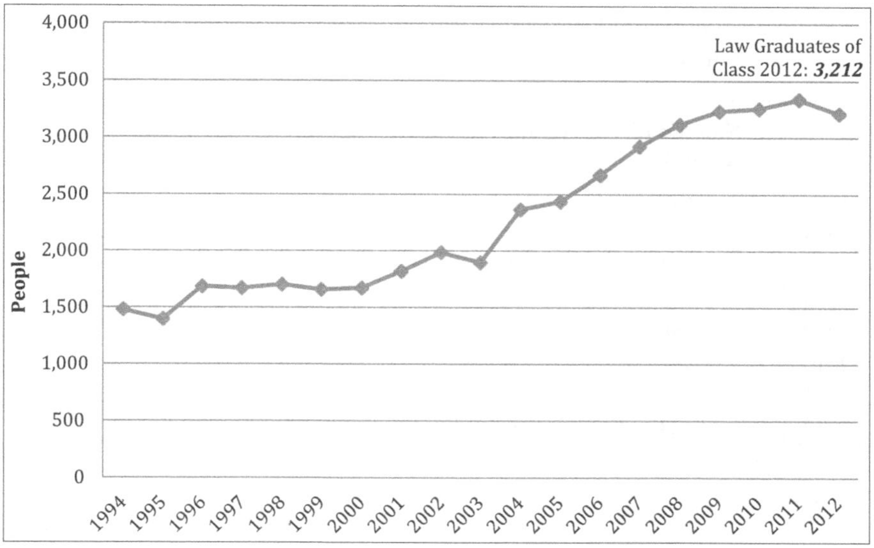

Figure 16.2 Increase in number of law graduates in Taiwan (1994–2012) (undergraduate only)[114]

Table 16.1 Number of bar examination applicants and passage rates in Taiwan (2005–12)[115]

Years	Number of Applicants	Actual Takers of the Examinations	Number of Applicants Passed	Passage Rates
2005	7,502	5,300	427	8.06
2006	7,942	5,546	448	8.08
2007	8,266	5,677	455	8.01
2008	8,469	6,128	494	8.06
2009	8,947	6,644	536	8.07
2010	9,822	7,482	600	8.02
2011	10,545	9,055	963	10.64
2012	10,249	8,619	915	10.62

on the website of the Department of Statistics via following link: https://stats.moe.gov.tw/files/main_statistics/u.xls, accessed August 16, 2015.

114 *Id.*

115 Ms. Hsin-Yu Chiang (江心瑜) created this table based on Examination Statistics of the Republic of China published by the Ministry of Examination under the Examination Yuan, http://wwwc.moex.gov.tw/main/content/wfrmContentLink.aspx?menu_id=268, accessed January 15, 2014.

Table 16.2 Number of judicial examination applicants and passage rates in Taiwan (2005–12)[116]

Years	Number of Applicants	Actual Takers of the Examinations	Number of Applicants Passed	Passage Rates
2005	5,602	3,819	165	4.32
2006	6,305	4,603	140	3.04
2007	6,384	4,660	141	3.03
2008	5,980	4,519	190	4.20
2009	6,558	5,150	121	2.35
2010	7,961	6,245	146	2.34
2011	7,982	7,144	71	0.99
2012	7,488	6,501	75	1.15

116 *Id.*

Chapter 17
Globalization and Legal Education in China Today

Wang Zhenmin[1]

China's legal construction has made great progress since the reform and open policy of 1978. In 1997, the Chinese authorities decided to adopt a new guiding principle which is "to govern the country according to law, building a socialist country under rule of law". Rule of law has become China's fundamental development goal. At the same time, Chinese legal education has seen significant changes over the past three decades. In 1977, there were only three universities in China which had law schools, and altogether they only enrolled 223 students. At present, however, over 620 institutions of higher education offer law degree programs, with some 400,000 students majoring in law. In China, basic degrees in law range from bachelor to doctorate, covering LLB, JM (Chinese version of JD program in Northern America), LLM as well as JSD (PhD in law). There were only some 200 lawyers in China back in 1980, but the number has reached nearly 200,000 up to now. The shortage of legal professionals is no longer a problem.

Our current problem is neither absence of laws nor shortage of legal professionals. On the contrary, we have too many of both to some extent, and the composition is somehow unreasonable. That's why the reform of legal education has been the subject of heated discussion in Chinese law schools recently.

China has been less impacted directly by the global crisis. That is because China keeps an independent financial system and implements strict supervisions to regulate banks. However, in terms of legal education, there remains much room for introspection and improvement. Law schools have two major tasks: one is to cultivate qualified legal professionals; the other is to conduct academic research on legal issues. Based on these two aspects, law schools shoulder special responsibilities in preventing the re-occurrence of global crisis.

Legal Education Should Retain its Independence and Maintain the Nature of Public Interest

Constructing the rule of law throughout society is significant for the future of every country and even that of mankind as a whole. And it should start from

1 School of Law, Tsinghua University.

legal education both domestically and internationally, that is, to cultivate legal professionals with ideals, ethics, ambitions and responsibilities. We have to admit the fact that a lot of problems exist in legal education throughout the world.

The Over-Commercialization of Legal Education

One of the major problems is that legal education is over-commercialized. In some places, it has almost become another kind of business education. Law has lost its original features: independence and the purpose of public welfare. Instead of being a noble career practicing for fairness and justice, it has become a way of reaping large profits. We can see from the curriculum of the law schools that more and more business-related courses are added to the course list while those theoretical or historical courses are becoming fewer and fewer. Legal education, as a vocational education, is interpreted as money-making education or technical education without grand ideals. Law schools are walking away from the beliefs they once shared. Evaluation agencies usually put great emphasis on the income level of the graduates when they rank law schools. People studying law are becoming more and more utilitarian, discarding the lofty aims of public good. Therefore, law schools are becoming more like business schools and lawyers are becoming more like businessmen.

People often compare law schools to business schools. In fact, law is an ancient subject with lofty ideals and aims. It is reasonable that the earliest universities in modern times only had three specialties: medicine, theology and law, for these three represented the initial purposes of humans: with medicine to cure the injuries of the body; theology to solve the problems of the mind; and law to solve the problems of the human society by providing a fair order. Only recently have business schools become commonplace. Oxford University once refused to establish a business school, hoping to maintain its purely academic image, but they finally yielded to reality. Actually, practicing business activities doesn't need much special training, for making money is a kind of human instinct. However, to pursue fairness, justice and order is not a human instinct. Thus, it needs college education and that is the purpose of our legal education.

If legal education is getting more and more commercialized, it means that law schools are giving up their pursuit for justice, fairness, order, development, harmony and peace. That will be terrifying, just like banks after commercialization, which gradually have forgotten their social responsibilities, solely working for money and finally leading to the financial crisis. The commercialization of our legal education will draw us away from our initial commitments. To speak more objectively, people handling legal issues, as well as people managing finances, are responsible for the financial crisis. The rules of the world were created by us and thus we contributed to the chaos of the world.

Why was legal education commercialized? One major reason is that both the government and society failed to invest enough. Law schools have to find a way to survive and the only way is to increase tuition fees. These exorbitant fees have made it difficult for law students to separate the study of law from that of business, and also made it difficult for students to continue to treat law as an art of fairness and justice. To keep the fairness of law, legal education must be independent from business practices; law schools should get subsidies from the government and support from non-profit foundations.

Transformation of the Development of Law Schools in China

With regard to the situation in China, the development of law schools has undergone significant transformation in the past 60 years, namely from government-led to self-controlled. Most of the law schools founded in the 1950s, as well as those established in the late 1970s and early 1980s, were led by the government, that is, they were set up in accordance with government planning.

The transformation first started in the 1990s. The government began to fade away, or to play a minor role in the process, letting universities and NGOs set up law schools themselves, as is true for many schools established since the 1990s. Within this framework there were two different options. Universities with greater educational autonomy were able to make the decision to set up law schools on their own. For instance, the restoration of the Tsinghua Law School in 1995 was a decision made by the university itself instead of the government. The other option was for the provincial government to establish law schools directly. Although these schools were financed by the government, it was the universities themselves, not the government, who actively decided to invest money in developing legal studies. It became obvious that the government, as a result, lost much of its initiative in putting money into law schools. Clear evidence of this might be the fact that since the 1990s, for almost every law school in China, the money to build new teaching buildings was raised by the universities themselves, not funded by the government. If the construction of a legal system is a national project, surely government should invest in this. However, as we can now see, the development of law schools is mainly funded by universities, with little input or effort from government.

So how should we look at such phenomenon? Is it beneficial or harmful? Why should universities set up law schools with their own money? It is simple and clear that the government grooms professionals to study theories of the law that our nation needs. You may ask then, what is the sole purpose for colleges to establish law schools? Why use a tight budget to nurture legal professionals? I believe that it is a professional obligation for jurists to set up institutes of law under most circumstances. The healthy development of the Chinese society requires the rule of law, and therefore legal professionals are in great demand. People already in the legal field are far more aware of the importance and the urgency of the development of the legal system than the government. This explains why law schools in China have been developing at unprecedented pace and scale though with little governmental investment in recent years.

There are two important consequences of the reduced government intervention and investment. The first is that the development of law schools becomes disordered with no common standard. Law schools are set up casually and enrolment is expanded disorderedly. Among all the subjects in universities, legal education has the greatest need to be unified. In order for the law in a country to be uniform, judiciary and enforcement must be uniform. Our legislation is uniform, but it depends on the scattered judiciary and enforcement to execute, and it depends on law schools to train legal professionals with unified standards. Another severe consequence is that, due to the reduction of government investment, law schools have to make a living by as many means possible to solve their financial problems. One important way is by increasing tuition fees. As a popular profession, many students choose to major in law. Although most universities, whose purpose and motivations are justified, work to offer legal professionals to help with the nation's promotion of the rule of law, it can't be denied that some universities treat their law schools as money-making machines.

As we all know, in order to have a transparent government free from corruption, it's important to increase the salaries of civil servants. But more importantly, we must provide adequate protection for the independence of the judges, for the judiciary is the last line of defense for social justice. Still I think professors in law are more important than judges, and it's more important to raise their salaries because legal education is the last line of defense of judiciary. Administrative problems aren't too bad because the judiciary can monitor and correct them, while judicial problems are a very bad thing for the country. However, as long as the legal education in our country is able to cultivate high-quality legal professionals and we are under the guidance of correct legal theories, there is hope. The most terrifying problems lie in legal education. As legal education is the most upstream of a nation's legal system, and if the water's upstream turns bad, the whole river will be polluted. The achievements of building the rule of law in our countries is partly owed to the efforts of legal education. However, we are also to blame for any problems caused. Therefore, we should make a great commitment to reforming legal education. State and society should increase investment, keep legal education independent and working for public welfare, and avoid trends towards commercialization. After all, the realization of social justice is the permanent theme and the fundamental objective of the government. And realizing social justice should begin from legal education. So I appeal to the government and society to increase investment in legal education.

Absence of Education of Professional Ethics in Lawyers

I mentioned law schools' external reform above, primarily the financing channels, and the relations with government and society. As for the matter of the teaching activities within law schools, there are still many problems. Among them, the most serious one is the absence of professional ethics education in lawyers. Law is a double-blade sword that can do good deeds as well as bad ones in lawyers' hands. If lawyers break the law, the results will be very serious. In ancient China, people who wanted to learn Kungfu had to learn Kungfu ethics. Nowadays, a lack of teaching courses in ethics is resulting in law gradually losing the human touch, and to be alienated from human kindness. Therefore, we should develop a set of compulsory courses in professional ethics.

As for the cultivation of legal professionals, I believe that what we can do is to keep our integrity, stay back, to a certain extent, from business, and to strengthen the education of professional ethics. We hope to foster lofty ideals in our law students.

In the long run, tertiary education as a whole also needs reform to face the recurrence of the global crisis. Previously, the universities used to talk too much about the business while paying too little attention to economics and the future. Both law schools and business schools should place more emphasis on economics than business. For sustainable development we can only live in an economical way.

On June 19, 2010, Alexander Medvedev, the President of Russia, raised the idea in his speech at The International Business Forum in St Petersburg that people should abide by the edification of the great Chinese philosopher and thinker Laozi to manage the crisis. He said, "If we follow the teachings of the Chinese philosopher, I think we can find balance and stand the tremendous test". He quoted from the Tao Te Ching written by Laozi, "Which one is more harmful, gains or losses? The more people like something, the more they must pay; the more people collect precious things, the sadder they feel when they lose them. Therefore, people will have no humiliation if they are content with their lots and will not be in danger if they stop where they should stop and thus will last long". In other words, the inordinate love should pay more for this and the over-accumulation of wealth will definitely bring about more devastating losses. Therefore, we will not be humiliated if we understand the philosophy of being satisfied, and no dangers will occur once we are more moderate. In this way, we can gain the lasting safety. From my point of view, this is extremely inspiring and meaningful for education in law schools and business schools.

The Global Financial Crisis Has Raised New Issues for Legal Research

The non-commercialization of law schools does not mean that they should not research commerce further. On the contrary, more emphasis should be placed on the study of both commercial and financial issues in law. The outbreak of the global financial crisis has had a great impact on legal studies as follows.

More Attention Should be Paid to the Studies on Rule of Law in Financial and Commercial Aspects

People are becoming more and more aware of the fact that, although there are various causes of the outburst of the financial crisis, the imperfection of conducting the rule of law is among the most crucial ones. Thanks to the rule of law, human behavior has changed from unconscious to conscious, and human activities have become rational and scientific, which can be seen as major evidence of the progress of human civilization. However, we have to admit that several fundamental aspects of human life are yet to be controlled by the rule of law; in other words, the rule of law has not played an effective role in the social context. For example, some commercial and financial practices often go beyond the effective coverage of laws. The line between the legal and illegal are blurred. This challenges the existing human ethics. On all accounts, the loose or zero control of the finance industry should be among the most blameworthy causes. In order to avoid further turmoil, we must strengthen the rule of law in the commercial and finance industries.

It cannot be denied that much could be done to improve conduct with respect to the rule of law in the financial industry, especially through the strengthening of legal enforcement to optimize the banking industry and reduces its speculative tendencies. So far, the rule of law has been mostly accountable to public supervision, a situation that needs to be improved by restoring the traditional aspect of supervision over private financial activities. This should be the lesson we learn from the financial crisis. Previously, the financial regulations of socialist states were too rigid. All banks were run by the state. The state-owned banks never had to worry about how to make profits – they could get by with zero profit or even a deficit. Banks then worked for the public welfare, which was one of the two extremes. The other was that capitalist states handed down the right of founding and managing the banks to private institutions and left everything to the adjustment of the market itself. How to obtain an equilibrium between these two positions is one of the key issues of today's legal studies.

Both developing countries and developed countries need to optimize their financial laws and legal supervision over banks.

The Government Needs More Administrative and Supervisory Authority

Financial and commercial law is not an independent existence, but a part of the country's entire legal system. In order to thoroughly solve the problem, we also have to reform the entire legal system and improve the legal environment. This is especially true concerning the rule of law in government, as this has often been viewed in a negative light, and perceived to be too harsh. Now we should pass laws giving government more regulatory power, enabling government to have greater access to the personal sector to enforce law so as to safeguard social equality and justice as well as to maintain a proper order of competition. Meanwhile, we have to avoid the government's abuse of power. In the face of the global crisis, how to define the authority of the government so that it possesses enough regulatory power but not so much as to lead to power abuse is an issue worth studying.

In addition, many countries are still falling behind with regard to the input of judicial power. There is still a shortage of qualified judges and prosecutors; the status of judges is not independent enough. All these are calling for immediate and profound improvement.

Legal Supervision of the Legal Profession Itself Needs to Be Strengthened

When strengthening the rule of law, we must also strengthen the legal supervision of the legal profession itself. Perhaps many people think that all legal professionals understand laws and there is no need to use too many laws to control them. In fact, legal professionals are ordinary people in the first instance, sharing the same problems as the rest of us. The occurrence of the global crisis has dealt another heavy blow to people's trust in professionals. In this regard, we need, on one hand, to strengthen professional ethics education and reinforce professional discipline. On the other hand, we must strengthen legal supervision of the profession and the norms of the legal profession itself. The legal professionals provide legal restrictions to other people almost every day, but it's time to designate legal boundaries for them. This is an important part of a country's legal governance, which has long been overlooked or ignored.

Legal Governance Needs to Be Supported at an International Level

We should also support projects and research concerning global legal governance. The financial crisis has exposed not only the loopholes in the laws of various countries but also the lack of legal governance at the international level. Perhaps the legal governance in each country is very good, being able to achieve social justice and orderly governance. But we have to admit the reality that the human world as a whole still appears disorganized and often even lawless. Everyone has an age. Children or teenagers are often naughty and uncivilized, showing contempt for law and order, but as they get older, people tend to be more civilized. Sociologists believe this is also true for a nation. However, it is sad to see that a country is always hovering around the age of 10 – that's to say, a country is never going to grow up. The relationships between countries are far less civilized than those among people. Achieving legal governance among nations is thus much more difficult and important than that within a country. Strengthening international legal governance is an important indicator and method towards human civilization. There are especially many major defects or even large research gaps (blank space of study) in the field of international finance law. Although many international organizations have already made valuable efforts in these aspects, I think there is still much more to be done.

Nowadays, great changes have taken place in our living environment, and we are faced with more and more severe challenges. Great human impacts can be identified behind the causes of natural disasters, which indicates that the root of these so-called natural catastrophes lie, in essence, in human behaviors. We are now moving further and further away from the sustainable development mode, which is becoming replaced by suicidal or devastating development. We cannot control volcanic eruptions, earthquakes or hurricanes fundamentally, nor can we create laws for nature. What we can do is to control ourselves, to make laws for human beings and to constrain our own behaviors so as to reduce the occurrence of disasters. In order to contain the malignant development, the best way is to actually constrain ourselves. Law schools must intensify research into global legal governance to create a peaceful, harmonious and restrained environment for the whole human race.

Conclusion

We cannot condemn Mother Nature for the outbreak of the financial crisis. It is totally different from volcanic eruptions, earthquakes or hurricanes, but is a completely man-made crisis. We cannot avoid natural disasters from occurring again, but the man-caused disasters, such as the financial crisis, are absolutely evitable. We must reflect upon our education and laws to prevent the crisis from happening again. In terms of improving legal education and rule of law, law schools shoulder an unshrinkable duty. The Law School of Tsinghua University is willing to work together with all of you to make a fair, reasonable, scientific and sustainable legal environment for all human beings through our legal education and academic research.

Chapter 18
The Ideal and Path of Legal Education Reform in China[1]

Ji Weidong

Using the Excellence Plan to Promote Legal Education Reform

The first decade of the twenty-first century has seen a huge change in legal education reform both in China and in the international situation. There is an increasingly diversified social demand for innovations in the methods of response and integration mechanisms. Under the "Going Out" strategy, Chinese enterprises have to face entirely new investment environments, a large number of trade frictions and complicated decision-making risks. Thus, they have to pay more attention to the effect of compliance and internal control, business law matters and consultant lawyers. The outbreak of the financial crisis in 2008 resulted in early participation by the Chinese Government in global governance. The problem of international competitiveness, for example in institutional soft power and talent resources, was also becoming obvious. In 2012, top-level leadership agreed that government power should be restricted and this meant that the rule of law order was again placed on the agenda. With these trends as a background, the Ministry of Education introduced a plan to establish the "Education and Training Bases for Excellent Legal Talents", which had a very clear target of meeting the challenges of marketization, diversification, internationalization and legalization by way of legal education reforms.

Until now, legal education in China has not clearly specified the training target and course contents of the LLB and Juris Master programmes. As a result, the system of professional legal education at the advanced level has not been established and there are some mistaken ideas. "Cramming" is the principal teaching method and students place great emphasis on memorizing statutes and standardized answers for examination. Meanwhile, training in professional qualities and skills is insufficient. The curriculum and teaching methods are stuck in a rut, and are divorced from legal practice and social needs, falling far short of the international standard. During the rapid increase in the number of law schools, there was a prevalent atmosphere of emphasizing the quantity but ignoring the quality, which led to a widespread homogenized mode of expanded reproduction with low cost.

---

1 This paper was translated into English by Mr Gu Yuxuan. Trainee Solicitor Candidate at Linklaters and PCLL Candidate at CUHK.

In 2013, there were 670 higher education institutions offering the LLB programme and about 310,000 students at faculties of law or graduate schools of law schools, with this number increasing to approximately 450,000 if postgraduate students are included. However, the average employment rate of law students was the lowest among the arts majors. It is reported that the average annual passing rate of law graduates in the National Judicial Examination was set at about 10%, but only half of the candidates who passed the Examination would choose a career as a lawyer, a judge or a procurator. There is a huge over-supply of talents in the low end of the legal market but the shortage of talents in the high-end legal market is also extreme. It is necessary to recognize that there is a striking imbalance amongst the investment, production and demand in legal education.

Therefore, it is necessary to trim down and control the size of legal education through significant reforms and then clarify the target and method of legal education. Otherwise, it would be difficult to satisfy the significant social demand of establishing a rule of law state, participating in global governance, operating business in compliance of law and resolving different disputes. The plan of establishing the "Education and Training Bases for Excellent Legal Talents" provides an excellent handle or experiment platform for legal education reform, and to properly co-ordinate and connect undergraduate education and the advanced professional legal education. It can foster the change from the homogenized mode (emphasizing quantity and reduction of cost) to the differentiated mode (emphasizing quality and increase of options). The differentiated mode is, on the basis of ensuring the education quality and standard of knowledge and skills, to encourage innovation and cultivate different types of legal talents according to the diversified demands. It also combines general education and specialization effectively.

Based on the above recognition of using the plan of training excellent legal talents to foster legal education reform in China, we can make the following statements about the direction of future development. First, use subjects such as theory of justice and legal professional ethics as well as pro bono activities to enhance the sense of identity and cultivation of basic qualities. Although the legal concepts are abstract and difficult to grasp, they are important to the "interpretative community" of the legal profession, development of excellent talents, and improvement of discernment and comprehensive judgment. Second, take a series of co-ordinated measures, including improving the curriculum, textbooks and reference materials, to establish an appropriate basic knowledge system of law. Apart from the 16 core courses, it would be advisable to have interdisciplinary courses, comprehensive application courses and courses covering the academic frontiers. Third, adopt teaching methods such as case discussion, dialogue, negotiation, legal clinics, simulation and problem solving workshops to enhance the training of professional skills. Teachers of substantive and procedural laws, as well as full-time and part-time legal practice teachers (practitioners), should be encouraged to start "unibus" courses. These enhance the students' ability to break down the barriers between different subjects and to freely use different knowledge and experience to solve practical problems. Fourth, to broaden the international visions and option of thoughts of the students, it is necessary to attach importance to courses in international law, comparative law and laws of foreign countries. It is also significant to improve communication with overseas institutions and provide opportunities of studying and visiting abroad.

"3 + 3 System": Innovation of the Mode of Cultivating Legal Talents

Large numbers of students undertake legal education in China, but only a small proportion of law graduates go on to become lawyers, procurators or judges. Most students will be employed in enterprise or government departments. Thus, the target of cultivating talents at the undergraduate level should not be limited to the legal professional qualities and skills. Rather, it could be blurred and the contents and methods of the courses need to be diversified. The substantive advanced professional legal education should be conducted at the postgraduate level, with the number of students reduced and the quality of students increased according to the standard of "fewer and better". It is self-evident that this is the basic purpose of the plan of establishing the "Education and Training Bases for Excellent Legal Talents". To achieve the purpose stated above, it is necessary to re-determine the position of the undergraduate legal education and the Juris Master education for non-law undergraduates; otherwise, it will lead to chaos. In comparison, litigation lawyers, procurators and judges require more professional and specialized training, and this could be incorporated into the institutional path of "LLB-Juris Master". Legislators, administrative officers, non governmental organization (NGO) leaders, business lawyers, government consultant lawyers, managerial staff of enterprises, heads of legal affairs in companies and senior officers in international dispute resolution institutions need more comprehensive training and they can be included in the established sphere of "non-law undergraduate – Juris Master". To achieve the plan of training excellent talents in the Juris Master period, although the career path of the graduates can be diversified and is not to be confined to one form, the teaching target should be clear, unified and specific, that is, to cultivate ideal professional legal practitioners (especially lawyers).

When considering the institutional design of "LLB–Juris Master" as a whole, it can be observed that it is necessary to reduce the law courses in the LLB and shorten the period of study. The key part of professional education should be switched to the postgraduate period. LLB education should place more emphasis on the elementary law courses and absorbing more social science knowledge and it should require the student to master IT skills and several foreign languages. The basic qualities of being law-abiding citizens and the ability to resolve legal problems, especially the ability to express, communicate and make proper judgments, should be developed by mingling humanities and professional knowledge. The purpose of the advanced professional legal education at the postgraduate level is to cultivate excellent legal talents with a strong sense of justice and responsibility, as well as superior knowledge, international vision and creative thinking ability. The significant legal professional skills to be developed include the following: the ability to sort out complicated factual relationships, and discover the importance and relevance of the facts; the ability to research appropriately on the laws, precedents and rules based on the factual relationships; the ability to apply the law to the facts correctly in order to satisfy the clients' needs; the ability to deal with ethical and thorny problems properly; the ability to appropriately express the facts and opinion in writing or orally, and the ability to finish tasks effectively within a limited period of time. Moreover, considering the needs to do internships systematically and study abroad (for example, getting an LLM degree from a law school in the US), a two-year course is clearly insufficient.

Based on the above analysis and judgment, the KoGuan Law School of Shanghai Jiaotong University innovated upon the legal education reform of "LLB–Juris Master" and started the "3 + 3" Distinctive Law Class in 2009. The Distinctive Law Class was to cultivate outstanding legal talents by way of a specialized LLB–Juris Master programme. It selects the excellent candidates who will study the professional legal courses of postgraduate level in advance in their fourth year of LLB study. They receive a longer term, more systematic and specialized professional education. In practice, a number of outstanding candidates are chosen from third-year LLB students and they start their postgraduate study in their fourth year of LLB. The students receive advanced legal professional education via a connected LLB–Juris Master programme and they obtain the Juris Master degree in six years (LLB included). The basic aim of the Distinctive Law Class is to provide advanced legal professional education meeting the needs of judicial and foreign-related legal practice. In particular, it emphasizes the development of the following three kinds of capacity: first, international vision and the ability to make legal analysis and judgments; second, the training of practical skills for leading legal practitioners; third, the cultivation of awareness and spirit of people who protect the legal order. Compared with the relatively convenient LLB–LLM "4 + 2" mode of the current system, the Distinctive Law Class of "3 + 3" mode does not waste the LLB students' time because of the sloppy internships in the fourth year of LLB. It allows the advanced legal professional education to connect better with the LLB in terms of time and makes the content more in-depth and comprehensive. It leaves more time for students to receive a half-year systematic training for practice and study in leading overseas universities (for example, the double degrees programme of Juris Master in China and LLM in the US) or to do research.

The students of the "3 + 3" Distinctive Law Class cannot be selected by the National Entrance Examination for Masters held every January and they can only be selected according to their merits at the end of their third-year of study by way of recommendation. Considering the convenience within the system, in the first two years the candidates of the Distinctive Law Class are limited to the outstanding LLB students of the KoGuan Law School of Shanghai Jiaotong University. Thus, at the end of LLB students' third-year study, the KoGuan Law School offers a number of students (around 15) a place in the Distinctive Law Class according to the ranking of their cumulative grade point average and a test of comprehensive qualities. Since the third year of admission in 2012, apart from selecting outstanding students from the KoGuan Law School, the Distinctive Law Class also selected a number of (approximately 25 at the moment) outstanding LLB students from other leading law schools in China through the Summer Camp for Excellent Lawyers in July and the recommendation and second-test in September. For those candidates selected from law schools other than the KoGuan, the programme has a flexible study scheme based on academic credits. Specifically, the selected candidates from law schools other than the KoGuan Law School formally join the Distinctive Law Class after having finished their undergraduate study and obtained their LLB degree. They can study the courses with students of the Distinctive Law Class from the same or different years. For some elective courses, the Distinctive Law Class recognizes the credits obtained by candidates not from the KoGuan Law School in their LLB study, with a maximum of 15 credits.

The characteristic of the "3 + 3" Distinctive Law Class is that both the entry (selecting high-quality candidates) and the exit (providing more opportunities) are strict and it provides an appropriate process management for the personal growth and career planning of outstanding legal talents. This mode is not only suitable for "LLB–Juris Master" education, but can also be enlarged to "non-LLB–Juris Master" education. After repeated negotiation, the KoGuan Law School and the School of Foreign Languages of Shanghai Jiaotong University started to jointly enrol high school graduates nationwide (tentatively 20 students per year). The programme also adopts the six-year undergraduate and postgraduate study scheme and its target is to develop composite advanced legal talents dealing with foreign-related affairs. In the first three years of undergraduate study the students study in the School of Foreign Languages and the main target is to fully master two official languages of the United Nations or minority languages and professional knowledge of international business. In the fourth year of undergraduate and during the two years at the postgraduate level (three years in total) the students will receive advanced legal professional education. They will obtain the bachelor of foreign languages and the Juris Master degrees. If we can win the support of the Ministry of Education, we may enrol third-year undergraduate students majored in foreign languages, foreign trade and diplomacy from other foreign-related higher education institutes. The problems of connecting the study schemes and degrees would be solved so that the range of selection and the cultivation of composite advanced legal talents for foreign-related matters would be further enlarged. It is evident that the "3 + 3" system, as a mode of legal education reform in China, can be copied and promoted. It has a wide modelling effect and it can be used to develop outstanding legal talents with different disciplines.

Apart from traditional judicial organs, for example the public security organs, procuratorates, courts and judicial departments in the government, and the law firms, a considerable amount of law graduates will work in executive administration, public administration and business management positions.

However, law schools seldom consider their needs to systematically design the curriculums. Thus, legal education reform in the future should also adjust the curriculum for the cultivation of excellent legal talents in accordance with the diversified social needs. The law schools may jointly offer compulsory and elective courses with the School of Public Administration and the School of Economic Management. Under the circumstances of the increasing outbound investments and international trade frictions, the KoGuan Law School regards the development of elite corporate heads of legal and company lawyers as an important target during the education reform of "non-LLB–Juris Master" programme. Therefore, we established an overseas internship base for corporate heads of legal in Tokyo, Japan. The Corporate Law Research Centre was established in May 2011 and the KoGuan Law School offered a series of course with special topics on several modules including intellectual property (IP) law, commercial and financial law, and foreign-related economic law developed from the teaching system. If the agreement can be reached, it is possible to jointly cultivate talents on corporate law and government law with relevant schools by the "3 + 3 System" mode. In fact, the KoGuan Law School is preparing to start an interdisciplinary degree programme of "Corporate Legal Risk Management" with the Antai College of Economics and Management. The design proposal is finished and it is waiting for approval.

The Curriculum Design of Law Schools Requires New Ideas

Until now, law schools in China have tended to teach the knowledge in books and the difference between the cultivation of practical talents and research talents has not been fully reflected in the curriculum design and teaching methods. Although the civil law tradition emphasizes doctrines and the logical relationship between concepts and propositions, over-emphasizing the systematic study may easily neglect the connection between theory and practice and it is difficult for talents to emerge in legal practice. The same criticism can also be heard in Germany, France, Japan and South Korea. On the other hand, education in common law countries uses precedents as the material and places more emphasis on practicality and the training of legal thinking and practical skills. However, there is an over-emphasis on litigation, private law and personal issues, and education in these countries has not fully recognized the great impact of a more organized and industrialized legal profession. In fact, although the Langdell case method does not use the constitution, statutes or doctrines but instead uses appellant precedents for material, it is consistent with the civil law teaching method in that it applies legal principles to the specific facts by close analysis and logical deduction. This method of teaching law can no longer accommodate the increasing complicated and risky social reality. As a result, it seems that reforming the contents and teaching methods of legal education is becoming a common phenomenon internationally.

In terms of teaching content, it is particularly useful to look at the fundamental curriculum reform of the Harvard Law School in the US started in 2006, after it completed three years of research and looked at the transformation taking place in medical schools, business schools and schools of public policy. It was regarded as the second revolution of legal education after the Langdell case method. The most important changes in the first-year curriculum include: (1) Making international law and comparative law a compulsory subject, the purpose of which is to give law students a clear picture of the global legal landscape and allow students to correctly determine the position of national law in the framework of international society. Although compulsory, students can select from a range of courses in this areas, including public international law, law and international economy, constitutional law and international order, comparative private law doctrines and institution and Chinese law (or other foreign law). (2) Due to the increasing extension of the legislative and executive power, "Legislation and Control" has been made a compulsory subject. This course focuses on how professional legal practitioners should deal with statutes and administrative rules, especially how judicial organs and law enforcement agencies interpret and apply these rules. (3) Offering a new compulsory subject called the "Problem Solving Workshop". This is an unprecedented innovation, which has changed the scene of the classroom of the junior year and has been highly praised by the professors and students. It will certainly have a great impact on the US and other countries.

The "Problem Solving Workshop" is a teaching method that sees participants deal with certain cases or problems under the supervision of a full-time teacher with some experience in practice. It is a core course that closely combines theory and practice. Here, the students act like lawyers and solve the problems step by step, starting from taking the instruction from the client and preparing the case. The whole process of dealing with cases cultivates the students' ability to observe, apply the knowledge and make judgments. According to the design of the course, it takes approximately three days for the team to complete its assignments and discuss the case. Each team comprises four or five students and they spend three weeks dealing with seven cases. Usually, the teacher will briefly talk about the case on the morning of the first day and give a list of relevant statutes and cases as well as articles for the students to reference. After that, each team will start their work and in principle they must submit their assignment in the evening. The following day, students have a two-hour class during which time they can discuss the previous day's assignment. After that the students will continue their work and submit the second assignment before that evening. On the morning of the third day the teacher will hold a final discussion about the case and close it, then introduce the next case for students to undertake. Solving the case as a team and within a limited timeframe creates an intense and exciting atmosphere, motivating students to innovate and use their initiative. Harvard Law School's 2010 curriculum offered seven topics within the "Problem Solving Workshop", namely: administrative law and contract law, financial regulation and international finance, property law and conflict of laws, internet law, law and economics, dispute resolution institution, and legal professional institution and ethics. Each topic is taken on by teams of four or five students.

The reform of compulsory courses for senior-year students at Harvard Law School gave students more options and large autonomy in course selection. To avoid the imbalance of knowledge structure resulting from the freedom of course selection, Harvard Law School prepared a handbook to guide the credit planning of different categories of courses. There are two methods which guide the course selection. The first method is to categorize all subjects and seminars into 18 categories, with each category having its own course list. The second method is to confirm the senior-year research project and advise students on which subjects they should study within a specific area. For example, there were six research projects in 2011, including law and government, law and business, international law and comparative law, law and science and technology, law and social changes and criminal law and justice. Each research project comprises elementary courses, advanced courses, seminars, legal clinic experience, relevant research areas and interdisciplinary subjects. Although these reforms were based on the conditions of US and may not be suitable for legal education in other countries, it provides a useful example for curriculum reform in order to cultivate excellent legal talents in China.

In recent years, the KoGuan Law School of Shanghai Jiaotong University has made significant reforms to the curriculum to meet the needs of cultivating outstanding legal talents. One important measure of the reform is to enhance the training of practical skills. Thus, the Training Centre for Legal Experimental Teaching was established and there are five full-time teachers responsible for its operation. A new teaching mode was carefully designed and it provides a series of attractive course lists, which cover different modules including practice courses, clinical education, moot court, negotiation training, competition projects and legal aid centre. According to statistics, there are 23 full-time teachers involved in practical teaching and the skill training courses represent 20% of all courses in the KoGuan Law School. The KoGuan Law School co-operates with government departments, arbitration and judicial organizations, industrial organizations, international enterprises and top-20 law firms in Shanghai, and 25 "Practical Teaching Bases" and "Overseas Practical Teaching Bases" have been established. Every year more than 150 undergraduate and postgraduate students work as interns in these bases. In the fall semester of 2010, the KoGuan Law School started a Mooting on Intellectual Property Law course, which adopted the Chinese–English bilingual teaching method and was mainly for Juris Master students. Using the experience of Harvard Law School as an example, the KoGuan Law School started a "Legal Negotiation" course with prestigious law firms in 2011. In 2009, the KoGuan Law School started to establish a "Virtual Law Firm" system with reference to the Glasgow Mode, which has been an elective for law students since 2014. This project aims to enable students to learn the methods and skills to deal with complicated legal disputes in a multi-party and multi-threaded virtual environment by using the internet.

Restructuring of Law Schools and Assessment Criteria

The 1960s was the golden era for the continuous expansion and prosperity of universities in the US. In those days, the growth of the youth population and the increase of budget for higher education undoubtedly led to the development of higher education. However, in the early 1980s, the difficulty in the enrolment and employment of students as well as the deficit of the universities began to affect the higher education industry in the US. The number of students in the universities in 1989 was 40% smaller than 1983 and it dropped a further 60% in 1997, which was a big surprise. In the 1990s, the decrease in the youth population, which was a structural change, led to fiercer competition between universities in Japan. The establishment of the independent administrative legal personality of national universities and the reorganization of private universities came onto the agenda in this context. In sharp contrast, higher education in China has expanded for more than 20 years. However, with the recent decrease in birth rate and an aging population, concerns about the stringency of universities have begun to appear. If universities in China face the crisis of recession and bankruptcy in the near future, the already over-sized legal education industry would be the first to suffer. Taking this into consideration, the plan of establishing the "Education and Training Bases for Excellent Legal Talents" looks to the future. It involves a significant adjustment of the faculty–university–department layout over the next 15 years and will further stimulate competition within the legal higher education industry. The elimination mechanism will improve the standard of law school operation and the quality of talent cultivation. In order words, the Excellence Plan will restructure the legal education industry in China.

During the process of "the fittest survive", the significance of assessment, recognition and ranking will be more obvious and these activities will to some extent affect the allocation of resources. Thus, establishing a reasonable and authoritative quality assessment system is a basic task that cannot be avoided. It is easy to measure and compare the quantity, but quality includes values that are difficult to measure, for example tradition, reputation, tone of a school, brand name, support for graduates and fundraising capacity. These factors will have a great impact on the social position of the higher education institutes and it is a very complicated question to determine the relevant indicators. In terms of the plan to establish the "Education and Training Bases for Excellent Legal Talents", quality is more important because in this concept "quality" means excellent performance or effectiveness. The education results can be self-evaluated by the education suppliers, the education consumers and third parties. However, the most important evaluation is to be conducted by the standard recognition agencies, independent evaluation agencies, public media and preparatory schools for examinations (the third person). It is arguable that the third-person evaluation is the basic guarantee of the quality of education and research. Generally speaking, continuous evaluation and recognition of the quality of law schools by an organization consisting of the governmental education departments, legal institutes and users of legal service as an independent third party is an appropriate way to maintain the standard of quality and has a stronger credibility.

The evaluation of national universities and their law schools is usually conducted by the government department in charge and its main purposes are to maintain and improve the quality, determine the allocation of resources, hold the management accountable and disclose information. Therefore it is necessary to establish a national standard to ensure the objectiveness and justice of the evaluation. Although the evaluation systems differ from each other, the objective criteria usually include the following items: first, research – number of articles published in anonymously reviewed journals, the number of articles being referred to, the number of publication of monograph, the number of speeches made in international academic conferences, the number of papers and conference reports of postgraduate students, the application of research results, the number of policy consultation reports being adopted and the number of research projects and research grants; second, cultivation of talents – the degree of activity of the graduates in academic research and the society, the employment status of the graduates in overseas universities or research institutes, acceptance of visiting students, degree awarding and the efforts made in the curriculum and teaching methods of cultivating excellent legal talents; third, internationalization – the number and percentage of degree students studying abroad, the number and percentage of short-term students studying abroad, the number and percentage of foreign degree students accepted, the number of subjects taught in foreign languages, the number of degrees awarded to foreign students, the international experience of professors, the number of papers published in foreign languages, research with foreign academics and the percentage of foreign teachers; fourth, social contribution – receiving scholarships, donations, research instruction and co-ordinated research, the instructions from industry and companies to the professors, legal aid and legal consultation, participation in the government and public bodies' policy consultation and the consultation of international bodies; fifth, conditions and mechanisms of operation – the efficiency of the organization, the implementation of external evaluation, environment and support for education and research (libraries, IT and relevant facilities and equipment).

For the subjective quality evaluation, it is very difficult to use a set of specific criteria to regulate. The key is to establish the method or mechanism of self-evaluation, peer evaluation and external evaluation and its sustainability. For example, every teacher may be required to submit a written report on his teaching and research periodically (every year or every three years). The report will be evaluated by the faculty and the evaluation result will be reported to all teachers. The teachers can listen to each others' classes or study from each other and conduct evaluation. The faculty should conduct self-evaluation and external evaluation on its education and research periodically and publish the relevant data to fulfil the obligation of explanation. For the law schools, the passing rate of the Judicial Examination can, to a certain extent, be an important indicator of teaching quality evaluation. From another perspective, the Judicial Examination can be the baton of legal education. Thus, it is necessary to connect the reforms of these two systems. If serious defects exist in the Judicial Examination system and personnel system, the effect of legal education reform will be affected however it is carried out and the plan of cultivating legal talents may lose its realistic impact.

Chapter 19

Legal Education in the Global Context: The Case of Hong Kong

Johannes Chan[1]

Overview: The Impact of Globalization

Partly as a result of globalization, a few recent trends in legal education are noticeable. Firstly, the pace of changes in the modern era is unprecedented. On the one hand, knowledge has a much shorter life-span these days and factual knowledge becomes outdated much more quickly than before. On the other hand, many new problems have emerged that require innovative solutions within a very short period of time. The advance of modern technology and means of communication, which present a new virtual world with novel and complex legal relationships is a prime example. Secondly, advances in technology mean that a huge amount of information is available on any topic. It also greatly shortens the distance between different legal systems and legal cultures. Very few legal systems can be insulated from external influences these days, and there is an increasing need for knowledge and familiarity of legal systems other than that of our own. Thirdly, legal issues have become increasingly multi-disciplinary in nature. Climate change, town planning, trade relations and so on are just some obvious examples. Fourthly, it is rare these days that graduates will stay in one career throughout their life. Instead, we have seen university graduates, and not just law graduates, have become or have to become increasingly versatile. It is also an increasingly popular phenomenon that law graduates, by their own choice, decide not to stay in or even enter into the legal field.

As legal education has become increasingly globalized and competitive, more and more legal education institutions are adopting an outward looking attitude. This has enhanced academic collaboration and exchange, to the benefit of both students and teachers. The other side of the coin is that tertiary institutions are increasingly concerned about international ranking. Education is to be quantified so that they can be compared and ranked. Factors that are more difficult to measure such as quality of teaching or impact on students tend to be ignored, or worse, twisted for the sake of quantification. In the process there is a danger that we have forgotten what the mission of a university or a law school should be, or in the words of a former Dean of Harvard University, tertiary institutions are pursuing excellence

1 Professor of Law and former Dean, Faculty of Law, The University of Hong Kong.

sometimes at the expense of a soul.[2] What is the place of teaching as opposed to research in legal education that is offered by the tertiary institution? What is the role of teaching of ethics, and how should it be done? Increasing globalization in legal practice also results in some cases in the domination of corporate, commercial or financial work. The demand for knowledge in these rapidly developing areas of practice in turn exerts pressure on the law school curricula, which brings to the forefront the aim of legal education and what should be expected of a graduate fresh from law school. The problem is only to be aggravated by the dictation of a law curriculum through the requirements of a national Bar examination, which is a common phenomenon in Asian countries such as Japan, Taiwan or Korea. In many jurisdictions, the Bar examination is said to set a minimum entry standard in core competences. In practice, the minimum standard becomes the maximum amount of knowledge, as anything that is not within the syllabus of the Bar examination curriculum attracts little interest among students. Inadvertently, the national Bar examination reduces diversity and creativity in the teaching and learning of the law, and the law school curriculum becomes something just to help students pass the Bar examination. Should this be the case? Does it produce better lawyers? And more fundamentally, who should pay for the cost of legal education?

All these changes prompt us to review what legal education is about, and what a modern law curriculum should look like in light of these changes. Many law schools have undergone major curriculum reforms in recent years. Hong Kong is no exception. A major review of legal education took place at the turn of the century, and a decade since then, another major legal education review is on its way.

The Hong Kong Scene

The legal profession in Hong Kong is a relatively small and separate profession comprising barristers and solicitors. As of Jan 2015, there were about 1,275 practising barristers, among them 93 were Senior Counsel (80 male; 13 female). As at 31 December 2014, there were 8,279 solicitors with a current practising certificate, among them 6,239 were in private practice working in 836 firms,[3] including 79 foreign law firms. Of the local law firms, 382 or 46% were sole practitioners. Of all the sole practitioners, 40% have no assistant solicitor. Foreign lawyers are allowed to practise in foreign law in Hong Kong. A total of 1,253

2 Harry R. Lewis, *Excellence without a Soul* (Perseus Books Group, 2006).

3 Among the solicitors in private practice, 2,489 of them were partners or sole practitioners, 3,750 were employed as assistants or working as consultants. The remaining 2,040 solicitors holding valid practising certificates were not in private practice. Of all 8,279 practising solicitors, 53% were men and 47% were women; 82% of practising solicitors were ethnic Chinese. Among 836 law firms, a total of 984 trainee solicitors were employed, among whom 39% were male and 61% were female.

foreign lawyers were employed by both local and foreign law firms.[4] Their number has doubled in the last seven years. Solicitors and barristers are governed respectively by the Law Society and the Bar Association.

In mid-2014, the population in Hong Kong stood at 7.24 million. While Hong Kong has a per capita income comparable to many developed countries, it has also one of the largest income differential ratios between the rich and the poor in the world. Tertiary education has traditionally been and remains one of the key means of upward social mobility. Admission to tertiary institutions is basically determined by academic merit. Tertiary undergraduate education is mainly funded by public revenue and is provided at a substantially subsidized rate. It is due to the meritorious admission system and through the publicly funded tertiary education that some of the most talented students have been able to enter into the legal profession and become distinguished legal practitioners and prominent leaders of the community today. Although the community has in general become more affluent these days, it remains an important feature of our legal education system that no one is denied an opportunity to enter law school and the legal profession for want of financial means.

In general, until recently, legal education has been an undergraduate curriculum. However, a unique feature of legal education in Hong Kong is that, for historical reasons, the professional qualification, namely Postgraduate Certificate in Laws (PCLL), which is a common qualification for entry to both the barristers' and the solicitors' branches of the legal profession, is conferred by the university. The PCLL is a one-year full-time course of study.[5] PCLL graduates who wish to join the Bar will have to undertake one-year pupilage with a practising barrister, and those who wish to become solicitors will have to serve two years of traineeship with a solicitors' firm. There is no further qualification examination after the PCLL. Apart from the PCLL, the only other route of entry to the legal profession is through the Overseas Lawyers Qualification Examination (OLQE) for admission to be a solicitor and the Barristers Qualification Examination for admission to the Bar. Only overseas lawyers with at least three years' post-qualification experience are eligible to take these examinations, which are conducted by the legal profession and have a much lower passing rate than that of the PCLL. Thus, the bulk of lawyers admitted to the legal profession each year come largely from the PCLL graduates. In other words, the university becomes the primary gate-keeper of the quality and the number of new entrants to the profession. In recent years, this situation has become a thorny issue between the universities and the professional bodies, and sets the context for recent reform in the legal education curriculum in universities in the last decade. At the same time, there is a sharp increase in recent years in the number of overseas lawyers who are admitted through the

4 There were 79 foreign law firms employing 1,253 foreign lawyers. Among them, 918 foreign lawyers were employed in local law firms. And 335 in foreign law firms.

5 HKU offered a part-time PCLL programme in 2006–07.

OLQE.[6] In 2012–13, there were a total of about 650 PCLL graduates from the three law schools. In 2012, 256 candidates sat for the OLQE; 168 of them passed the examination and were admitted as registered foreign lawyers.

The first law school in Hong Kong was set up at the University of Hong Kong (HKU) in 1969.[7] The second law school was established at City University of Hong Kong (City U) in 1988, almost 20 years later. The third law school was set up at the Chinese University of Hong Kong (CUHK) in 2006. Apart from the undergraduate Bachelor of Laws (LLB) programme, each of the three law schools offers its own PCLL programme. They also introduced, at various points in time, a graduate Juris Doctor (JD) programme.

Apart from the three universities, a number of overseas universities, such as the University of London and Manchester Metropolitan University, offered overseas law degrees (for example, LLB) or professional programmes (for example, Common Professional Exam (CPE), Graduate Diploma in Law (GDL)) in conjunction with a local partner in Hong Kong. Their graduates will still have to take and pass the PCLL course in order to be eligible for admission to Hong Kong's legal profession. As from 2008–09, overseas law students are required to demonstrate competence in some conversion subjects before they are eligible for admission to the PCLL. These conversion course requirements were introduced to ensure that overseas students are equipped with adequate knowledge of substantive law that is required for a skills-based PCLL course.

A Response to Global Challenges: A Twenty-First Century Curriculum

With globalization comes an increasing expectation and demand on the qualities of law graduates, which in turn pose challenges on the mission of the law school. On the one hand, the legal profession increasingly expects law graduates to be competent, not just in general skills and knowledge, but also in specialized areas like securities, listing and other commercial practices. Global legal practice may also require students to be familiar with international law and different cultures and legal systems. At the same time, the competition and the pressure on passing the Bar examination result in students not interested in anything other than those subjects required to do so. This phenomenon is most obvious when law is pursued as a graduate programme where students enroll in the programme with full knowledge of the investment and the opportunity cost that they have incurred and would want to recover them in pursuing a legal career. At the other end of the scale, with rapidly changing career paths and, in some jurisdictions, the lack of

6 There were 777 registered foreign lawyers in 2005. The number rose to 1,041 in 2007; 1,203 in 2009; 1,431 in 2012: *South China Morning Post*, 15 Aug 2012. The number dropped to 1,253 in 2014. On average, about 200 candidates sat for the OLQE each year in the past six years since 2008 and the overall past rate was about 70% during these periods.

7 It was first established as a Department of Law within the Faculty of Social Sciences.

opportunities in the legal profession, the law curriculum may have to be designed in such a way that it could adequately prepare law graduates for a career other than law. At the same time, law schools, as an academic institution, would like to offer an educational experience that is intellectually interesting, challenging and rigorous. A twenty-first century law curriculum will have to address and balance all these conflicting demands, taking into account the history and characteristics of each institution. Thus, in a recent review, Oxford has decided to retain its century-old curriculum with in-depth teaching on a small number of subjects with little choice of electives, whereas others may decide to go for a broad liberal curriculum, and some others may find themselves constrained by the Bar examination.

HKU has always taken the view that 'the study of law is not only meaningful and useful as a preparation for a career in the legal profession, but also as a vehicle for cultivating general intellectual and linguistic skills, learning about how society, politics, and the economy work, and being nourished by the moral and ethical values that form the foundation of a civilized and humane society'.[8] The aim of liberal education is to develop intellectual curiosity and a critical analytical mind through the legal context, and to appreciate law and legal values in a wider community through broad-based knowledge and education. There is no reason to believe that a legal career is the only form of employment for law graduates, and with its intellectual rigour, legal education should be able to prepare law graduates to embark on other careers.[9]

---

8 Prof Albert Chen, Message of the Dean, *Faculty of Law Prospectus 2001–02*. See also *Roper–Redmond Report*, below, at pp. 119–26, para 73.

9 Ibid. Until recently, legal education in Hong Kong has largely followed the recommendations of the *Ormrod Report*, which emphasized that proper legal education at university level is an indispensable component of legal education. It recommended that there be three distinct stages of legal education, namely:

an academic stage taken at university or its equivalent;
a professional stage comprising:
organized vocational training in an institution; and
apprenticeship involving practical experience in a professional setting under supervision; and a continuing legal education stage.

As to the aims of legal education, it states:

'The professional lawyer requires a sufficiently general and broad based education to enable him [sic] to adapt himself successfully to new and different situations as his career develops; an adequate knowledge of the more important branches of the law and its principles; the ability to handle fact, both analytically and synthetically, and to apply the law to situations of fact; and the capacity to work, not only with clients, but also with experts in different disciplines. He must acquire the professional skills and techniques which are essential to practice, and a grasp of the ethos of the profession; he must also generate a critical approach to existing law, an appreciation of its social consequences, and an interest in, and a positive attitude to, appropriate development and change. To achieve these aims, a combination of

A comprehensive review of legal education and training in Hong Kong was carried out in 2001. The *Roper–Redmond Report*, as it was generally known,[10] basically adopted the three stages of legal education outlined in the *Ormrod Report*, and reaffirmed that the undergraduate law degree is a valuable preparation not only for the practice of law but also for a variety of other careers.[11] It noted that there was no necessary conflict between law as liberal arts education and law as legal education, as the generic or generally transferable intellectual skills and competencies common to most university education in the humanities and social sciences are essential to legal education.[12] Hence the goals of the academic stage should include the development of intellectual skills and competencies specific to the discipline of law. They should draw upon general transferable skills of analysis and problem solving but take on a cast of thought and intellectual method that is specific to the discipline of law. The Report also emphasized the importance of English language proficiency in the common law system, and advocated engaging students in the teaching and learning of law so that the learning experience is one of active and not passive learning.[13] It further recommended extending the then three-year LLB curriculum to four years during which law and non-law subjects are taken concurrently.[14] It, however, did not advocate turning the undergraduate LLB programme into a graduate programme, but highlighted the needs for a part-time law degree and a graduate programme of a shorter duration than the four-year LLB.[15]

These recommendations on the aims, content and teaching methods at the academic stage and the proposal to extend the LLB study to four years were generally well received. Indeed, HKU has long advocated for a four-year programme which would provide the much needed space for liberal education. The only constraint has been budgetary. The University Grants Committee (UGC) eventually agreed to fund the four-year programme and it was introduced in September 2004.

As far as HKU is concerned, the new four-year LLB is not merely an extension of the existing programme. Instead, the curriculum was restructured to reflect the emphasis on core legal competencies and transferable skills, broad-based education and the nurturing of a global perspective. The curriculum is conceived as a two-

---

education at university level and apprenticeship in its widest sense is necessary' (*Report of the Committee on Legal Education* (Cmnd 4595, HMSO, London, 1971).

10 *Legal Education and Training in Hong Kong: Preliminary Review*, a Report of the Consultants to The Steering Committee on the Review of the Legal Education and Training in Hong Kong (Aug 2001) (hereafter referred to as the *Roper-Redmond Report*).

11 At pp. 13–15, para 2.1.1.

12 At p. 119, para 7.3.1.

13 At p. 162, para 7.6.3.

14 At p. 136, para 7.4.3.

15 In 2012–13, the Hong Kong Government introduced a further major change in university curriculum. All undergraduate programmes were extended by one year, with the exception of law, which will remain as a four-year programme.

tier structure: the first two years being foundation years with mostly compulsory subjects, and the last two years being senior consolidation years with mostly electives. In the first two years, the focus is on teaching core legal competencies and transferable skills in the legal context (for example, case reading, analytical, research, writing, oral communication skills, problem solving skills and so on). Different subjects are assigned, as far as possible, to focus on different aspects of these skills. An intensive legal research and writing programme, which lasts for two years, was introduced. The five-module course is designed in such a way that each module builds upon another, and culminates in a major piece of research work with oral presentation.

At the same time, compulsory broadening courses on law and society, legal theory and critical thinking are introduced. These courses are in addition to the general requirement of language and information technology proficiency courses and general broadening courses in sciences and technologies for arts and humanities students. These broadening courses were further revamped and formed a rigorous common core curriculum since 2009–10 where all undergraduate students were required to do, initially four, and since 2012–13, six one-semester common core courses in four areas of inquiries (global studies, China studies, arts and humanities, science and technology). These courses aim to provide students with a broad knowledge basis and are taught primarily with an inter-disciplinary approach. All common core courses have to satisfy certain criteria and are vetted in terms of content and standard by a university committee to ensure their intellectual rigour. In 2013–14, about 150 common core courses were offered.

The final two years are designed to provide a diverse range of experience and options. HKU offers a wide range of law electives, as well as non-law subjects up to a maximum of 20% of the curriculum. For law electives, HKU emphasizes inter-disciplinary studies (for example, law and literary studies) and comparative law approach so as to enrich students' understanding of the strengths or weaknesses of our legal system and to have a good appreciation of different legal traditions and approaches. Cross-subject advanced seminars are also offered to break down artificial barriers arising from traditional subject classifications by adopting an integrated approach to problem solving – the so-called capstone experience. Those who take law electives in one of the specialized streams (for example, Chinese law; commercial, corporate and financial law; international trade and economic law) may obtain specialization in that stream. Those who have taken all non-law subjects in a specific discipline may obtain a minor degree in that discipline (for example, psychology, global studies). A particular challenge is where and how to teach ethics. This includes not only the professional code of conduct, which is taught in the PCLL year, but also general ethical issues in legal practice. While selected ethical issues are raised in different subjects such as criminal law or law and society, a series of informal dialogues are run with practitioners and judges who share with students the day-to-day ethical issues that they encounter in their daily practice.

Another characteristic of HKU's teaching is the importance placed on experiential learning. This is done through mooting, alternative dispute resolution, exchange programmes, clinical experience and internship. Mooting is used pervasively as a form of teaching. Apart from a compulsory moot for all students, they also participate in various international and regional mooting competitions each year. This provides students with invaluable opportunities to compete and share experience with students from some of the best law schools in the world. Since 2013–14, the mooting programme was been extended to cover mooting and dispute resolution, which is a one-semester course with theory and simulation exercises. In response to the challenges of globalization, HKU has engaged in an extensive exchange programme to provide students with opportunities for overseas exposure. The University has exchange arrangements with over 200 universities in the world. Each year about 20–30% of law students go abroad on exchange for one semester or one academic year. In return, the Faculty receives a substantial number of exchange students from overseas and the Mainland each year, and these help to provide a truly international learning environment at home for the students.

As far as teaching is concerned, HKU emphasizes interaction and participation through small group teaching (group size of about 10–12) for each subject in the first two years of foundation studies. It is all too often that curriculum changes at the university are not accompanied by a corresponding change in teaching methods and assessment. A curriculum is only as good as how it is delivered. Hence, alongside HKU's curriculum reform, the methods of teaching and assessment have been reviewed to ensure that they are consistent with the overall objectives of the curriculum. Teaching and learning seminars are organized to facilitate teachers to move towards a more engaging approach. There is also a shift from the traditional in-hall examination to a great variety of assessment methods, such as research projects, mooting, stimulation exercises and so on. Teaching and assessment have been kept under regular review, which forms part of a continuous process of teaching enhancement.[16]

Apart from the LLB programme, HKU has introduced four double degree programmes since 1999, which have proved to be very competitive and have attracted the best group of students. These are five-year programmes, covering business and law, government and law, civil engineering and law, and law and literary studies. Students are equipped with training in two different disciplines which give them a stronger competitive edge and a more flexible career choice in the highly globalized economy. Another impact of globalization is the recent trend of international collaboration. A number of leading law schools are offering joint or collaborative programmes which can leverage on the strengths of the respective partners. For instance, the National University of Singapore (NUS) offers a Dual LLB/Master of Law (LLM) degree in collaboration with New York University (NYU). London School of Economics and Political Science (LSE)

16 Indeed, the Department of Law of HKU was awarded Excellence in Teaching Quality Work in 2002 in the Teaching and Learning Quality Process Review conducted by the UGC.

offers a joint JD/LLM degree with Columbia University Law School (so is King's College London and University College London). Cambridge offers a joint JD/LLM programme with Harvard Law School. HKU runs various double degree programmes with University of British Colombia (UBC), King's College London (KCL), University of Pennsylvania Law School (U Penn), Zurich University and Peking University. These are exciting developments and will no doubt reflect a modern trend that no law school could afford to be isolated in the global village. At the same time, a successful joint programme depends on a whole range of factors, not least that the joint programme has to be able to leverage on the strengths of the partners and is not just a combination of two parallel programmes.

Another major challenge comes from technological advancement. Distance learning or real time collaboration through the internet becomes a real possibility. In the early days, there were various ambitious attempts to offer joint or collaborative degrees through distance learning. Yet so far very few of these ideas have flown, let alone become sustainable. One difficulty is that many law schools have underestimated the amount of resources and investment required to deliver a really successful programme, let alone a coherent joint academic programme. Even cross-border collaborative teaching of a single individual course through internet or video-conferencing has not been very popular, partly because they depend on the initiatives of the teachers involved who may not have the incentive or support to do this, and partly that, despite technological advancement, distance learning can at best be a supplement rather than a replacement for traditional face-to-face teaching. Having said that, law schools have in general been slow to take advantage of technological advancement in facilitating teaching, and the potential of collaboration through technology has not been fully explored. In recent years, the introduction of a standard open platform such as Massive Open Online Courses (MOOCs) poses a promising breakthrough. The success of the MOOC model lies in the fact that these courses are offered by leading universities in the world for reputational rather than financial purposes. While these courses invariably attract tens of thousands of students, it appears it is unlikely to be able to replace the more structured traditional form of legal education. Human interaction is an important facet of any form of education and could only be supplemented and not substituted by technology. How this mode of education would change the global scene of legal education remains to be seen.

Graduate or Undergraduate Programme?

Whether law should be taught as an undergraduate or a graduate programme is a matter of policy choice. Britain and many common law jurisdictions opt for the former whereas North American jurisdictions opt for the latter. In recent years, a graduate law programme has been gaining popularity in Asian jurisdictions such as Japan, Korea, Australia, the PRC and Hong Kong. This phenomenon is to some extent a reflection of the North American experience that law may be best taught at a postgraduate level to students with some degree of maturity and a good sense of the world. In Hong Kong, a JD programme was first introduced in 2004–05 by City U, followed by CUHK in 2006–07, and HKU in 2010–11. In all three universities, the graduate JD programme runs alongside an undergraduate LLB programme. In contrast, Melbourne Law School has decided to move to a graduate JD programme by giving up its LLB offering.

As a JD programme is targeted at people who intend to join the legal profession and in view of its relatively short duration (typically two to three years), it inevitably covers mainly the core courses that are necessary for admission to the legal profession. Thus, a JD programme could have a fairly narrow scope and offer a relatively narrow perspective of law. This limitation is compounded by the existence of a part-time programme. Because of its professional orientation, a JD programme will likely lean towards preparing students for the Bar examination. This seems to be the experience in Japan and Korea, and to some extent, Taiwan. In contrast, the common law jurisdictions are able to maintain a JD programme that could still offer sufficient intellectual rigour and diversity.

Another potential weakness is that academic research is unlikely to be emphasized in a practice-oriented course. The response of Melbourne University is to maintain a parallel stream of LLM to sustain academic research and excellence, whereas a dissertation is retained as a compulsory requirement of the HKU JD programme.

A further issue is that, in many jurisdictions, undergraduate study is state-funded. Thus, an advantage of providing legal education as an undergraduate programme is that it will better guarantee equal access to legal education. Legal education is expensive, and the cost is borne by the students in a typical graduate programme. While scholarships and bursaries may be available to alleviate financial difficulties of law students in a graduate programme, the North American experience is that many law students are heavily indebted by the time they graduate.

Thus, in short, for any law school that wishes to embark on a graduate law programme, it is essential to ask why it wants to do it, what kind of graduate programme it wishes to launch, and how it would fit into the mission and vision of the law school.

Bridging the Gap: From Academic Study to Legal Practice

Law schools are traditionally good in providing intellectual academic training. Law students may learn all the legal principles governing contract law or banking law, but they may never come across a real commercial contract or a banking document in their academic study and may be at a complete loss when they are asked to advise on or draft a commercial contract. Yet when they graduate from law school, law firms may expect them to be able to complete commercial transactions, to be effective in engaging clients, and to be competent in conducting negotiations. In a recent discussion with leading practitioners, they were amazed that law graduates did not understand financial documents such as 'paid through notes', 'equity linked notes' and so on. The gap between the expectations of the profession and that of the law schools is getting wider. This in turn raises the questions of what should be realistically expected of the law schools, how to bridge the ever-widening gap between academic study and legal practice, and who is responsible for doing what.

It is obvious that there is a big gap between academic study of law and legal practice. It is equally obvious that it would be unrealistic to expect a law graduate to be able to function as a fully qualified lawyer on the day of his or her graduation. Practical training is best done in practice. While the law schools could strengthen their practical training, they could only realistically and fairly be required to produce law graduates who are competent trainees rather than fully operating qualified lawyers upon graduation. There are various models to bridge the gap. A national examination is unlikely to be able to provide effective practical training. Indeed, many law firms in North America lament that the national Bar examination has not been able to provide good quality trainees, and the cost of training falls onto the law firms. In times of economic downturn, more and more clients are unwilling to finance the training of trainees. In Singapore, some corporate clients even refuse to pay the bill for work done by a trainee. The alternative model is to introduce vocational course providers. This has been the case in the UK where the teaching for the Bar examination or the Law Society Qualifying Examination is provided by a number of accredited professional schools. They provide well-structured skills and professional training that prepare a law graduate for legal practice. In Hong Kong, such practice training is provided by the three law schools in the form of a one-year programme, the PCLL, which has the benefit of having substantial professional input and is subject to rigorous scrutiny to ensure its relevance to practice.

The PCLL programme has undergone many changes in recent years and is designed to help students to transit smoothly from the academic stage to the practice stage of their legal career. It is a successful model of collaboration between the profession and the universities, as professional input is sought at every stage of the planning and delivery of the curriculum. The professional bodies also set out the benchmarks to be met by the programme. This model has an advantage of providing a buffer between legal practice and academic study of law, thereby shielding the law schools from the pressure of a Bar examination in designing their undergraduate law curriculum which in turn encourages intellectual rigour and academic diversity. It does not completely resolve the problem of a widening gap of expectation from the legal profession and what can be realistically achieved within a one-year training programme. There is probably no quick solution apart from a regular dialogue between the programme providers and the legal profession.

Recently, the Law Society has advocated for the introduction of a single Solicitor Qualifying Examination, primarily on the grounds that it needs to maintain consistency in standard when the PCLL programme is offered by multiple providers. This is not a novel issue and there are various ways to achieve consistency other than a single unifying examination. As pointed out above, a single examination may provide apparent consistency, but it may also result in a more narrowly-focused professional training programme. The real question is whether a unified entry examination will result in better lawyers, or whether it will only introduce a further hurdle to entering the profession. Experience elsewhere suggests that a unified examination is unlikely to produce better lawyers than a sustained structured training programme.

Access to the Legal Profession

This gives rise to another set of issues, namely whether there should be multiple entry points to the legal profession. In most jurisdictions, a law degree is a necessary pre-requisite to entry to the legal profession, though this is not invariably the case. In Hong Kong, the *Roper–Redmond* study emphasized the importance of providing an alternative entry route other than an undergraduate law degree. This recommendation has prompted the introduction of JD programmes in Hong Kong, which is intended to provide graduates who do not study law an alternative route of entry to the legal profession. In contrast, in the PRC, anyone who has a university degree can take the national Bar examination. In the UK, there are multiple entries to the legal profession and a law degree is not required.

It has never been doubted that one can become a doctor only by following the medical curriculum in a medical school, or an architect or an engineer only by doing the prescribed curriculum in the respective disciplines. As law has become an increasingly sophisticated profession which shoulders a heavy public responsibility of handling their clients' life, liberty or property, let alone a high calling to defend justice and the rule of law, it would be startling if a lawyer is not required to undergo the most stringent professional and academic training. The responsibility of academic education is squarely and rightly placed in the university, in which training is to be supplemented by a period of training in cce. This is not about equal access, but about ensuring quality and competence in the public interest. Equal access is guaranteed by equal access to admissions to universities on merits. It is not granted by giving any person who aspires to be a lawyer to take a professional examination without going through any proper training or education.

Conclusion

A twenty-first century law curriculum has to meet many conflicting expectations. As an academic programme, the study of law should provide an intellectually challenging experience and a broad education, and equip students not just with knowledge of the black letter law but also its broader context and the role of law in the wider local and international communities. While this may be shared by the profession at a general level, the increasingly sophisticated legal practice prompts them to expect more specialized and focused training for legal practice in the law curriculum. As a professional programme, it is fair to expect law graduates to be competent to provide a high standard of legal services to the community.

There are tensions between the provision of solid general legal knowledge and nurturing specialized legal expertise, and between offering rigorous intellectual and academic training and honing practical legal skills. While these are not novel issues, the gap between the expectations of the law school and the legal profession is getting ever wider as a result of globalization. The increasingly consumer-oriented approach in universities may drive the content of the law curriculum towards meeting the market demands for admission to the legal profession and, inevitably, the requirements of the professional examination. In this regard, it is ironic that in some Asian jurisdictions such as Korea, Japan or Taiwan, where the passing rate of the Bar examination is dismally low, the law curriculum is not designed to prepare students for a career other than law, whereas in some other Asian jurisdictions such as Singapore and Hong Kong, where the focus of legal education is to provide a broad liberal education, most of the graduates end up in the legal profession.

Advancement in technology offers a new dimension to internationalization, and may facilitate international collaboration in a manner that has not been possible before. Yet the potential, as well as the necessary infra-structural and resources support, has not been fully explored. Despite these possibilities, some law schools may decide to focus on their traditional strengths; others may decide to expand and capitalize on their international exposure. There are new challenges, and with these come new opportunities. There is no single ideal model, and each law school will have to take into account its own history, culture, characteristics and strengths, as well as wider issues such as the cost of legal education and national legal environment, in developing its own responses. If anything, globalization should lead to greater diversity rather than greater convergence.

Index

Figures and Tables are indexed in **bold**.